MAGILL'S
SURVEY
OF
WORLD
LITERATURE

MAGILL'S SURVEY OF WORLD LITERATURE

Volume 2

Christie–Gogol

Edited by

FRANK N. MAGILL

Marshall Cavendish Corporation
New York • London • Toronto • Sydney • Singapore

REF
809
CAV
VOL. 2
1995

Published By
Marshall Cavendish Corporation
2415 Jerusalem Avenue
P.O. Box 587
North Bellmore, New York 11710
United States of America

Library of Congress Cataloging-in-Publication Data
Magill's survey of world literature. Edited by Frank N. Magill.
    p. cm.
    Includes bibliographical references and index.
    1. Literature—History and criticism. 2. Literature—Stories,
plots, etc. 3. Literature—Bio-bibliography. 4. Authors—Biogra-
phy—Dictionaries. I. Magill, Frank Northen, 1907-   .
PN523.M29 1992
809—dc20
ISBN 1-85435-482-5 (set)   92-11198
ISBN 1-85435-484-1 (volume 2)   CIP

Second Printing

PRINTED IN THE UNITED STATES OF AMERICA

CONTENTS

MAGILL'S SURVEY OF WORLD LITERATURE

MAGILL'S
SURVEY
OF
WORLD
LITERATURE

AGATHA CHRISTIE

Born: Torquay, England
September 15, 1890
Died: Wallingford, England
January 12, 1976

Principal Literary Achievement

As the foremost writer in what has been called the golden age of crime fiction, Christie was instrumental in bringing the genre to new heights of literary achievement.

Biography

On September 15, 1890, Agatha Mary Clarissa Miller was born in Torquay, Devonshire, England. Her father, who died when she was eleven, was American, and her mother was British. At this point in time, formal schooling for young women usually took place in the home. At sixteen, Agatha went to Paris to study piano and singing. She became an accomplished pianist and was fluent in French. This linguistic knowledge helped her to create realistic dialogue for her famous character the Belgian detective Hercule Poirot, whose English was fractured and frequently included French expressions.

In 1912, Miller became engaged to Archibald Christie, a young officer in what would become the Royal Air Force in 1918. They were married on December 24, 1914. During World War I, he was stationed in France and Mrs. Christie became a member of the Voluntary Aid Detachment in a hospital at Torquay. Her work in the pharmacy would be invaluable, as she became familiar with many of the poisons that she would later use in her novels. She was writing short stories at this time, and a few were published. In 1916, after a challenge from her sister that she could not write a detective novel, Christie produced *The Mysterious Affair at Styles: A Detective Story* (1920), featuring Poirot. The book was rejected by a number of publishers before it was finally published by Bodley Head in 1920. It was not a great financial success, but the publication did encourage Christie to continue writing.

Between 1920 and 1926, Christie published six novels and introduced several new primary characters. Among these were Tommy and Tuppence Beresford, who made their debut in *The Secret Adversary* (1922), and Colonel John Race, who was introduced in 1924 with the publication of *The Man in the Brown Suit*. The author also published *The Secret of Chimneys* (1925), which featured Superintendent Battle, the

only major Christie detective who was affiliated with Scotland Yard. In 1926, *The Murder of Roger Ackroyd* was published and provoked a violent debate among both reviewers and readers alike. Christie, according to some, broke the rules of fair play often associated with mystery novels by allowing the narrator, Ackroyd, to be the murderer. Christie responded with the defense that the reader must suspect all the characters. This novel is now regarded as one of her highest achievements.

At this point, Christie's life began to change dramatically. Her mother died soon after the publication of *The Murder of Roger Ackroyd*, and her marriage to Colonel Christie was quickly falling apart. On December 4, 1926, she took her car and drove away from her Berkshire home, supposedly for a short drive. Colonel Christie called the police when she did not return after a reasonable time. Her car was found two days later—its wheels hanging over a cliff. The entire country seemed involved in the search for the missing author, whose life appeared to be taking on the characteristics of one of her books. Two weeks after her disappearance, staff members at a Yorkshire hotel identified her among their guests. She had registered as Teresa Neele of Capetown. "Mrs. Neele" had appeared completely normal to the staff and guests of the hotel. The doctor who later examined her concluded that she had a legitimate case of amnesia that had been brought about by stress.

In 1928, she was divorced from Colonel Christie and spent her time traveling while her daughter Rosalind was in school. She met her second husband, Max Mallowan, an archaeologist, in 1930 while visiting Ur in what is now Iraq. They were married on September 11, 1930. From that time on, she spent several months a year at digs in Iraq or Syria. During World War II, while Mallowan worked as an adviser on Arab affairs for the British military government in North Africa, Christie again volunteered as a nurse. She was assigned to the pharmacy at University College in London. Once again, this experience enabled her to gain valuable information on poisons. Because she had little to do in the evenings, Christie continued writing, and two of her most famous books, *Sleeping Murder* (1976) and *Curtain: Hercule Poirot's Last Case* (1975), were written during this time. These were the "last cases" of Jane Marple and Hercule Poirot. They were originally intended to be published posthumously. The success of the film version of *Murder on the Orient Express* in 1974, however, convinced Christie that the books should be published sooner. Thus, *Curtain* was published in 1975 and *Sleeping Murder* in 1976. Christie published her autobiography (*An Autobiography*) in 1977.

Christie was made a Fellow of the Royal Society of Literature in 1950. The year 1952 saw the opening of Christie's *The Mousetrap* in London—a work that has the distinction of being the longest-running legitimate play in history. In 1955, she received the New York Drama Critics Circle Award for *Witness for the Prosecution* (1953). She was made a Commander of the Order of the British Empire in 1956, received an honorary doctorate of literature from the University of Exeter in 1961, and was made a Dame of the British Empire in 1971. Madame Tussaud's Wax Museum measured her for a wax portrait in 1972. After a brief period of failing health, Christie died in her home in Wallingford on January 12, 1976.

Analysis

Christie is known for her crime-fiction novels, especially those that feature Poirot, introduced in *The Mysterious Affair at Styles*, or Miss Marple, an elderly spinster introduced in *The Murder at the Vicarage* (1930). Her other detectives include Tommy and Tuppence Beresford, Superintendent Battle, and Colonel John Race. Christie began writing during what has been called the golden age of crime fiction. This time period can be roughly defined as the years between World War I and World War II. It was a time of world recovery, tinged with hardship as well as a certain amount of optimism. People were anxious to forget their daily troubles, and crime-fiction novels often provided this escape. Following the publication of *The Murder at the Vicarage*, Christie was on her way to becoming a well-established author. At about the time of World War II, her novels became quite popular, and she firmly established her place as a leader in the genre.

Christie can be characterized as a traditional mystery writer, depending on imagination and intelligence, rather than technological marvels, to solve crimes. That is one of the reasons that she has remained popular. She was always careful to "play fair" and provide her reader with all the information necessary to solve the crime, plus enough red herrings to make this task challenging. By the time Christie died in 1976, many new scientific discoveries had revolutionized police departments around the world. While she did not ignore modern methods, she did make it clear that all the scientific apparatus in the world would not solve a crime if there was not a thinking individual to work with the machinery.

One of her two most popular thinking individuals is Hercule Poirot, a fastidious and curious Belgian with a large mustache. Poirot is painted as a dandy, about whose appearance others often make jokes. Scoffers often find themselves rebuffed, however, because Poirot's sometimes semicomical fastidiousness hides a keen mind and a nature that demands that he search for the truth in all matters. In this search, Poirot employs his "little grey cells" in order to distinguish the truth from fiction. He often accomplishes this by asking seemingly irrelevant questions. These questions do, however, turn out to be relevant and often important in terms of uncovering information previously hidden.

Christie's other well-known detective is Jane Marple, a spinster who resides in the village of St. Mary Mead. One of the characteristics that has set Miss Marple apart from other detectives is her age. She is in her seventies or eighties, but the reader should not underestimate her. Miss Marple uses her knowledge of human nature to solve crimes. In addition, Christie uses the anonymity that Miss Marple can assume. Miss Marple looks so innocent that no one could ever suspect her of having any dealings with the police. She is everyone's old-fashioned aunt and blends in quite well with the scenery.

Several factors account for Christie's popularity. First, her plots are well constructed. She takes the reader through a logical series of actions to an equally logical conclusion. In addition, enough red herrings are dragged across the reader's path to ensure continued interest in the activities. Characterization is also an important factor. While

Poirot and the Beresfords, especially, are occasionally parodies of themselves, they are still believable. Their eccentricities are not so outlandish as to be thought impossible. In addition, Christie has an ear for dialogue. Her characters consistently speak in a manner appropriate to their roles in the novels. Her characters also continually act in a manner consistent with roles created for them.

Christie was also interested in looking at human nature in general; thus, her plots revolve around the motivations that cause people to act in a desperate manner. These include greed, jealousy, a desire for power, and revenge. This tendency to construct crimes around common motives rather than esoteric ones enables the reader to relate easily to the characters involved.

Through the course of her career, Christie developed a particular style and stuck with it. In her novels, the reader can expect a clever plot, believable dialogue, and engaging characters. This adherence to a pattern that worked has contributed greatly to the popularity of her novels.

THE MURDER OF ROGER ACKROYD

First published: 1926
Type of work: Novel

In this novel, Dr. James Sheppard leads the reader through an account of the murder of his friend, Roger Ackroyd.

The Murder of Roger Ackroyd was Christie's sixth novel and was published in 1926. It was the third novel that featured the Belgian detective Hercule Poirot. Like many of her other novels, the book is set in a small town and focuses on the interactions between characters who are well known to one another.

When the novel was first published, critical reactions were mixed because of the unusual narrative structure. Christie chose to have the murderer tell the story from his point of view. This device caused some consternation because some believed that Christie was not "playing fair" with her readers. They reasoned that, in crime fiction, if the novel is to be fair, the reader should be able to follow the same path the detective does in order to solve the crime. Some believed that by having the narrator as the murderer, the reader would not be able to follow the path of the clues, since the murderer would, in order to protect his identity, conceal certain key pieces of information.

Christie circumvents this problem in several ways. First, Dr. Sheppard is an extremely believable character. Because of the remorseful tone he assumes at the beginning of the novel, the reader immediately trusts him and his observations. In addition, Poirot appears to trust Sheppard, including him in discussions with the police and, as Poirot admits, using Sheppard as a substitute for Captain Hastings, who had played Dr. Watson to Poirot's Sherlock Holmes in previous novels. Thus, the reader is led to trust Sheppard because Poirot trusts him.

Sheppard also establishes an intimate rapport with the reader through the use of first-person narrative. The reader is privy to what are assumed to be the doctor's private thoughts about Ackroyd's murder. Poirot also confides in Sheppard and often asks his opinion of people within the town. Again, this action on the part of Christie serves to inspire confidence in the narrator; the reader does not suspect him because Poirot does not, and because Christie has, as in previous novels, established Poirot as a reliable source and a good judge of human nature.

Another aspect to the novel in regard to the narration is the comparatively small role that Poirot plays. The reader is accustomed to seeing him as the main character—almost as a master puppeteer who guides the movements of all around him. In fact, the readers expect Poirot to manipulate them, for this is the nature of crime fiction in general: The reader is manipulated by the detective to see things his or her way. Christie, however, chooses to depart somewhat radically from this formula. Instead of Poirot manipulating the reader, Sheppard manipulates both the reader and Poirot. The reader is unaware of this subterfuge, however, until the end of the novel, when all the other probable suspects have been eliminated and only Sheppard remains. The reader is then privy to Sheppard's confession, and all the pieces to this very complex puzzle fall into place.

A POCKET FULL OF RYE

First published: 1953
Type of work: Novel

Jane Marple travels to Yewtree Lodge to try to discover who has murdered her former maid, Gladys Martin.

A Pocket Full of Rye opens with the death of Rex Fortescue, a successful but not universally liked financier. Curiously, rye is discovered in one of his pockets. In addition, it was not his afternoon tea that poisoned him, but something that he had eaten at breakfast that contained taxine, a derivative of yew. Before long, Gladys Martin, the parlor maid, has been strangled, and Rex's attractive second wife, Adele, has received a dose of cyanide in her tea.

The police are baffled, both by the methods the murderer has chosen to employ and by the number of motives. Adding to the confusion is the sudden appearance of Lancelot Fortescue and his wife Pat. Years before, Lance had moved to Africa after his father had turned him out of the house for ostensibly forging a check. According to him, he and his father had made their peace, and he has come back to enter the family business, much to the dismay of the oldest son, Percival, who resides at Yewtree Lodge with his wife, Jennifer. All parties stand to gain from the death of Rex Fortescue. Consequently, there are nearly as many motives as there are suspects, and no one can adequately account for his or her time. Adding to the confusion are the rye in Rex's pocket and a clothespin clipped to the nose of Gladys Martin.

Miss Marple enters the Fortescue home as a former employer of Gladys Martin. She wants to see the girl's murderer found. Inspector Neele quickly finds that Miss Marple is a valuable asset and asks that she lend a hand in finding out information about the family. Miss Marple is aided in her endeavors by Miss Ramsbottom, Rex Fortescue's eccentric sister-in-law from his first marriage. She likes Miss Marple because Marple is sensible, and she insists that Marple stay at Yewtree Lodge.

The continued presence of Miss Marple unnerves the household, with the exception of Miss Ramsbottom, but greatly aids Inspector Neele, who finds her observations invaluable. In addition, Miss Marple is the quintessential objective observer. She does not know anyone in the household except the late Gladys Martin and so is in a position to evaluate objectively the various members of the family.

Throughout the novel, the reader sees Christie employ her own powers of observation to bring the characters to life. As in most of her novels, the setting is sketched and the reader is left to fill in the fine details. With the characters, however, Christie takes great care to see that all necessary details are supplied for the reader. Facets of the characters are often revealed through dress and everyday actions.

This novel also serves to give the reader a fairly complete portrait of Jane Marple. Christie herself described her as "dithery," and that she is. This behavior, however, is more camouflage than anything else. Miss Marple does indeed take in everything around her. Christie also uses this novel to show the benefits of age. Inspector Neele does not see the significance of the pocket full of rye, the clothespin on Glady's nose, or the fact that Adele was poisoned while eating scones with honey. Yet when Miss Marple reminds him of the rhyme from Mother Goose, several pieces of the puzzle fall into place.

The overriding theme of this novel is that justice must be served. Miss Marple gets involved in the murders because of Gladys Martin, a not-very-bright parlor maid. It is definitely Miss Marple's belief that her murder deserves as much attention as the murder of a wealthy business executive. It is a theme present in many of Christie's works: Justice is not simply for those who are privileged, but for all.

Summary

Taken as a whole, Agatha Christie's crime-fiction novels constitute some of the best-known works in the genre. Her primary detectives, Jane Marple and Hercule Poirot, are some of the best-known characters in popular fiction. Christie's talents include the ability to weave a cunning plot, construct realistic dialogue, and create believable characters. All these traits combine to create novels that are entertaining and engaging. While Christie's writing is somewhat old-fashioned, she uses realistic motivations that enable readers to relate easily to the situations at hand.

Bibliography

Bargainnier, Earl F. *The Gentle Art of Murder: The Detective Fiction of Agatha Christie.* Bowling Green, Ohio: Bowling Green University Popular Press, 1980.
Christie, Agatha. *An Autobiography.* New York: Dodd, Mead, 1977.
Fitzgibbon, Russell H. *The Agatha Christie Companion.* Bowling Green, Ohio: Bowling Green University Popular Press, 1980.
Keating, H. R. F., ed. *Agatha Christie: First Lady of Crime.* New York: Holt, Rinehart and Winston, 1977.
Tynam, Kathleen. *Agatha.* New York: Ballantine, 1978.

Victoria E. McLure

CICERO

Born: Arpinum, Italy
January 3, 106 B.C.
Died: Formiae, Italy
December 7, 43 B.C.

Principal Literary Achievement

Universally regarded as the greatest of the Roman orators, Cicero was also a competent poet whose epics showed the possibilities of the rhymed hexameter and thus paved the way for the works of Vergil.

Biography

Marcus Tullius (Tully) Cicero, the son of a Roman knight, was born in Arpinum (Arpino) on January 3, 106 B.C. He was the elder son of Marcus Tullius Cicero and Helvia. He was also one of several famous Romans, such as Gaius Marius, who made the Latium region of Italy famous. His family was upper-middle-class, and he was well educated in law, rhetoric, and Greek literature and philosophy, attending schools in both Rome and Greece. In 89 B.C., he commenced military training under Pompeius Strabo, the father of Pompey the Great, the Roman general who became the rival of Julius Caesar; he also served with Lucius Cornelius Sulla, who was the commanding general in the campaign to drive Mithridates, king of Pontus, back to Asia. Cicero first appeared in the Roman courts in 81 B.C., and his celebrated defense of Sextus Roscius, the great actor who had taught him elocution, established him as a preeminent defense lawyer. Within a decade, he had won many important legal battles, including the prosecution of Gaius Verres (governor of Sicily, 73-71 B.C.) for extortion and other forms of maladministration. In this famous case, Cicero displayed remarkable versatility: He delivered a brief speech, notable for its thundering rhetoric and its inclusion of evidence by witnesses.

Cicero was made praetor in 66 B.C. and consul in 63 B.C. His first speech as consul was against the agricultural policy of Servillius Rullus and in the interests of Pompey, with whom be maintained a lifelong friendship. At this time, he discovered the conspiracy of Lucius Sergius Catilina (Catiline) to murder the consuls, generate uprisings, and burn Rome. After escaping an attempt on his life, Cicero on the same day delivered one of his greatest prosecution speeches. The conspirators were apprehended and executed on the authority of Cicero himself. Marcus Porcius Cato, who outdid Cicero in vituperation, argued for execution; Julius Caesar argued against

413

it. When Cicero announced the death of the conspirators with the single word *vix-erunt* (they are dead), he was hailed by Quintus Catulus as the father of his country—a title later accorded to President George Washington in recognition of his having saved the United States from its enemies.

Because he had acted on his own authority, Cicero was criticized for the execution of the Catiline conspirators—which he never regretted, though it was legally questionable because it was carried out without a formal trial. Cicero went into voluntary exile for a year, but on his return to Rome he became a great advocate of the republican form of government, against Caesar's concept of a popularly supported dictatorship. During his absence, however, the politician Publius Clodius Pulcher had a bill passed that forbade the execution of a Roman citizen without trial, tried to have Cicero declared an official exile and ordered the destruction of Cicero's beautiful villa at Tusculum.

From August 4, 57 B.C., when he landed at Brindisi in the south of Italy, Cicero was warmly welcomed by the populace, who were favorable to his political theory of *concordia ordinum* (harmony among the several social classes). His monthlong journey to Rome helped to establish his popularity; however, he faced formidable obstacles in his plan to reestablish himself in the world of politics, because Pompey and Caesar formed an alliance. After promptings by Pompey, Cicero agreed to align himself with them politically, though he found distasteful some of the legal cases that he was obliged to accept. Accordingly, he decided to devote himself increasingly to writing, *De oratore* (55 B.C.; *On Oratory*), *De republica* (54-51 B.C.; *On the State*), and *De legibus* (52 B.C.; *On the Laws*) being some of his main publications. He was pleased when Titus Milo assembled a gang to try to defeat the gang controlled by Clodius, which kept Rome in constant fear, and Cicero agreed to defend Milo when Clodius was killed on the Appian Way. Cicero was so intimidated by Pompey, however, who was given plenipotentiary powers to restore order, that he did not deliver his speech at the trial. Milo was exiled, joined an insurrection, and was captured and killed. Only later did Cicero publish his defense speech as *Pro Milone* (52 B.C.; *For Milo*).

During the civil war (49-45 B.C.), Cicero was given charge of recruiting soldiers from Campania for Pompey's armies, but he did not leave Italy with Pompey and his men, though he later joined them for a while—until illness forced him to retire. When Caesar defeated Pompey's army at Pharsalus in 48 B.C., Cicero was offered safe conduct and returned to Rome, where he continued his efforts for a republican polity and against Caesar's dictatorship. There began his second intense period of literary works, which included *Brutus* (46 B.C.), a study of Roman orators, indicating their strengths in the five divisions of rhetoric: ideas, arrangement, diction, delivery, and memory, and *Orator* (46 B.C.; *The Orator*), composed in the form of a letter addressed to Marcus Junius Brutus that answers a request for a picture of the perfect speaker. It is the latest of Cicero's rhetorical studies and offers a defense of his own career as an orator, as well as a detailed examination of the five canons of rhetoric. In particular, *The Orator* defends the florid, or Asian, style against critics who favored the Attic, or plain, style, and it asserts the validity of vitality, exuberance, digressions, and rhythmical language in the composition of effective speeches. That is, Cicero favored the speech style of the public orator rather than that of the cool, collected, logical courtroom advocate of his era. That his point of view had merit may be gathered from the almost universal belief that he is the unchallenged master of Latin prose style.

Cicero took no part in the assassination of Caesar on the Ides of March, 44 B.C. Two days later, on March 17, he delivered a conciliatory speech in the Roman senate, supporting a general amnesty. Later, he delivered the fourteen great Philippic orations (so named because they resemble the great Greek orator Demosthenes' speeches against Philip of Macedon) that marked his return to politics. Cicero thought that he could "use" Caesar's adopted son Octavian, but Octavian was astute and could not be manipulated. The latter's march against Rome made him consul. When the Second Triumverate of Octavian, Marc Antony, and Marcus Lepidus was formed, Cicero was proscribed, caught, and killed near Caieta in Formiae, on December 7, 43 B.C. Marc Antony and his wife, Fulvia, had Cicero's head and hands nailed to the rostrum in the Roman forum.

Analysis

For many readers, the most interesting of Cicero's works are his letters to Titus Atticus, the Roman philosopher and patron of literature, who was perhaps his closest friend; to his brother Quintus; or to Marcus Junius Brutus, the principal assassin of Caesar. For others, his philosophical works have a special interest, since they expound a fundamentally Stoic position and address such topics as friendship, old age, duty, the good, the nature of the gods, and the goals of life and politics. Yet for those interested in rhetoric and oratory, his three treatises—*On Oratory*, *Brutus*, and *The Orator*—constitute a major investigation and analysis of those subjects. These three works have justified placing Cicero in the company of Aristotle and Quintilian as the three great classical writers on the subject of public speaking. In many ways, Cicero's *On Oratory* is the most important of his three books: It gives full consideration to all the aspects of the subject, and it lacks the self-justification of the more epistolatory *Brutus*. *On Oratory* is the theoretical study, *Brutus* is the exemplification, and *The Orator* is a consideration of the ideal, as one critic has phrased it. *On Oratory* is written in three books and is offered as a reconsideration of earlier thoughts and writings on public speaking; it was intended as edification for his brother Quintus, who had inquired about the functions of the orator. In addition, it defends Cicero's view that the good speaker is a well-educated person.

For centuries, the very term "Ciceronian" suggested everything that was elevated and admirable in the art of rhetoric, whether written or spoken. Cicero was the consummate stylist, the model advocate. His strengths in the use and manipulation of language were admitted by all, and his weaknesses or defects were few or trifling. Whether speaking for the prosecution or for the defense, his advocacy was considered exemplary. Hugh Blair, an eminent eighteenth century critic who was professor of rhetoric and belles lettres in the University of Edinburgh, offered his appraisal of

Cicero in one of his *Lectures on Rhetoric* (1783): "He is always full and flowing, never abrupt. He is a great amplifier of every subject; magnificent, and in his sentiments highly moral. His manner is on the whole diffuse, yet it is often happily varied, and suited to the subject." Blair thought that some of Cicero's great achievements were his ability to gain the attention of his audiences and to influence them, his ability to arrange his arguments with the greatest force and propriety, and his reluctance to bring the emotional proofs into force before he had prepared the way with logical conviction. Blair concluded that "no man knew the power and force of words better than Cicero." Yet even Blair discerned certain weaknesses in Cicero, and he proposed that they amounted to a predilection for show (for "eloquence" in the old terminology), which had the effect of leaving on the minds of both readers and hearers "the impression of a good man, but withal, of a vain man."

Over the years, concepts of appropriate style have changed somewhat, and today "Ciceronian" implies the use of long and elaborate sentences—usually of the periodic form—that end with great force and climax. The term also suggests parenthetical elements, doubled elements, appositives, such tropes as triads, and periphrasis. Yet in his many great speeches he knew how and when to use the demotic, the conversational, and the formal styles to serve the purpose of the occasion. Their amalgam in his magnificent speeches on Milo and Catiline, for example, is still worthy of study by students of courtroom speaking; for the ordinary person who relishes language used at its best, there are few authors who are more satisfying.

ON ORATORY

First published: *De oratore*, 55 B.C. (English translation, 1742)
Type of work: Essay

In the form of a Platonic dialogue with other famous orators, Cicero offers his philosophy of rhetoric as more than the mastery of certain rules; rather, it is the training of the whole person to speak effectively.

On Oratory takes the form of a dialogue, though it is fictional: It is merely a vehicle for Cicero to state his theory of public speaking, supported by the views of some other famous orators of his time. These are Licinius Crassus, Marcus Antonius, Sulpicius Rufus, and Caius Aurelius Cotta. Others participate in sections of the book; the most notable of them is Quintus Mucius Scaevola, the elderly lawyer and Stoic.

In book 1, Cicero offers *On Oratory* as his principal contribution to the discussion of rhetoric (the art of persuasion in all of its forms), indicating that it is to supersede all of his earlier statements on the subject, and that it is prompted by his brother Quintus' inquiry about the matter. Great orators are rare, says Cicero, not owing to a dearth of men of ability, but because of the difficulty of the art itself, in spite of its great rewards, both in compensation and in fame. Cicero calls for a liberal education (a wide general knowledge), mastery—not just fluency—in the language, psychological insight and sophistication, wit (sharpness of intellect), humor, excellent delivery (voice and gesture), and outstanding memory. All of these demands are to be satisfied if the speaker is merely to be competent to meet the usual demands of public life; leadership requires that they be mastered to a high degree, and that the speaker must first have attained a knowledge "of all important subjects and arts."

"There is, to my mind," says Crassus, "no more excellent thing than the power, by means of oratory, to get a hold on assemblies of men, win their good will, direct their inclinations wherever the speaker wishes or divert them from whatever he wishes." In every free society that has enjoyed the fruits of peace and prosperity, the art of rhetoric has always flourished and reigned supreme; it is indeed puzzling that so few men have been given the power to use language to move others. Scaevola objects that Crassus values rhetoric too highly and proposes that its main uses are to be seen in the law courts and in political situations only. Crassus replies that rhetoric alone is insufficient: The great orator must be well versed in moral and political philosophy; his language must rival that of the poet, and his style must reveal his depth of education. Answering Scaevola, he admits that few can attain the ideal of a true liberal education, but that all should aspire to it. There follows Cicero's view that "in an orator we must demand the subtlety of the logician, the thoughts of the philosopher, a diction almost poetic, a lawyer's memory, a tragedian's voice, and the bearing almost of the consummate actor. Accordingly, no rarer thing than a finished orator can be discovered among the sons of men."

Cicero's discussion of the art or science of rhetoric follows the Greek model, most clearly stated by Aristotle in his *Rhetoric*: There are three speech types (forensic, or courtroom; deliberative, or parliamentary; and panegyric, or speeches of praise and blame); speeches have three sections (introduction, discussion, and conclusion); and the act of speaking covers the arrangement of ideas, style, and delivery (involving voice, gesture, and memory). The competent speaker practices frequently. He or she writes themes to improve fluency and style, paraphrases poetry and prose extemporaneously and occasionally impromptu, delivers speeches upon all subjects and as often as the opportunity allows, practices gestures and trains the voice, engages in close reading of literature, and debates both for and against as many propositions as possible.

Book 2 takes the form of a second day's discussion of the topic of oratory. Antonius proposes that oratory is not a science but that many useful rules can be derived from the observation of successful speakers: Oratory covers all good speaking and on all subjects. He suggests that the most difficult kind of oratory is forensic—courtroom speaking. There, the speaker is required to meet argument with argument and appeals to the emotions by appeals to the opposite emotions. Cicero proposes that wit and humor are natural gifts and cannot be taught; he suggests that there are two types of wit, irony and raillery, and that they are often particularly effective in court cases. Antonius resumes his contribution, proposing that the strongest argument should be placed either at the beginning or at the end of the speech.

Book 3 is devoted to a discussion of style, which Crassus holds to be inseparable from matter. Further, he says that various styles are necessary and admirable, but that the first consideration of the orator is clarity of diction. Embellishment should be produced naturally, not as an extravagance. Always, style should be adapted to a specific audience and occasion. Style depends on correctness, lucidity, ornateness, and appropriateness to the subject and occasion; but style without effective delivery is impotent, and effective delivery depends in large measure on a pleasing variety in vocal qualities: "This variation . . . will add charm to the delivery."

Summary

Charles Sears Baldwin, a Columbia University professor of rhetoric in the 1920's, noted that Cicero sympathized with the views of both Antonius and Crassus: Both orators are right in almost all of their views, which are actually complementary. Further, Baldwin believed that book 1 has been the volume studied most by readers because it "has most of the Ciceronian message" which can be summarized rather easily: The effective speaker is the well-educated individual who has studied the speeches of the great orators of the past, has studied the component parts of the oration and their requirements, and has practiced diligently to strengthen wit, voice, and bodily delivery—always remembering that any good speech must be adapted to both the occasion and the audience.

Bibliography

Baldwin, Charles Sears. *Ancient Rhetoric and Poetic Interpreted from Representative Works*. Gloucester England: Peter Smith, 1959.

Cicero. *De Oratore*. Translated by Edward W. Sutton and Harris Rackham. 2 vols. Cambridge, Mass.: Harvard University Press, 1942-1948.

Cowell, Frank R. *Cicero and the Roman Republic*. Harmondsworth, Middlesex, England: Penguin Books, 1956.

Haskell, Henry J. *This Was Cicero*. Greenwich, Conn.: Fawcett, 1942.

Mitchell, Thomas N. *Cicero*. New Haven, Conn.: Yale University Press, 1979.

_____. *Cicero the Senior Statesman*. New Haven, Conn.: Yale University Press, 1991.

Ramson, Elizabeth. *Cicero: A Portrait*. Ithaca, N.Y.: Cornell University Press, 1983.

Thonssen, Lester, and A. Craig Baird. *Speech Criticism: The Development of Standards for Rhetorical Appraisal*. New York: Ronald Press, 1948.

Wilkin, Robert N. *Eternal Lawyer: A Legal Biography of Cicero*. New York: Macmillan, 1947.

Marian B. McLeod

ARTHUR C. CLARKE

Born: Minehead, Somersetshire, England
December 16, 1917

Principal Literary Achievement

A prolific writer of novels, short stories, and nonfiction, Clarke is one of the best-known and most influential science-fiction writers.

Biography

Arthur C. Clarke was born in the village of Minehead, Somersetshire, England, on December 16, 1917. His parents were Charles Wright Clarke and Norah Mary Willis Clarke. Even as a boy, he was interested in science and writing. In 1931, he read *Last and First Men* (1930) by W. Olaf Stapledon, a book that changed his life. A strong advocate of space exploration, he joined the British Interplanetary Society in 1935, serving as its chair from 1946 to 1947 and again from 1950 to 1953.

Clarke did well in mathematics but could not afford to attend a university. Instead, he took the civil service examination and in 1936 found employment as an assistant auditor in His Majesty's Exchequer and Audit Department. He continued to read widely and began to publish short fiction in 1937.

From 1941 to 1946, Clarke served in the Royal Air Force. Because of his poor eyesight, he was unable to qualify for pilot training. He was sent to electronics and radar school and worked as a technical officer on the first trials of ground control approach radar. He also served as a radar instructor. A technical paper that he wrote describing the possibility of communications satellites was published in the October, 1945, issue of *Wireless World*, an engineering journal. After leaving the Royal Air Force in 1946, he received a grant to enter King's College, London; he received a degree in physics and mathematics in 1948. From 1949 to 1950, he was an assistant editor for *Science Abstracts*, a technical journal.

During the 1950's and 1960's, Clarke published prolifically, both fiction and nonfiction. *Childhood's End* (1953) was the first work to win critical acclaim. In 1956, he won the Hugo Award for his short story "The Star." Between 1964 and 1968, Clarke wrote the novel *2001: A Space Odyssey* (1968) and collaborated with Stanley Kubrick on the 1968 screenplay. This book and its sequels, *2010: Odyssey Two* (1982) and *2061: Odyssey Three* (1987), are probably his best-known works. Clarke won virtually every award for science-fiction writing, an Academy Award conomination for the screenplay of *2001: A Space Odyssey*, and a number of awards for science writing.

Clarke wrote an astonishing number of nonfiction books and articles, some for the general public but many for scientific and technical journals. He also became interested in underwater exploration and published several books and articles on this subject as well.

Clarke married Marilyn Mayfield in 1953; they were divorced in 1964. He moved to Sri Lanka in 1956 but continued to make frequent trips to England and the United States.

Analysis

In his introduction to *Time Probe: The Sciences in Science Fiction* (1966), Clarke explains his views on what science fiction should be. In the first place, it must incorporate some principles of science and technology. He strongly emphasizes, however, that "the prime function of a story is to entertain—not to instruct or to preach." In addition, the story must contain some intellectual substance if it is to have lasting value. All of these are evident in his own writing.

Clarke was educated as a scientist and can write about the future in a remarkably detailed, believable manner. He became a staunch advocate of space travel; books such as *Prelude to Space* (1951) are mostly propaganda with many scientific details to show how some technical accomplishment might be possible. Clarke sees space travel as opening new horizons for human civilization, rather like the exploration of the Western Hemisphere did several centuries ago.

Other stories show his skill as a storyteller, often including some surprising revelation that changes the readers' perspective. In *Childhood's End*, the extraterrestrial creatures who seem to be acting as humankind's guardian angels turn out to look like devils. Another example is "The Star." It tells about a Jesuit priest who, while traveling on a starship, discovers the ruins of an ancient civilization that was destroyed when its sun became a supernova. By calculating the time when the light from this star would have reached Earth, he determines that this civilization was destroyed to create the star of Bethlehem.

Clarke's writing can be a combination of the mundane with the lyrical and mystical; *2001: A Space Odyssey* includes both. On the one hand, readers learn all about space travel down to what makes a toilet work in zero gravity. On the other hand, the ending describes astronaut David Bowman traveling through time and space to some other type of existence, into a truly transcendental experience.

Most of Clarke's writings deal with two main themes: the belief that human beings are not alone in the universe, and the outcome of human evolution. Clarke is convinced that life has evolved on many other planets and that it is merely a matter of time before contact is made. In stories such as *2001: A Space Odyssey*, the extraterrestrial being plays a key role in the development of the human race; in others, such as *Rendezvous with Rama* (1973), the aliens are indifferent. In all cases, the first contact with another race shows that humans are members of a galactic community.

The question of what is to become of humans has troubled writers since Charles Darwin first published *On the Origin of Species by Means of Natural Selection* in

1859. Some, such as H. G. Wells in *The Time Machine* (1895), have taken a pessimistic position, predicting that the human race will simply expire. Others, such as W. Olaf Stapledon in *Star Maker* (1937), suggest that human beings may eventually evolve into new, superior creatures: Clarke belongs to the latter group.

Clarke sees the evolution of humans as something they cannot control, but he also sees the possibility of some type of transcendent mutation, one in which the mind is freed from matter—and therefore from decay and death. That is certainly the case of Vanamonde in *Against the Fall of Night* (1953), of the children in *Childhood's End*, and of David Bowman in *2001: A Space Odyssey*.

Even if humans cannot be sure of their evolutionary future, Clarke thinks that change and potential progress are preferable to stagnation. In *Imperial Earth* (1976), Duncan Makenzie is the latest in a long line of clones. Because of an inherited genetic defect, cloning is the only way the family can perpetuate itself. Makenzie has the resources to make one clone and is expected to make a genetic duplicate of himself. Instead, he decides to have his dead friend cloned because the friend had intellectual gifts and because that clone would be able to have children and thus contribute to the genetic pool; thus the potential for change would exist.

Clarke takes a mostly optimistic view of the future. Although humans cannot know what lies ahead and cannot to a large extent control it, they should trust their potential.

CHILDHOOD'S END

First published: 1953
Type of work: Novel

While Earth is being supervised by extraterrestrial Overlords, humans suddenly evolve into a new type of creature.

Childhood's End begins with this unusual statement: "The opinions expressed in this book are not those of the author." Although Clarke's books usually promote space exploration, this one shows that humans are not ready to travel to the stars.

Many writers have speculated about the first encounter between the human race and extraterrestrial beings and what the relationship between those two races will be. *Childhood's End* begins with a description of just such an encounter. Some thirty years after the end of World War II, just as the Americans and the Russians are both about to launch their first rockets to the Moon, spaceships appear over every major city on Earth. The Overlords, as the extraterrestrials come to be called, are intellectually and technologically superior to humans and quickly assert their authority.

Their directives result in an improved standard of living for all the creatures on Earth. Some object to their domination, mostly because the Overlords are secretive and have never explained why they have come to Earth. No one has ever seen one, and only Rikki Stormgren, the secretary general of the United Nations, ever speaks to them. Karellen, the head Overlord, explains to Stormgren that he is not a dictator but "only a civil servant trying to administer a colonial policy in whose shaping I had no hand." He does not say who sent him. After fifty-five years, the Overlords finally show themselves to humans. Although their actions make them seem like the guardian angels of humankind, they look exactly like the ancient legends of devils with horns, barbed tails, and leathery wings.

The Overlords have prohibited space travel, and people such as Jan Rodricks resent this because they want to learn what is out there. Rodricks is a stowaway inside a whale model that is being shipped to the Overlords' home planet and becomes the first and last of his species to travel in space. He learns, however, just how vast and unknowable the universe is and how paltry humans are in comparison. He understands why the Overlords have said, "The stars are not for Man."

The Overlords represent science and reason and spend much time learning about humans. One of them, Rashaverak, attends a party because the host owns one of the best libraries on paranormal phenomena. When the last few guests experiment with a sophisticated Ouija board, Rashaverak does not participate but sits outside the circle and observes. One of the guests wonders if Rashaverak is like an anthropologist watching a primitive religious rite he does not understand. Apparently, the Overlords are not omniscient.

When the children of the planet begin their transformation into a new type of creature, Karellen finally announces the Overlords' true purpose: They were sent to Earth by some superior force called the Overmind to help humans through the transition from their present form to a new type of existence. They can help with the birth of a new species and can observe it, but they themselves lack the potential to evolve any further.

The other major question in *Childhood's End* is what will be the next step in human evolution. The Overlords engineer the first stage by creating a utopia in which humans learn to live in a cooperative society. All the major problems such as war and famine have been solved, but no more real progress occurs; no more major scientific breakthroughs are made and no notable works of art are created.

When the final change occurs, it is triggered not by the humans' intellectual or technological advances but by their paranormal powers. All the children are soon affected by the "Total Breakthough," and a new species evolves. They lose their individual personalities; each becomes like a single cell in a larger brain. Eventually, they lose their need to exist in material form and join with other races from other planets in the Overmind, free to roam the universe.

The species known as *Homo sapiens* comes to an end as Jan Rodricks, the last man on Earth, watches the final joining take place. He expresses a sense of achievement and fulfillment and sends a message to the Overlords, now on their way home: "I am sorry for you. Though I cannot understand it, I've seen what my race became. Everything we ever achieved has gone up there into the stars."

The Overlords, who seemed so powerful in the beginning, do not have the potential to evolve. Humans do not possess their great intellectual powers, but do have paranormal powers and therefore can evolve into a new species. The stars are not for the present race but rather for its descendants.

2001: A SPACE ODYSSEY

First published: 1968
Type of work: Novel

A team of astronauts is sent to discover the destination of a strange signal emitted by a monolith excavated on the Moon.

2001: A Space Odyssey is Clarke's best-known work, partly because of the popularity of the 1968 film version. From 1964 to 1968, Clarke and Stanley Kubrick collaborated on the novel and the screenplay, with Kubrick having control over the film and Clarke being responsible for the novel. Both works were extensively revised, and Clarke later published some material cut from the novel in *The Lost Worlds of 2001* (1972).

In the epilogue to *2001: A Space Odyssey*, Clarke says the book "was concerned with the next stage of human evolution." The beginning of the book describes creatures not yet human, the middle shows modern humankind, and the ending speculates on what humanity might become. Black monoliths appear in each section and provide connections between each section.

When the book opens, three million years in the past, man-apes have reached a crucial point in their development. Unable to obtain enough food, they will perish if they do not learn to use tools to hunt. Space-traveling extraterrestrials recognize their potential and teach them how to use bones as weapons. The first monolith is a teaching device, but it also transforms Moon-Watcher, one of the smarter apes; the structure of his brain is altered and the change will be passed on to his descendants. Without this almost divine intervention, the human race would not have evolved. Moon-Watcher also discovers, on his own, that the weapons can kill others of his own species.

In the next section, humans have developed a sophisticated technology that enables them to travel to the Moon—and also to create increasingly lethal weapons. They, too, are at a crucial point in their history: Will they continue to progress or will they destroy themselves and the planet?

Clarke sees technology as a necessary step forward. In "The Sentinel," the short story on which *2001: A Space Odyssey* is based, a scientist discovers an ancient device on the surface of the Moon. When disturbed, it emits a signal. The scientist speculates, "They would be interested in our civilization only if we proved our fitness to survive—by crossing space and so escaping from the Earth, our cradle."

In *2001: A Space Odyssey*, scientists discover a similar device, this time another black monolith. When uncovered after three million years, it emits a powerful signal toward Saturn. Humankind now knows that it is no longer alone in the universe.

Undaunted, not waiting for the extraterrestrials to come to Earth, the humans launch a mission to Saturn. David Bowman, the one astronaut to survive that trip, discovers a third monolith on Japetus, one of the moons of Saturn. This one is a "star gate," an extremely advanced machine that shuttles him through time and space to a distant part of the universe. In this odyssey, he discovers that the beings who left the monoliths have themselves evolved, first into mechanical bodies that could last forever, and finally into creatures of energy no longer dependent on matter for their existence.

Bowman undergoes a transformation, first aging rapidly, then dying and being reborn as the infant Star Child. He is the first human to make this evolutionary jump. Again the extraterrestrials have intervened to make it possible.

Whether this evolutionary jump has resulted in a better creature, or whether humankind will be doomed to repeat the mistakes of the past, is not clearly answered. At the very end, Star Child completes his journey back to Earth, where he discerns some atomic bombs in orbit and detonates them. Does he merely destroy the bombs, making the world a safer place, or does he destroy humankind in the process? The description of Star Child discovering his new powers is almost identical to the description of Moon-Watcher discovering his new power: Both are like children who learn through play.

The people in *2001: A Space Odyssey* tend to be detached, unemotional men of science. Hal, the computer, seems more human than the humans. Hal may represent another evolutionary path to intelligent life. Although he is a machine, his electronic brain can reproduce most of the mental activities of which a human brain is capable. He becomes "neurotic" and "dies" when Bowman disconnects his higher mental functions. In the sequel *2010: Odyssey Two* (1982), the extraterrestrials permit the lonely Star Child Bowman to choose a companion. He chooses the revived Hal, who is then transformed into a creature of mental energy like Bowman. Once again the extraterrestrials are controlling the evolutionary process.

Summary

Arthur C. Clarke's stories are grounded in scientific fact, but they also deal with a future that cannot be known. For the most part, he is optimistic about that future and the role humans will play in it, and he sees space travel as an invigorating force. He believes that life exists on other planets and that eventually humans will make contact with it. Although the human race may reach the end of its evolutionary development, it has the potential to become something better.

In *Profiles of the Future* (1962), one of his nonfiction books, Clarke writes that he is not trying "to describe the future, but to define the boundaries within which possible futures must lie." When considering the future, he says, the one fact "of which we can be certain is that it will be utterly fantastic."

Bibliography

Hollow, John. *Against the Night, the Stars: The Science Fiction of Arthur C. Clarke*. San Diego: Harcourt Brace Jovanovich, 1983.

Olander, Joseph D., and Martin Harry Greenberg, eds. *Arthur C. Clarke*. New York: Taplinger, 1977.

Rabkin, Eric S. *Arthur C. Clarke*. Mercer Island, Wash.: Starmont House, 1980.

Samuelson, David N. *Arthur C. Clarke: A Primary and Secondary Bibliography*. Boston: G. K. Hall, 1984.

Slusser, George Edgar. *The Space Odysseys of Arthur C. Clarke*. San Bernardino, Calif.: Borgo Press, 1978.

Eunice Pedersen Johnston

JEAN COCTEAU

Born: Maisons-Laffitte, near Paris, France
July 5, 1889
Died: Milly-la-Forêt, France
October 11, 1963

Principal Literary Achievement

Cocteau's protean achievements, which encompass most literary genres and media, secured for him a place as one of the most influential French avant-gardists of the twentieth century.

Biography

Jean Maurice Eugène Clement Cocteau was born on July 5, 1889, in Maisons-Laffitte, on the outskirts of Paris, France, where he would spend most of his diverse, prolific, and well-publicized artistic career. A fragile child, he was introduced early to the arts by his family and their acquaintances. At the age of nine, his father, Georges, committed suicide, an event never mentioned in any of Cocteau's works; Cocteau then began his intense preoccupation with the circus, the theater, and classical music. He attended primary school from the ages of eleven to fourteen, and his three failures at the *baccalauréat* clearly showed his lack of taste for the regimented French educational system, which he later called being "badly brought up."

Cocteau's adolescence was spent living with his stylish and independently wealthy mother, Eugénie, whose influence he admits never diminished even with his artistic successes. Although his attempts at independence, including marriage to the actress Madeleine Carlier, failed, his mother received with hospitality his homosexual friends, and Cocteau pursued an active career in Paris' *fin de siècle* high society and artistic circles. After the 1908 performance of several of his poems, he was introduced to the director of the Ballets Russes, Sergei Diaghilev, and to the innovative composer Igor Stravinsky, with whom he first collaborated in *Le Potomak* (1919). Cocteau served in the medical corps during World War I, returning to Paris to collaborate with Erik Satie, Diaghilev, and Pablo Picasso on a ballet, *Parade*, in 1917.

Cocteau's most important friendship was with the young novelist Raymond Radiguet, whom he met in 1919; the period produced a farce, *Les Mariés de la Tour Eiffel* (1921; *The Wedding on the Eiffel Tower*, 1937), and the novels *Thomas l'Imposteur* (1923; *Thomas the Impostor*, 1925) and *Le Grand Écart* (1923; *The Grand Écart*, 1925), before the tragic death of Radiguet at the age of twenty. Heartbroken, Cocteau

retired to the French Riviera and turned first to the use of opium and then to religion. The next few years, in and out of opium asylums, were spent collaborating with the painter Christian Bérard on several works, including the play *La Voix humaine* (1930; *The Human Voice*, 1951) and the film *La Belle et la bête* (1946; *Beauty and the Beast*, 1947). During this time, Cocteau was involved with twenty-year-old Jean Desbordes, who inspired *Le Livre blanc* (1928; *The White Paper*, 1957). He also completed *Les Enfants terribles* (1929; *Enfants Terribles*, 1930; also known as *Children of the Game*) and the first version of *Orphée* (1927; *Orpheus*, 1933).

With the publication of *Children of the Game*, Cocteau achieved notoriety and success. In February of 1930, he produced his one-act, one-man play *The Human Voice*, which was decried by the Surrealists, who finally forgave him in 1938. Along with successes on the stage, his first film, *Le Sang d'un poète (1930; The Blood of a Poet*, 1932), was presented and well received in January of 1932 and was followed by his version of Oedipus, in *La Machine infernale* (1934; *The Infernal Machine*, 1936). During World War II and Germany's occupation of France (1940-1950), he had many premiers, including *Les Monstres sacrés* (1940; *The Holy Terrors*, 1953) and his neo-Sophoclean tragedy *Antigone* (1922; English translation, 1961). The success of his film *L'Éternel retour* (1943; *The Eternal Return*, 1948) was followed by the loss of two friends, one to pneumonia in a concentration camp, and the other to Gestapo torture.

With the end of the war, Cocteau presented numerous ballets, plays, and films, including his enduringly successful *Beauty and the Beast*. Cocteau finally left Paris for good in 1947 and moved to Milly-la-Forêt, where he lived with a young painter, Édouard Dermit. While writing *Bacchus* (1951; English translation, 1955) and his *Journal d'un inconnu* (1952; *The Hand of a Stranger*, 1956), he concentrated upon the fine arts, especially his paintings and illustrations, first exhibited in Munich in 1952. He also worked in pottery, glass, mosaic, tapestry, stained glass, and architecture.

He was elected to the Belgian Académie Royale and the Académie Française in 1955, was received into the French Legion of Honor in 1957, and died quietly at Milly-la-Forêt, France, on October 11, 1963.

Analysis

Cocteau constructed for himself a complete aesthetic universe; he wrote the texts, designed the scenery and costumes, selected the dancers, arranged the choreography, wrote the music, directed, and often performed in the production, and illustrated the published book. As much as any one since the composer Richard Wagner, Cocteau demanded of his productions and publications that they be "total artistic experiences" under the control of a single aesthetic imperative, and of his audiences that they appreciate his work on its own terms, free from modish evaluations or conservative intolerance. There is a curious combination in Cocteau's work of an intense insistence both on classicism and on artificial convention and upon radicalism and individualism. The most sustained exposition of his thoughts on art and literature is his late work *La Difficulté d'être* (1947; *The Difficulty of Being*, 1966).

Rather than allying himself with fashionable authors of the day, most notably the Surrealists, Cocteau designates as his inspiration the Renaissance essayist Michel de Montaigne, who described his own writings as being "consubstantial with their author"—both mystically and physically inseparable from their author. Cocteau persistently credits the contributions of his friends to his work and insists upon the direct relationship of his own lived experience to that which he artistically represents. Yet his work is not simply an autobiographical expression of a personal experience to be assimilated exactly to the copious personal remarks and records that the author has left behind. Indeed, critics have even accused Cocteau of a lack of artistic and theoretical originality. Even as familiarity with such biographical details as the artistic society of the Café aux Deux Magots, frequented by the philosopher Jean-Paul Sartre and the Parisian avant-garde, is necessary to the full appreciation of the satire that opens the 1950 film *Orpheus*, for example, so, too, a knowledge of Cocteau's theoretical indebtedness is crucial. Cocteau never claims to be original and often attributes his theoretical and artistic borrowings, claiming in this scholarly respect, as well as in other artistic aspects, to strive for clarity and lucidity, to "show darkness in broad daylight."

Cocteau's emphasis upon neoclassical simplicity and order in works such as *Orpheus* and *Antigone* stands in apparent contradiction to his recurrent interest in many of the metaphysical questions raised by German Romanticism in particular. In many of his works, from *The Blood of a Poet* and *Bacchus* to *Children of the Game*, as well as *Beauty and the Beast* and *Orpheus*, Cocteau develops commentaries upon, and versions of, central Romantic themes such as the inextricability of love and death, divine poetic intoxication, the unavoidability of suffering for the artist, and the incomprehension and lack of appreciation of bourgeois society for radical art. Cocteau himself cites as inspirations the importance of the philosopher Friedrich Wilhelm Nietzsche's theory of Dionysiac poetic inspiration and of the unparalleled polymathy of the German writer Johann Wolfgang von Goethe. Perhaps the single most persistent theme in Cocteau is that love can only be perfected in death. Like his precursor French Romantic poet and novelist Victor Hugo, Cocteau sees the poet as the *écho sonore*, whose voice echoes both the events of the external world and such intense internal orphic realizations.

If love and death is a central theme, then the conduct and destiny of the poet is his dominant theoretical preoccupation. For Cocteau, "poetry" encompasses all media, and his own corpus contains experiments in dozens of literary genres and artistic media. For Cocteau, poetry is not an esoteric preoccupation of an elite group of aesthetes. Although often criticized as being precisely such a precious enterprise destined for a marginal coterie, Cocteau's "poetry," like the productions of so many artistic movements of the first half of the twentieth century, insists upon the universal relevance and importance of poetry as that alone that makes life worthwhile in a materialistic age, as the only remaining "spiritual luxury." Cocteau's work is committed to the double imperative both continually to shock its audience and uncompromisingly to create a radically individualized system of its own artistic fabrication.

The phenomenon of Cocteau, patron of new talent, scintillating conversationalist, homosexual, opium addict, and *grand maître* of the French avant-garde, especially after his self-imposed exile from Paris, often obscures the substance of his artistic achievement. Perhaps more so than any of his extraordinary fictional poets, Cocteau himself has become one of his own *monstres sacrés*.

ANTIGONE

First produced: 1922 (first published, 1928; English translation, 1961)
Type of work: Play

Antigone, the cursed descendant of Oedipus, must decide between familial duty and the laws of the state in order to bury her brother.

Cocteau chose in 1922 to translate Sophocles' famous tragedy *Antigone* (441 B.C.; *Antigone*, 1729) into French. Cocteau himself, in his diaries, declares that he was motivated by a feeling of sympathy with the heroine, who like Joan of Arc, Jean-Jacques Rousseau, and Jean Genet, shares the condition of being both persecuted and inspired. For Cocteau, the persecution of Antigone will be based on her purity, which distinguishes her from the rest of corrupt society. The first production of *Antigone*, in 1922, was given at the Atélier in Paris with settings by Pablo Picasso, music by Arthur Honegger, and costumes by Gabrielle "Coco" Chanel. Charles Dullin and Antonin Artaud played the parts of Creon and Tiresias; Cocteau himself took the part of the Chorus, and Genica Atanasiou played Antigone. This collaboration of innovators in all fields of the arts is typical of Cocteau's productions and films.

Cocteau's text shortens Sophocles' tragedy, adapting the Greek tragedy to a unified French dramatic form, and shifts many of the psychological and verbal emphases of the ancient play. Cocteau's prose is itself shortened; it is often not only concise but abrupt, giving a feel of avant-garde modernity to the play's language. Cocteau describes his effort as a reduction and "scouring" of language to the point at which the play "hurtles toward its conclusion like an express train." At the same time that the play is accelerated by Cocteau's streamlined language, it is transformed from the record of the majestic actions of kings, a traditional definition of a tragedy, to a minimalist melodrama that restricts and schematizes the characters and the scale of their actions. Even with stage directions, its text can never adequately record the rich visual and auditory experience of the play in performance. Many of the stage directions and costuming directions suggest, but cannot represent, the boldness of the play's staging:

> beneath the masks one could make out the actor's faces, and ethereal features were sewn onto the masks in white millinery wire. The costumes were worn over black bathing suits, and arms and legs were covered. The general effect was suggestive of a sordid carnival of kings, a family of insects.

The theatricality of the performance, such expressionist stage directions as "Antigone . . . braces herself for the day ahead," and all the mentions of musical interludes indicate the multimedia nature of this piece of "performance art." This version of Sophoclean theatricality, which also relied upon masks and music, both insists upon the connection between Cocteau's piece and the Greek original and emphasizes the degree to which it has transformed the classical material that it invokes. Cocteau emphasizes both the translation of the Antigone myth by time and the persistence of the importance of myth and its accompanying spectacles.

In scenes such as the encounter between Creon and Antigone, Sophocles himself carefully presented and questioned the nature of legal justice and its relationship to human emotions and familial duty. With Cocteau's treatment of the myth, another issue emerges clearly, however, that of Antigone's nature as a poet. Other playwrights, notably Cocteau's contemporary Jean Anouilh, insist upon the defiant heroism of Antigone in the face of political oppression in their adaptations of Sophocles' play. In Cocteau's version, such political, or even religious or familial, defiance gives way to her emphasis upon her autonomy and upon her status as a poet. She does not present an elaborate defense of her actions; instead, she offers the spectacle of her demise as the gesture that will testify to her innocence. Creon corroborates the theatricality of the play, when, in the last moments of the play, he describes his plight as the cause of three deaths, as "not knowing where to look."

CHILDREN OF THE GAME

First published: *Les Enfants terribles*, 1929 (English translation, 1930)
Type of work: Novel

Two children, Paul and Elizabeth, play a dangerous and amoral game that substitutes fantasy for reality and finally kills them.

Much of *Children of the Game* is drawn from Cocteau's experiences from 1900-1903 as an unhappy student at the "Petit Condorcet," in the rue Amsterdam. Indeed, the opening description of a visit to the Cité des Monthiers, a hidden courtyard of artists within an international diplomatic neighborhood of Paris, is a recollection of many such visits made with school friends by Cocteau himself. Cocteau uses the same autobiographical material in his *Le Sang d'un poète* (1930; *The Blood of a Poet*, 1932), which represents a development of ideas raised by *Children of the Game*, and in the famous *film noir* version directed by Jean-Pierre Melville. The symbolic meanings that will be assigned to the later cinematographic versions of the story are already present in the story of these children, who, Cocteau will say later in his journals, did not recognize their own poetry, who "were not playing horses but actually became horses."

Written in three weeks in 1929 while Cocteau was being treated for opium addiction, the novel focuses on the theme of the adolescent, a new creation of the years following the end of World War I, whose sense of prestige and freedom in the first half of the decade would decay into disenchantment in the second half. The plot of the novel itself is simple and absolute in its construction, revolving around the promise made between Paul and Elizabeth to adhere to a pact, which excludes the rest of the world and love. They are "angelic," in the sense of being both innocent and uncompromising. For a few years, they are granted a carefree life, in their world of childish, if nightmarish, performances and images, before the encroachment of a race of adults perverts and destroys them. The novel opens and closes with snow scenes, which establish the emotional coldness of the life that it depicts. Like the falling snow, which blocks out the world, the children's game substitutes their nocturnal performances and an absolute code of rules for all the accepted ways of ordering reality.

The novel opens with the school bully throwing a deadly snowball at Paul. This childhood rite of initiation, which is repeated in the autobiographical *The Blood of a Poet*, forms an ominous frame for the whole novel. Although scarcely present in the novel, Dargelos remains a haunting threat, an avenging angel, from whom the children retreat into their symbolic world of the game. He finally sends poison, a more incontrovertibly lethal symbol than the snowball, into that children's room, whence the rules of the game originate. Only with Paul's death, Elizabeth's suicide, and the poisonous invasion of their sacred, and yet horrendous, magical space, the "theater of the bedroom," will the curse be lifted. Cocteau consistently emphasizes the theatricality of their game through a careful attention to stage lighting for their vignettes, an attention that slowly seeps beyond the room to alter the balance of light and dark in the real world outside the room. Even natural phenomena are subject to distortion in this ever-expanding theater of cruelty. The unnerving combination of perversion and order within the constructed security of the children's game-world will be accompanied in the film version not only by *chiaroscuro* lighting but also by the deceptively soothing music of Johann Sebastian Bach and Antonio Vivaldi.

Elizabeth's suicide appropriately ends the game, for she has always been the stronger player, controlling both Paul's behavior and that of his friend Gerard. Although brutalized and terrified by her brother, Elizabeth finally causes the death of her brother when he breaks their childhood contract and falls in love with Agatha. Elizabeth, in a fever both jealous and physical, shoots both her already poisoned brother and herself in the head with a revolver. As an avenging Electra, she brings a final terrifying consummation of the tragic ritual, on a white and snow-covered stage, by playing the horror absolutely according to the rules.

Summary

At the age of forty-one, in his 1930 account of opium addiction, Jean Cocteau would write that even a poet cannot write his own biography. In the broadest sense, however, Cocteau's life was an exercise in being as many different poets as possible. In media ranging from fresco to film to the novel, Cocteau attempted to bring together a perfection of classical form and a wildly innovative modernity. By placing the debris of World War I on the stage of Greek tragedy behind a veil of medieval mysticism, he created a revolution not only in art but also in society. As flamboyant in life as in art, his agility and intensity continue to impress and sometimes to offend.

Bibliography

Bentley, Eric. *The Playwright as Thinker*. New York: Reynal & Hitchcock, 1946.

Brown, Frederick. *An Impersonation of Angels: A Biography of Jean Cocteau*. New York: Viking Press, 1968.

Cocteau, Jean. *The Journals of Jean Cocteau*. Edited and translated by Wallace Fowlie. New York: Criterion Books, 1956.

_____. *Past Tense*. Translated by Richard Howard. New York: Harcourt Brace Jovanovich, 1983.

Crossland, Margaret. *Jean Cocteau*. London: Peter Nevill, 1955.

Esslin, Martin. *The Theatre of the Absurd*. 1961. Reprint. Harmondsworth, Middlesex, England: Penguin Books, 1980.

Fifield, William. *Jean Cocteau*. New York: Columbia University Press, 1974.

Knapp, Bettina Liebowitz. *Jean Cocteau*. Boston: Twayne, 1989.

Oxenhandler, Neal. *Scandal and Parade: The Theater of Jean Cocteau*. New Brunswick, N.J.: Rutgers University Press, 1957.

Steegmuller, Francis. *Cocteau, a Biography*. Boston: Little, Brown, 1970.

Elizabeth Richmond

J. M. COETZEE

Born: Cape Town, South Africa
February 9, 1940

Principal Literary Achievement

The recipient of numerous prestigious writing awards, Coetzee is a respected writer of fictional and scholarly works that examine the sociopolitical context of human experiences.

Biography

John Michael Coetzee was born in Cape Town on February 9, 1940. His grandparents were farmers who descended from a long line of white Afrikaners who had immigrated to South Africa in the seventeenth century. J. M. Coetzee's father was an attorney, and his mother was a schoolteacher. As a child in the 1940's, Coetzee grew up in and around the Karoo desert, which was to provide him with many observations of the arid South African landscape for his novels. According to Allen Richard Penner in his book about Coetzee, *Countries of the Mind* (1989), the author spoke English at home and, after attending various English-language schools, also became knowledgeable in Afrikaans, Dutch, and several other languages.

Coetzee's wide intelligence is reflected in his academic degrees, as well as in his publications in a variety of disciplines. He received two bachelor of arts degrees from the University of Cape Town, one in English and the other in mathematics. In 1963, he also received an M.A. in English from the university. After graduation, he entered the private sector in England and worked for International Business Machines (IBM) in London and for International Computers in Bracknell, Berkshire.

In 1965, he began his doctoral education in English at the University of Texas at Austin under a Fulbright scholarship. There, he completed his dissertation on the modern writer Samuel Beckett and, even before he was graduated, was offered a teaching position at the State University of New York (SUNY) at Buffalo in 1968. Although he left Buffalo in 1971, he returned to the United States in 1983 and 1986 for one-year stints as visiting professor at SUNY-Buffalo and Johns Hopkins University. Since 1972, he has taught linguistics and literature at the University of Cape Town.

Coetzee's first novel, *Dusklands*, was published in 1974. It was followed by *In the Heart of the Country* (1977), which won the South African Central News Agency (CNA) Award and the Mofolo-Plomer Prize. Both these novels rely on first-person

perspectives to convey the manner in which the country has dehumanized its inhabitants. Successive novels also won critical acclaim for their portrayals of introspective characters living in South Africa at various historical periods.

In 1980, Coetzee published *Waiting for the Barbarians*, an allegorical account of the success of a ruling empire, which *The New York Times* selected among its Best Books of 1982. It also won the South African CNA Award, the Geoffrey Faber Memorial Prize, and the James Tait Black Memorial Prize. The enigmatic *Life and Times of Michael K* (1983), with echoes of Franz Kafka's *Der Prozess* (1925; *The Trial*, 1937), won two awards, the prestigious Booker-McConnell Prize from Britain in 1983 and the French prize, Prix Fémina Étranger, in 1985. For his achievements, Coetzee was also awarded the Jerusalem Prize for the Freedom of the Individual in Society in 1987.

Foe, a version of the Robinson Crusoe narrative by Daniel Defoe, was published in 1986, and *Age of Iron* was published in 1990. These two novels are narrated by women characters who, as their stories are progressively revealed, become deeply troubled and affected by their respective societies.

In addition to writing novels, Coetzee is a prolific scholar who has published essays on continental writers such as Samuel Beckett, Fyodor Dostoevski, Leo Tolstoy, D. H. Lawrence, Franz Kafka, and Vladimir Nabokov. He has also written articles on less canonical writers such as Yvonne Burgess, Alex La Guma, C. M. van den Heever, and Sidney Clouts. More notable, perhaps, are his nonliterary essays, which deal more specifically with his training in linguistics and mathematics. His many scholarly articles have appeared in noted journals such as *PMLA*, *Comparative Literature*, and *Critique*. In 1988, Yale University published his collection of essays entitled *White Writing: On the Culture of Letters in South Africa*, which examines the literary production of his native country. The essays are as much a historical view of South African literature as they are political perspectives of those who write under a restrictive regime.

Analysis

For the uninitiated reader, Coetzee's fictional texts are so highly sophisticated in their construction that it is easy to become lost in matters such as plot development and character formation. Furthermore, the mostly short novels are dense in their allusion to historical and political facts, which contribute to the difficulty of their comprehension.

Besides being accused of being impenetrable, Coetzee's novels are sometimes criticized for not taking a more overt stance against South Africa's commitment to a racist regime. Although the author has publicly denounced the social and political policies of the ruling white government, the Nationalist Party, it is also accurate that Coetzee does not explicitly state this opposition in his novels. For example, unlike the white South African writer Nadine Gordimer, who has more directly reflected the political circumstances of the country in her novels, Coetzee has opted for a markedly different literary approach. Instead of holding a mirror to the devastation of South African politics in his novels, Coetzee has created fictional characters who express a wide spectrum of physical, emotional, and psychological experiences. Very often, the novels are constructed from interior monologues, in which the narrator seems to be speaking to himself or herself. The specifics of historical time and space are inferred from the characters' plights. In this way, Coetzee allows the personalized experiences to speak the "truth" of the social and cultural situations.

In his first novel, *Dusklands*, Coetzee seems to indicate that South Africa does not have a monopoly on human cruelty. The two-part novel consists of two "reports" on the warfare that the government has waged against civilians. The first report is narrated by Eugene Dawn, a specialist for the United States military, who is making a report to a supervisor named Coetzee on war against the North Vietnamese in the twentieth century. The second part is written by Jacobus Coetzee in the eighteenth century, and it is translated by a Dr. S. J. Coetzee. Of the two narrators in the novel, Eugene Dawn and Jacobus Coetzee, one is introspective and sensitive, while the other is arrogant and aggressive. By naming the supervisor of the first part, and the narrator and translator of the second part, after his own last name, Coetzee seems to be making an indictment against the white settlers who, centuries earlier, had migrated to South Africa. The fictional character, Jacobus Coetzee, expresses his cruelty in a series of violent acts directed against the natives, whose land he has invaded. His report contains vestiges of Joseph Conrad's *Heart of Darkness* (1902), a short novel that deals with the white penetration into Africa.

It is difficult to assess which "side" is necessarily good and which is bad in his novels because, Coetzee seems to say, all human acts involve both. He makes this equivocation essential in his second novel, *In the Heart of the Country*, which was also published in the United States as *From the Heart of the Country* (1977) and contained the Afrikaans language in the novel's dialogues. For the English-language edition, Coetzee himself translated the dialogues.

The narrator of the second novel records her observations in the form of a journal. As events emerge, however, there are apparent inconsistencies, and they provide the reader with an essential clue to the ways in which isolation from other people might direct the narrator to think and behave in a disturbing manner. Magda's madness or perversion may be the product of the South African farm itself.

The theme of a hostile environment and the human isolation that that hostility produces also appears in the next novel, *Waiting for the Barbarians*. The Magistrate, like Coetzee's other characters, is an introspective narrator who seems pitted against a variety of circumstances over which he has little control. Under the Magistrate's watchful eye, the war between the unnamed Empire and the natives (or "barbarians," as the Empire refers to them) unfolds, and, as he observes, the Magistrate begins to sympathize more and more with the victims of the regime.

Coetzee's novels always seem to present two sides of the issue, as they emphasize the cruelty of which all human beings seem capable against one another. Sometimes, as in the case with the Magistrate, people realize too late their roles in helping to advance the cruelty. Other times, people choose to disappear altogether from society.

That appears to be the case with the main character, a gardener named Michael, in *Life and Times of Michael K*. From birth, Michael is an outcast who spends his childhood in an orphanage among other unwanted children.

The novel focuses on Michael's journey to the farm where his mother spent part of her girlhood. Mother and son begin the journey after a series of unpropitious delays by the bureaucratic government, only to have Michael's mother die on the way to the farm. Michael resumes the journey, taking her ashes with him. He finds the farm, where he manages to live from his harvests for a while, until he is captured by guerrilla soldiers who mistake his withdrawal from society as a revolutionary act.

The second part of the novel is narrated by a young pharmacist who is assigned to Michael's care after the capture. The third part shows Michael's return to Cape Town, where he accepts the charity of a group of vagabonds. The novel ends on the enigmatic observation that people do what they can under the circumstances, and, in this way, "one can live."

Human survival is an important theme in Coetzee's next two novels. *Foe* is narrated by the survivor, Susan Barton, who went from a capsized ship to a desolate island inhabited by Cruso (in contrast to Defoe's Robinson Crusoe) and Friday. Much of Susan Barton's relationship to Cruso and Friday is prompted by her own instincts to record the experiences. The two men seem unconcerned whether other people will ever know of their existence, while Barton desires not only to survive the island experience but also to live to tell or write about it. When Barton returns to England, she takes the mute Friday along with her. There, Barton confronts the writer Daniel Foe and asks that he help her record her experiences. The novel becomes Barton's own retelling of what occurred on the island, as well as a new version of the "real" Crusoe story told by the "actual" author, Daniel Defoe.

The layers of telling and retelling of a single story occur with variation in Coetzee's next novel, *Age of Iron*. As in *Foe*, there is an implied audience to the narrator's story. In *Age of Iron*, Mrs. Currens tells her grown daughter living in the United States the story of a vagabond named Vercueil, who one day appears at her home. Mrs. Currens and Vercueil become involved in unraveling the murder of two young black boys in one of the townships. When she is questioned by the police for her concern, Mrs. Currens shows the reader that her allegiances are no longer simply to the state; her knowledge of death and violence has rendered her desensitized to the way that her government operates.

IN THE HEART OF THE COUNTRY

First published: 1977
Type of work: Novel

The narrator, Magda, keeps a journal that reflects a psychological disorientation attributable to living on a South African farm at the beginning of the twentieth century.

The narrator of Coetzee's second novel, *In the Heart of the Country*, is a white woman named Magda, who appears to be living at the beginning of the twentieth century on a South African farm with her father and several servants and field hands. Her story is told in the form of a journal, and there are 266 numbered passages that constitute the novel. Magda's father appears to be a hard and rugged ruler of the farm, and, as the narrative progresses, it becomes evident that Magda's relationships with her father and some of the servants are complicated by the isolation of farm life.

In conventional literary terms, Magda's narrative may be considered "unreliable," because of grating inconsistencies in the sequence of events and in the manner of presentation. For example, in one scene, Magda brutally kills her father and his new bride with an axe while they are in bed; a little later, her father is up and about, although the "bride"—if indeed there had been a bride—seems to have disappeared; a little later still, Magda shoots her father from below his bedroom while he is having sex with one of the servants; and toward the novel's end, after an elaborate and illegal burial of the father, Magda is conversing with him. In other scenes, especially those with the servant Hendrik and his bride, Klein-Anna, Magda also expresses inconsistencies in her narrative. There appear to be a variety of sexual encounters, but these seem to arise from Magda's wishful imagination, rather than as a record of actual happenings. Clearly, though, Magda's record of events—not unlike those of Eugene Dawn and Jacobus Coetzee—are motivated by highly intense and personal desires.

Magda's isolation from people unrelated to the life of the farm seems to provoke some of the inconsistencies. Magda's rendition of the events is profoundly literal, and a careless reader is apt to miss the many tensions that inform her reported actions. Specifically, there are sexual undercurrents in her relationships with the two men, her father and Hendrik; even her conversations with Hendrik's young wife, Klein-Anna, seem filled with erotic tensions. In one scene, Magda makes a proposition to the couple that suggests the existence of a love triangle.

Throughout the novel, it is difficult to determine which event is "true" and which are colorful versions told by the spinster, Magda. If the accounts themselves appear dubious to the reader, however, they are perhaps accurate renditions of the narrator's own troubled psychological state. Coetzee seems to pose this question throughout the novel: What is real, what is reality? At the heart of the journal entries, what is actual may remain forever unknown, but what is real or genuine is the disorientation that Magda experiences as a result of her alienation.

WAITING FOR THE BARBARIANS

First published: 1980
Type of work: Novel

> The Third Empire wages a war with natives who are governed by the Magistrate; he soon learns who are really the victims and who are the barbarians.

Waiting for the Barbarians is a short novel narrated by a man known only as the Magistrate. The time and place of the situation in the novel are also unspecified, and these indeterminacies allow the reader to perceive the events as universal. In fact, the name of Third Empire may be a combination of the Roman Empire and Germany's Third Reich during World War II; the Empire in the novel acts as atrociously as the two historical empires.

The novel begins with the arrival of Colonel Joll from the Third Empire, which has declared war against the "barbarians," the natives of the surrounding land governed by the Magistrate. Among the captives, the Magistrate witnesses the killing of an old man and the torture of a young boy. Later, he encounters a young woman whose body bears the visible cruelties of the Empire.

It is in his relationship with the young woman that the Magistrate begins to reexamine the goals of the Empire. Before Colonel Joll's arrival, the Magistrate had lived without incident among the natives and "fisherfolk," and some of his leisure time was spent excavating and deciphering the artifacts of those who had lived there before him. In the young "barbarian" woman, the Magistrate begins to understand that he, along with those in the service of the Third Empire, helped to destroy an innocent and peaceful civilization. After the Magistrate embarks on an ill-timed journey to return the woman to her people, he is perceived as an enemy of the State and, upon his return, is summarily imprisoned without a trial. He makes the full understanding that it is the rulers of the Third Empire who are the real barbarians.

All the events are narrated by the Magistrate, whose ideological transformation becomes evident by the end of the novel. The "destroyers" leave after Colonel Joll realizes that their atrocities have been so thorough that there is nothing left to conquer. Most of the natives have also left the village for other places, and those too old or feeble to leave remain with the Magistrate. At the end, the Magistrate is trying to make a record of the Third Empire's devastation, and momentarily, it seems that order and productivity will be restored. The ravaged land, however, has become too arid and infertile to produce enough food to eat. The Magistrate and the rest simply wait and wait for something else to occur, but, deep down, he understands the futility. He sees himself "like a man who lost his way long ago but presses on along a road that may lead nowhere."

Summary

J. M. Coetzee's novels are dense and filled with philosophical awareness of the plight of people living under oppressive circumstances. In most cases, the novels do not appear as joyous celebrations of human lives. Yet neither do the novels depict a dismal vision of the state of affairs.

Rather, in creating realistic interior and external worlds that reflect human cruelty and atrocity, Coetzee never lets the reader forget that all existence comprises positive and negative acts. The novels are difficult to comprehend at times because the subject matter and the characters that inhabit the devastated worlds do not lend themselves to easy simplifications. Their inherent complexity reflects the general difficulty of confronting the pain and suffering of human lives.

Bibliography

Coetzee, J. M. "Interview with J. M. Coetzee." Interview by Jean Sévry. *Commonwealth* 9 (1986): 1-7.

──────────. "Two Interviews with J. M. Coetzee, 1983 and 1987." Interview by Tony Morphet. *TriQuarterly* 69 (1987): 454-464.

Penner, Allen Richard. *Countries of the Mind: The Fiction of J. M. Coetzee*. New York: Greenwood Press, 1989

Ward, David. "J. M. Coetzee." In *Chronicles of Darkness*. London: Routledge & Kegan Paul, 1989.

White, Landeg, and Tim Couzens, eds. *Literature and Society in South Africa*. New York: Longman, 1984.

Cynthia Wong

SAMUEL TAYLOR COLERIDGE

Born: Ottery St. Mary, Devonshire, England
October 21, 1772
Died: Highgate, London, England
July 25, 1834

Principal Literary Achievement

Coleridge is one of the most important and prolific English Romantic poets. His contributions to the art and philosophy of the age include some of the greatest literary criticism ever written, as well as one of humanity's most innovative biographical documents.

Biography

Born in Ottery St. Mary, at the vicarage of a small town in rural Devonshire, England, on October 21, 1772, Samuel Taylor Coleridge was the tenth and last child of the Reverend John and Ann Bowden Coleridge. John was an ambitious and scholarly man who served his community not only as parish priest but also as headmaster of the local grammar school, the site of his youngest child's first formal education. Many of Samuel's early family associations seem fraught with anxiety and pain. His elderly parents doted upon their clever and eager child, which his siblings resented, and Samuel developed an intense dependency upon those whom he perceived to be stronger and better than he—a pattern that persisted throughout his life. Thus, intellectual precocity brought him much attention and affection at the same time that nearly insatiable appetites, manifest as greed for books and food, prevented his ever feeling fully satisfied and cherished.

Whatever possibilities might have existed for bliss at home were thwarted, however, when John Coleridge died suddenly when the boy was about to turn nine. His mother was nearly destitute, so her youngest son was dispatched to London to attend Christ's Hospital Grammar School, originally a charity school for the children of indigent clergy. The boarding school was conservative and strict, but Coleridge, despite claims of homesickness and loneliness, flourished in the urban academic environment under the unflinching and at times painfully demanding tutelage of James Bowyer, who encouraged the youth's poetry writing and guided his inaugural study of Continental philosophy, which continued throughout his life. Moreover, Coleridge

was viewed by many of the other boys as gregarious and charming, although his lifelong friend Charles Lamb, also enrolled there, wrote later of Coleridge's unhappiness at Christ's Hospital.

Shortly before his twentieth birthday in 1792, Coleridge matriculated at Jesus College, Cambridge University, on a scholarship designated for those intending to take Holy Orders in the Church of England. From an initially rigorous regimen of mathematics and the classics, Coleridge drifted by his third and final year toward no less intensive but more idiosyncratic and less respectable pursuits. For a youth of slender means, he contracted sizable debts and became a supporter of religious and political radicals such as William Frend and William Godwin. England, in the initial period following the start of the French Revolution, harbored a number of young and idealistic sympathizers to the French, and Coleridge found himself in intelligent and congenial company. Overcome by guilt for his financial state, however, which was also undermining his chances with a young woman with whom he was in love, Coleridge impulsively and secretly enlisted in the Light Dragoons as Silas Tomkyn Comberbacke, preserving the initials by which he preferred to be known. The Dragoons were cavalry units, requiring equestrian skills beyond those of Coleridge. After a month, he appealed to his brothers, who paid off his debts and the cost of his discharge.

Returning to Cambridge in the spring of 1793, Coleridge met Robert Southey, another improvident young intellectual poet, recently at Oxford and also unwillingly destined for the Church. They instantly became great friends, with Coleridge virtually idolizing Southey, sharing ideas and interests and formulating Pantisocracy, a utopian community to be established in the United States along the Susquehanna River in Pennsylvania. In Bristol, where Coleridge began delivering successful public lectures on various literary and philosophic topics, he contributed journalistic articles and essays, wrote poetry, and undertook in-depth study and reflection, which he recorded in notebooks and the margins of published books. All of these occupations lasted his entire life.

In October, 1795, Coleridge wed Sara Fricker. They settled in Clevedon on the Bristol Channel, while he prepared to launch his own (short-lived) weekly newspaper, *The Watchman.* Idyllically happy, Coleridge wrote one of his most famous poems, "The Eolian Harp," in which he explores the idea of the "One Life."

Around this time, too, Coleridge met William Wordsworth, also a young, restless, and penurious Cambridge radical and aspiring poet. As he had with Southey (with whom Coleridge had now quarreled), Coleridge fell into a kind of hero worship of Wordsworth, although in many ways their relationship was mutually sustaining.

Coleridge's first book of poems appeared in 1796, along with the first issue of his paper, but neither was very successful. This same year, Coleridge was reconciled with Southey, who was now his brother-in-law, and Coleridge's first son, Hartley, was born. Coleridge decided to move his young family to Nether Stowey in the rural west of England, where he had been born. The year was also marked by an outbreak of facial neuralgia, for which Coleridge amply medicated himself with laudanum, the common alcoholic tincture of opium of the day; at that time, laudanum was as readily used as aspirin is today and was a recourse that was already habitual with Coleridge.

Coleridge had had a sickly childhood. When he was eighteen, he had developed serious rheumatic fever and very likely received a considerable amount of laudanum for anesthetic relief. In addition, opium initially offered him an escape from his inadequacies. Despite some periods of remission, the rheumatic fever seems to have become a chronic condition progressing over the course of his life to rheumatism and rheumatic heart disease. As a result of his ill health, coupled with his dependent personality, Coleridge swiftly capitulated to opium addiction, which itself compromised his health, as well as the conduct of his life.

While living in Stowey, Coleridge labored on a play, *Osorio,* completed in 1797 and destined for the Drury Lane Theatre in London—which, however, rejected it. (In 1813, revised and renamed *Remorse,* it triumphed at that theater.) Meanwhile, he also wrote more conversation poems, including "This Lime-Tree Bower My Prison," about a walk in the country made by a group of his friends whom he was unable to accompany because Sara had spilled hot milk on his foot, and "Frost at Midnight," in which he pledges a childhood nurtured by nature for baby Hartley, unlike his own London-bound experiences at Christ's Hospital. Coleridge also is thought to have written the mysterious, exotic "Kubla Khan" around this time.

During the last years of the eighteenth century, Coleridge was increasingly drawn to Wordsworth. In discussing their craft, the two poets decided to collaborate first on a poem, then on a collection. The poem was to be a narrative about the wandering, guilt-ridden Cain; the idea dissolved into Coleridge's magnificent *The Rime of the Ancient Mariner* (1798), which was published as the first poem of their joint *Lyrical Ballads* (1798). This collection is generally seen as heralding the English Romantic movement. The volume ends with Wordsworth's masterpiece "Lines: Composed a Few Miles Above Tintern Abbey," the philosophic underpinnings of which are clearly Coleridge's notion of the One Life, transmuted through Wordsworth's childhood mysticism. Shortly after writing *The Rime of the Ancient Mariner,* Coleridge wrote the fragmentary *Christabel* (1816), and the Wedgwood family of pottery wealth, whose sons were sympathetic to Coleridge's writing, settled a £150 annuity on the perpetually indigent poet. It was well timed, for the Coleridge family now included a second son, Berkeley.

One of the reasons for publishing *Lyrical Ballads* was to underwrite a winter in Germany, which Coleridge believed was the essential place to study. He had originally planned to write the age's great philosophic poem; now he turned the responsibility for that work over to Wordsworth, typically deferring to one deemed superior. (Wordsworth accepted the charge and felt burdened by it for life, haunted by Coleridge's specter, though Coleridge himself by no means escaped the self-inflicted obligation of producing a magnum opus). The Wordsworths and Coleridge, with his wife and family left in the care of friends, set sail before the collection appeared, toward the end of 1798. The Wordsworths were cold, poor, lonely, and miserable in Goslar, while Coleridge reveled in the social and intellectual ferment at the university town of Göttingen. In April, he finally received word that Berkeley had died two

months before, although he did not return to Stowey until July, which aroused ac-
cusations of neglect. Once back in England, Coleridge decided that he and his family
would follow the Wordsworths to the Lake District, and he installed his family in
Greta Hall in Keswick. In 1800, a third son, Derwent, was born, and Coleridge devoted himself for a time to journalism to support his family.

Coleridge's health, as a result of both genuine malady and the opium use, was
suffering, and his marriage was seriously foundering. Although he and Sara had seemed
ecstatically happy at first, the full burden of the household had fallen to Sara, who
was unable to rely upon her husband for assistance or steady financial support. Moreover, he had, since his earliest married days, been unable to stay in one place or at
one task for very long; he was alternately indolent, fidgety, moody, and infirm of
purpose and of place, for which the encumbered Sara had no sympathy. For emotional and physical sanctuary, he fled frequently to the Wordsworths in Grasmere,
where he encountered the sister of Wordsworth's intended bride, Sara Hutchison,
whom he rendered anagrammatically as "Asra" when he fell madly in love with her.
A verse letter to her, much revised, became his moving and melancholic paean to his
inability to feel and, ironically, to write. It became "Dejection: An Ode." His ardor
for Sara seems not to have been consummated.

Coleridge increasingly chose prose over poetry to channel his emotional and creative furies. At times, he tried to make his marriage work, and his last child and only
daughter, Sara, was born at the end of 1802. Coleridge, however, effectively ceased
being a member of his family after young Sara was born. His marriage was virtually
over, though divorce, in keeping with the mores of the day, was never seriously con-
templated. In 1804, Coleridge set off for Malta, to recover his health in a foreign and
presumably more hospitable climate, to break his addiction, and to produce some
serious writing, including some philosophical notes to buttress Wordsworth's grand
poem. He traveled around southern Europe, skirting the movements of Napoleon's
armies, and returned to England in 1806, still addicted, still ill, and claiming that the
notes for the poem had been lost at sea. In the meantime, Wordsworth was writing
his great autobiographical *The Prelude: Or, The Growth of a Poet's Mind* (1850), which
he always considered as his poem addressed to Coleridge. Nonetheless, Coleridge
had clearly tried and expended the good favor of his friends.

Although Coleridge remained in touch with his family, his base of operations was
henceforth London, where he lectured to great acclaim on poetry, both contemporary and Renaissance, and philosophy, publishing a journal, *The Friend* (1809-1810,
1818), which was notable but insolvent. His youthful radicalism had almost entirely
eroded, so that now he wrote positively and enthusiastically about the English establishment and the Church of England, trying to contrive his magnum opus now in
religious terms.

In 1810, Coleridge moved in with the Montagus, who endeavored to cure his addiction, although Wordsworth, their friend, warned them of the hopelessness of helping
Coleridge. When Wordsworth's warning came true, they revealed it to Coleridge, who
thereupon broke off all relations—already somewhat cooled—with Wordsworth. The

breach, celebrated at the time, was healed two years later, although the two were never what they had been to one another, despite a joint trip to Germany in 1828.

In 1815, Coleridge began what became an innovative document, the unfinished *Biographia Literaria: Or, Biographical Sketches of My Literary Life and Opinions* (1817). Two years later, he published *Sibylline Leaves* (1817), a late collection of verse, and a small volume containing, for the first time, *Christabel* and "Kubla Khan."

For the remainder of his life, Coleridge resided, first, for about six years with the Morgan family, wealthy admirers who failed to eliminate his dependency on opium, and, then, with Dr. James Gillman in Highgate, who seems to have finally controlled the habit. Coleridge was particularly fortunate in this hospitality, for his health remained very poor, and in 1812 he willingly surrendered his annuity when the Wedgwoods experienced financial reverses. He continued various writing projects, which earned for him some economic relief and growing respect as a literary critic and as an architect of a modern temperament in art.

Coleridge regretted the unfolding patterns of the lives of his abandoned children. His son Hartley, who had seemed the quintessential Romantic child, had to leave Oxford and great academic promise owing to alcohol abuse, drifting into alcoholism and homelessness. The brilliant daughter Sara had married her cousin Henry Coleridge; the blood relationship concerned her father, although they proved their devotion by serving as the first editors of Coleridge's writings. Drawing upon his faith at the end, Coleridge died of a massive heart attack compounded by rheumatic hypertension on July 25, 1834, in London, and was buried at Highgate cemetery.

Analysis

As one of the three primary figures of the first generation of the traditional canon of English Romantic poets, Coleridge is responsible along with Wordsworth for the *Lyrical Ballads*, which is generally viewed as the opening salvo of English Romanticism. Coleridge's masterwork is that great vision of sin and Redemption, *The Rime of the Ancient Mariner*, which begins the volume, but he wrote other magnificent poems and contributed substantially to literary theory.

In fact, in many respects, English Romanticism might not have occurred without the synergy of the two poets in the mid- to late 1790's and into the first decade of the nineteenth century. Critics have interpreted Wordsworth's "Peter Bell" and "The Idiot Boy" as reactions to or attempted corrections of *The Rime of the Ancient Mariner.* Also, Wordsworth's "Ode: Intimations of Immortality" is often seen as engaged in a "lyrical dialogue," to use critic Paul Magnuson's expression, with Coleridge's "Dejection: An Ode," in which both poets ponder emotional despair and what it means for themselves in the world and as poets, as well as what each thinks of the other's ideas.

One of Coleridge's earliest contributions to English Romanticism was the "conversation poem," a form that he invented, which critic M. H. Abrams later termed the "greater Romantic lyric." In this form, a speaker describes to a silent listener the physical surroundings and the passage of his thoughts until some insight, related to the landscape and yet also transforming it, and him, arises. Other Romantic poets borrowed the form (William Wordsworth's "Lines: Composed a Few Miles Above Tintern Abbey," Percy Bysshe Shelley's "Mont Blanc," and John Keats's "Ode to a Nightingale" might be considered examples), but no one surpassed the compact power of "The Eolian Harp," "This Lime-Tree Bower My Prison," and "Frost at Midnight."

For Coleridge, the conversation poem was particularly well suited to his evocation of the One Life, a philosophy of pantheism with which he was much taken in the 1790's. In brief, this philosophy holds that the Creator and the created are one, that God suffuses and interfuses the universe, and that all that lives is in and of God. Coleridge, however, was uncomfortable subscribing to this idea for very long, and age, care, and experience seem to have taken their toll and restored him to the Church of England. Nonetheless, his restless imagination explored the implications of the established religion, as well. Late in life, his prose works reflected these interests.

Many of Coleridge's projects share the recurring Romantic characteristic of fragmentation. For the Romantics, the fragment was testament to the partiality of the human ability to understand and to re-create the world. For Coleridge, in particular, the fragment also testified to his own tendencies to start vast projects that would, for a variety of reasons, fail to be realized in their entirety. Nonetheless, in the Romantic period great merit was located in the portion that abided, and fragments by Wordsworth, Shelley, Keats, and George Gordon, Lord Byron, have all been published, while Coleridge's "Kubla Khan," and *Biographia Literaria* are all billed as incomplete. Despite their tentativeness, however, they are triumphs of artistry, celebrating the mystery of the universe coupled with the insatiable and indestructible talent to fabricate, which Coleridge understood, both as practitioner and as philosopher.

Coleridge devised theories to account for the functioning of the imagination and offered inspired commentary on many other great writers, including William Shakespeare and John Milton, as well as his former collaborator, Wordsworth. For Coleridge, creativity imitated the divine act recorded in the biblical book of Genesis, not as blasphemy but as homage and as the best of which humanity was capable. Also, aesthetic value, he believed, derived from the degree to which art achieved or approached organic form rather than stylized or artificial construction. Thus, he linked art with the vitality of the living thing, which he saw as also celebrating multifaceted integrity, what he called "multeity in unity"—a phrase that sums up, as well, the varied legacy subsumed under the name of Samuel Taylor Coleridge.

THE RIME OF THE ANCIENT MARINER

First published: 1798
Type of work: Poem

On a long sea voyage, a sailor kills the faithful albatross, which then brings down upon him ghostly punishment and penance.

Coleridge's masterpiece, *The Rime of the Ancient Mariner*, was first published as part of the *Lyrical Ballads* (1798), which thereby secured its position as one of the landmark poems of its age, despite its archaic ballad form. Structured as a frame narrative, the poem begins with the Mariner's detaining a guest on his way to a wedding with the spellbinding account of a most strange ocean voyage. The Mariner tells of a southbound voyage to the Antarctic. He describes how the ship, as it clears the horizon, ominously dips below the Church and below all of civilized and conventional authority, descending toward the unknown, the wild, and the hellish. Reaching the frozen, seemingly blank, polar world, the sailors call to and feed a white albatross, a large sea bird, as an apparent friend or messenger from another realm. The Mariner inexplicably shoots it, sacrificing it, innocent and pure, with his crossbow (echoing Easter imagery). Thereupon, the ship idles without wind to move it while the superstitious crew grows increasingly thirsty and hangs the dead bird around the Mariner's neck to punish him for his cruelty, which they feel in some way has stalled their trip.

At last, a ship is sighted, but it is a skeleton ship, carrying the Spectre-Woman, "Life-in-Death," and her mate Death, who are types of avenging spirits of the albatross. The two of them toss dice to determine who will decide the fate of the Mariner's ship, and the Woman wins. She imposes a penance on the Mariner, which begins with the death of the crew while the Mariner lives on, unable to die, unable even to sleep. Watching the now-beautiful phosphorescent water snakes, which earlier looked monstrous to him, the Mariner is impelled to bless them, and at once the albatross slides off his neck into the sea. His unconscious action restores a balance upset by his murder of the albatross, although his penance is not finished, as disembodied spirit voices assert.

The Mariner is now able to sleep, and he dreams while the ship sails home, manned by spirits animating the crew's corpses. At length, the ship escapes the haunted universe to return to home port, but then it suddenly sinks, while the Mariner is rescued and immediately absolved of his sins, if only for a time, by the Hermit of the Wood. Nonetheless, his need for penance remains, for the Mariner must wander endlessly and solitarily, until an agony seizes him, and he in turn seizes one whom he knows must hear his tale. The Wedding Guest misses the marriage ceremony, but he has been irrevocably changed by the Mariner's words.

The poem has given rise to a multitude of interpretations, stressing the existential, meaningless murder of the albatross in an incomprehensible world; the Christian pattern of sin, confession, and penance within a sacramental universe; the functioning of the symbolic or nightmare imagination as the Mariner's fate unfolds; and the necessity, even the desperation, of narration. Coleridge himself after the first publication appended marginalia that recapitulate the poem in an effort to clarify (though what it actually does is to retell the plot at a slant and thereby distances the author, as well as the frame, from the poem's peculiar and disturbing nature, relinquishing responsibility for interpretation to each reader).

CHRISTABEL

First published: 1816
Type of work: Poem

The maiden Christabel finds the mysterious, serpentine Geraldine in the woods at midnight and brings her home to her castle with subsequent emotional chaos.

Christabel has two parts, written in 1797 and 1800, with the second part a distinct falling-off from the preceding. In the first part, the maiden Christabel, rather unwisely for a defenseless young girl, goes into the woods at midnight to pray for her betrothed knight, where she discovers the beautiful but evil Geraldine, who claims that she has been abandoned by five would-be rapists. At once, the idea of sexual violation comes into the poem. Christabel takes pity upon her and brings her to the home that she shares with her father, Sir Leoline. Geraldine, like evil spirits traditionally, cannot cross the threshold of the castle, so poor, duped Christabel carries her, in an ironic inversion of the marriage ritual.

Christabel brings Geraldine to her bedchamber and tells her guest about her mother's having died when she was born. They undress, Geraldine revealing her magic and mystery in an undescribed horror visible on her chest and side. Naïvely, Christabel sleeps with her visitor. In the conclusion to the first part, the narrator acknowledges that Geraldine now has Christabel at her mercy and that only the unlikely aid of the spirit of Christabel's mother can save her. Geraldine probably is a lesbian vampire, as is most persuasively argued by James Twitchell and Camille Paglia (in Harold Bloom's collection of essays).

The second part of the poem concerns the day after the previous waking nightmare. Sir Leoline arises to note that he awakes to a world of death, which clearly characterizes the experience to which his daughter is now subject. He meets Geraldine, who discloses that she is the daughter of his youthful best friend, from whom he is now estranged. He decides to use this visit to mend fences, while the watching Christabel is reminded of how chilled she was when she touched Geraldine the night before.

Similarly, Bard Bracy, the resident poet who is by virtue of his craft gifted with the artist's intuition of truth, describes a dream that he has just had, in which Sir Leoline's pet dove, named for his daughter, has been captured by a green snake. Moreover, Christabel, under the magnetic but malevolent influence of Geraldine's serpentine eyes, reflects the same diabolic appearance, which renders Sir Leoline, interpreting it as jealousy, enraged at his evidently inhospitable child. Christabel's troubles are only just beginning, it seems, as the poem breaks off.

Coleridge talked of completing the poem, but, starting as it does with the rise of evil, he was uncomfortable pursuing that to its anticipated and un-Christian triumph. It remains, then, a provocative fragment of innocence in the grasp of potent, malicious, and unconventional female sexuality.

KUBLA KHAN

First published: 1816
Type of work: Poem

In a fragment of an opium dream, the Mongol emperor builds a crystal palace; then an Abyssinian maiden and a flashing-eyed prophet reproduce it.

"Kubla Khan," tagged as a fragment, has two parts. The first is a mostly prose introduction in which Coleridge recounts the circumstances under which he composed the following lines of verse. He confesses to having fallen asleep after having taken medication for a minor complaint while meditating upon a voluminous travelogue. Asleep, he dreams the images that, upon waking, he dashes down as the poem. Unfortunately, he is interrupted by a man from Porlock, a nearby town, and when he is again able to write, he recalls little more. Additionally, Coleridge announces that he is publishing this fragment, written years before, only at the behest of the deservedly famous (as he ingenuously notes) Lord Byron. Thus, in short order, Coleridge blames a book, sleep and dreams, drugs, a visitor, and Byron for this curious and cryptic poem rather than bravely taking responsibility for it himself.

Coleridge's insecurities prevented his claiming a masterpiece. The poem proper is also bipartite. Its first section describes how, godlike, Kubla Khan creates an entire world, a kind of Eden, merely by utterance. His decree animates a world of fountains and rivers, caves and gardens, energy and peace, an enchanted and hallowed place that seems to represent the origins of life, consciousness, and art. Within this Eden, conflict, a fall, is predicted, for the emperor hears ancient war prophecies.

Abruptly, the poem switches to a dream of an Abyssinian dulcimer-playing maiden singing of a holy mountain. The poet declares that, were he able to recall her song, which in a way he has just done with lines that evoke her, he would also be able to duplicate Kubla Khan's invention, which he has actually also just done in writing the foregoing, and his witnesses would attest to his inspiration, his art, and his prophecy.

What Coleridge has done is to celebrate his poetic artistry and its kinship with the creative and prophetic powers of religion and humanity's deepest desires.

BIOGRAPHIA LITERARIA

First published: 1817
Type of work: Autobiography

In an unfinished autobiography, Coleridge considers his childhood, the rules of poetry, Wordsworth's poetry, the nature of creation, and German philosophy.

The *Biographia Literaria*, ostensibly a literary biography, is also one of the greatest works of literary criticism. Coleridge begins by discussing his secondary education, particularly in classical poetry, under James Bowyer at Christ's Hospital Grammar School. From there, he launches a discussion of Wordsworth's poetry, to which he later returns. Coleridge takes Wordsworth at face value and applies to Wordsworth's poetry what Wordsworth in his 1800 preface to the *Lyrical Ballads* claimed to do. Coleridge shows that Wordsworth's protestations that his craft was the common language of common people was not strictly true, that his poetry is nonetheless artifice, consciously crafted and not the unreflective, thoughtless speech he said it represented. Still, Coleridge argues that Wordsworth is the finest contemporary poet and an example of poetic genius. He also gives his version of the origin of the *Lyrical Ballads* of 1798, saying that Wordsworth was to write of natural scenes made extraordinary by his craft, while Coleridge was to write of the supernatural rendered credible by his art. This interpretation is somewhat at odds with Wordsworth's emphasis in his preface on the volume's intended singular purpose.

Coleridge also proffers his definition of imagination. He distinguishes the "primary," which he describes as the divine ability to create, the source of all animate power. The "secondary" imagination is the human ability to create, through the inventive perception and recollection of images. Last is the "fancy," which is simply the ability to remember.

Coleridge, in addition, discourses at length on philosophy. Beginning with Thomas De Quincey, however, who was himself later similarly charged, critics have noted, censured, or excused the extensive portions of the *Biographia Literaria* that correspond to translations of the German philosopher Friedrich Wilhelm Joseph Schelling. Commentator Thomas McFarland has pointed out that Schelling did not consider his work to have been plagiarized and that in large measure what Coleridge was doing was registering a congruence of his thinking with that of Schelling, before both diverged in opposite directions. Moreover, McFarland notes that Coleridge fully intended to return to the manuscript later to insert his own words for the words of the German, which were at the moment merely holding a place in the text, as it were, for Coleridge's words. Alas, Coleridge never returned, never substituted, and never completed the work. Thus, it might be described most accurately as an "anatomy," as critic Northrop Frye defines it, a congeries of digressions, meditations, and reflections, the unity of which may be unclear but the sum of which clearly exceeds its parts.

Summary

Samuel Taylor Coleridge was justly celebrated during his lifetime for his wide learning and wonderful powers of conversation, which competed personally with devastating opium addiction, deep-seated miseries, and emotional insecurities. Yet he is also remembered for his poetic gifts, which enabled him to explore extraordinary worlds opened up by creative powers, and his philosophical inquiries, which attempted to account for those worlds, those powers, and his own complex self.

Bibliography

Bate, Walter Jackson. *Coleridge*. New York: Macmillan, 1968.

Bloom, Harold, ed. *Samuel Taylor Coleridge: Modern Critical Views*. New York: Chelsea House, 1986.

Holmes, Richard. *Coleridge: Early Visions*. New York: Penguin Books, 1989.

Lefebure, Molly. *Samuel Taylor Coleridge: A Bondage of Opium*. New York: Stein & Day, 1974.

McFarland, Thomas. *Coleridge and the Pantheist Tradition*. Oxford, England: Clarendon Press, 1969.

_____. *Romanticism and the Forms of Ruin: Wordsworth, Coleridge, and Modalities of Fragmentation*. Princeton, N.J.: Princeton University Press, 1981.

Magnuson, Paul. *Coleridge and Wordsworth: A Lyrical Dialogue*. Princeton, N.J.: Princeton University Press, 1988.

_____. *Coleridge's Nightmare Poetry*. Charlottesville: University Press of Virginia, 1974.

Newlyn, Lucy. *Coleridge, Wordsworth, and the Language of Allusion*. Oxford, England: Clarendon Press, 1986.

Roe, Nicholas. *Wordsworth and Coleridge: The Radical Years*. Oxford, England: Clarendon Press, 1988.

Twitchell, James. *The Living Dead: A Study of the Vampire in Romantic Literature*. Durham, N.C.: Duke University Press, 1981.

Laura Dabundo

COLETTE

Born: Saint-Sauveur-en-Puisaye, France
January 28, 1873
Died: Paris, France
August 3, 1954

Principal Literary Achievement
Colette is one of France's most popular novelists, noted especially for her depictions of love, animals, and nature.

Biography

Sidonie-Gabrielle Colette was born in Saint-Sauveur-en-Puisaye, a small town in southwest France, on January 28, 1873, to Jules-Joseph Colette and Adèle-Sidonie Landoy Robineau-Duclos. Jules-Joseph was a retired army captain turned tax collector, and it was this new profession that had led the family to Saint-Sauveur-en Puisaye. At first things went well, and Colette enjoyed a happy childhood in her easygoing, free-thinking family. Jules-Joseph, however, was too easygoing; he was not very industrious, and he did not have much of a head for business. In 1890, the family was forced to sell its house and move in with Colette's older brother Achille Robineau-Duclos, a doctor in a nearby village.

It was there, in 1891, that the family received a visit from Henri Gauthiers-Villars (later known simply as "Willy"), the son of a former colleague of Jules-Joseph in the military. Willy had rejected his father's scientific orientation in favor of literature, aided by his father's contacts in the publishing industry. Willy was fifteen years older than Colette, but the age difference apparently did not pose a problem. They were engaged within the year, and in 1893 they were married. To what extent Colette was in love with Willy is a question that has preoccupied biographers ever since. It is certain that Colette had a considerable amount of difficulty leaving behind her mother, to whom she remained strongly attached, when the couple moved to Paris that year. Not much is known about the early years of Colette's marriage, but it was clearly a period of disillusionment. Willy, it transpired, was something of a philanderer and without real literary talent. Colette fell ill, no doubt partly as a result of her depression. It was Sido (as Colette called her mother) who came and nursed her back to health, a further testimony to the close bond between mother and daughter.

As a way to lift Colette out of her depression, Willy suggested that she become one of his ghostwriters and write down some of her schoolgirl memories with a bit

of added spice to make them sell. The first result of their collaboration, *Claudine à l'école* (1900; *Claudine at School*, 1956), was published in 1900 and became an immediate success. Willy and Colette quickly followed with *Claudine à Paris* (1901; *Claudine in Paris*, 1958) the following year, *Claudine en ménage* (1902; *The Indulgent Husband*, 1935; also translated as *Claudine Married*, 1960) in 1902, and finally *Claudine s'en va* (1903; *The Innocent Wife*, 1934; also translated as *Claudine and Annie*, 1962) the year after that. The series was a resounding success and led to a "Claudine craze" that made the authors household names.

All four novels contained a strong autobiographical element, characteristic of all Colette's work, and as the heroine Claudine evolved through each story, so, too, did Colette. Like her heroine, she had left school, got married, moved to Paris, and grown more and more independent. By 1904, Colette no longer needed Willy as coauthor and her first "solo" novel appeared, signed merely by "Madame Colette Willy."

Colette's new confidence and independence put increasing distance between her and Willy. The stress on their relationship was intensified by the death of Colette's father in 1905, and in 1906 the couple separated and Colette's life entered a new phase. She began appearing on the stage, notably in mime-dramas that often led to controversy because of the roles that she played. She also became involved in a relationship with the Marquise de Belboeuf (known as "Missy"), which would last for several years. During this time, Colette continued publishing, and several important novels appeared during this period, including *La Retraite sentimentale* (1907; *Retreat from Love*, 1974) and *La Vagabonde* (1911; *The Vagabond*, 1955).

In 1912, a death in the family once again precipitated a change. Colette had been living with Henri de Jouvenel, whom she had met the previous year. Henri was then a vigorous newspaper editor and a thirty-five-year-old divorcé with two children. In September, 1912, Colette's mother, Sido, died. In December, Colette married Henri, and their daughter (also named Colette) was born the following year. Family life was interrupted by World War I, but Colette continued to write, travel, and publish. Her work was recognized after the war, in 1920, when she was awarded membership in the French Legion of Honor in recognition of her contributions to literature. This award coincided with the publication of one of her best-known novels, *Chéri* (1920; English translation, 1929), in 1920. The novel was successfully adapted for the stage the following year.

In the early 1920's, Colette's relationship with Henri began to deteriorate. He was very busy, was having affairs with other women, and would occasionally disappear without explanation. In 1923, Colette announced her intention of divorcing him, a process completed the following year. Shortly afterward, Colette met Maurice Goudeket, a pearl dealer some eighteen years her junior, in the south of France. Although they were not married until 1935, this quickly became the central relationship in Colette's life and it would last until her death nearly thirty years later.

Colette was by now a very successful writer, with an apartment in Paris and a house near St. Tropez in the south of France. She was kept busy writing, adapting for the stage, and traveling. She published a number of novels, including *Le Blé en herbe*

(1923; *The Ripening Corn*, 1931; also translated as *The Ripening Seed*, 1955), *La Fin de Chéri* (1926; *The Last of Chéri*, 1932), *La Naissance du jour* (1928; *A Lesson in Love*, 1932; also translated as *Break of Day*, 1961), and *La Chatte* (1933; *The Cat*, 1936).

Domestic and professional happiness were once again interrupted by war when the Germans invaded France in World War II. Colette left Paris briefly but returned in 1941 to endure the Occupation. She was forced to be separated from Maurice, who was first arrested by the Germans and then fled to the unoccupied zone to avoid further danger. Colette was far from idle, however, and it was during the war, in 1944, that one of her most popular works, *Gigi* (1944; English translation, 1952), first appeared. Published originally in a periodical in Lyon in 1942, it was published as a book in 1944 and later became an Academy Award-winning film that brought Colette an international reputation.

Gigi was the last novel that Colette would write, but she continued to receive honors. She was promoted within the Legion of Honor (she received the Grand Cross in 1953); she was elected to the Académie Goncourt (in 1945) and later became the president of that prestigious literary body; finally, when she died in Paris on August 3, 1954, she became the first French woman to be honored by a state funeral. She was, however, as controversial in death as she had sometimes been in life. The Catholic church would not permit a religious funeral because of her two divorces, a stand that generated considerable criticism.

Analysis

The majority of Colette's works are so short as to call into question whether they should be labeled "novels" or "short stories." Although relying heavily on description and evocation of mood, her works are not given to prolixity. Her literary output was nevertheless quite prolific, one edition of her complete works stretching to fifteen volumes. The consistent quality of this large volume of works, their style and themes, brought Colette popularity and recognition during her lifetime and have contributed to the maintenance and spread of her reputation since her death.

Colette was not a deep or philosophical writer, and she left no profound thesis on the meaning of her writing, but she was a keen observer of life and of nature, and she possessed a gift for turning those observations into stories that illuminated human experience with charm and humor, stories that appealed to and were admired by her vast readership. The Claudine stories illustrate the devices that initially gained for her a following and continue to entertain today. Based heavily on autobiography, the subjects of the stories are unpretentious: In the first volume of the series, the young Claudine shares her memories of schooldays, using the provincial school as a forum to observe the vagaries of human behavior. Colette would often draw on such autobiographical sources for the inspiration for her stories. For all of this, her work does not suffer from a lack of originality, for not every author shares Colette's ability to see the interest of a subject or her ability to set the scene so delicately.

Thus, in *Claudine at School*, the reader shares Claudine's glimpses of budding, burgeoning, and dying love, for example—a subject that might be banal in the hands of a less talented writer but that takes on a universal quality when treated by Colette. Moreover, the fact that some of these moments occur between women seems perfectly natural when presented through Claudine's eyes. All human beings are entitled to their happiness as well as to their weaknesses, and Claudine's nonjudgmental attitude illustrates Colette's talent for showing the human side of everyone. The same openness and sympathy are evident in Colette's presentation of marginal social figures such as the courtesans of *Chéri* and *Gigi* and the homosexual character Marcel, Claudine's friend in *Claudine in Paris*. It is also evident in the more complex *Ces Plaisirs* (1932; better known as *Le Pur et l'impur*, 1941; *The Pure and the Impure*, 1967), a work of memoirs and biography that some critics find the most challenging of Colette's works, but which presents memories of Colette's personal acquaintances in the same nonjudgmental way.

Colette's gift for evoking credibility and sympathy is such that her ability to render human qualities extends even to animals. One of her most popular novels, *The Cat*, depicts a love triangle between a husband and wife (Alain and Camille) and the husband's cat, Saha. Colette depicts the bond between a man and his cat with such insight that the intrusion of a cat into a marriage does not appear at all farfetched, and the reader is quickly caught up in the tensions of the conflicting pull of emotions.

Because of the autobiographical nature of her work, many of Colette's novels are told from the perspective of a first-person narrator (again, the Claudine series offers an illustration), but a number of works are written in the third person. Even so, the narrator is not an intrusive presence, and the stories somehow seem to tell themselves. This narrative strategy and Colette's use of dialogue perhaps explain why so many of her works were successfully adapted to the stage.

Colette created a number of characters who are remembered vividly by readers. Chief among these is the figure of the gamine, the assertive but endearing girl represented by (among others) Claudine and Gigi. While Colette does not neglect male characters (the figure Chéri must certainly be mentioned here), many of her creations are women, and it is no doubt Colette's attention to the problems and intricacies of women's lives that has earned for her a large following among women readers.

CHÉRI

First published: 1920 (English translation, 1929)
Type of work: Novel

The handsome Chéri falls in love with an older courtesan, whom he leaves when his mother arranges a marriage.

One of Colette's contemporaries suggested that *Chéri* was one of the most important love stories ever written. Despite the many unconventional aspects of the story—

love between an older woman and a younger man, the sympathetic depiction of a courtesan, and the willingness with which Chéri submits to an arranged marriage—the novel indeed remains an engrossing portrait of doomed love.

Léonie Vallon, known as Léa de Lonval, a courtesan nearing the end of her career, falls in love with Fred Peloux, known as Chéri, the son of one of her rivals. Although they live together for several years and seem to love each other, their relationship is precarious, and indeed when Chéri announces that he is going to marry Edmée for money, Léa accepts the inevitable breakup. She maintains a strong exterior so as not to give her rivals the satisfaction of seeing her pain. The reader, however, sees a different side, as the narrator shows Léa's loneliness and desperate attempts to fill the time. The reader is also made aware that Chéri is not entirely happy and comes to see—even before Chéri himself is aware of it—that Chéri misses the comfort and love of his former mistress. The climax comes after Léa returns from a mysterious vacation, and Chéri, more aware of his feelings for having missed her, shows up one night to confess his love.

A happy ending would have satisfied many readers, but Colette does not compromise for effect: After Chéri spends the night with Léa, he returns the next morning to Edmée. The bittersweet ending reveals Colette's preoccupation with harmony rather than happiness. The story achieves its resolution from the fact that Chéri realizes his true feelings. This confrontation with the past frees him to continue his relationship with Edmée in the present. Avoiding facile wish fulfillment, Colette instead offers a profound insight into human nature.

THE LAST OF CHÉRI

First published: *La Fin de Chéri*, 1926 (English translation, 1932)
Type of work: Novel

Chéri attempts to revive a former love, but when it fails, he commits suicide.

While the first volume of Chéri's story, set in the pre-World War I Paris of 1912, conveyed the light, carefree mood of the *belle époque*, *The Last of Chéri* has the somber, sober mood of postwar France, when many illusions had been lost. Five years have passed since Chéri left Léa, but he has been unable to find a purpose in his life to replace his lost love. His thoughts turn back to this idealized past, as many in France also thought back to prewar days with nostalgia, and he decides to revive his relationship with Léa.

Chéri's attempt to recapture the past, however, fails. When he does see Léa again, he does not even recognize her because she has changed so much. She has stopped trying to disguise her age and appears transformed into an unattractive old woman. Significantly, when Chéri sees her, he thinks of his mother. With this realization that he cannot return to the past and yet cannot live with or in the present, Chéri resolves that the only remaining choice is suicide. In this act, he symbolically returns to his happy prewar days with Léa by surrounding himself with pictures of her as he remembers her, as a beautiful young woman, at the moment of his death.

Once again, Colette maintains a light touch in a novel that has philosophical underpinnings in its representation of human attempts to recapture the past. Chéri appears as a tragic hero who has brought about his own suffering by giving up love for money, and who now pays a fatal price for his blindness, but the tragic elements never dominate the narrative. Subtle comparisons (Chéri compares Léa to the war, for example, to explain his inability to come to terms with the present), well-chosen adjectives placed for effect—these are the techniques whereby Colette suggests to her readers that the story of Chéri may have a more universal message than its unusual aspects might at first suggest.

GIGI

First published: 1944 (English translation, 1952)
Type of work: Novella

Gigi, reared to be a courtesan, instead marries the rich Gaston Lachaille.

Colette once again provides an indirect comment on contemporary France. With Paris occupied and in the grip of war, readers of Colette's *Gigi* are transported to a less complicated and painful time. Set in 1899, the story once again orchestrates a small but intimate cast of characters in a personal drama with a twist. The plot focuses on the "gamine" character of Gigi (a nickname for Gilberte), a young woman who has been reared by her grandmother and great aunt to follow in their profession as a courtesan. They hope to make her the mistress of Gaston Lachaille, but Gigi instead becomes his wife. This conclusion introduces an ironic twist. In the conventional love story, the resolution of the plot through marriage is usually the desired outcome, but in *Gigi* marriage appears as a frustration rather than a fulfillment of plans. The story serves as a lighthearted reminder that the best laid plans may go astray, especially if love is involved.

In once again portraying the charm and humor of an independent and mischievous adolescent, Colette comes full circle in her career, ending her writing with a character very similar to the one who made her reputation, Claudine. It is through her ebullience and love of life that Gigi wins Gaston's true affection, a message of optimism and faith in the power of love.

Summary

Colette's state funeral was a symbol of the popularity that her works had gained by the time of her death. Her numerous works of fiction were accessible and highly readable, yet they presented a unique perspective on everyday human problems and experiences. From the girlish figures of Claudine and Gigi to the lonely old women such as Léa, from finely drawn tragic figures such as Chéri to the almost human Saha, Colette's characters are memorable individuals. Her twists on conventional love stories are imaginative and frequently more complex than their superficial simplicity and light tone would suggest.

Bibliography

Cottrell, Robert D. *Colette*. New York: Frederick Ungar, 1974.

Crosland, Margaret. *Colette: The Difficulty of Loving*. London: Peter Owen, 1973.

Davies, Margaret. *Colette*. New York: Grove, 1961.

Eisinger, Erica M., and Mari Ward McCarty, eds. *Colette; The Woman, the Writer*. University Park: Pennsylvania State University Press, 1981.

Goudeket, Maurice. *Close to Colette*. New York: Farrar, Straus and Cudahy, 1957.

Marks, Elaine. *Colette*. New Brunswick, N.J.: Rutgers University Press, 1960.

Massie, Allan. *Colette*. Harmondsworth, Middlesex, England: Penguin Books, 1986.

Richardson, Joanna. *Colette*. London: Methuen, 1983.

Sarde, Michèle. *Colette: Free and Fettered*. New York: Morrow, 1980.

Stewart, Joan Hinde. *Colette*. Boston: G. K. Hall, 1983.

Melanie Hawthorne

WILLIAM CONGREVE

Born: Bardsey, Yorkshire, England
January 24, 1670
Died: London, England
January 19, 1729

Principal Literary Achievement

Congreve is considered the most brilliant of the Restoration dramatists, a writer who used sharp wit, vision, and comic dialogue to expose the hypocrisies of society.

Biography

William Congreve was born in Bardsey, Yorkshire, England, on January 24, 1670. In 1674, his father, William, an army officer, was stationed in Ireland. Congreve was sent to school in Kilkenny, where he met Jonathan Swift, the future satirist. The two formed a lifelong friendship. In 1686, Congreve entered Trinity College, Dublin, earning his M.A. in 1696. Around 1688, the family moved to the Congreve home at Stretton, Staffordshire, where Congreve's father was estate agent to the earl of Cork. Congreve entered Middle Temple, London, to read law in 1691, but he soon abandoned his studies to write. He produced a light novel, *Incognita: Or, Love and Duty Reconcil'd*, in 1692. The following March, Congreve was catapulted to fame with the production of *The Old Bachelor* (1693), a play he wrote to amuse himself while recovering from an illness. It was an enormous success, highly praised by the poet and essayist John Dryden, who remained an enthusiastic supporter of Congreve's work.

His next play, *The Double Dealer*, opened later in 1693. Though now considered a much better play than his first, it was unpopular with audiences of the time. *Love for Love* followed in 1695, enjoying great success as the first performance staged for the new theater in Lincoln's Inn Fields. Congreve became one of the managers of the theater, promising to write a new play every year—a promise that he failed to keep. The year 1696 saw publication of Congreve's essay "A Letter Concerning Humour in Comedy."

By now, Congreve was firmly established as a man of letters. The government rewarded him with a salaried position somewhat of the nature of a sinecure. He was made a commissioner for licensing hackney coaches—the first of several undemanding yet lucrative civil service posts that he accumulated throughout his life. In 1697, a tragedy, *The Mourning Bride*, was produced at Lincoln's Inn Fields theater. In 1698,

Jeremy Collier published a vicious attack on Congreve in *A Short View of the Immorality and Profaneness of the English Stage*. Congreve replied with his *Amendments of Mr. Collier's False and Imperfect Citations* (1698). Two years later, in March, 1700, Lincoln's Inn Fields produced Congreve's greatest work, *The Way of the World*. In spite of a brilliant cast, the play was poorly received. Congreve is said to have appeared on stage at the end to rebuke the audience.

Congreve never wrote another full-length play, though he did produce other work: a masque, *The Judgement of Paris* (1701), an opera, *Semele* (1710), a prose tale, and several unremarkable poems. The Collier attack and the cold reception given *The Way of the World* are often cited as reasons for his early retirement from writing for the stage. Other contributing factors may have been poor health—he suffered from gout—and his affluence. His civil service posts, added to a private income, meant that he did not need the modest earnings that his plays had generated.

Some scholars suggest that Congreve had always placed a higher priority on cultivating high society than on writing. They cite an occasion in 1726 when the French writer Voltaire came to request an audience with Congreve and was granted it only on the condition that he be considered a "gentleman" rather than a playwright. Voltaire replied in disgust that if that were the case, he would not have bothered to visit. Congreve's remark is, however, open to interpretations other than the snobbery imputed to him by Voltaire. It could as easily have been prompted by weariness caused by illness and a reluctance to defend and explain plays written more than twenty years previously. Indeed, Congreve was known for his constant and warm friendships with people from all social circles, from his early companions in Ireland to the nobility of England. His literary friends (including Swift, John Dryden, the poet Alexander Pope and dramatist John Gay) were unanimous in their warm praise of his character as well as his writing.

Congreve never married, but his mistress of many years was the actress Anne Bracegirdle, who played many of his female leads. In his later years, he formed a devoted attachment to Henrietta, second duchess of Marlborough, and it is probable that he fathered her second daughter, Lady Mary Godolphin, later duchess of Leeds. Congreve never fully recovered from a carriage accident in Bath in 1728, and he died in London on January 19 the following year. He left two hundred pounds to Anne Bracegirdle and the rest of his large fortune to the duchess of Marlborough.

Analysis

Congreve has become known as the most brilliantly witty of the group of Restoration dramatists that included Dryden, George Etherege, and William Wycherley. Restoration drama is a comedy of manners showing a metropolitan society in pursuit of pleasure. It takes a satirical view of the hypocrisy, sexual freedom, and moral degradation of the sophisticated class of people that would have formed its audience. Congreve's characters are variations on Restoration stock types: On one side, there are the fools, including "coxcombs," "fops" (vain, self-deluded followers of fashion), and dullards pretending to wit. In this category also are the predatory old men and women who set their sights on handsome young spouses. On the other side of the fence are the people of sense—characters who carry the audience's sympathy because they have a higher degree of awareness of self and others, and a genuine wit.

The desired outcome in these plays is the marriage between a young couple of sense and their secure possession of the fortune due to them. Working against this desired outcome are schemes engineered by the old, deluded, or wicked against the young couple. The prizes at stake are a young and handsome spouse and the fortune. Sometimes the fortune is already in the possession of the young person, becoming part of the prize. More often, it is still in the control of the old and foolish and will only descend to the young person at the old person's discretion.

The Double Dealer and *The Way of the World* are remarkable among Restoration comedies; though they feature many brilliantly caricatured schemers driven by folly and weakness, such characters are not the primary engineers of trouble. Instead, the seeds of evil are sown and tended by villains of almost tragic status—Maskwell in *The Double Dealer* and Mrs. Marwood (and, to a less intense degree, Fainall) in *The Way of the World*. Characters such as Lady Touchwood and Lady Wishfort, powerful though they be in their ability to frustrate the desired outcome, are instruments in the hands of these grand destroyers of happiness.

Many of Congreve's characters are drawn with a complexity and insight not seen in other plays of the type. The witty "whirlwind" character of Millamant in *The Way of the World* remains a challenge for any actress. Foolish characters evoke pathos even as they do laughter—for example, Lady Wishfort in *The Way of the World*, with her hopeless attempts at reconstructing her long-lost beauty by artificial means, and Sir Paul Plyant in *The Double Dealer*, nightly swaddled in blankets that prevent him from fathering the son for whom he longs. More than any other Restoration dramatist, Congreve saw the tragedy underlying the ridiculousness of his subjects.

In the world of Congreve's plays, values are inverted, and characters pretend to be the opposite of what they really are. Mirabell's epigrammatic couplet at the end of the first act of *The Way of the World* summarizes this unnatural moral condition: "Where modesty's ill-manners, 'tis but fit/ That impudence and malice pass for wit." Hence, in *The Double Dealer*, Brisk's obsession with his "wit" belies his true status as a "pert coxcomb"; Lady Plyant's harping on her "honour" as she capitulates without much resistance to Careless's seduction reveals her promiscuity. The constant abuse of such terms by hypocritical or foolish characters makes them gain ironic weight at every repetition. The pointedness and brilliance of Congreve's wit have remained unrivaled, except possibly in the plays of Oscar Wilde three centuries later. Congreve's dialogue has a rhythm, cadence, and rhetorical structure at times approaching the status of poetry.

THE DOUBLE DEALER

First produced: 1693 (first published, 1694)
Type of work: Play

In a sophisticated social circle of fops, wits, fools, and hypocrites, two schemers try to foil the intention of a young couple to marry.

The action of *The Double Dealer* is governed by the Machiavellian schemes of Maskwell and the manipulative Lady Touchwood, with whom he is in league. Maskwell and Lady Touchwood both want to break the intended match between the innocent couple Cynthia and Mellefont—Maskwell, because he wants Cynthia for himself, and Lady Touchwood, because she wants Mellefont for herself. Most of the characters' lives revolve around hidden motives, secret intrigues, and deception. Nobody, except Mellefont and Cynthia, is what he or she seems. Sir Paul and Lady Plyant pretend to the world to be the happiest married couple; Lady Plyant pretends to her husband that she is too chaste to grant him her sexual favors, while enthusiastically pursuing intrigues with others. The fop Brisk sets himself up as a wit; the giggling Lord Froth affects solemnity; the vacuous Lady Froth sees herself as a writer of heroic epic poems.

The supreme embodiment of deception is Maskwell. He pretends to be Mellefont's loyal friend, defending him against Lady Touchwood's plotting and supporting the marriage with Cynthia. In fact, he is using every weapon in his armory to discredit Mellefont in the eyes of his uncle and benefactor-to-be Lord Touchwood, and his bride's parents Sir Paul and Lady Plyant. Such is Maskwell's skill that he prevails upon the unwitting Mellefont to conspire in his own undoing: In a seeming effort to put an end to Lady Touchwood's activities, Maskwell suggests that Mellefont appear in her bedroom at a time calculated to compromise her; Maskwell, however, ensures that it is Mellefont who is compromised and risks the wrath of Lord Touchwood. Neither Mellefont nor anyone else sees through Maskwell's guise until Cynthia points out a discrepancy in his instructions to her and Mellefont toward the end of the play. Others are also fooled: Lord Touchwood almost disinherits Mellefont in favor of Maskwell; and, ironically, Lady Touchwood herself mistakenly believes that Maskwell is motivated by his attachment and obligations to her.

Maskwell creates a labyrinth of confusion, symbolized by the many references to private stairs, hidden passages, and back ways and put into words by the baffled Mellefont: "I am confounded in a maze of thoughts, each leading into one another, and all ending in perplexity." Maskwell's controlling genius lies in his ability to play upon the desires and weaknesses of his dupes. As he says, those who want to be deceived will be: "and, if they will not hear the serpent's hiss, they must be stung into experience, and future caution." The theme of willful self-deception is strong. Even when

Sir Paul has written evidence of his wife's intended infidelity thrust into his hands, he is eager to swallow her and Careless' hastily engineered explanation, once again submitting to being swaddled in blankets in the marital bed.

The unpopularity of *The Double Dealer* in and after Congreve's time may have been attributable to unease at the extreme nature of the evil represented in it. Maskwell's coolness and single-mindedness in plotting evil, his flawless mask of honesty and loyalty, and his unrepentant silence after his villainy is finally unmasked recall William Shakespeare's villain Iago in *Othello* (1604) and place him beyond the conventions of Restoration comedy. Lady Touchwood, too, attains a sinister status beyond that of a hot-tempered woman scorned; in the scene with Mellefont in her chamber at the end of act 4, against all odds she makes herself appear innocent and Mellefont appear the criminal in Lord Touchwood's eyes. As she leaves, she turns and smiles malevolently at Mellefont—a truly spine-chilling image.

That this uncompromising sense of evil was intentionally created by Congreve is suggested by constant references to witchcraft, possession, and the devil used in connection with Maskwell and Lady Touchwood. The good-evil polarity is reinforced by the strong visual symbolism of the final expulsion of Maskwell and Lady Touchwood by Mellefont and Lord Touchwood dressed in parson's costumes. The schemers are undone by their own machinations, in the absence of any conscious campaign on the part of the good characters, and the young couple are free to marry. As Brisk says, Love and Murder will out—in the unfoldment of time and by the workings of Providence.

THE WAY OF THE WORLD

First produced: 1700 (first published, 1700)
Type of work: Play

A deceiver in league with his lover plots to prevent the marriage between Mirabell and Millamant and to secure Millamant's fortune.

The Way of the World is generally viewed as the supreme example of its genre. Its characters—the vengeful and ultimately pathetic Lady Wishfort, the sparring lovers Mirabell and Millamant, the dark and devious Mrs. Marwood—remain in the mind long after the play is over. The complexities and subtleties of relationships are observed with a keen psychological insight: the domineering nature of Lady Wishfort turning to abject dependence on her mentor Mrs. Marwood; the carefully manipulated shifts of power between Fainall and Mrs. Marwood; the passionate attraction between Mirabell and Millamant, disguised beneath a covering of mockery and indifference.

As in *The Double Dealer,* covert motives and hypocrisy govern the action of the play. Old Lady Wishfort has loved Mirabell since he pretended to love her in order to woo her niece Millamant: Her ostensible motivation in opposing the young couple's marriage is to protect her daughter from a deceiver, but her actual motivation is to avenge herself on Mirabell. Mirabell counters with an equally underhanded plan to foil Lady Wishfort's plots with a decoy—his servant Waitwell disguised as wealthy suitor Sir Rowland. Waitwell is to prepare to marry Lady Wishfort, and Mirabell is to reveal his servant's true identity and release her from the match on condition that she release Millamant's fortune and grant Mirabell her hand in marriage.

Mrs. Marwood, at the center of the scheming, exploits Lady Wishfort's dislike of Mirabell to pursue her own ends. Throughout, her ostensible desire is to protect Lady Wishfort's interests. Her actual desire, however, is to fan the flames of Lady Wishfort's fury against Mirabell and to persuade her to disinherit Millamant in favor of Fainall, Mrs. Marwood's lover. Fainall, meanwhile, means to denounce his wife (Lady Wishfort's daughter) publicly for infidelity with Mirabell in an effort to blackmail Lady Wishfort into making over Mrs. Fainall's estate to him. The blatant hypocrisy of his scheme becomes evident in the light of his true motivation: to have his wife's fortune under the control of himself and his mistress, Mrs. Marwood. Congreve depicts a constant satirical tension between outward self and inward self, between the mask and the face behind it.

Deception is not only an interface between the characters and the world; it also serves to illustrate the characters' view of themselves. Lady Wishfort's attempt to turn back the years by painting herself a new face is an image whose symbolism reverberates throughout the play. It is a visual illustration of the affectations in which the foolish characters indulge. In the same vein, Petulant pays prostitutes to hire a coach and call on him in order to give the impression that he is in demand among ladies; and Mrs. Marwood makes a great show of hating men even while her actions are motivated by desire for them. All these characters are, metaphorically speaking, painting their own faces—cultivating appearances that are at odds with reality. Hence, Mirabell's premarital condition to Millamant—"I article, that you continue to like your own face, as long as I shall: and while it passes current with me, that you endeavour not to new-coin it"—suggests a conscious rejection of the affectation and pretense that characterize the foolish sector of society.

The appearance of the unsophisticated, country-bred Sir Wilful Witwoud shows the extent to which this world has become divorced from the natural order. Lady Wishfort condemns his uncouth manners as barbaric—though shortly afterward she displays true cold-blooded barbarity in her relish at the prospect of Mirabell's slowly starving to death. The metropolitan Witwoud disowns his brother (Sir Wilful Witwoud) because it is not fashionable to acknowledge relations in town. One treasures Sir Wilful's ingenuous response to Witwoud's snub: "The fashion's a fool; and you're a fop, dear brother."

Mirabell and Millamant, with their wit and good sense, stand in contrast to the fops and fools. They embrace the pleasures of the town—indeed, Millamant is uncompromising in her disdain for the country—yet are not blind to its folly. The famous scene in which Mirabell and Millamant barter conditions and provisos for their life together shows a couple who see their world as it is and prefer not to waste time pretending it is otherwise. It is significant that Mirabell's clear-sighted, if cynical, understanding of "the way of the world" helps him foil the plot against Mrs. Fainall and restore himself to Lady Wishfort's good graces. Lacking faith in Fainall's integrity, Mirabell had previously ensured that Mrs. Fainall's estate was made over to him in trust, making her husband's claim on it ineffective. Lady Wishfort is happy to offer Millamant to Mirabell in exchange for her daughter's honor and fortune intact, and the prospect of their marriage makes a satisfying resolution to this complex plot.

Summary

The satirical vision and pointed wit of William Congreve's plays expose the hypocrisy, affectation, and moral degradation of the affluent society of his time. The extreme complexity of his plots makes his plays notoriously difficult to follow on the page. It is on the stage that their superb entertaining quality is most evident: The rapid-fire wit of the dialogue, lively action, and psychological truth of the characterization carry the audience through labyrinthine twists and turns of plot. Indeed, the plays' complex form aptly reflects the confusion created by the manipulative and self-deceiving characters, for whom no word or action is straightforward, simple, or what it seems. In Congreve's universe, inverted or perverted values predominate, but truth and good sense must finally prevail.

Bibliography

Lindsay, Alexander, and Howard Erskine-Hall, eds. *William Congreve: The Critical Heritage*. New York: Routledge, 1989.

Lyons, Patrick ed. *Congreve Comedies: A Selection of Critical Essays*. London: Macmillan, 1982.

Morris, Brian, ed. *William Congreve*. Totowa, N.J.: Rowman & Littlefield, 1972.

Van Voris, W. H., ed. *The Cultivated Stance: The Designs of Congreve's Plays*. Dublin: Dolmen Press, 1965.

Williams, Aubrey L., ed. *An Approach to Congreve*. New Haven, Conn.: Yale University Press, 1979.

Claire Robinson

JOSEPH CONRAD

Born: near Berdyczów, Poland
December 3, 1857
Died: Oswalds, England
August 3, 1924

Principal Literary Achievement
One of the most original and innovative writers of English prose, Conrad was a pioneer of the psychological novel, and his characters reflect the moral dilemmas of the modern world.

Biography
Joseph Conrad was born in Poland, spent much of his childhood in Russian exile with his parents, was orphaned at an early age and reared by his uncle, lived as a young man in France, and then, after a career with the British merchant marine, became one of the major writers in English literature. He lived a life as adventurous as that portrayed in any of his novels, and, in fact, many of the episodes of Conrad's later fiction were rooted in his own experiences.

He was born near Berdyczów on December 3, 1857, and christened Jósef Teodor Konrad Nałęcz Korzeniowski. Conrad was particularly proud of his ancestry, which, rooted in the Polish nobility, had a long and distinguished history. Apollo Korzeniowski, his father, was a Polish intellectual and writer whose works included original verse and translations of William Shakespeare. Apollo Korzeniowski was also a fervent Polish patriot at a time when Poland was a part of the Russian Empire. In 1861, his activities with the Polish independence movement caused his arrest and exile by Czarist authorities. He along with his wife Ewa and his young son, Jósef, was sent to Vologda, a dismal town northeast of Moscow.

At Vologda, the climate was severe and living conditions were harsh. Ewa, who suffered from tuberculosis, died in April, 1865, when Jósef was only seven years old. A few years later, Apollo was released from exile because of his own ill health. Shortly after returning to his native Poland, he died, and at eleven years old Jósef was left to the care of his maternal uncle. Fortunately, the uncle was a kindly man who provided for Jósef's education and supported him for many years.

Because of his painful memories and his own intense Polish patriotism, Jósef found life in occupied Poland unbearable; when doctors recommended a seaside environment to improve his health, he gladly moved to Marseilles, France, in October, 1874.

In Marseilles, he lived on funds from his uncle and made several voyages as a sailor on French ships. In 1877, he was part of an attempt to smuggle weapons to royalist rebels in Spain, a cause that excited his romantic nature, but their plot was betrayed and the vessel, the *Tremolino*, had to be deliberately run aground to avoid capture.

About this time Conrad seems to have had an unhappy love affair. The details are unclear and not totally convincing, but in the spring of the following year Jósef attempted suicide. The cause may have been his unhappy romantic attachment; or it may have been the loss of all of his money while gambling at Monte Carlo. Whatever the reason, the wound was minor, and within a month he was able to sign aboard his first English ship, the *Mavis*. On April 24, 1878, Jósef Korzeniowski, soon to be known as Joseph Conrad, became an English sailor. He would remain with the British merchant marine for the next seventeen years, serving on eighteen different vessels, rising through the ranks as second mate, first mate, and finally captain, commanding the *Otago,* in 1888. He became a British citizen in 1886.

During these voyages, Conrad traveled to the settings that inspired his later stories. In 1883, he was second mate on board the *Palestine*, which caught fire and later sank, leaving the crew to survive in open boats until it reached land. The events are brilliantly re-created by Conrad in his short story, "Youth." In 1890, Conrad was in the Belgian Congo as part of a European trading company but left before the year had ended. His health was seriously weakened by malaria, and his psychological and moral senses were severely shaken by the ruthless, amoral exploitation of the natives by Europeans desperate for ivory. These experiences remained with Conrad for many years and found their powerful, searing expression in the short novel *Heart of Darkness* (serial, 1899; 1902).

Conrad had grown increasingly despondent about his opportunities in the merchant marine. Although he was a competent, even outstanding officer, commands were difficult to obtain and the financial rewards were small. Conrad concluded that his seafaring career was unsuccessful; he had already started work on his first novel, *Almayer's Folly* (1895). In January, 1894, Conrad ended his seagoing career, determined to make his living as a writer. *Almayer's Folly* gained favorable critical notice, mostly for its exotic setting and characters. Conrad's next work, *An Outcast of the Islands* (1896), seemed to mark him as a talented but perhaps limited author of exotic romances. With the appearance of *The Children of the Sea: A Tale of the Forecastle* (1897; republished as *The Nigger of the "Narcissus": A Tale of the Sea*, 1898), however, the literary world was forced to take note of a new and strikingly original talent.

After the turmoil and adventures of his earlier life, Conrad's middle and later years were relatively peaceful and uneventful, marred only by tight financial conditions, a situation not uncommon for writers. Conrad settled at Pent Farm, in Kent, with his wife Jessie George, to whom he was married on March 24, 1896. The Conrads had two sons, Alfred Borys and John Alexander. The family life of the Conrads does not appear to have been especially close, largely because of Conrad's own innate reserve and aloofness. He was also plagued by bouts of severe illness and the anguish of composition, which, for him, could be almost unbearable.

As an author, Conrad was critically acknowledged but not popular until fairly late in his career. Classic novels such as *Lord Jim, A Tale* (1900), *Nostromo, A Tale of the Seaboard* (1904), or *Under Western Eyes* (1910) had relatively modest sales. Even collaboration with the well-known English author Ford Madox Ford failed to bring wide sales. To supplement his income, Conrad frequently contributed short fiction to popular magazines, and eight volumes of these stories were collected and published during Conrad's lifetime.

It was not until 1913 that Conrad wrote his first truly popular work, *Chance.* Ironically, many literary critics have marked this novel as the beginning of his decline as an artist. Its success, however, gave Conrad financial stability, and in 1919 he moved to a country estate at Oswalds, near Canterbury, England. It was there that Conrad spent the remaining years of his life. He declined a knighthood in 1924 and, that same year, after a long struggle with ill health, died in Oswalds of a heart attack on August 3. He was buried at Canterbury.

Analysis

Conrad is notable for three major contributions to English and world literature: his unique style, his addition of new settings and genres to serious writing, and his creation of the psychological story. Conrad's style is remarkable, not least because he was already an adult by the time he had learned to speak and write English. In early works such as *Almayer's Folly*, or *An Outcast of the Islands*, the descriptions of jungle or exotic landscapes are remarkable for their precision and detail. In the short story "The Lagoon," the landscape itself becomes a character in the tale rather than merely a setting or background.

The early stories, as critics have noted, tend to be static and somewhat slow-moving, and Conrad's style accounts for much of this, especially his extensive descriptions. These tendencies, however, were refined by Conrad as his career developed so that his language, still using numerous modifiers, was able to express action concisely and vividly. His mature style is capable of both description and action, so that a story such as "Youth" easily combines rousing action at sea with delicate, almost elegiac memories.

Conrad's second contribution to modern literature was his introduction of new settings and types of novels, which extended the range of literature. Conrad used exotic locations, such as the Far East, the African jungle, or the Caribbean, which had traditionally been reserved for light romantic or escapist fiction, and made them the settings for serious literature. This device also allowed Conrad to develop his characteristic themes in appropriate settings, most notably the confrontation of conflicting moral and ethical codes.

A second expansion of literature by Conrad was accomplished with his creation of political fiction—in fact, what might be termed the spy novel. In works such as *The Secret Agent: A Simple Tale* (1907) and *Under Western Eyes*, Conrad literally established this particular genre of literature, creating the prototypical characters and situation that have remained constant through such later authors as Graham Greene and

John le Carré. Conrad's novels of espionage and intrigue are always more than exciting adventures because they inevitably contain considerations of deep moral and ethical dilemmas, highlighted by the shadowy situation in which the characters are
placed.

The emphasis on the interior lives of his characters, on their hidden motivations
and desires, is undoubtedly Conrad's most famous and lasting accomplishment. Working at a time when Sigmund Freud's writings and other psychological theories were
opening new aspects of human personality, Conrad in his stories and novels delved
deeply into facets and features that earlier fiction had either neglected or treated
briefly and often superficially.

Conrad's single greatest achievement was his virtual creation of the psychological
story, in which the interior lives of the characters achieve an immediacy and importance comparable to actual life. In stories such as "The Secret Sharer" or *Heart of
Darkness*, the events are filtered through the perceptions and minds of characters
who are changed by what they see and experience. The novel *Lord Jim*, one of Conrad's most famous and impressive works, contains many vivid and exciting scenes,
but its essential action is internal and takes place within the mind and soul of its title
character.

Even when Conrad's stories are spread across a vast canvas with a number of characters, as is the case with *Nostromo*, much, if not most, of the key action remains
internal and psychological. In this fashion, Conrad's works are not simply stories of
adventure but contain full and fully believable human beings whose actions, however
exciting or unusual, still spring from recognizable human impulses and causes.

LORD JIM

First published: 1900
Type of work: Novel

Having failed his own inner moral code in a moment of crisis, a man struggles
to redeem himself.

Lord Jim, A Tale, Conrad's most famous work, is also his most extensive examination of a persistent theme, the conflict between an individual's inner moral code and
his or her outward actions. Throughout Conrad's short stories and novels, his characters are often afraid, even obsessed, with the concern as to how their personal standards will bear up under the stress of events. This situation is explicit in *Lord Jim*.
As a young boy learning the sailor's craft, Jim is certain he will meet the test of
moral courage, but later, while serving as a first mate on the *Patna*, an old, unsea-
worthy steamer carrying Moslem pilgrims across the Indian Ocean, he fails the test.
The *Patna* strikes an unknown object in the night and seems ready to sink. The
crew, including Jim, abandons the ship and its passengers. When the drifting *Patna*

is discovered and the events are revealed, Jim becomes an outcast, both literally and morally.

These events occur quickly, and the bulk of the novel consists of Jim's personal and moral redemption. For a while, he drifts from port to port, leaving when his identity is discovered. Finally, he abandons the world of Europeans altogether and heads upriver to a small Malay village. Even there, however, he finds he cannot escape the demands of his sensitive moral feelings and must prove to himself that he is not a coward.

Jim's early efforts win praise, especially when he rids the countryside of the notorious bandit, Sherif Ali. Yet this is not enough for Jim, who intuitively senses that his honor has not been restored nor his moral balance satisfied. That occurs only at the end of the novel, after Jim has inadvertently caused the death of a Malay friend, the son of a powerful local chief. Knowing that it will mean his own death, Jim accepts his responsibility without hesitation or fear, and his action redeems the long years of exile caused by his moment of fear and indecision on the *Patna*.

Such a relatively simple tale might seem more suitable for a short story than a full-length novel, and when *Lord Jim* was first published, many critics complained that it was too long. Such is not the case, however, for the power and impact of *Lord Jim* lie not in narrative actions but in psychological nuances and meanings.

Once again, Conrad uses Marlow as both a character and a narrator. Marlow, who went through his own testing experiences in the short story "Youth" and was more severely tested in *Heart of Darkness*, comes to know Jim by accident and then follows his career as if by fate. It is Marlow, for example, who obtains Jim's positions after the *Patna* incident, and it is Marlow who visits Jim in the small Malay village of Patusan, which is the setting for the second part of the novel. Throughout the story, Marlow is concerned, even obsessed, with Jim's actions and thoughts.

The presentation of these actions is not straightforward; Conrad's narrative seldom is, especially when he is concerned with revelation of character. Marlow is less interested in what Jim does than what those actions reveal of the inner man. Much of the novel concerns Marlow's speculations on Jim's actions, and often Marlow seems to be the central character of the book.

In the end, however, the actions of the mysterious Jim command the reader's attention. Significantly, Conrad allows his title character no last name, letting him be known by his Malay title of Tuan Jim, or Lord Jim. This title is given sincerely by the Patusan villagers, but Jim and the reader both understand the implicit irony of the title, an irony that can be resolved only by Jim's final, deliberate actions.

NOSTROMO

First published: 1904
Type of work: Novel

Caught in the moral ambiguities of a South American revolution, an essentially good man finds his innocence corrupted.

Nostromo, A Tale of the Seaboard is Conrad's most expansive and ambitious political novel, a story that examines how both societies and individuals are adversely affected by the process of government in its most brutal form. The book combines several of Conrad's recurring themes, most notably the harmful effects of imperialism, the baleful influence of wealth, and the evil results of individuals acting without the restraints of inner moral codes.

The story is set in the Occidental Province of Costaguana, a nation in Central America. Isolated behind an almost impassable mountain range and situated on a broad but windless bay, the Golfo Placido, Sulaco, the capital city of the Province, has for centuries remained outside of events. Sulaco's only importance comes from the riches of its nearby silver mine, known as the Gould Concession because it is operated by an English family of that name. The Goulds, who have lived in Costaguana for three generations, are permitted to work the mine so long as they pay sufficient bribes to whatever government happens to control Costaguana. Charles Gould, who has brought the mine to its greatest productivity, has grown tired of this endless extortion and resolves to throw his great wealth behind a revolution that will finally bring a responsible government to power in Costaguana.

The novel also follows the career of its title character, an Italian immigrant who is the leader of the stevedores and other dock workers in Sulaco harbor and whose real name is Gian' Battista Fidenza. Fidenza has been given the nickname "Nostromo," meaning "one of ours," by the Englishmen who operate Costaguana's shipping line and is valued by his English masters for his ability to discipline his fellow workers. He is also a brave and resourceful individual, and when the Gould-inspired government seems about to collapse following another revolution, Nostromo is ordered to transport a shipment of silver to safety outside Costaguana. After his small craft is nearly wrecked by a passing ship during the dangerous night crossing, Nostromo hides the treasure on a deserted island in the Golfo Placido. When he learns that Gould and the others believe the silver lost, Nostromo resolves to keep it for himself. Nostromo's realization of the loss of his integrity weighs heavily on him, and although his death at the novel's end comes from a tragic mistake, Conrad makes it clear that the real cause is Nostromo's sense of overwhelming guilt.

As is typical of Conrad, these events are not related in strict chronological sequence or through simple narrative. Instead, the novel moves forward and backward in time, arranged more by themes than events. Following a natural metaphor suggested by the silver mine, Conrad pursues each vein of his story until it seems exhausted, then turns to another. Only gradually, as the narrative strands are connected, does a total picture of events and characters emerge. Because nothing is simple in Costaguana, Conrad implies, its history must also be told in an oblique fashion.

Conrad uses several different narrators. Much of *Nostromo* is told by a third-person narrator who seems to have visited the place and perhaps even participated in some of the actions. Two of the most important accounts of the novel's central events, the defeat and resurgence of the Gould-backed revolution, are told indirectly. The first is presented in a letter written by one of the revolutionaries, Decoud, to his sister. The second is retold years after the events by another character, the Englishman, Captain Mitchell. Ironically, neither man understands fully what he has related; only the reader can place their stories into perspective.

Such irony, an essential trait of Conrad, runs strongly through *Nostromo*. Not only do the characters engage in actions whose importance and results they cannot comprehend, their very names signal a gulf between perception and reality. Most notable, of course, is the title character himself. Nostromo, as he is called by his supposed masters, is anything but "one of ours," and his real name, Fidenza, or "Faithful," becomes a cruel joke when he steals the silver he has been entrusted to preserve.

For Conrad, irony was inevitable in a political situation because politics is the exploitation of the split between the real and the perceived. In such a fashion, Charles Gould defends his silver mine and his backing of yet another revolution for Costaguana because they will bring "law, good faith, order, security." As he tells his wife:

> That's how your money-making is justified here in the face of lawlessness and disorder. It is justified because the security which it demands must be shared with an oppressed people. A better justice will come afterwards. That's your ray of hope.

"Afterwards," Conrad implies in *Nostromo*, never comes. There will always be one more revolution, one more justification for money-making above justice itself. In Conrad's most ironic novel, nothing is more bitterly ironic than Charles Gould's "ray of hope."

HEART OF DARKNESS

First published: 1899
Type of work: Novel

On a voyage up the Congo River, a man confronts the savagery and inner darkness that is part of all human nature.

Heart of Darkness was based upon Conrad's own experiences in the Congo as first mate on the riverboat *Roi des Belges* in 1890, during which he was overwhelmed by intense moral revulsion at the degradation and exploitation of the natives by the ruthless European traders. Conrad noted that, in turn, the savage jungle quickly eliminated the slight beneficial effects that civilization gave to the white plunderers. His observations and reactions to this situation were transmuted into one of his most powerful works.

The character of Marlow, introduced in the short story "Youth," reappears as the narrator and central character of *Heart of Darkness*. The center of *Heart of Darkness* is a trip by Marlow up the Congo River in search of a mysterious Mister Kurtz. The events that take place during this river voyage constitute both a literal and a symbolic journey by Marlow into that "immense heart of darkness" that is both the African jungle and the human soul.

The events of the story are relatively simple. Marlow finds himself, as sailors often do, without a position, a situation Conrad knew well. Against his better judgment, Marlow contracts to serve as a riverboat captain for a Belgian company that exports ivory from the Congo. Exactly as happened to Conrad, however, Marlow's boat is wrecked before he arrives, and he is assigned to serve as a mate on a company steamboat sailing upriver. Marlow goes willingly because he wishes to meet the famous Mister Kurtz, a man who has become renowned equally as a trader of ivory and as a champion of civilization.

Marlow learns, however, that Kurtz is more than an ivory trader, and that the man's vision of civilization and progress has been changed by contact with the African wilderness. When Marlow arrives at Kurtz's station, he finds that Kurtz has reverted to savagery and is alternately feared or worshiped by the terrified natives whom he oppresses. Kurtz's station is ringed with posts decorated with human skulls, and unspeakable rites are celebrated there in honor of the man-god Kurtz. Marlow loads the sick, delirious Kurtz on the boat and hurries back down the river, narrowly escaping an ambush by the terrified and outraged natives. Kurtz dies on the journey.

Marlow takes Kurtz's belongings, including his precious journal, back to Kurtz's fiancée in Europe. Having carefully removed the increasingly frenzied and desperate passages that occur toward the end of the diary, Marlow lies to the woman, claiming that Kurtz died as he had wished and as she herself would have wanted, as an apostle for civilization and Christianity. Still, Marlow must recognize the truth that he has witnessed.

The impact of *Heart of Darkness* comes from the nearly devastating effects Marlow experiences in the Congo. As the story unfolds, the world in which Marlow finds himself grows both more corrupted and more corrupting, so that nothing is left untouched or untainted. Marlow's adventures become stranger, and the characters he meets grow increasingly odd, starting with the greedy traders whom Marlow ironically describes as "pilgrims," through an eccentric Russian who wanders in dress clothes through the jungle, to Kurtz himself, that figure of ultimate madness. Only the native Africans, whether the cruelly abused workers who slave for the trading company or the savages who serve Kurtz out of fear and superstition, retain some of their original dignity. To Marlow, however, they are initially beyond his comprehension. *Heart of Darkness* shows the reader the world through Marlow's eyes, and it is a strange and terrifying place where the normal order of civilized life is both inverted and perverted.

In *Heart of Darkness*, Conrad presents his narrative in a carefully distanced fashion; little is told directly. The story begins with Marlow and four friends aboard a small boat on the Thames River, talking about their experiences. One of the listeners, who is never named, is the actual narrator of the story he has heard from Marlow; while readers may believe they are listening directly to Marlow, actually they hear his story secondhand. Within this narrative framework, the tale shuttles back and forth as Marlow recounts part of his story, then comments upon it. At times, Marlow makes additional reflections upon his own observations. It is only by retelling the events that Marlow comes to understand them, a gradual revelation that is shared by the reader.

Heart of Darkness makes substantial use of symbolism. Conrad used symbolism— the literary device that uses the images of a work to underscore and emphasize its themes and meanings—in many of his works, especially in his descriptions of the landscape, which grows denser and darker as Marlow's journey progresses. The technique is essential for *Heart of Darkness*; the underlying meanings of the story are too terrifying and bleak to be expressed openly. Conrad also uses imagery throughout his story to underscore the meaning of events as Marlow comes to understand them. Opposites are frequent, so that brightness is contrasted with gloom; the lush growth of the jungle is juxtaposed with the sterility of the white traders; and the luxuriant, even alarming, life of the wild is always connected with death and decomposition. Running throughout the story are images and metaphors of madness, especially the insanity caused by isolation. In particular, the decline of Kurtz is a powerfully symbolic expression of the weaknesses of supposedly civilized Europeans. The dominant symbol for the entire work is found in its title and final words: All human nature is a vast "heart of darkness."

THE SECRET SHARER

First published: 1910
Type of work: Short story

A young ship's captain hides a murderer in his own cabin to maintain his own inner moral code.

"The Secret Sharer" is Conrad's most famous short story and one that has long puzzled readers and critics. The story's central character is a young captain, whose name the reader never learns, who has just assumed his first command. The man is nervous, wondering if he will be able to fulfill the obligations of his new position and, more important, his own ideals. As he paces the empty deck of his ship during the night, he is startled to discover a naked man swimming by his ship's side. Once aboard, the swimmer, Leggatt, confesses that he is fleeing from his own ship, the *Sephora*, because he murdered a fellow sailor. As the young captain and Leggatt talk, it appears that the act was justified because the *Sephora* was in danger during a violent storm and Leggatt had to strike the man down in order to save the ship. Because the letter of the law makes no provision for this particular situation, however, Leggatt is condemned as a criminal and will be punished, perhaps executed, if captured. That places the young captain in a moral dilemma: Should he hide Leggatt or turn him over to the authorities? Almost without hesitation, the captain puts Leggatt in his own cabin, where the fugitive remains hidden until the captain sails his new ship dangerously close to land, allowing Leggatt the chance to swim for safety and escape.

The young captain upholds his own moral code by pledging and keeping his word to the mysterious murderer Leggatt, even though his code stands in opposition to conventional law and morality. By taking this action, which some might see as willful, even perverse, the young captain demonstrates to himself that he is capable of fulfilling that "ideal conception of one's personality every man sets up for himself secretly." This ideal conception is not presented explicitly in the story. Rather, readers see the captain's code in action and perhaps assess its consequences but must decide for themselves what the young captain considers his standards and why he must uphold them even in the face of danger and disgrace.

Creating and living by a morality that must be a secret, in this case literally so, is an instance of irony by Conrad and a central paradox of "The Secret Sharer." The captain's code requires him to protect a murderer and to risk his own ship and crew. He faces this danger when he steers dangerously close to shore, risking shipwreck. Since the captain cannot tell his crew the true reason for his baffling action, another secret is present in the story. When the captain succeeds, however, he feels a secret bond between himself and his ship.

"The Secret Sharer" hides these mysteries in the mask of a straightforward narrative, and all of its ambiguity and double meanings are presented in a simple fashion. Even the title is multiple: Since only the captain knows about Leggatt, Leggatt's presence is indeed a secret. On another level, however, the murderer and the young commander also share common secrets—Leggatt's presence on board the ship and the "ideal conception of one's personality" that seems to be their joint moral code.

Doubling, in the physical and moral sense, is found throughout "The Secret Sharer." The young captain and Leggatt are so similar that they seem to be twins, an identification that Conrad clearly intends the reader to take in more than one sense. Both men feel themselves to be outcasts, Leggatt actually so, because of his crime; the captain, psychologically, because of his newness to the ship and its crew. Leggatt can be regarded as the alter ego of the captain, perhaps a reflection of the darker, even criminal, aspects of the captain's personality. Some readers have argued that Leggatt does not even exist but is only a figment of the young captain's imagination.

"The Secret Sharer" is one of the most complex and multilayered short stories in literature. Without resorting to technical devices such as using several narrators or switching back and forth in time, Conrad tells a story that presents the reader with a mystery that cannot be resolved even as it cannot be ignored.

Summary

Joseph Conrad's mastery of the psychological story and his creation of memorable and highly complex characters established him as one of the most important authors in world literature. In exploring such concepts as the double and the human subconscious, Conrad both anticipated and complemented many modern psychological theories.

In addition, Conrad is one of the most original and influential of modern English prose stylists. His densely written and often highly descriptive passages reflect perfectly the complex world of his narratives and his often mysterious but always memorable characters.

Bibliography

Bloom, Harold, ed. *Joseph Conrad's "Nostromo."* New York: Chelsea House, 1987.

Gillon, Adam. *Joseph Conrad.* Boston: Twayne, 1982.

Graver, Lawrence. *Conrad's Short Fiction.* Berkeley: University of California Press, 1969.

Leavis, F. R. *The Great Tradition.* London: Chatto & Windus, 1948.

Meyers, Jeffrey. *Joseph Conrad: A Biography.* New York: Charles Scribner's Sons, 1991.

Najder, Zdzislaw. *Joseph Conrad, A Chronicle.* Translated by Halina Carroll-Najder. New Brunswick, N.J.: Rutgers University Press, 1983.

Tennant, Roger, *Joseph Conrad: A Biography.* New York: Atheneum, 1987.

Michael Witkoski

PIERRE CORNEILLE

Born: Rouen, France
June 6, 1606
Died: Paris, France
September 30, 1684

Principal Literary Achievement

Corneille helped to create neoclassical theater in France. His thirty-three plays, written between 1629 and 1674, attained a standard of excellence and a psychological depth equalled in the seventeenth century only by Molière and Jean Racine.

Biography

Pierre Corneille was born in the Norman city of Rouen on June 6, 1606. He was the eldest of the six children born to Pierre and Marthe Corneille. His younger brother Thomas also became a very successful playwright. Between 1615 and 1622, the younger Pierre Corneille studied at the Jesuit high school in Rouen. Pierre was a learned Latinist and remained a fervent Catholic for his entire life. In 1624, he received his law degree and was admitted to the bar in Rouen. It is not known if he ever practiced law. He lived in his native city until 1662, when he moved to Paris with his family.

Beginning in 1629, Pierre Corneille began writing plays for Parisian theater companies. His early plays revealed both his skill as a dramatist and the diversity of his interests. He wrote witty comedies, a powerful tragedy titled *Médée* (1635; *Medea*), and *L'Illusion comique* (1636; the theatrical illusion), which contains a series of plays-within-a-play. His 1637 tragicomedy *Le Cid* (*The Cid*, 1637) provoked an extremely positive reaction from Parisian theatergoers and much criticism from writers who were clearly jealous of Corneille's success. The decade that followed the first performances of *The Cid* was a very productive period for him. He wrote a series of excellent plays inspired largely from Roman and Spanish sources; these works established his reputation as the most creative and influential French playwright of his generation. Plays such as *The Cid, Horace* (1640; English translation, 1656), *Cinna: Ou, La Clémence d'Auguste* (1640; *Cinna*, 1713), *Polyeucte* (1642; English translation, 1655), and *Le Menteur* (1643; *The Liar*, 1671) are considered masterpieces of French theater. They are regularly performed by modern French theatrical companies and are frequently studied in courses on French theater.

In 1641, Corneille married Marie de Lampérière. The Corneilles had seven chil-

dren. In 1647, he was elected to the French Academy, whose meetings he attended quite regularly until 1683, when he became very ill. The money that he received from theatrical troupes and the annual grants that he received from King Louis XIV for his contributions to the cultural life of France enabled the Corneilles to lead a comfortable life in Rouen.

Between 1648 and 1653, however, there was a civil war in France called the Fronde. The resulting social instability caused a decrease in theater attendance in Paris. After the first performances of his tragedy *Nicomède* in 1651 (English translation, 1671), Corneille stopped writing plays for several years. Between 1651 and 1656, he worked on a verse translation of Thomas à Kempis' influential Latin book of lay piety *Imitatio Christi* (c. 1400; *The Imitation of Christ*, 1696). *Imitation de Jésus-Christ* (1656) contained more than thirteen thousand lines of poetry. He was very interested in religious subjects and, in 1665, he published *Louanges de la Sainte Vierge,* a fine translation of Saint Bonaventure's literary work on the Virgin Mary. His contemporaries were greatly impressed by the quality of these translations. For the 1660 edition of his works, Corneille undertook a systematic revision of his earlier plays and also wrote three very influential essays of dramatic criticism. These essays are generally considered to be the clearest descriptions of such conventions of neoclassical French theater as the importance of respecting social decorum and the three rules requiring the unities of time, place, and action.

Although the nine plays that Corneille wrote between 1659 and 1674 reveal that his skills as a dramatist had not diminished, Parisian theatergoers responded more favorably to the plays of Molière and Racine than to those of Corneille. Discouraged by this popular reaction to his later plays, Corneille retired definitively after the first performances of *Suréna* (1674; English translation, 1960) in 1674. Although Parisian theatergoers reacted coolly to *Suréna* during its first run, critics now consider *Suréna* to be a brilliant tragedy. During the last ten years of his life, Corneille wrote occasional poems, corresponded with fellow writers, and continued to attend the meetings of the French Academy. Very poor health prevented him from leaving his house in Paris after August, 1683. He died there on September 30, 1684, and was succeeded in the French Academy by his brother Thomas.

Analysis

Corneille is famous for his skill in creating dramatic tension by placing sympathetic characters in situations that require them to make difficult moral choices. As a lawyer, Corneille understood that the motivation for human behavior is rarely simple. Individuals wish to believe that their personal search for happiness should not conflict with the allegiance owed to state and family, but this is not always the case. In both *The Cid* and *Horace*, Corneille shows that characters can react very differently during the same moral crisis. In several plays, he made effective use of blocking characters who created problems that would not have existed if all the characters had been tolerant and understanding. The Roman tragedy *Horace* illustrates nicely how Corneille integrated moral conflicts into his plays.

From the opening scenes in *Horace*, audiences realize that several generations of Albans and Romans have lived together in peace and that numerous marriages between Albans and Romans seem to have cemented the links between their two countries. At the beginning of *Horace*, one cannot imagine what could possibly destroy the stability and peace between Rome and Alba. Sabine (an Alban noblewoman) has married the Roman nobleman Horace, and his sister Camille is in love with Sabine's brother Curiace and hopes to marry him. The Roman king decides, however, to invade Alba in order to expand his political power. Corneille's audiences understand that this is a totally unjustified and unnecessary invasion, because the Albans have not the slightest desire to threaten the security of Rome. They simply want to live in peace with their more powerful neighbors in Rome. The Roman invasion provokes extreme reactions from both Sabine's husband and her father-in-law, the older Horace. Both affirm that Romans must prove their loyalty by hating the Albans. Neither the younger nor the elder Horace believes that one can separate political service to one's country from commitment to one's beloved. Both the younger and older Horaces are fanatics who refuse to accept the fact that Camille can love Curiace and still be a loyal Roman. In combat, Camille's two other brothers and Curiace are all killed. The grieving Camille tells Horace that Rome has dishonored itself by killing peaceful Albans. The enraged Horace takes out his sword and kills his sister offstage. In a very real sense, the war between Alba and Rome was the equivalent of a civil war, the two countries having lived together in peace for generations. In *Horace*, Corneille shows that the combination of civil war and blind patriotism can transform otherwise decent people into violent characters. Patriotism is an admirable virtue, but one should never allow patriotism to corrupt moral judgment. Blinded by his hatred for Alba, Horace concludes that killing Camille was "an act of justice." It is obvious that this murder of his sister had absolutely nothing to do with "justice" and represented, on the contrary, the moral degeneracy of Horace.

Corneille lived during a very turbulent period of French history. During his childhood in Normandy, peasant revolts against the royal forces were suppressed with incredible cruelty. During the 1630's, the intolerance of Cardinal Richelieu (the French prime minister under King Louis XIII) caused much suffering among French Protestants. The abuse of power by Cardinal Mazarin (the French prime minister during the early years of the reign of King Louis XIV) created great resentment and provoked a civil war that lasted from 1648 until 1653.

Several of Corneille's most effective plays, such as *Horace, Polyeucte*, and *Suréna*, illustrate the extraordinarily destructive effect on society when political power is used abusively or arbitrarily. The action in his major plays takes place in different countries, but the game of political power unfolds in very similar ways. Corneille's political plays warn that the misuse of political power can have a long-term negative effect on society as a whole. Corneille created much sympathy for characters who adhered to high ethical standards and refused to commit amoral actions in order to advance their careers, but these same morally admirable characters are frequently destroyed by those who played the political "power game" more ruthlessly and effectively.

Corneille is justly famous for the finely crafted speeches that his characters use in order to defend their political decisions. The formal eloquence of these speeches is not misleading once it is realized that selfish and intolerant characters such as Horace use specious reasoning in order to justify their refusal to respect the basic freedom and dignity of other characters. When Horace tries to justify his murder of his sister Camille, the audience is not persuaded by his arguments.

It would be hasty to conclude that Corneille did not believe in the basic goodness of people. He spent years translating into French Thomas à Kempis' *The Imitation of Jesus Christ*, a famous work of lay piety that affirmed that systematic meditation and prayer can enable all Christians to develop a rich understanding of the divine perfection in every believer. Corneille felt that people can attain true happiness and spiritual growth in their personal lives as long as they are not tempted by the Machiavellian world of politics.

THE CID

First produced: *Le Cid*, 1637 (first published, 1637; English translation, 1637)
Type of work: Play

In the feudal society of medieval Spain, the sympathetic lovers Rodrigue and Chimène must choose between duty and love.

Although it was Corneille's eighth play, *The Cid* was his first great popular and critical success. He transformed the medieval epic legend of the Cid into a very intimate play in which Rodrigue and Chimène suffer unnecessarily because of the selfishness of their fathers. Rodrigue and Chimène love each other very much and want to get married. Instead of considering the happiness of their adult children, Don Gomès (Chimène's father) and Don Diègue (Rodrigue's father) become involved in a petty argument that turns violent. Each claims to merit the honor of serving as the governor to King Fernand's eldest son, a purely honorary position. The king's decision is totally arbitrary and does not imply any criticism of the man not chosen. When Don Gomès realizes that his rival will receive this appointment, he loses his temper and slaps Don Diègue, who interprets this not as the crime of battery but rather as an offense against his family's honor. He demands that his son avenge this insult by killing Don Gomès in a duel—a request that places Rodrigue in a terrible situation and does not give him enough time to consider an alternative. As a lawyer, Corneille knew that there were obvious legal remedies available for Don Diègue. Charges should have been brought against Don Gomès, and a court should have tried him for his physical attack against Don Diègue, who could also have begun a civil suit against his attacker. Death was an excessive penalty for the crime of battery. In act 1, both Don Diègue and Rodrigue pronounce monologues that create very negative impressions on listeners, who conclude that both characters are irrational and violent men who do not respect the absolute value of human life.

After the death of Don Gomès, the king finds himself in a very delicate situation. As an absolute monarch, he has the authority to judge criminal cases. Although Rodrigue is a military hero, the king cannot excuse Rodrigue's crime because it is very dangerous for individuals to place themselves above the law. Society cannot permit young soldiers to kill elderly gentlemen in duels. Although Chimène demands justice, she does not want to have Rodrigue executed for the murder of her father. King Fernand is a patient and objective judge. He comes to understand that it was the fanaticism of Don Diègue that caused Rodrigue to commit his heinous crime. There were extenuating circumstances. Although Rodrigue is guilty, the king pardons him and allows him to resume his military career. King Fernand suggests that after an appropriate period of mourning Chimène may want to marry Rodrigue. He strongly recommends that Chimène take at least one year before deciding whether she can forgive Rodrigue for his crime.

The Cid shows that chaos may result if individuals place their own desires above the needs of society as a whole. Whatever his motivation may have been, Don Diègue did not consider the effect of his fanaticism on others. Only the wisdom and compassion of King Fernand enabled him (Fernand) to propose a solution that both preserved the rule of law and spared the life of Rodrigue. King Fernand accorded equal importance to both justice and mercy.

When he first published *The Cid*, Corneille referred to it as a tragicomedy, although he later decided to call it a tragedy. There is, however, no tragic vision of the world in *The Cid*. Although this play explores serious themes, such as death and justice, it does have a relatively optimistic ending. King Fernand may well succeed in restoring order to his kingdom while at the same time allowing Rodrigue and Chimène to live emotionally satisfying lives.

POLYEUCTE

First produced: 1642 (first published, 1643; English translation, 1655)
Type of work: Play

Polyeucte describes the heroism of converts to Christianity who willingly accept martyrdom.

The action in *Polyeucte* takes place in the Roman colony of Armenia. Emperor Decia hates Christians and insists that all of his governors enforce his draconian laws against them. Practicing Christianity is a capital offense. Polyeucte has married Pauline, the daughter of Félix, the Roman governor in Armenia. Although she loved Sévère, she acceded to her father's wishes and married Polyeucte because he was then richer than Sévère. Things have changed, and Sévère is now an influential adviser to

Emperor Decia. Polyeucte seems to be a very ordinary person. No one expects any surprises from him, but his friend Néarque persuades him to embrace Christianity. Both Polyeucte and Pauline speak of her recurring nightmare in which she sees Polyeucte's death. He does not take this nightmare seriously, but she is terrified. Although he wants to become a Christian, he does not want to anger Pauline and Félix, who hold Christians in contempt. After much hesitation, Polyeucte publicly reveals his conversion.

This development creates an immediate problem for Félix, Sévère, and Pauline. Should Decia's arbitrary law against Christians be enforced? At first, Félix thinks that he can profit from Polyeucte's martyrdom if Pauline then marries the influential Sévère. Pauline rejects this proposal and vows never to marry Sévère; she appeals to Sévère's love for her and begs him to intervene with her father. Félix is intransigent but gives his son-in-law one last opportunity to avoid death. He forces Polyeucte to watch the execution of Néarque offstage. Far from discouraging him, this martyrdom only serves to strengthen Polyeucte's commitment to his new religion, and he is executed. The martyrdom of Polyeucte unexpectedly affects Félix and Pauline, who are so moved by his courage that they both convert to Christianity. As this tragedy ends, Sévère expresses admiration for Christians and promises not to persecute them. He believes that Félix and Pauline can serve both God and Decia.

Polyeucte is a very powerful tragedy that explores with much sensitivity the importance of courage, loyalty, and personal commitment to ethical and religious beliefs. Although Polyeucte had no intention of converting to Christianity before his conversations with Néarque, he comes to realize that his life would have no meaning if he were to deny his faith. He refuses to lose his immortal soul in order to save his life. Although Pauline would have preferred to marry Sévère, Polyeucte is her husband and she admires his courage. Her love and respect for him made her ready to accept the gift of faith after his execution. Similarly, Félix was displeased that his son-in-law was not as skilled a politician as Sévère, but he did recognize Polyeucte's honesty. Félix's conversion to Christianity has struck many critics as almost incredible, but one cannot question his sincerity. Félix tells Sévère: "I made him a martyr, his death made me a Christian." *Polyeucte* continues to fascinate readers and theatergoers by its very effective representation of heroism through characters who refuse to compromise their moral beliefs.

Summary

Pierre Corneille was a gifted playwright who has remained justly famous for his treatment of moral problems. Audiences can identify with the universal moral dilemmas he described so well. In depicting the feudalism in *The Cid* or the Roman imperial power in *Horace* and *Polyeucte*, Corneille described problems that exist even today. Like Pauline, Polyeucte, Rodrigue, and Chimène, one recognizes that there are still conflicts between one's personal ethical beliefs and the demands that society imposes on the individual.

Bibliography

Abraham, Claude. *Pierre Corneille.* New York: Twayne, 1972.

Brereton, Geoffrey. *French Tragic Drama in the Sixteenth and Seventeenth Centuries.* London: Methuen, 1973.

Harwood, Sharon. *Rhetoric in the Tragedies of Corneille.* New Orleans: Tulane University Press, 1977.

Mallinson, G. J. *The Comedies of Corneille.* Manchester, England: Manchester University Press, 1984.

Muratore, Mary Jo. *The Evolution of the Cornelian Heroine.* Potomac, Md.: Studia Humanitatis, 1982.

Nelson, Robert J. *Corneille: His Heroes and Their Worlds.* Philadelphia: University of Pennsylvania Press, 1963.

Pocock, Gordon. *Corneille and Racine: Problems of Tragic Form.* Cambridge, England: Cambridge University Press, 1973.

Edmund J. Campion

DANTE ALIGHIERI

Born: Florence, Italy
May, 1265
Died: Ravenna, Italy
September 13 or 14, 1321

Principal Literary Achievement

Dante introduced the use of vernacular language in poetry and pioneered the secular use of allegory, creating verse which is simultaneously historical, universal, and intensely personal.

Biography

Dante Alighieri was born in Florence sometime in May, 1265. His family was of the minor nobility, though neither wealthy nor particularly famous. What details exist concerning his background and career come from his own writings, from the sketch written by his neighbor Giovanni Villani, from the eulogy written after his death by Giovanni Boccaccio, and from the fifteenth century biography written by Leonardo Bruni. The miscellaneous nature of these sources, the fictive element incorporated in Dante's own biographical references, and the welter of legend that surrounds his life make it difficult to isolate fact from fiction; nevertheless, certain things are clear.

Dante's family name was Alagherius in its latinized form, was spelled Alaghieri during his lifetime, and was written Alighieri in the centuries following his death. His given name is a shortened form of Durante. He was deprived of both parents relatively early in his life, his mother having died when he was a boy and his father (who had subsequently remarried) in the year 1283. His father's death thus corresponds exactly to Dante's coming of age. He had a half brother, Francesco, and a half sister, Tana, both children of his father's second marriage. There was another sister, though it is impossible to say whether she was Dante's full or half sister. Based on Dante's own testimony, he had a happy childhood.

It is clear that Dante came from a family that valued education. He had his elementary training from the Dominicans, and he attended the Franciscan school of Santa Croce in his youth. His writings indicate a close familiarity with country, as well as city, life, which he acquired at a relatively early age.

Dante's interests in youth thus paralleled those of other young men from his class and background; they included travel, a knowledge of art and drawing, music, but,

most of all, an abiding interest in poetry.

The most important early counsel that Dante received in his youth came from Guido Cavalcanti, who was twelve years Dante's senior and who came from the wealthy Cavalcante family. Guido would become Dante's first friend in the personal, as well as the literary, sphere. More questionable insofar as its desirability was Dante's early association with Forese Donati, brother of Corso Donati. Corso was the leader of the Florentine political faction known as the Blacks. It was Corso who massacred and expelled the opposing Whites in 1301. The story of Corso's death appears in *Purgatorio* 24 of *La divina commedia* (c. 1320; *The Divine Comedy*, 1802), related by Forese. These political involvements would provide an important element in Dante's poetry but would also be the source of his personal frustration and the reason for his eventual exile from the city. It was possibly at the urging of Forese that Dante took part in the Battle of Campaldino on June 11, 1289, the decisive engagement of Florence's campaign against the neighboring town of Arezzo. By this time, Dante was a young husband, having married Gemma Donati, a fourth cousin to Forese and Corso, sometime between 1283 and 1285. It was an arranged marriage with a relatively wealthy family, the dowry set as early as 1277, but it also solidified Dante's political connections with the Donati family.

Subsequent to his marriage, between the years 1287 and 1289, Dante was in Bologna, possibly for university-level studies. The deep debt into which he fell between the years 1290 and 1300 was likely aggravated by the cost of these studies combined with those of Dante's growing family. He and Gemma would have two sons, Pietro and Jacopo, and one daughter, probably named Antonia Beatrice. Nothing is known of a child named Giovanni, whose signature appears on a contract drafted at Lucca in 1308, except that he calls himself the "son of Dante Alieghieri of Florence."

Dante's first involvements in the political life of Florence date from 1295. He worked tirelessly during this period for Florentine independence and against extension of papal political influence. For two months during the summer of 1300, he served as one of the six priors of the city, served as Florence's representative to San Gimignano in the same year, and was commissioned in 1301 to supervise the widening of a street. While on a mission to Rome, opposing political factions indicted him on a trumped-up charge of embezzlement and condemned him first to payment of a fine, then to exile, and then to death. It is likely that Dante could have restored himself to the city through payment of a fine; yet he refused to do this. Instead, he spent the first few months of 1302 in conspiracy with other Florentine exiles, but soon thereafter, disgusted by their violent radicalism, he went his own way and accepted the life of an exile. His wife and family, however, remained in Florence, so the years that followed were increasingly lonely and filled with frustration.

Fortunately, Dante could turn for assistance to several wealthy friends and patrons during his years as a wandering exile, and the first of these was the Scala family of Verona. Alberto della Scala and his three sons Bartolommeo, Alboino, and Francesco (Can Grande) held sovereignty in Verona from 1262 to 1329 and brought a period of unparalleled peace and stability to the city. Each would provide the Florentine exile, at various times of his wanderings, with the support necessary to sustain him.

Dante left Verona in 1304, likely after the death of Alberto's eldest son, Bartolommeo. He returned to Bologna at this time, probably to the university, where he had been known as early as 1287. His wanderings subsequently brought him to Padua and in the same year, 1306, to Lunigiana, the city of the Malaspina family. The period at Lunigiana is documented by Dante's service to the Malaspinas both as negotiator and attorney, assisting in their conclusion of an agreement of peace with the bishop of Luni. Boccaccio and Villani report Dante's subsequent travels throughout northern Italy, following the course of the Arno and perhaps, from 1307 to 1309, establishing residence in Paris.

When Henry VII (Henry of Luxembourg) became Holy Roman Emperor in 1312, Dante hoped that some rapproachement of church and state would be possible. Three letters that Dante wrote in 1310-1311 praise Henry's idealism and indicate the poet's support for the imperial program. Still, Henry's invasion came to naught; the papacy, which had promised its support, turned against him, and Henry died near Sienna in 1313. Dante's own hopes for triumphant return to Florence died with the emperor.

Two cities offered Dante sanctuary from the political turmoil that attended Henry's death: Verona and Ravenna. Francesco (Can Grande) della Scala of Verona provided immediate asylum, though Dante would spend his final years under the patronage of Guido Novello da Polenta of Ravenna. Guido was a nephew of Francesca da Rimini, whose illicit love for Paolo da Malatesta had by this time been immortalized by Dante in *Inferno* 5 of *The Divine Comedy*. Ravenna would be Dante's home until his death. He spent his final years engaged on occasional diplomatic missions for Guido, one of which was an embassy to Venice. Though he never returned to Florence, he died hoping that Can Grande, influential among the Ghibellines, would bring stability and an end to factionalism in northern Italy. Dante died in Ravenna, Italy, on September 13 or 14, 1321.

Analysis

Political alignments caused Dante's exile, but exile broadened Dante's historical perspective and thus provided an important dimension for his verse. The attribute one most closely associates with Dante's mature poetry is, indeed, his ability to universalize particular historical details. He is able to see all human experience in terms of his own, and there is little doubt that his long period of wandering and his life as an exile, begun in middle age and continued through the rest of his life, furnished the salvation metaphor central to *The Divine Comedy*.

From the earliest period of his life, Dante was fascinated with the possibilities of vernacular Italian as the medium for his poetry. Even in his student verse, he had moved away from classically inspired convention and what he considered its artificiality. His relationship to the classical past is something that he clearly acknowledges; it is implied by the fact that he elects to have Virgil, the preeminent poet of Latin literature, lead his Pilgrim through Hell and Purgatory. It is also the writers of classical Greece and Rome who welcome the Pilgrim as one of their fraternity in the Limbo of the Poets (*Inferno* 4). This reception and its location in the region of the unbaptized indicate that, at the beginning of his journey, and correspondingly at the beginning of his career as a poet, Dante derived satisfaction from his relationship to the classical tradition. Correspondingly, the fact that the Pilgrim leaves Virgil behind when he enters Paradise implies more than that only the baptized can enjoy the Beatific Vision. In effect, the progress of the Pilgrim equals the progress of the Poet. The wandering exile, the man searching for meaning in his own life and in life generally, the poet who is ambitious and who seeks to surpass the poets who have influenced him—all of these are simultaneously Dante.

Still another indication that Dante would accept such a description of his life and work (which became for him synonymous) appears in his treatment of Brunetto Latini in *Inferno* 15. Brunetto, his former teacher, appears among the sodomites. This sensational context, seen in terms of Dante's aesthetics, becomes, however, an argument against stultifying imitation, a verbal sodomy that feeds upon the conventions of the past and thus inhibits genuine progress. In truth, the meaning of the Brunetto canto is one of the most disputed in Dante's poem; yet, this view of its meaning, that it provides an important key to Dante's philosophy of composition through the criticism that it implies, does not preclude the debt that Dante felt to Brunetto as his teacher. If anything, it underscores the difference between a teacher (who privileges the value of the past and transmits it) and the superior creative artist (who uses the past but privileges innovation and originality).

One measure of Dante's ability to make innovative change appears in the figure of Beatrice. It is likely that he based his creation upon the daughter of Folco dei Portinari, a wealthy Florentine who died in 1289. It matters relatively little whether one accepts this testimony, provided by Boccaccio. If so, however, it makes the relationship poignant and Platonic, for this Beatrice died a young bride (the wife of the banker Simone dei Bardi) at the age of twenty-four. What is important for Dante's aesthetics is that Beatrice illustrates the remarkable way that Dante alters the conventions of courtly love as it had appeared in medieval poetry.

If one believes the tradition, Dante saw Beatrice for the first time when she was nine years of age, on May 1, 1274. His love grows, documented in *La vita nuova* (c. 1292; *The New Life*, 1861), though his lady remains unnamed and never reciprocates the poet's attentions. The unnamed persona of *La vita nuova* finds her ultimate development in the *Paradiso*, the final canticle of *The Divine Comedy*. In this context, she literally shows the Pilgrim the way to blessedness, and she figuratively allows the Poet to describe infinite love through finite language. She intercedes to secure the Pilgrim's initial impetus toward salvation, but she simultaneously employs Virgil, whose *Aeneid* (c. 29-19 B.C.; English translation, 1553) had helped inspire the formation of the Poet, as the primary agent of that salvation.

LA VITA NUOVA

First published: c. 1292 (*The New Life*, 1861)
Type of work: Poetry

This collection of verse and commentary traces the progress of the poet's love for an unnamed woman and the progress of the poet in the pursuit of his art.

La vita nuova is a logical precursor of *La divina commedia* (c. 1320; *The Divine Comedy*); both involve the figure of Beatrice, and both show a marked concern with the aesthetics of writing verse. Both also deal with love, though at this point arises the important distinction: Though pure in both works, the love in *The Divine Comedy* is divine and therefore infinite. It engineers the Pilgrim's salvation through the figure of Beatrice and guides the Poet's progress as would a Muse. The unnamed woman of *La vita nuova*, identifiable with Beatrice, is closer, as portrayed, to the feminine persona of courtly poetry, and the love that she represents is transcendent.

The poems of *La vita nuova*, though arranged as chronological narrative, were not written as a cycle; indeed, many date from Dante's youth. The first, for example, is an extraordinary dream poem originally sent for comment to Guido Cavalcanti. Guido was older than Dante and a proud, disdainful Florentine Guelf. He was quick to seize on the sonnet's strong psychological implications. Love appears as a feudal lord. In his arms he holds a sleeping woman, who is naked except for a blood-red cloak thrown about her. In his hand he holds the poet's heart. Love then awakens the woman, convinces her to eat the poet's heart, then departs with her, and the dream ends. Though written considerably earlier than *La vita nuova*, this sonnet sets the psychological tone for the entire work. Without knowing, the lady has consumed the poet's heart and, by extension, his soul and his life; the poet's own love is the means by which she has done this.

Poems, however, constitute only one part of *La vita nuova*. Accompanying them are two kinds of commentary. The first is prose narrative that illuminates the verse that follows it. The second, which immediately follows and appears whenever the poet deems necessary, is a commentary on the poem's prosody itself. For example, the commentary on the dream poem notes that it is divided into two parts, that it initiates a response and resolves it, and that it was controversial when Dante had first circulated it, but that it ultimately won for him a special friend and mentor (Cavalcanti), who, however, remains unnamed.

This second variety of commentary breaks the narrative of the prose commentaries that introduce and link the verse; nevertheless, the commentaries on prosody indicate that the process through which Dante created *La vita nuova* is just as important to him as the work itself. Admittedly, Dante handles his concern with aesthetics less gracefully in this work than in *The Divine Comedy*; still, the privileged place that he implicitly assigns to prosody by including technical commentaries indicates his clear thesis that a poet grows artistically in direct proportion to the poem as it is written.

Even at the point when Beatrice dies, the logical climax and the place where one might expect some particularly personal element to appear, Dante refuses to allow it. Instead, he introduces a quotation from the lamentations of The Book of Jeremiah to suggest the depth of his grief, notes that he cannot provide details about her death, and in the following section precisely calculates by the Arabic method the hour, day, and month on which she died. The result is that the reader dwells upon the mystical nature of the experience. The poet first encounters the woman as she begins her ninth year, and she dies on the ninth day of the ninth month. Thus, although one can calculate that the unnamed love dies on June 8, 1290 (by the Roman calendar), the affair becomes universalized, even stylized, in a way that implies a symmetry in the stages of life.

The depersonalization of the poet's style underscores the poet's thesis: to fix upon those moments that mark the beginnings of a new life. To provide every detail would limit the experience to only those persons immediately concerned. Leaving such details unwritten makes memory, that of the reader, as well as of the poet, essential to a reading of the work. *La vita nuova* thus marks an important stage in the poet's development as a poet. It logically precedes *The Divine Comedy* insofar as it lacks the latter poem's highly personal references; yet it resembles this work as a journal of universalized human experience.

La vita nuova provides additional linkages that unify its discontinuous narrative. Besides the numerology that frames the poet's encounters with the Beatrice figure, the three meetings themselves occur at times that mark stages of the poet's own life. The first, discussed above, is the childhood meeting that occurs at the end of the poet's ninth year and the beginning of the Beatrice figure's ninth year. This point marks the poet's boyhood; he realizes that the encounter is meaningful, for it affects his vital, animal, and natural spirits. Yet this tumult is sexless; what has taken place is a fundamental alteration in the poet's perceptions and a basic development in his personality.

The second encounter takes place nine years later in the ninth hour of the day. Now the poet sees the Beatrice figure, who actually greets him. The physical dimension adds to the nature of the experience. Again, the poet has reached a new stage in his life. He retires to his room and experiences the dream noted above. The personification of Love, his declaration *Ego dominus tuus* (I am your master), the naked Beatrice figure clothed only with a crimson cloth, and her eating of the poet's heart all add to the sexual innuendo. That the woman is the same one who greeted the poet is clear. She is both *la donna de la salute* (the lady of the greeting) and the lady of the poet's salvation. The poet inquires of many *trovatori* (troubadours), somewhat naïvely, the meaning of the dream, and this juncture introduces his *primo amico* (first friend), the otherwise unnamed Cavalcanti. Again, the poet realizes that he has reached a new stage in life but senses even more that the physical dimension has lessened the spirituality of his love. The overwhelming emotion is regret, not lust, and the screen-love device, the poet's substitution of another woman for his true love, represents his attempt to preserve the purity of the original experience. Appropriately, it is the Love persona himself who counsels the poet to adopt this ruse, and it succeeds so well that the poet acquires the reputation of a roué. When Beatrice next passes him, she withholds her greeting. The greeting in this context assumes the dimension of a benefaction, akin to the creative inspiration that a Muse might furnish. That it is withheld signals a nadir of the poet's creative activity, just as it indicates another stage in the poet's life.

Sorrow is the predominant emotion at this point, and the Love figure reappears to counsel that the poet abandon his screen-love ruse. The Love figure, who speaks only in Latin, declares that he is the center of a circle at which all points of the circumference are equidistant. In other words, the poet, though he recognizes the transcendence of love, cannot know love's eternity. That, in essence, is the creative problem with which Dante as a poet must grapple; indeed, it is one that he manages to surmount only in *The Divine Comedy*.

Fate increasingly informs the pattern of life after this experience. At a wedding reception, the poet suddenly senses the presence of Beatrice. He attempts to distract himself by looking at the paintings that adorn the walls of the house, then raises his eyes only to discover Beatrice herself. Again, he swoons and observes that at this point he has moved to that stage of life beyond which it is impossible to return to what had been. Death and the poet's awareness of his mortality intrude when a young woman dies, when Beatrice's father dies, and when the poet himself falls seriously ill. In the ninth day of his illness, the poet reflects on the inadequacy of life and its brevity. Again a dream intrudes, this time a nightmare, in which disheveled women in mourning first warn the poet of his mortality then declare him dead. Beatrice is among them, and in the same dream a friend appears to tell the poet that Beatrice herself has died. The landscape clouds over, and the natural world appears fundamentally changed, much as it had at the death of Christ. Even so, the poet now witnesses his beloved's assumption into heaven. The poet recognizes the beatitude that attends death, and he himself wishes to die.

This vision foreshadows the actual death of Beatrice. The poet sees her death as a divine judgment that the world had been unworthy of one so perfect. Following the death of Beatrice, a young woman pities the poet in his mourning. He accepts her pity and thereby recognizes the mortal, as well as the transcendent, power of love. His sorrow thus passes beyond mortal bounds and arrives at the Empyrean, the largest sphere of First Cause, in which Beatrice herself dwells for all time.

THE DIVINE COMEDY

First published: *La divina commedia*, c. 1320 (English translation, 1802)
Type of work: Poetry

Through the medium of secular allegory, Dante simultaneously individualizes, universalizes, and describes symbolically the circularity of life's journey.

The Divine Comedy represents the mature Dante's solution to the poet's task enunciated in *La vita nuova*. Its three canticles (the *Inferno*, the *Purgatorio*, and the *Paradiso*) display a nearly limitless wealth of references to historical particulars of the late Middle Ages and to Dante's life. Even so, its allegorical form allows these to function as symbols. The Pilgrim's journey through Hell to Heaven thus becomes an emblem of all human experience and a recognition of life's circularity. The "Comedy" of its title is, therefore, the situation of life and the accumulation of experience that attends it.

Correspondingly, however, chronological placement of the narrative from Good Friday through Easter Sunday, 1300, particularizes the experience even as it implies the death and rebirth that attends a critical stage of any person's life. The poet tells his readers in the first line of the *Inferno* that he is midway through life, and indeed Dante would have been thirty-five years of age in 1300. Though he maintains present tense throughout the poem, he is, however, actually writing in the years that follow the events that he describes. This extraordinary method allows the Poet to place what amounts to prophetic utterance in the mouth of the Pilgrim. Dante thus maintains and further develops the thesis of *La vita nuova*, that the progress of the Pilgrim corresponds directly to the progress of the Poet. The literal journey that the Pilgrim undertakes toward the Beatific Vision succeeds only insofar as the Poet can transcend the finite barriers that signification imposes upon language.

If one understands the task of the poem in these terms, the exponential symbolism of *The Divine Comedy* becomes inescapably clear. Like every human being, Dante carries the intellectual burden of what has formed him. At mid-life, this includes the historical influences of his time and the artistic influences of what he has read. His task is to use these to direct his life's journey and, if he is able, to transcend them. His inspiration for doing this is the same feminine persona that appears in *La vita nuova*, though in *The Divine Comedy* Dante specifically identifies her as Beatrice. Her name implies the grace that she represents, and it is noteworthy that she intercedes with St. Lucy, patroness of the blind, and with the Blessed Virgin Mary to set the Pilgrim on the course toward Paradise. Beatrice thus represents efficient grace, Lucy illuminating grace, and Mary prevenient grace. Collectively, they oppose the three visions of sin (Leopard, Lion, and She-wolf) that obstruct the Pilgrim's path.

The women logically employ the Roman poet Virgil as the Pilgrim's guide through

Hell and Purgatory. Virgil represents the achievement of pre-Christian antiquity. His poem the *Aeneid* (c. 29-19 B.C.; English translation, 1553) is the logical forerunner of the poem that Dante hopes to write. Dante, if successful in his journey as Pilgrim and Poet, will synthesize the epic of classical antiquity with the allegory of biblical literature. Understandably, the Pilgrim protests to Virgil that he is neither Aeneas nor St. Paul. This protestation reflects the Poet's awareness of the daunting artistic task of fusing pre-Christian and Christian thought as much as it does the Pilgrim's awareness of the long distance between Hell and Heaven. In reality, they are one and the same journey, and Dante undertakes both tasks simultaneously in *The Divine Comedy*. Appropriately, Virgil can guide the Pilgrim only through Hell and in the ascent of Mount Purgatory. Past that point the pre-Christian past cannot venture. St. Bernard and ultimately Beatrice will guide the Pilgrim through Heaven; yet Virgil (and the pre-Christian wisdom that he represents) offers enough direction to ensure that the Pilgrim reaches Heaven's threshold.

The sinners whom the Pilgrim beholds as he descends through the circles of Hell correspond generically to the three specters that had haunted him in the wood before Virgil's arrival. The sins of the Leopard are serious but unpremeditated. Paolo da Malatesta and Francesca, the adulterous lovers of *Inferno* 5, are good representatives of this grouping. For political reasons and as an alliance of families, Francesca was married to the deformed Gianciotto, son of Malatesta da Verrucchio and ruler of Rimini, but she fell in love with Gianciotto's handsome younger brother Paolo. Gianciotto caught Paolo and Francesca in adultery and murdered them both. Dante bases his depiction of their affair upon these historical personages; Francesca was aunt to Guido Novello di Polenta, Dante's friend and host at Ravenna during his years of exile. Even so, he makes the immediate cause of their adultery their reading of a book, the tale of Guinevere and Lancelot. Guinevere, too, had married a man older than she, King Arthur of Camelot; like Francesca, she fell in love with a handsome younger man. Lancelot thus corresponds to Paolo, Guinevere to Francesca, and Arthur to Gianciotto. Dante thus describes seduction by language, calling the book that Paolo and Francesca read a panderer. Its language has seductive charms but was wrongly directed. Paolo and Francesca burn intertwined in a single flame in punishment for their sin, but their punishment effectively extends their passion into eternity.

The Brunetto Latini episode of *Inferno* 15, the soothsayers canto of *Inferno* 20, as well as many of the other encounters that the Pilgrim has with sinners stress wrong use of language. Brunetto's was wrong because it pridefully paid too great a debt to the past and did not seek transcendence. When Dante's Virgil recounts a version of the founding of his native Mantua, which differs from that which the Roman poet had provided in his own *Aeneid* 10.101, then makes the Pilgrim promise to believe only that which he has now spoken, Dante questions in another way the timeless signification of words with reference only to the natural order. He also implies that there is nothing inherently mantic about a poem, not even Virgil's *Aeneid*, and makes Virgil himself articulate the thought.

The topography of Dante's Hell, Purgatory, and Heaven violates the conventional

Christian conception of these states because of his use of the gyre to describe each. As the Pilgrim descends Hell's circles, the sinners appear more bound to their sin. Paolo and Francesca burn in perpetual consumation of their passion at Hell's top, but at its frozen core Vanni Fucci curses God, and Judas Iscariot stands frozen beside Satan. The topographical arrangement implies degrees of offense, yet all sinners in Hell have mortally offended God. Gyre imagery continues as the Pilgrim and Virgil ascend Mount Purgatory. Though its gyres are more discrete than those of Hell, the chaos of sin rules within each of its precincts, mitigated only to the degree that the sinners trust in the divine mercy that will allow them to reach Heaven.

Dante's Mount Purgatory consequently has three major regions through which the Pilgrim and Virgil ascend: ante-Purgatory, occupied by those who failed to use the grace that divine mercy had provided them in life; lower Purgatory, the region for the proud, envious, and wrathful; and upper Purgatory, reserved for the slothful, covetous, gluttonous, and lustful. At its summit is an earthly paradise corresponding to Eden, as well as to the Elysium of *Aeneid* 6. Logically, Virgil cannot venture beyond this stage both because of his status as pre-Christian and because of his achievement as a poet. As Purgatory implies the reconstitution of a soul, its mountain requires an ascent that corresponds to the descent through Hell. The process that it imposes upon its sinners is purificatory rather then penal, and so it is appropriate that all of its souls at some period, whether on arrival or after preliminary cleansing in ante-Purgatory, must pass through Peter's Gate. After the sinners have demonstrated their desire for Heaven by ascending the three steps of penitence (confession, contrition, and satisfaction), an angel inscribes seven *P*'s upon their foreheads (*peccata*) for the seven capital sins (pride, covetousness, lust, anger, gluttony, envy, and sloth). These vanish singly as the soul ascends each cornice. Once again, signification emerges as a dominant aspect of Dante's allegory. Inscribing the *P*'s enforces the souls' awareness of the sin that had existed hidden in life. The Pilgrim grows in his appreciation of the unspoken word as the Poet grows in his ability to express the ineffable in words whose signification is conventionally finite.

It is in *Purgatorio* 30 that the Pilgrim, awakened in the Edenic paradise by the approach of Beatrice, realizes that Virgil is no longer with him. The fears of the Pilgrim at this apparent abandonment by his guide correspond to those of the Poet, who realizes that from this point the artistic task is his alone. This realization creates impressive tension between the status of the journey, whose successful outcome would appear assured, and the task of the Poet, whose task of reconciling heavily weighted allegorical language with the limitless signification of the infinite necessary to describe the nature of Heaven grows more challenging.

The poetry of *Paradiso* does assume a more mystical character, which enlists the full imaginative powers of the reader. In a way impossible in either the *Inferno* or the *Purgatorio*, the reader becomes participant in the transforming experience that Heaven imposes. The gyres recur, though as circles of the blessed grouped around the Beatific Vision. Even among those saved, the capacity to appreciate the infinite varies directly with their distance from the Vision itself. The Poet thus asks the reader to accept a paradox, which once granted, allows finite language's reconciliation with the Logos itself. It is Dante's most extraordinary achievement of all, and it is the key to an appreciation that is worthy of the *Paradiso*.

Beatrice now assumes an active role in the direction of the Pilgrim. They rise from the earth into the heavenly Empyrean, the abode of God, within which revolves the Primum Mobile, the swiftest and outermost of the heavens. The light of the sun, the music of the spheres, and the gaze of Beatrice, all representing spiritual illumination and enlightenment, increasingly fill the cantos of the *Paradiso* and replace the doubt, darkness, and periodic faintings of the Pilgrim on his passage through Hell and Purgatory.

Much emphasis rests upon the degrees of happiness that the blessed of Heaven experience. Piccarda dei Donati and the Empress Constance both reside in a lesser sphere of bliss; both had been forced to leave the spiritual life that they would have preferred and enter into forced marriages. Even so, Piccarda and Constance experience a full measure of happiness. In another paradox, they know the infinite bliss of Heaven to the full measure of their ability to comprehend it. Their joy is no less than that of the souls that are closer to the Beatific Vision, even though they reside within a considerably lower sphere.

In the Ptolemaic cosmos, which informs *The Divine Comedy*, all the planets (including for Dante the sun and moon) orbit the earth upon a series of transparent concentric spheres. These celestial spheres provide the external order that characterizes Heaven. They guide the seven heavenly bodies that circle the Earth: Moon, Mercury, Venus, Sun, Mars, Jupiter, and Saturn. Beyond the planets is the Sphere of Fixed Stars, and still further is the Primum Mobile. Beyond all nine spheres lies the Empyrean, Dante's unmoved, eternal, boundless region in which the Logos and the saints reside. This conception of Heaven is another means by which the Poet allows his poem to move beyond limited signification and approach the unchanging infinity of First Cause.

Central to portrayal of the Primum Mobile is the symbol of the Celestial Rose. It is a circle of white light within which is a golden center of God's glory. White petals rise in a thousand tiers, and upon these sit the blessed: saints of the old law at one side, saints of the new on the other; little children arranged immediately around the golden center; virtuous women in one descending portion, saintly men in another opposite location. Beams of divine glory, comparable to sunbeams but carried by angels, bear divine love to the created world, not of necessity but from divine graciousness.

As the Pilgrim nears the Beatific Vision, he comprehends all the contradictions that had filled his life's journey. He compares himself to the geometer, who knows it is theoretically possible to square the circle, yet he recognizes the limitations that language imposes upon any attempt to describe accurately what he sees. The image of divinity seems self-sufficient, self-defined, simultaneously that of the Pilgrim and of all humanity. The single word that allows the Poet to describe it is "love," the boundless ability that is assuredly human but that also moves the sun and stars.

Summary

Love's transcendent power directs both *La vita nuova* and *The Divine Comedy* to their conclusions. Though entirely different in their scope and complexity, both works ratify this transcendence through the signification of language and the figure of Beatrice. Still, one indication of the aesthetic distance between the two works is that the former emphasizes that love offers the means by which life evolves while the latter identifies pure love as the First Cause of the cosmos itself. It is a mark of Dante Alighieri's artistry that he manages to universalize the highly personal situations upon which both works depend. Ultimately, in *The Divine Comedy*, the mode of allegory allows him to do that even as he retains thousands of particularized references; yet the anonymity of *La vita nuova* is a clear indication that he had always sought the *dolce stil nuovo* ("sweet new style") that he would realize in his maturity.

Bibliography

Alighieri, Dante. *The Divine Comedy*. Translated by Charles S. Singleton. 3 vols. Princeton, N.J.: Princeton University Press, 1970.

Auerbach, Eric. *Dante, Poet of the Secular World*. Translated by Ralph Manheim. Chicago: University of Chicago Press, 1961.

Boyde, Patrick. *Dante's Style in His Lyric Poetry*. Cambridge, England: Cambridge University Press, 1971.

Dronke, Peter. *Dante and Medieval Latin Traditions*. New York: Cambridge University Press, 1985.

Freccero, John, ed. *Dante: A Collection of Critical Essays*. Englewood Cliffs, N.J.: Prentice-Hall, 1965.

_____. *Dante: The Poetics of Conversion*. Cambridge, Mass.: Harvard University Press, 1986.

Gilson, Etienne. *Dante and Philosophy*. Translated by David Moore. New York: Harper & Row, 1963.

Limentani, Uberto. *Dante's Comedy: Introductory Readings of Selected Cantos*. Oxford, England: Oxford University Press, 1985.

Quinones, Ricardo. *Dante Alighieri*. Boston: G. K. Hall, 1979.

Sayers, Dorothy L., and Barbara Reynolds. *The Comedy of Dante Alighieri the Florentine*. 3 vols. New York: Penguin, 1949-1962.

Robert J. Forman

ROBERTSON DAVIES

Born: Thamesville, Ontario, Canada
August 28, 1913

Principal Literary Achievement
One of Canada's leading novelists, Davies meshes comedy and serious discussions of complex philosophical issues to produce works that are both enjoyable and thought-provoking.

Biography

William Robertson Davies was born in the small town of Thamesville, Ontario, on August 28, 1913. Davies' father, William Rupert Davies, had emigrated with his parents to Canada from Wales in the 1890's and had married Florence Mackay, a woman of Scottish-Dutch descent whose family had been in North America since the 1680's. By the time Robertson Davies was born, Rupert Davies had become an influential newspaper publisher. Both of his parents had strong personalities and greatly influenced Davies' intellectual development. They read often to their children; in an interview, Davies remarked that these stories "marked me forever as a lover, and victim, of myth."

When Davies was five years old, his father bought a newspaper in the small Ontario town of Renfrew and moved the family there. Davies went to the country school with the children of farmers and woodcutters, and his experiences there—he was teased, beaten, and terrorized—parallel those of Francis Cornish in *What's Bred in the Bone* (1985). The family lived in Renfrew until 1925, and it was in his father's Renfrew paper that Davies got his first taste of publication at the age of ten. Everyone in the family was expected to be able to write clearly and accurately, and Davies was sent to report on a slide show and lecture on William Shakespeare's England.

In 1925, Davies' father took on a newspaper in the college town of Kingston, Ontario. In 1928, Davies began attending Upper Canada College, a prestigious boys' school. Davies won prizes for speech and acted in school plays and recalled that he was "capable of learning anything that interested me in record time, but cretinous in my failure to comprehend whatever I did not like." He did not like mathematics and failed both geometry and algebra in his matriculation examinations, which meant that he could not attend university as a regular student.

Queen's University in Kingston, however, allowed Davies to enter as a "special student." He was able to take classes but would receive no degree. He took courses in

505

literature, drama, and history and, as at Upper Canada College, participated as often as possible in drama productions. He finished at Queen's University in 1935. While Davies was at Queen's, his father, while on a trip to Britain, inquired about admission to Oxford, and Davies was accepted by Balliol College. Davies thoroughly enjoyed the Oxford atmosphere and did very well there. He soon joined the Oxford University Dramatic Society and stage-managed and acted in several productions. He read Elizabethan drama and was awarded a bachelor of literature degree in 1938. He was able to publish his university thesis in 1939 as *Shakespeare's Boy Actors.*

After finishing at Oxford, Davies toured with a theater company for several months before going to London and joining the Old Vic, which was then managed by Tyrone Guthrie. He was assigned minor acting roles, but his chief duties were to teach theater history in the school attached to the company and to act as a literary assistant to Guthrie. The Old Vic disbanded in 1939 because of World War II; Davies tried to enlist but was rejected because of his poor eyesight.

At the Old Vic, Davies had met Brenda Mathews, an Australian woman who worked as a stage manager for the company. On February 2, 1940, they were married and in December had their first child. Upon their return to Canada that same year, Davies worked briefly for his father's newspaper in Kingston before being offered the job of literary editor at *Saturday Night*, which was then a well-respected Canadian paper. He wrote on music, theater, and ballet as well as literature.

Davies stayed at *Saturday Night* until 1942, when his father bought the Peterborough *Examiner.* Davies became the editor of the paper; during his years there, the paper was well respected and his editorial comments were often quoted elsewhere. Davies created the character of Samuel Marchbanks for the *Examiner*, and the column in which Marchbanks acidly and wittily commented on the mores of the times appeared in several other newspapers as well.

During his time in Peterborough, Davies helped form the Peterborough Little Theater. He wrote plays for it and for professional companies, and his plays *Eros at Breakfast and Other Plays* (1948) and *Fortune, My Foe* (1948) won the awards for best production at the Dominion Drama Festival. In 1951, Davies published his first novel, *Tempest-Tost*, which drew on his knowledge of nonprofessional acting companies in its comic portrayal of a Little Theater production of Shakespeare's *The Tempest* (1611).

From 1953 to 1959, Davies, while continuing to edit the Peterborough *Examiner*, also wrote for *Saturday Night's* book column. In 1953, Davies was elected to the board of directors of the Stratford Shakespeare Festival, on which he served until 1971. In 1955, Davies' second novel, *Leaven of Malice* (1954), was published and received the Leacock Medal for humor in Canadian writing. This second novel is also set in the fictional town of Salterton and with *Tempest-Tost* and *A Mixture of Frailties* (1958) forms a loose trilogy.

In 1960, Davies spent a year as a visiting professor of English at Trinity College, University of Toronto, and in 1963 he was appointed the first master of the newly opened Massey College, University of Toronto. He taught English and drama at the university until his retirement in 1981. In 1970, he published *Fifth Business*, the first novel in the Deptford Trilogy, which has brought him much acclaim. *The Manticore* (1972) and *World of Wonders* (1975) followed. During the 1970's, Davies also wrote a number of critical studies.

In his retirement, Davies continued writing, publishing a third trilogy during the 1980's that began with *The Rebel Angels* (1981) and continued with *What's Bred in the Bone* (1985) and *The Lyre of Orpheus* (1988). In 1991, his novel *Murther and Walking Spirits*, a kind of fictional history of Canada, was published. Davies continued to live in Toronto with his wife.

Analysis

In *Stage Voices: Twelve Canadian Playwrights Talk About Their Lives and Work* (1978), edited by Geraldine Anthony, Robertson Davies said that his work might be categorized as

> comedy, in the broadest sense of the term. But I take it to include a great measure of romance, of pathos, of the rueful awareness that life is short in time and that what we understand of it is only a trifle of the whole. . . . The greater part of life is lived in the mode of comedy.

Davies' comment applies to his novels quite as much as to his plays; they are comedies in the broadest sense of the term. His novels are witty and occasionally even slapstick, as when Professor Vambrace, in *Tempest-Tost*, attempts to eat grapes while declaiming one of Prospero's speeches. In a somewhat more technical sense, Davies' novels are comedies because they are about real human frailties and limitations. If tragedy can be described as the great brought low through the actions of their faults, then perhaps comedy can be defined as the ordinary muddling through while occasionally appearing ridiculous because of their faults. In *Tempest-Tost*, Hector Mackilwraith, a middle-aged teacher of mathematics, attempts to hang himself in the middle of a production of the *The Tempest* because he loves a young woman who he knows will never love him. Instead of being tragic, Hector's suicide attempt is ridiculous: He is told off by the director for disrupting the play and has broken a number of bottles of homemade champagne in his fall, so that at first everyone thinks he is merely drunk. There is pathos in this account of Hector's misery, but not tragedy.

Hector's fault is that he has lived an almost purely intellectual life and disregarded, or buried, his emotional side. Even when he ponders being attracted to Griselda (the young woman), he makes a list of the pros and cons of pursuing her. This theme of the overreliance on intellect to disastrous effect appears also in *Fifth Business* and, more explicitly, in *The Manticore*, in which it is treated much more seriously than in *Tempest-Tost*. In fact, it is a theme that reappears in one guise or another in most of Davies' novels. In *The Rebel Angels*, it appears as a conflict between a beautiful graduate student's "root" and "crown" (using the metaphor of a tree): Maria Theotoky wants to jettison her emotional, irrational Gypsy background, her root, while living in the intellectual ivory tower of the university, her crown. In *A Mixture of*

Frailties, Monica Gall must learn to release the emotion trapped inside her if she wants to become a great singer. Dunstan Ramsay, in *Fifth Business*, spends his life intellectually examining the lives of saints, something that is at heart intuitive and emotional, and at fifty his "bottled-up feelings have burst their bottle and splashed glass and acid everywhere." It is in *The Manticore*, however, that Davies illustrates this theme most effectively. David Staunton's whole life has been an attempt to bury his emotions and live by his intellect. He wrongly believes that this is the only way he can survive; upon his father's mysterious death, emotion breaks through and he decides to enter Jungian analysis to bring order back into his life. The analysis brings David's true feelings to the fore, and David must acknowledge these feelings before he can be "cured."

The Manticore is also the book that most explicitly makes use of the work of Carl Jung. As David undergoes analysis and works through his memories and dreams, Davies explains some of the archetypes that Jung identified in his work, such as the shadow, friend, and anima; the aim is to acknowledge and accept these elements in oneself and so achieve a wholeness and knowledge of oneself. David, in his diary, dreams of escaping "the stupider kinds of illusion." Jung's ideas are important in most of Davies' works. In the Cornish Trilogy, especially in *The Lyre of Orpheus*, Davies makes much of the idea that "we all have a personal myth . . . that has its shape and its pattern somewhere outside our daily world." Simon Darcourt, a character in *The Lyre of Orpheus*, learns that his myth is not that of servant, as he had once thought, but of Fool—the Fool on the Tarot card who is being pushed by instinct, represented by a dog, into making discoveries that would otherwise remain in mystery. In the same novel, Arthur, his wife Maria, and Geraint, the father of Maria's baby, are playing out the roles of the cuckolded King Arthur, Guenevere, and Lancelot. Dunstan Ramsay, in *Fifth Business*, is Fifth Business, the man in opera who, while not the most important character, "knows the secret of the hero's birth, or comes to the assistance of the heroine when she thinks all is lost." To Davies, a myth is a way of approaching the archetypes that are true for all people at all times. It provides people with the "power to see themselves objectively" because it is an outside measure, not one made up by the individual. Personal myth acknowledges one's place in the scheme of things; it allows one to know what and who one is while escaping "the stupider kinds of illusion."

In identifying Dunstan Ramsay as Fifth Business, Davies uses characters from opera that are essentially melodramatic: the Hero, the Heroine, the Villain, the Rival, and Fifth Business. Davies has written that "Melodrama is an art in which Good and Evil contend, and in which the dividing line between Good and Evil may often be blurred, and in which Good may often be the winner." In *World of Wonders*, the hero, Magnus Eisengrim, undergoes severe mistreatment as a child; he is abducted and sodomized by a magician with a traveling carnival, made to spend long hours hidden inside a mechanical effigy, working its machinery so as to impress the carnival-goers, and is otherwise abused and ignored. That is certainly evil. Yet the result is that Magnus becomes a very great magician, a master illusionist, something that he would never have become had he spent his life in Deptford, where he was born. Here the dividing line between good and evil is blurred, and it seems that good is the winner.

Davies also employs elements of satire, especially in his earlier works. In *Tempest-Tost* and *Leaven of Malice*, particularly, Davies pokes fun at some of the social conventions of Salterton, the town in which they are set, and deflates the pretensions of some of the characters. Yet rather than satire, which Davies claims he never intended to write, perhaps one should use the term "comedy of manners" to describe these novels. He examines the follies of the opinions and behaviors of various characters, and his favorite target is the person with a self-deluding sense of importance. In *Leaven of Malice*, he pokes fun at a character who tries to apply psychological precepts facilely: "The chapter on Freudian psychology in his general textbook had not, after all, equipped him to deal with a tiresomely literal professor of classics who knew Oedipus at first hand, so to speak."

Davies is convinced of the importance of the individual; but it is the individual who knows or comes to know himself or herself, not the self-deluding fool, with which he is concerned. The books of the Deptford Trilogy, in particular, written for the most part in the first person, are about the growth in self-knowledge of the individual. Several of Davies' books are *Bildungsromane*: They recount the development, the education, of a young person reaching for maturity. *World of Wonders* is one such novel; so is *A Mixture of Frailties*, the third novel in the Salterton Trilogy. In it, Monica Gall leaves her family and Canada for England, where she has several teachers who each, in their way, teach her not only music and singing but also how to value herself and her opinions. Monica comes from an essentially anti-intellectual, culturally deprived background; part of her development is learning which parts of her background are part of her and valuable to her and which are not.

This tension between family and individual is a recurrent pattern in Davies' novels. In *Tempest-Tost* and *Leaven of Malice*, Solly Bridgetower and Pearl Vambrace each have an overpowering parent to overcome; in *A Mixture of Frailties*, Solly's mother even exerts her dominance beyond the grave in her humiliating will, which says that Solly will not inherit until he and Pearl have a son. Making a break between domineering parent and submissive child is not the only way to portray and deal with the tension between the two, however; that would be far too simplistic. Both Monica in *A Mixture of Frailties* and Maria in *The Rebel Angels* have to come to terms with their parents, accepting them for what they are. Maria fights her mother's Gypsy inheritance but must acknowledge it if she wants to be wholly herself.

Davies includes a huge amount of ideas, themes, and arcane knowledge in his books. *What's Bred in the Bone* discusses undertaking, art, alchemy, astrology, and spying. *The Rebel Angels* includes François Rabelais, Paracelsus, Gypsy lore, the tarot, and more. Davies does not expect his reader to be knowledgeable about these things, too; what the reader needs to know is adequately, and often amusingly, explained.

THE DEPTFORD TRILOGY

First published: *Fifth Business*, 1970; *The Manticore*, 1972; *World of Wonders*, 1975
Type of work: Novels

A snowball thrown with a stone in it has consequences for the lives of three men.

The publication of *Fifth Business*, the first novel in the Deptford Trilogy, marked a deepening of Davies' novelistic talents. His previous novels (the Salterton Trilogy), while amusing and certainly not devoid of ideas, lack the depth of thought and power that characterizes *Fifth Business*. Davies has said that when he began *Fifth Business*, he had had no intention of writing a trilogy; the subsequent two novels arose because he found that he had more to say about some of the characters. Each novel can stand completely on its own, yet there is a link between the novels. They express some of the same ideas and themes in different ways, and the reader is richer for having read the others.

In a speech transcribed in *One Half of Robertson Davies* (1977), Davies commented that *Fifth Business* arose from his examination of the extent to which one is responsible for the outcome of one's actions and when this responsibility begins. He decided that

> it began with life itself, and that a child was as responsible as anyone else if it chose a course of action knowingly. In *Fifth Business* . . . a boy makes a choice: he wants to hurt his companion, so he throws a snowball at him, and in the snowball is a stone. . . . The consequences of the snowball with the stone in it continue for sixty years, and do much to shape the lives of three men.

The boy who threw the stone is Percy Boyd Staunton; he aimed it at Dunstan Ramsay, and it hit the mother of Magnus Eisengrim. *Fifth Business* examines the life of Ramsay; *The Manticore* looks at Boy Staunton's life and the effect it has had on his son, David Staunton; and *World of Wonders* concerns Magnus Eisengrim.

Fifth Business begins at 5:58 P.M. on December 27, 1908, in a small Canadian town in Ontario called Deptford. That is the exact time that Percy Boyd Staunton threw the snowball that Dunstan Ramsay sidestepped. Ramsay took evasive action knowingly and feels guilty when he realizes that the snowball meant for him has caused Mary Dempster to lose her wits and to have her baby, Paul, prematurely. This scenario is the beginning of Ramsay's involvement with Mrs. Dempster, who becomes more than simply a responsibility to him; she becomes what Ramsay sees as a saint. Whether or not she is a saint is important, really, only to Ramsay. An old Jesuit questions him: "who is she in your personal world? What figure is she in your personal mythology? . . . [Y]ou must find your answer in psychological truth, not in objective truth." What Mary Dempster has done is to enrich Ramsay's life. Through her ability to love without fear, she has given him an entry into the world of the spirit.

After being wounded at Passchendaele, Ramsay's is not a particularly unusual life. He attends a university, gets a position as a teacher of history at a boys' school, and begins writing books on saints for travelers as well as producing a book on the psychology of myth and legend. Finally, on a sabbatical to South America visiting churches and studying local legends of saints, he again meets Paul Dempster, who has become Magnus Eisengrim, and meets Magnus' manager, Liesl Vitzlipützli. Liesl is a gargoyle of a woman who, along with Mrs. Dempster and the Jesuit priest, becomes one of Ramsay's most important teachers. She forces him to find out who he is in his "personal world": "Who are you? Where do you fit into poetry and myth? Do you know who I think you are, Ramsay? I think you are Fifth Business."

Fifth Business quite accurately reflects the role Ramsay has played in his relationship to Boy Staunton. Boy considers Ramsay an eccentric and old friend but one who is unsuccessful in the way in which Boy measures success. If Fifth Business "knows the secret of the hero's birth," then Ramsay fits the bill, for he knows Boy's beginnings, his traits established from boyhood, better than Boy does himself. Ramsay's final act as Fifth Business in Boy's life is to force him to examine his actions and take responsibility for them: "I'm simply trying to recover something of the totality of your life. Don't you want to possess it as a whole—the bad with the good?" Possessing one's life as a whole—the bad with the good—is essentially what *Fifth Business* is about.

Ramsay, over many years and with the help of such teachers as Liesl, is able to come to know himself essentially through his own efforts. In *The Manticore*, David Staunton, the son of Boy Staunton, has inherited his father's lack of self-knowledge and goes to Switzerland for Jungian analysis in an attempt to put his life back together. Boy's ignorance of his true nature has a lasting detrimental effect on his son: David struggles very hard before he can break down the false image his father has created and see him as he was and before he can stop putting himself on trial for not living up to his father's standards of manliness.

Like *Fifth Business*, *The Manticore* is written in the first person: It is David's record of his analysis. His analyst asks him to prepare a "brief"—David is a successful Toronto lawyer—which consists mainly of a chronological account of David's childhood memories. Like *Fifth Business*, the plot of *The Manticore* does not reveal a life wildly unusual, but the events of David's life show why he is who he is. He has taken refuge from his feelings because, in effect, every time he had strong feelings he was punished for them. By denying them and creating a shell of rationality, he protects himself. One of his tasks under analysis is to recall and recognize his true emotions.

David's analysis only goes so far in helping him recognize and accept both sides of himself, the emotional and the intellectual. His analyst helps him identify the ways in which Jungian archetypes apply to the people in his life and helps him strip the archetypes away again to allow these people to be themselves, real people and not images created by David. It takes an encounter with Liesl, however, to truly put him on the path to wholeness. Liesl, whom David has met in a chance encounter with Ramsay during the Christmas holidays, takes David to a cave in the mountains where the remains of a group of primitive men have been found. She leads him further into the mountain, forcing him to crawl and wriggle through the narrow passageway to a kind of holy of holies, the place where these primitive men worshiped bears. David is uncomfortable and wants to go back to the light; darkness and bear-worship are unreasonable to him, and he wants to run back to rationality. On the way out, David becomes severely frightened and empties his bowels. Before this trip, Liesl has suggested that learning "to know oneself as fully human" must involve a kind of "rebirth": "It's more a reentry and return from the womb of mankind. A fuller comprehension of one's humanity. . . . It's not a thinker's thing." David's trip back from the cave is his rebirth: The terror is something he feels deeply. It gives him the "glimmering" of his own humanity and perhaps the ability to face the "inner struggle" to become whole, which is what Liesl describes as heroic behavior.

World of Wonders presents the life of the third man affected by that stone-filled snowball. Unlike Ramsay's and David's, Paul Dempster's life has been far from ordinary. Eisengrim (the name Paul Dempster has finally taken) is asked to tell his story as a kind of "subtext" for a film he is starring in about the life of the magician Jean-Eugène Robert-Houdin. He tells it to Ramsay, Liesl, and the director, cinematographer, and producer of the film and begins with what he calls his descent into hell.

His particular hell is Wanless' World of Wonders. He has stolen fifteen cents to go to the fair, and five of that buys him entry to a carnival show—the World of Wonders—where he sees a fat woman, a man who writes with his feet, and Willard the magician. After the show, Willard, on the pretext of showing Paul a trick, rapes him and then, in a panic, abducts him. Paul spends the years of his adolescence and young adulthood being sodomized by Willard and shut inside a mechanical effigy called Abdullah, used to fool carnival-goers. After Willard's death, Paul travels to England, where he joins a theater troupe as the double of the leading man, Sir John Tresize, in a series of melodramas. After Sir John's death and a period of odd jobs, he travels to Switzerland, where he gets a job repairing mechanical toys that have been smashed to bits by the adolescent Liesl, who suffers from a disease that has thickened the bones of her head, distorting her features. Magnus teaches her to be human again, and they later perform a magic show that makes Magnus into the world's greatest illusionist.

During most of his life, Magnus has been forced to be someone other than himself, to the point of being given names not of his own choosing. Yet he comes out of this not as a nonperson but as a very great magician who knows himself very well. Out of evil has come good. Liesl attributes this to what she calls Magnus' "Magian World View": "It was a sense of the unfathomable wonder of the invisible world that existed side by side with a hard recognition of the roughness and cruelty and day to day demands of the tangible world."

All three of the Deptford novels have this concern with the "invisible world." In

Fifth Business, it expresses itself in Ramsay's concern with saints; in *The Manticore*, it is represented by the cave in which David is at last freed to have feelings; in *World of Wonders*, it is this "Magian World View" that finds art in low places. Magnus has survived and prospered because he has always had an art to sustain him—conjuring with Willard, acting with the Tresizes, and fixing clocks in Switzerland. Art has allowed Magnus to remain an individual who is wholly himself.

THE CORNISH TRILOGY

First published: *The Rebel Angels*, 1981; *What's Bred in the Bone*, 1985; *The Lyre of Orpheus*, 1988
Type of work: Novels

The life of Francis Cornish and his influence after his death lay the groundwork for these novels.

The Cornish Trilogy shares many of the themes that run through the Deptford Trilogy, and it is these themes as much as the characters that link the three novels that can be read completely independently. Davies is once again concerned with finding one's personal myth, becoming fully oneself—something that often is connected with art or pure scholarship in these novels—and in each book he again approaches the topic somewhat differently.

The Rebel Angels is the only novel in the trilogy to be written in the first person; the main narrative voice is passed back and forth between Maria Theotoky, a beautiful graduate student who narrates the sections titled "Second Paradise," and Simon Darcourt, an Anglican priest and teacher at the university, who narrates the chapters called "The New Aubrey." Maria's sections focus on her love for Clement Hollier, her dissertation director, and her problems with John Parlabane, a renegade monk who teaches skeptic philosophy and was a boyhood friend of Hollier. Darcourt is one of Francis Cornish's executors, along with Hollier and Urquhart McVarish, and his chapters attempt to provide a broader view of the university, especially of its personalities. As Darcourt's and Maria's experiences overlap, the effect of two separate narrators is not a disjointed story line but one that is dovetailed. Maria's voice, in fact, is much like Darcourt's, and while this is a weakness in terms of portraying Maria, it does give the novel a continuity and a unity of vision.

The main thrust of the story comes from the actions of Parlabane, who deliberately sets out to get everybody excited. He badgers Maria, poking and prying into her personal life and giving her long lectures on his philosophy, he cadges money from Darcourt and Hollier, and he plays the sycophant to Urky McVarish, the professor everyone else is united in loathing. At the end of the novel, he kills McVarish in a gruesome way and then kills himself, leaving a letter explaining the circumstances of the murder to Hollier and Maria. Parlabane also writes a long, rambling novel called

"Be Not Another's," which he thrusts on Hollier, Maria, and Darcourt, asking for their opinions and then ignoring them.

Parlabane—though his book is based on his own life, though he seems to obey no rules but his own, and though he gives perfectly good advice to Maria on knowing herself—does not fully know himself. For Dunstan Ramsay, David Staunton, and Magnus Eisengrim, knowing oneself involves a balance between intellect and wonder; Parlabane has no balance and relies on his intellect, despite his claim of belief in God. Parlabane is an egotist and, as such, cannot fully know himself, for he does not really accept anything outside his own authority. Nevertheless, he is able to become one of Maria's Rebel Angels, helping her to realize that she must accept her Gypsy background as much as her university education if she wants to be herself. Maria also calls Hollier and Darcourt her Rebel Angels (placing them in her personal mythology), for the Rebel Angels taught wisdom to men after being thrown out of heaven, and Maria believes that the three have taught her much about herself.

What's Bred in the Bone is the strongest novel of the Cornish Trilogy perhaps because it is the most focused. It tells the story of what is bred in the bone of Francis Cornish, the experiences and inheritances that make him who he is. It begins prior to his birth by describing the town of Blairlogie, Ontario, and the family into which he was born, and goes on to describe all the events that are important in forming Cornish's character, from his first discovery that the world is separate from him to his death. Francis discovers that art is his talent and develops it by sketching the corpses at the undertaker's, where his grandfather's coachman holds a second job. At the university, he practices drawing in the manner of the Old Masters, using silver point, and after Oxford he takes a job helping Tancred Saraceni in art restoration. When Saraceni challenges him to paint a picture in Old Master style, mixing paints as they would have done and using a wooden panel of the right age, Francis paints "the myth of Francis Cornish." It is done as a triptych of the Marriage at Cana, and every figure in it is significant for whom Francis Cornish has become.

In *What's Bred in the Bone*, Davies again strongly emphasizes the importance of discovering one's personal myth. In an early conversation with Francis, Saraceni says that modern artists "are painting the inner vision . . . but they depend only on themselves, unaided by religion or myth, and of course what most of them find within themselves is revelation only to themselves." One needs a connection with the "world of wonders" to produce a life that is meaningful. Davies does not imply that finding one's personal myth is easy or that knowing oneself solves all problems. Because Francis expresses himself best in Old Master style, he is effectively prevented from painting anything, for he would simply be accused of fakery. Though in his old age he seems to the world an "eccentric and crabbed spirit, there was a quality of completeness about him." Francis dies laughing, having recognized the allegory of his own life.

The Lyre of Orpheus, which further develops several of the main characters of *The Rebel Angels*, pursues several threads of plot. Simon Darcourt, whose discoveries while writing a biography of Francis Cornish provided the framing fiction of *What's*

Bred in the Bone, is putting two and two together about Francis' art and discovering his own personal myth in the process. His plan to prove and reveal Francis as a great artist and not a skillful faker leads him, with help from Maria's mother, to identify his personal myth as that of the Fool on the tarot cards, who is pushed by instinct, "something outside the confines of intellect and caution," into unconventional paths. Darcourt finds this identification of his personal myth gives him "a stronger sense of who he was."

The second major thread of plot involves the decision that the Cornish Foundation (headed by Arthur Cornish, Francis' nephew) makes to produce an opera called "Arthur of Britain, or The Magnanimous Cuckold." The opera and the characters involved in creating it take up a large part of the narrative, but the most important facet of it is the way the plot—Guenevere and Lancelot's betrayal of Arthur—is reflected in the lives of Arthur and Maria Cornish and Geraint Powell, the director of the opera and Arthur's friend. Maria's infidelity with Geraint does not exactly parallel Guenevere's, for she does not love Geraint, and in many ways Geraint's bedding of her reflects the way Uther came to Ygraine to sire Arthur more than it does Guenevere and Lancelot's affair. During a discussion of what plot the opera should use, Darcourt recalls Ovid saying that "the great truths of life are the wax, and all we can do is to stamp it with different forms. . . . If we are true to the great myth, we can give it what form we choose. The myth—the wax—does not change." Arthur and Maria must learn how to be true to "the great myth" in order for their marriage to be enriched rather than destroyed, and that lesson is expressed in the loving charity of Sir Walter Scott's lines used in the opera's libretto:

> It is the secret sympathy,
> The silver link, the silken tie,
> Which heart to heart, and mind to mind,
> In body and in soul can bind.

Summary

All the novels of the Deptford and Cornish trilogies are rich in character and complex in theme. They are engagingly written; Robertson Davies entertains at the same time that he makes the reader think. The foregoing analyses can cover only a small fraction of the ideas Davies brings to his writing and point out what is perhaps the overriding theme of both trilogies: the importance of recognizing the wonder of the world, whether one calls it God, myth, mystery, the realm of "the Mothers," the unconscious, or all of the above.

Bibliography

Cude, Wilfred. *A Due Sense of Differences: An Evaluative Approach to Canadian Literature.* Lanham, Md.: University Press of America, 1980.
Grant, Judith Skelton. *Robertson Davies.* Toronto: McClelland and Stewart, 1978.

Heintzman, Ralph H., ed. *Journal of Canadian Studies* 12 (February, 1977).

Jones, Joseph, and Joanna Jones. *Canadian Fiction.* Boston: Twayne, 1981.

Keith, W. J. *Canadian Literature in English.* New York: Longman, 1985.

Lawrence, Robert G., and Samuel L. Macey, eds. *Studies in Robertson Davies' "Deptford Trilogy."* Victoria, British Columbia: University of Victoria, 1980.

Monk, Patricia. *The Smaller Infinity: The Jungian Self in the Novels of Robertson Davies.* Toronto: University of Toronto Press, 1982.

Peterman, Michael. *Robertson Davies.* Boston: Twayne, 1986.

Karen M. Cleveland Marwick

DANIEL DEFOE

Born: London, England
1660
Died: London, England
April 26, 1731

Principal Literary Achievement

Generally considered the most typically English of the major early eighteenth century writers, Defoe was one of the great journalists and professional authors of his age and an important contributor to the development of the novel in English.

Biography

Daniel Defoe was born Daniel Foe in the parish of St. Giles Cripplegate, London, England, in 1660, the son of James Foe, a tallow chandler and butcher who later held several positions of authority in the City of London, and Alice Foe. (Defoe changed his name to its more aristocratic form sometime around the age of forty.) Because there are no surviving records of Defoe's birth, biographers have surmised, on the basis of two of his offhand statements, that he was born sometime in the autumn. Defoe's early years were eventful: When he was five, the Great Plague ravaged London and his family fled to the country; the next year, the Great Fire of London leveled thousands of houses and eighty-seven churches, including St. Paul's Cathedral. He grew up in a London wracked with political and religious controversy, and belonging as he did to a Dissenting family, he must have been more than a little interested in the events occurring around him.

Because the Foes were Presbyterians (a major Dissenting group), Daniel was denied an education at Oxford and Cambridge, from which Nonconformists were barred. Instead, from 1671 to 1679, with the intention of studying for the ministry, he attended schools founded for well-to-do Dissenters: James Fisher's school in Surrey, and the Academy for Dissenters, run by the Reverend Charles Morton, north of London. Unlike the traditional classical courses of study at Oxford and Cambridge, the curriculum at Morton's Academy emphasized modern philosophy and science, as well as the new English grammar. This practical education—especially the study of English— became the foundation on which Defoe built his later career as a professional writer.

Defoe left Morton's Academy around 1679, having at some point decided against the ministry. By the early 1680's, he had established himself as a hosiery merchant in

London, and in 1684, he married Mary Tuffley, with whom he had eight children.

For Defoe, the 1680's and the 1690's saw substantial business and political activity. Although, as a merchant, he traveled extensively in England and on the Continent— acquiring the geographical and linguistic knowledge that his writing would later reveal—he found time for involvement in the Duke of Monmouth's Rebellion in 1685, for his first published piece of writing (a pamphlet against the Catholic James II), and for participation in William III's triumphal entry into London in 1688. Defoe's business interests included not only hosiery but also wine, tobacco, land, and civet cats; he conducted business on a grand scale—and, like other aggressive merchants of his age, was entangled in a number of legal suits. In 1692, Defoe's businesses failed, leaving him seventeen thousand pounds in debt.

After his financial collapse, Defoe used his Whiggish connections to acquire various lucrative government positions. For half a decade, he served as a trustee of the government lottery, worked as an accountant for the government office that levied duties on glassware, and even functioned as a secret agent for the Crown. By 1694, he was able to set up a brick and tile factory near London and to pay off many of his debts; by the mid-1690's, he had prospered enough to purchase a new house, and a coach and horses. Sometime during these years, he also changed his name.

Defoe began writing at the end of the seventeenth century, publishing his first book, *An Essay upon Projects* (1697), and much Whig propaganda, culminating in his defense of the Crown in the satiric poem *The True-Born Englishman: A Satyr* (1701). With King William's death in 1702, resentment against Dissenters (whom the king had protected) grew. That December, Defoe published *The Shortest Way with the Dissenters* (1702), an outrageous proposal, supposedly from a High Church extremist, for prosecuting and killing those who did not conform to the Church of England. Arrested for sedition, Defoe was pilloried, fined, and jailed. His half-year sojourn in Newgate prison left him with huge debts and a failed brick and tile factory.

Released from prison at the behest of Robert Harley, the Tory speaker of the House of Commons, Defoe worked for Harley as a secret agent, traveling throughout England in search of political information, and writing and publishing a thrice-weekly Tory publication, *The Review* (1704-1713). Defoe also produced a considerable amount of other writing—journalistic pieces, familiar essays, poetry, allegories, letters, and book-length works on various topics. Although he kept his Tory connections secret and publicly remained a Whig, he was criticized by the Whigs, who suspected his affiliations. Criticism was not Defoe's only problem; from 1713 to 1714, he was arrested several times either for debt or for political reasons, and each time he was released as a result of government intervention.

With the death of Queen Anne and the fall of the Tory ministry, the pragmatic Defoe offered his services to Sir Robert Walpole, the powerful Whig politician. Defoe, until the year before his death, was Walpole's secret agent working in the Tory publication network, subverting Tory propaganda from within. He also published a popular series of conduct books, including the well-received *The Family Instructor, in Three Parts* (1715).

With the publication of *The Life and Strange Surprizing Adventures of Robinson Crusoe, of York, Mariner, Written by Himself* (1719; more popularly known as *Robinson Crusoe*), Defoe began yet another career, producing in the remaining decade or so of his life the fictional works that assured him of a place among England's literary greats. *Robinson Crusoe* was followed a few months later with *The Farther Adventures of Robinson Crusoe: Being the Second and Last Part of His Life* and with *Serious Reflections During the Life and Surprising Adventures of Robinson Crusoe, and His Vision of the Angelic World* (1720). The second and third volumes never earned the acclaim of the first; neither was worthy of the first. Defoe's success with Crusoe's story led to a number of long narratives, including those on which his enduring fame rests: *Memoirs of a Cavalier* (1720); *The Life, Adventures and Pyracies of the Famous Captain Singleton* (1720; more popularly known as *Captain Singleton*); *The History and Remarkable Life of the Truly Honourable Col Jacque, Commonly Call'd Col Jack* (1722; more popularly known as *Colonel Jack*); *A Journal of the Plague Year* (1722; also known as *The History of the Great Plague in London*); *The Fortunes and Misfortunes of the Famous Moll Flanders, Written from Her Own Memorandums* (1722; more popularly known as *Moll Flanders*); and *The Fortunate Mistress* (1724; more popularly known as *Roxana*). In addition, during that last decade of his life, he wrote several other book-length works on a variety of topics and continued to produce pamphlets, criminal biographies, political pieces, and other journalistic works.

Defoe died in London on April 26, 1731.

Analysis

Defoe's admirers sometimes call him the "father of the novel," sometimes refer to him as the "first great realistic writer." While neither phrase is completely accurate—there is no consensus about the identity of the first novelist, and there is controversy about when realistic writing first became popular—both descriptions reveal something about Defoe's major literary contribution. He was one of the best of the earliest writers of realistic fiction, the genre that eventually evolved into the novel as it is known today.

Defoe and his contemporaries did not invent fiction or even popularize it. Elizabethan and Jacobean England produced a number of writers whose chief oeuvre was fictional writing—imitations of classical models, prose romances, biographical accounts of criminals and rogues, picaresque tales, allegories, and even translations of the lengthy and complicated narratives so popular in France. To this tradition, Defoe added the realistic first-person narrative, featuring the humble everyday occurrences that constitute the life of the ordinary—not famous or notorious—human being.

All Defoe's long major works are fictional narratives that pretend to be true autobiographies. Defoe's skill at inventing realistic episodes and providing superbly realized detail makes it difficult for the average reader to believe that the tales are fictional, that they have no basis in actuality, that they are the creations of one man.

Defoe's fiction is notable for its verisimilitude—that illusion of reality or semblance of truth created through the use of concrete details, elaborate identifications of the sources of information or ideas, simple and unadorned prose, frequent reminders to the reader to beware of inaccuracies, and, most important, the first-person narrator. Verisimilitude is created through the naming of actual places and people, the inclusion of historical events as background, the inclusion of prefatory statements in which the narrator writes of material omitted because of lack of space or mentions corroborating testimony to the events in the narrative, and the creation of completely believable characters.

In *An Essay Upon Projects*, Defoe suggests the creation of a Society, modeled on the French Academy, "to polish and refine the English Tongue . . . to establish Purity and Propriety of Stile. . . ." Defoe's concern with language is evident in the fact that "Purity and Propriety of Stile" are the dominant characteristics of his prose. To Defoe, clarity and plainness—qualities learned at Morton's Academy—were not only necessary for understanding but also morally correct. Plain language was, for Defoe, the language of the everyday world that he inhabited, the diction and imagery of business people, the vocabulary of the middle class, the honest communication of the common English citizen. This stylistic plainness is completely appropriate to Defoe's intentions in his fiction and lends an air of authenticity to the autobiographical discourse of his characters. Plainness of language notwithstanding, Defoe's prose is not devoid of linguistic creativity; when it is appropriate, he skillfully uses aphorisms, proverbial phrases, figurative comparisons; he apostrophizes, he uses analogies, he constructs alliterative sequences and rhetorical questions. Like Alexander Pope, he is a master of periphrasis.

At first acquaintance, Defoe's first-person narrators seem unusual or uncommon—they are prostitute and courtesan, sailor and gentleman, criminal and Quaker—but they are very much of a type: They are practical, business-minded, middle-class folk who inhabit an active and vigorous world. These narrators—Roxana, Moll Flanders, Robinson Crusoe, Colonel Jack, Captain Singleton, the unnamed Cavalier—are possessed of a sturdy, irrepressible desire to conquer all circumstances; they are industrious and determined, and their ingenuity often proves their economic salvation. Indeed, Defoe's narrators seem always to be counting or tallying money or goods or movable property.

All Defoe's long narratives tell essentially the same story: An average, but prudent and hardworking, person is forced by circumstances into desperate straits but manages, through human ingenuity and determination, to gain success. Defoe's characters personify the heroic in common humanity, and their actions represent the religious significance of hard work and discipline. Defoe writes about everyday life and its temptations and compromises, but he also illustrates the workings of divine providence in the humblest of daily activities.

Defoe's fiction has often been criticized for its lack of discernible structure—he rarely uses chapter divisions, leaving no clues to the dramatic moments and internal climaxes in the narratives. He provides a stunning variety of richly detailed episodes that do little to advance what little plot there is, but which do create a sense of the importance of the mundane. Unlike the novelists who would follow him, Defoe avoids character analysis, preferring instead to concentrate on action and incident; his characters show little emotion and a considerable amount of calm reflection. Defoe's debts to allegory and the moral treatise are evident in the hortatory tone so characteristic of his tales; he moralizes frequently—to many readers' irritation—but always, it is in the service of his intentions, in the contexts of the solid middle-class fictional world that he has created.

ROBINSON CRUSOE

First published: 1719
Type of work: Novel

Shipwrecked on a deserted island, an English seaman manages to create, through hard work and ingenuity, a profitable and comfortable life for himself.

Robinson Crusoe was Defoe's first-published full narrative and his most popular, appealing to both middle-class and aristocratic readers with its combination of a believable and very human first-person narrator, realistic detail, allusions and references to actual places and people, imagery drawn from everyday life and the natural world, and an appealing, if somewhat unstructured, narrative line.

The title page of the book provides a considerable amount of information for the reader. *The LIFE and Strange Surprizing ADVENTURES of ROBINSON CRUSOE, of YORK. Mariner: Who lived Eight and Twenty Years, all alone in an un-inhabited Island on the Coast of America, near the Mouth of the Great River of Oroonoque; Having been cast on Shore by Shipwreck, wherein all the Men perished but himself. With An Account how he was at last as strangely deliver'd by PIRATES. Written by Himself.* That, in brief, is a plot summary. It also is evidence of the ordinariness of the narrator, a seaman from York (and therefore middle class) who is forced by circumstances to fend for himself in unfriendly surroundings, a practical man who manages to survive for twenty-eight years before his rescue. Finally, within this long title is the evidence of Defoe's insistence on realism—the use of real place names, the statement that the book is an autobiographical narrative.

That Robinson Crusoe is a Defoe character is evident from the moment he finds himself shipwrecked. He acts immediately in the interest of survival, salvaging such necessaries as he can from the stricken ship and building a rude shelter. Yet Crusoe's concern is not only for his physical well-being; he begins a journal in which he plans to record his spiritual progress as it is reflected in the daily activities that mark his sojourn on the island. For nearly two decades, Crusoe works to create a life for himself, building what he needs, improvising where he must, and ultimately replicating a little corner of England on the desert island. What he accomplishes is beyond basic survival; he fashions an English life that is dependent on the transformation of raw materials into the necessities of his culture. He plants grain that he bakes into bread, he domesticates goats so that he might have milk, he turns a cave into a cozy fortified dwelling that boasts comfortable furniture. When Friday arrives, Crusoe's little English empire is complete: The conqueror has mastered both the territory and its people.

Having survived the shipwreck, Crusoe has become strongly aware of his vulnerability as a human being, and throughout the narrative he insists that his life is proof of the workings of divine Providence. Consequently, he often reflects on the spiritual lessons to be learned not only from his experiences on the island but also from the events in his life that led to his sojourn so far from home. This reflection is typical of Defoe's narrators, who look on life's experiences as a series of symbolic occurrences pointing to the connections between the spiritual and the secular.

Defoe has created in Robinson Crusoe a man very like himself—and very much a typical eighteenth century Englishman. Crusoe's plebeian origins, his earnest industry, his tendency to see religious meaning in the mundane, his talent for overcoming misfortune are all Defoe's qualities. Like the average Englishman of his time, Crusoe is something of a bigot, and although he treats Friday well, the slave is never offered his freedom and must call Crusoe "Master." Crusoe triumphs over his circumstances and environment, and indeed he manages to provide himself with a little paradise on earth; but he is English to the core, and with the first opportunity he returns to England and settles down to family life.

Robinson Crusoe is often described as one of the major forerunners of the novel. Although written as a travel narrative, it displays many of the modern novel's major characteristics: realism (through verisimilitude, the first-person narrator, imagery from the natural world, copious detail), interesting and believable characters engaged in plausible adventures and activities, and an engaging story.

MOLL FLANDERS

First published: 1722
Type of work: Novel

Born into poverty, a resourceful and industrious woman works her way through moral lapses and misfortunes to repentance and middle-class respectability and comfort.

If *Moll Flanders* is Defoe's most highly regarded fictional narrative, Moll Flanders is probably Defoe's most memorable narrator, with her compelling account of a life spent largely in attempts to survive in a society hostile to unattached women.

Born to and abandoned by a convicted felon, Moll Flanders is reared first by Gypsies and then as a ward of the parish of Colchester. At fourteen, she is hired as a servant to a kind family who educates her along with their daughters. Moll, believing she is loved, loses her virtue to the oldest son, who later pays her to marry the youngest son, Robin. Widowed after five years, Moll is married four more times, to a draper who spends all of her money, to a sea captain who turns out to be her half brother, to a roguish Irishman (from whom she separates when he decides to continue highway robbery), and to a bank clerk (with whom she finds happiness until his death). Between the brother and the highwayman, she spends six years as the mistress of a gentleman whose wife is insane. Moll also bears several children to husbands and lover, but she seems ill-suited to motherhood. In the end, she is reunited with the great love of her life—Jemmy E., the charming Irishman—with whom she resolves to live respectably.

Because she has no social status and no real financial possibilities, Moll Flanders, like so many eighteenth century women, is dependent to a great degree on men—as husbands or keepers or employers—and on her own industry for survival. Her adventures following Robin's death are focused on marrying profitably: Moll learns to say little about herself, to pretend to wealth in order to attract men, to behave like a lady in order to appear worthy of gentlemen. Like so many women of the middle class and the aristocracy, her principal objects are money and security, and she employs all of her energy in the pursuit of a financially lucrative marriage. She has two embarrassing failures and achieves only modest success with the bank clerk, and when he dies, she is eventually tempted by her poverty to begin a criminal career that lasts for twelve years. By the time Moll is apprehended in the act of stealing two pieces of silk, she has become one of the wealthiest thieves in London.

In the story of Moll Flanders, the reader can recognize many of the concerns that Defoe addressed in his fiction. Moll is a sturdy, resourceful, intelligent woman, driven by her need to survive. She turns to a life of crime, is enabled by her industry and ingenuity to succeed to the point of minor wealth, and is forced by her Newgate incarceration to a recognition of her need for repentance.

The story of Moll Flanders' life and misadventures displays the stylistic traits for which Defoe is praised. Moll's world—eighteenth century London, with its crowded streets and throngs of humanity, with its gulf between rich and poor—is vividly realized in Defoe's attention to detail and in his frequent allusions to actual places and real people. The horrors of Newgate Prison are detailed in vigorous language that conveys strong images of confinement and inescapable poverty. Defoe's fascination with precise location and the intricacies of process allows Moll to elaborate on her plans for snaring rich husbands and on her techniques for stealing jewelry or other goods. So graphically located are Moll's exploits that at times the book reads like a criminal atlas of eighteenth century London streets or even like a manual for a would-be thief.

This focus on the minutiae of thievery, coupled with Moll's evident relish in telling stories that display her audacity and subtlety in criminal activity, her satisfaction with the expertise she developed, and her sense of triumph at acquiring wealth (albeit through crime), becomes the basis for Defoe's didacticism. The middle-class traits that Defoe admires—practicality, determination, focus on assets and liabilities—have been employed in a reprehensible life, and Moll must undergo a spiritual conversion and repent before the narrative ends.

Finally caught in the act, Moll is incarcerated in Newgate and condemned to death. She is visited by a clergyman, who prays with her and entreats her to repent her wicked past. Moved by the minister's words, Moll realizes that she must be concerned with her spiritual impoverishment. Her repentance is intensified by the imprisonment of Jemmy, her favorite husband, whose criminal life she now blames on her desertion of him. Moll and Jemmy escape execution and are transported to Virginia, where they purchase their freedom and become landowners. The elderly Moll Flanders who narrates the story is a woman who is determined to tell her story so that it can serve as a deterrent to anyone who might contemplate a life of crime, as an assurance to the sinner that no life is too despicable to be salvaged through repentance.

Summary

Daniel Defoe's narratives—in particular, *Robinson Crusoe*, *Moll Flanders*, and *Roxana*—are widely regarded as ancestors of the novel. The first two have each, at one time or another, been declared "the first novel," although the consensus is that both books lack two essential characteristics of the novel: character development and a well-structured plot.

There is more agreement on Defoe's contribution to the development of the new genre. From Defoe's work, the novel acquired realism, moral complexity, plain language, and a focus on everyday human life. He may not be the father of the English novel, but that genre owes much of its character to the fiction that he produced.

Bibliography

Backscheider, Paula R. *Daniel Defoe: Ambition and Innovation.* Lexington: University Press of Kentucky, 1986.

_____. *Daniel Defoe: His Life.* Baltimore: The Johns Hopkins University Press, 1989.

Bell, Ian A. *Defoe's Fiction.* Totowa, N.J.: Barnes & Noble Books, 1985.

Elliott, Robert C., ed. *Twentieth Century Interpretations of "Moll Flanders": A Collection of Critical Essays.* Englewood Cliffs, N.J.: Prentice-Hall, 1970.

Ellis, Frank H., ed. *Twentieth Century Interpretations of "Robinson Crusoe": A Collection of Critical Essays.* Englewood Cliffs, N.J.: Prentice-Hall, 1969.

Hunter, J. Paul. *The Reluctant Pilgrim.* Baltimore: The Johns Hopkins University Press, 1966.

Richetti, John J. *Daniel Defoe.* Boston: Twayne, 1987.

E. D. Huntley

CHARLES DICKENS

Born: Portsmouth, England
February 7, 1812
Died: Gad's Hill, Rochester, Kent, England
June 9, 1870

Principal Literary Achievement

Dickens' innovations in genre, serialization, and magazine publishing deeply affected the development of the nineteenth century novel. His social criticism had a direct influence on his country, and his extraordinary inventiveness left a legacy of memorable characters.

Biography

Charles John Huffam Dickens was born in Portsmouth, England, on February 7, 1812, the second child of John and Elizabeth Dickens. Following his father's work as a clerk in the Navy Pay Office, the family moved to the port town of Chatham in 1817, where for a time Charles enjoyed an idyllic middle-class childhood—fresh country air, decent schooling, and books to read in the attic on sunny afternoons.

It was a short idyll. By 1822, improvident John Dickens' fortunes were waning. Recalled to London by his office, he placed his wife and six children in a cheap and smelly little house in the ugly new suburb of Camden Town. In late January or early February of 1824, the seminal event of Dickens' life occurred: He was sent to work sticking labels on bottles of bootpolish alongside a group of ragged urchins in Warren's Blacking Factory, a tottering and rat-infested building next to the Thames River in old central London. Passersby could see him at work in the window: His degradation seemed complete.

To make matters worse, there was the loneliness. Within a month, in February, 1824, John Dickens was arrested for debt. His family joined him in the Marshalsea Prison—all, that is, except twelve-year-old Charles, who was left to survive on his own in London.

Buoyed by an inheritance, Dickens' father was released after only a few months in prison. Charles's mother, however, kept her son at the blacking factory—something he never forgot. Only after John Dickens had retired from the office and turned to free-lance journalism in March of 1825 was Charles sent back to school. The nightmare had lasted little more than a year, but a year is a long time to a sensitive, brilliant, and ambitious boy; such an experience, in the class-conscious society of

527

Victorian England, was for Dickens a deep source of shame. The adult Dickens told it only once, to his best friend and first biographer John Forster. His wife never knew.

In 1827, Dickens left school for a dull job as a lawyer's clerk. Two years later, he followed his father into journalism, first as a law reporter, then as the fastest short-hand reporter in the Houses of Parliament, moving in 1834 to one of the best newspapers in the country, the *Morning Chronicle*. Meanwhile, he was rejected in love, dabbled in amateur theatricals, and, in 1833, had his first short story published.

Success came fast. Under the penname of "Boz," Dickens rapidly published a series of London "Street Sketches" over the next two years. These were collected together as his first book, *Sketches By Boz* (1836). Original, brilliantly illustrated, and intensely observant of the new phenomena of urban life, it captured the public fancy, and Dickens was invited to collaborate on another project with top cartoonist George Cruikshank. The *Pickwick Papers* (1836-1837) followed, in twenty monthly serial parts—its resounding success was assured when Dickens invented Sam Weller, the archetypal streetwise low-life, and teamed him with genial, portly, gentlemanly Mr. Pickwick.

Dickens needed quick success. His craving for middle-class respectability led him rapidly into marriage to kindly and unassuming Catherine Hogarth in 1836, into a growing family, and into the solid comforts of a "proper" home. This situation was also graced by his teenage sister-in-law Mary, whose sudden death in his arms in May of 1837 profoundly shook him. That same year, keen to exercise control over his own writing and thereby to maximize his profits, he first tried his hand at magazine editing. The periodical *Bentley's Miscellany* (1836) seemed to need rejuvenating, and, although he was still in the middle of *Pickwick Papers*, he began serialization in the magazine of his *Oliver Twist* (1837-1839). That in turn overlapped with his next novel, *Nicholas Nickleby* (1838-1839). When *Bentley's Miscellany* folded in 1839, he launched his own magazine, the short-lived *Master Humphry's Clock* (1840-1841), and serialized in it, in forty weekly parts, *The Old Curiosity Shop* (1840-1841), which was both a pinnacle of Victorian sentimentality and a nightmare of threatened and dying childhood. He also published his historical novel *Barnaby Rudge: A Tale of the Riots of '80* (1841).

The year 1842 saw Dickens' first visit to America. His experiences produced a controversial travel book, *American Notes* (1842), and his picture of failed utopia, *Martin Chuzzlewit* (1843-1844). At thirty, he was already a figure of towering importance in Victorian society: Every novel addressed a pressing social issue; he was heavily involved with charities and pressure groups and was increasingly attracted by the stage. Meanwhile, his wife was pregnant with their fifth child. In 1843, he wrote *A Christmas Carol*, following its success every year with another holiday offering.

The writing of his next big novel, *Dombey and Son* (1846-1848), in Italy (which also produced another travel book, *Pictures from Italy*, in 1846), went slowly: Dickens missed the direct inspiration of late-night walks in the London streets. In 1849-1850 came his major autobiographical novel, *David Copperfield*. The next year (along with his ninth child) came his most successful venture into magazine editorship, the weekly *Household Words* (1850-1859), mixing entertainment with useful information. It ran until arguments with his publishers caused Dickens to shut it down and start again under the title *All the Year Round* (1859-1870); in it, Dickens helped launch such important fellow-novelists as pioneer "sensation" and detective-fiction writer Wilkie Collins.

Dickens' "other" career as a semiprofessional actor-director first started to merge with his career as a writer in December, 1853, when he gave his first public reading from his own works—a seasonal offering, not for profit, of *A Christmas Carol. Bleak House* (1852-1853) had been published the year before, and *Hard Times* (1854), his exposé of industrial inhumanity, was published the year after. In 1855, Dickens met again the first love of his life, the capricious and ornamental banker's daughter Maria Beadnell, who had toyed with him in the early thirties. She was now fat, forty, and silly. He had his revenge on her, and on the march of time, whose ravages he was himself starting to feel, in the character of garrulous Flora Finching in *Little Dorrit* (1855-1857).

In 1856, Dickens bought the gentleman's country house that he had once admired, as a boy, from the dusty highroad: Gad's Hill Place, in Kent. In 1857, while directing and acting in a play, he met the young actress Ellen Ternan. The following year, he separated from his plump and aging wife—trumpeting his self-justification in *Household Words*, and pointblank denying the obvious implications of his new liaison. The same year, he gave another, better performance—as the dramatic public reader of his own works: Eyewitness accounts testify to his extraordinary, almost hypnotic power over his audience, and his ability to transform himself into each of his own characters. Several weeks of London engagements were followed by a three-and-a-half-autumn reading tour of the provinces, Scotland, and Ireland.

The first issues of *All the Year Round* in 1859 contained the first installment of Dickens' romantic fable of revolutionary France, *A Tale of Two Cities* (1859). *Great Expectations* (1860-1861) began serialization in 1860, the year of Dickens' second season of public readings. The deaths of his mother and (in India) of his son Walter perhaps colored his shadowy last finished novel, *Our Mutual Friend* (1864-1865), a tale of deceit, betrayals, and violence.

By 1865, Dickens, at fifty-three, looked twenty years older: He had lived too intensely. Death was hastened when, against doctors' orders and family pleas, he added to his public reading repertoire an adaptation of the scene in *Oliver Twist*, where villain Bill Sikes murders the prostitute Nancy. What brought him back to the gory scene, after nearly thirty years—acting ambition, an obsession with sex, blood, and violence, murky impulses toward self-destruction—will never be satisfactorily explained. He died of heart failure on June 9, 1870, in Kent, England, leaving on his desk an unfinished tale of perversity and murder, *The Mystery of Edwin Drood* (1870).

Analysis

Dickens is one of the accidental giants of literature: Only William Shakespeare has commanded anything like the same level of both extraordinary popularity and critical esteem. Dickens was the first mainstream nineteenth century writer to reach out to hundreds of thousands of lower-class semiliterate readers, for whom he retained a conscientious concern that was only partly paternalistic: When one reads in *Our Mutual Friend* that the urchin Sloppy, who turns the washer-woman's mangle, is "a beautiful reader of a newspaper," because "He do the police in different voices," one can laugh yet be respectful. Dickens himself did much to bring his works within the reach of ordinary people: Monthly serial parts at a shilling (one twentieth of a pound), in an age when a standard novel cost more than thirty times as much, put fiction within the reach of the lower middle classes; the twopence weekly (a sixth of a shilling) that bought *Household Words* made quality entertainment and useful information available to a mass audience.

One secret of Dickens' success, as the detective novelist and critic G. K. Chesterton wrote in 1906, was that Dickens was both genius and Everyman: He wanted what the people wanted. That helps explain why about a dozen pirate adaptations of *Oliver Twist* were playing popular theaters across London before Dickens had even finished writing it, and why early cinema invested so heavily in his novels—the second British feature film, in 1912, was an adaptation of the very same novel. It partly accounts, too, for the wild fluctuations in his critical reputation during his lifetime and after. Other sources for this are probably his period sentimentality and his resounding anti-intellectualism—he was, above all, an instinctive performer and semieducated improviser, the master of the carnival, a self-made man who thought he had a few hard-won truths to tell but who, unconsciously, revealed considerably more. He was not really, Chesterton argues, a novelist at all, but "the last of the mythologists," whose god-like characters, from Pickwick and Sam Weller on, exist "in a perpetual summer of being themselves." A Dickens novel is theater, even circus. Not until *Dombey and Son* in 1846 did he (regretfully) move on from the episodic and freewheeling "life and adventures" structure of his early novels.

When the twelve-year-old Dickens walked alone through London to the blacking factory, the scene of his degradation, he learned step-by-step the map of the sprawling and frightening city that looms in nearly every one of his works, the first modern metropolis, where only one in two poor children would survive to precarious adulthood. It takes the first detective in fiction to penetrate such a labyrinth, and Dickens invents him, in *Bleak House*'s Police Inspector Bucket. To express the image of the great city, it takes an imaginative identification of people with their houses, like the kind Dickens achieves in *Little Dorrit*, or the intrusion of a gigantic symbol, such as the (real-life) dustheaps that loom over the urban wasteland of *Our Mutual Friend*, and through which scavengers sift for coins, spoons, rags, and bits of human bone.

The story of his childhood degradation was also the source of his relentless (even desperate) creative energy, and the core of the central myth that he created of lost and violated childhood. As if upping the stakes of helplessness and terror, in *The Old Curiosity Shop* and the much-later *Little Dorrit*, he projects his anguish through the female persona of Little Nell, to whose deathbed the narrative inevitably marches, and "little" Amy Dorrit, the child born and bred in the Marshalsea Prison, who rises by force of humility of spirit above its degradation. In *Bleak House*, perhaps his masterpiece, he speaks, still more startlingly, directly through another female character, illegitimate and unattractive Esther Summerson.

In every one of Dickens' novels is embedded an attack on a specific social abuse. In *Bleak House*, it is the dilatory injustice of the legal system. His portrait of vampiric lawyer Mr. Vholes, a minor character who might at any moment step to center stage, perhaps typifies Dickens' method and its biblical roots: Attempting to reassure a client, Vholes thumps his coffinlike desk, making a sound as if ashes were falling on ashes, and dust on dust. This very same example, however, points back toward the true source of Dickens' art: not a thirst for social justice, though he devoutly felt this, but an eye for the weirdness of the world and the estranged unfamiliarity of the ordinary—Vholes "skinning" his black gloves from his hands.

OLIVER TWIST

First published: 1837-1839 (originally published as *The Adventures of Oliver Twist*)

Type of work: Novel

An orphan survives the workhouse and London's criminal underworld, to be rescued by a rich benefactor.

The first chapters of Dickens' first "true" novel, *Oliver Twist*, which he began to write concurrently with the picaresque adventures of Mr. Pickwick, form a hard-hitting satire on the inhuman cruelties of the New Poor Laws of 1834. These dictated that society's jobless and desperate should be virtually imprisoned in harsh institutions known as "workhouses." Into one of these a little bastard boy is born—the lowest of the low, christened "Oliver Twist" by a pompous parish official, Mr. Bumble the beadle. Yet Oliver is in fact a gentleman by blood, with a fortune awaiting him, for his story is also a romance of origins, a battered child's wish-fulfillment.

"The Parish Boy's Progress" (to use Dickens' subtitle) really starts when Oliver draws the short straw among a group of starving workhouse boys, and must approach the master at dinnertime to utter his famous request: "Please, sir, I want some more." He is promptly sold to an undertaker, whose wife locks him up among the coffins for punishment. He escapes to London, where he is befriended by a streetwise boy, the "Artful Dodger," who initiates him into the all-boy household of an "old gentleman" called Fagin (the name of one of Dickens' companions at the blacking factory), a criminal mastermind. Innocent as ever, it is not until Oliver is mistakenly arrested that he realizes that his new friends are pickpockets. During his trial at the police court, the gentleman, Mr. Brownlow, whom he is supposed to have robbed, realizes Oliver's innate goodness and takes him into his home.

All seems safe—but Oliver knows too much about wily, demonic Fagin and his companion-in-crime, Bill Sikes. Sikes's woman, Nancy, a prostitute, is employed to steal Oliver back—an act that she immediately regrets and tries to repair. Sikes tries to seal Oliver's degradation and his power over him by employing him on a house-breaking expedition. The plan misfires when Oliver is shot crawling through the window of a country house and is taken in by the gentle people he is supposed to be robbing—an old lady and her ward, who eventually turns out to be Oliver's aunt.

As this excess of "coincidences" indicates, the second half of the novel is inferior to the first. Good eventually defeats evil, and Oliver inherits the heaven of respectable middle-classness (hardly a radical solution to a novel that trumpets its social criticism). Creative energy dissipates, however, when the action leaves the nightmare underworld of London, which seems almost a projection or map of Dickens' own childhood terrors. The real climax of the novel is Sikes's brutal murder of Nancy—one of the scenes that led some commentators to worry that the novel belied its author's fascination with the criminality that it denounced.

NICHOLAS NICKLEBY

First published: 1838-1839 (originally published as *The Life and Adventures of Nicholas Nickleby*)
Type of work: Novel

A young gentleman restores the flagging fortunes of his family and exposes the villainy of his uncle.

The title character of *Nicholas Nickleby* sets off to be a schoolmaster in the north of England when the death of his father leaves the Nickleby family in bad straits—a trial his pretentiously genteel and garrulous mother (a comic portrait of Dickens' own mother) finds hard to bear. At Dotheboys Hall in Yorkshire, Nicholas wins a test of strength with the evil headmaster Squeers, whose reign of terror has resulted in the abuse and deaths of his cringing charges, all of whom are orphans and unwanted children—a fictionalization of the real-life horrors that Dickens documented during a visit to Yorkshire with his illustrator.

Next, Nicholas becomes an actor in the hilariously inept touring company of Mr. and Mrs. Crummles, a development that allows Dickens to demonstrate both his knowledge and his affection for the theater. Meanwhile, the rather precarious main plot of the novel concerns the pathetic Smike, a handicapped boy whom Nicholas rescued from Dotheboys; its climax occurs when the boy is revealed to be the illegitimate son of Nicholas' evil uncle, Ralph Nickleby, who has also plotted against the innocence of Nicholas' sister, Kate. Father and son both perish, but a happy conclusion is brought about by the fairy-tale benevolence of the Cheeryble Brothers. Not surprisingly, they have long been targets of attack for critics who believe that Dickens has no practical or political solutions to offer to the abuses that he exposes.

DAVID COPPERFIELD

First published: 1849-1850 (originally published as *The Personal History of David Copperfield*)

Type of work: Novel

David Copperfield's autobiography duplicates the rags-to-riches shape of Dickens' own life: from castaway factory boy to famous author and self-made gentleman.

Dickens' eighth novel, his favorite, has an intimate relationship to his own story: "C. D." becomes "D. C." Some months before he began it, he had sat down to write the story of his childhood degradation, for the first and only time in his life. The experience was too painful, and Dickens abandoned the autobiographical attempt. Yet the material found its way, often word for word, directly into the first-person fiction of *David Copperfield*, which (as Dickens puts it semijokingly in the subtitle) the hero "never meant to be published on any account."

Fatherless David Copperfield's idyllic relationship to his pretty and childlike mother is utterly ended by her second marriage. Austere Mr. Murdstone lives up to the fairy-tale model of the wicked stepparent, whipping the terrified boy when he stammers over impossibly long sums, sending him away to school (where he meets and worships handsome Steerforth), and finally depriving David of his inheritance when his mother dies in childbirth, consigning him instead to the hell of Murdstone and Grinby's (that is, Warren's) factory. Comfort, however, is provided by the feckless, wordy, self-important Mr. Micawber, a masterly comic transformation of Dickens' own father, with whom the lonely boy takes lodgings. Micawber suffers the same fate of imprisonment in debtor's prison but remains convinced that his luck will change.

An important subplot, meanwhile, centers on the seafaring folk David meets through his devoted nurse, Peggotty: her brother Daniel, whose house is an upturned boat, the stalwart fisherman Ham, and "Little Em'ly," the reckless and beautiful girl who is eventually seduced and ruined by Steerforth, David's idol—an act Steerforth can only partially redeem by his death in a storm at sea, which also kills Ham, who had hoped to marry her.

When Micawber departs in search of his fortune, David also leaves London in quest of love and family. Robbed even of his clothes, he walks the long miles to Dover, to be rewarded by the half-unexpected affection of his cantankerous and eccentric Aunt Betsy. She provides the schooling proper to a gentleman, at Dr. Strong's academy, and sets David on the path to becoming a successful professional writer. The text pays little attention to his work, however: His romantic life looms far larger. He enters into an unsuitable marriage to sweet, frivolous, luxurious Dora Spenlow. She calls herself his child-wife.

On her deathbed—tragic but inevitable, given her inadequacies—Dora commends David to the woman who will be her successor, Dr. Strong's daughter, Agnes, an incarnation of the Victorian ideal of the domestic angel, and, as such, somewhat lifeless and unbelievable. Embedded in this development is a hint at Dickens' own dissatisfaction with his own marriage and his desire for escape. Yet several hurdles must be negotiated before David can be safely delivered into the haven of a proper Victorian marriage. Dr. Strong and Agnes must be rescued from the clutches of the reptilian, mock-humble Uriah Heep, largely through the agency of Micawber. "Little Em'ly" must be found and rescued: Old Daniel Peggotty finally emigrates with her to Australia—a treatment of the taboo fallen woman theme that was radical and humane for its time, and which reflects the lessons that Dickens learned in his ten-year involvement with a home for fallen women, Urania Cottage.

GREAT EXPECTATIONS

First published: 1860-1861
Type of work: Novel

The mysterious benefactor who turns Pip into a gentleman proves to be not the aristocratic lady he supposed but a runaway convict.

Not one of Dickens' child characters enjoys a happy and uncomplicated relationship with two living parents. Dickens, in his fiction, found it necessary not only to orphan himself of the parents who shamed him but also to re-create them in ideal shapes—and sometimes, too, to be fair to them. That is what happens in *Great Expectations*. What strikes one most powerfully about this compact and streamlined narrative—technically, perhaps Dickens' best—is the excessive and apparently unmotivated guilt of its hero: guilt, perhaps, for the terrible snobbery into which he falls as he tries to climb the social ladder, guilt at his rejection of his parents, or the guilt of the human condition.

Pip is a village orphan brought up roughly by his unmotherly sister (her bosom bristles with pins), the wife of gentle blacksmith Joe Gargery. In the first chapter of the novel, on the memorable day when he becomes aware for the first time of his identity and his place in a hostile world, Pip meets, in the graveyard where his parents lie buried, a shivering, ravenous, and monstrous man, an escapee from the prison ships across the marshes, who terrorizes Pip into stealing food and drink for him. The convict is eventually recaptured, but not before Pip (and Joe) has come to pity him or before he has lied that it was he who stole a pie and brandy from the Gargery larder.

Next, Pip also meets for the first time the rich, weird recluse Miss Havisham, who lives in a darkened and dusty room where time has stood still, dressed always in a yellowing wedding dress. He falls in love with her petulant and beautiful ward, Estella, whom the old woman is training to break men's hearts, as vengeance for her own abandonment at the altar.

Some years later, a lawyer named Jaggers appears at the smithy with the news that Pip, now Joe's apprentice, has been left a fortune, and is to become a gentleman. He leaves for London, and inevitably a wedge is driven between him and his best friend, illiterate Joe, of whom Pip sinks so low as to become ashamed. Miss Havisham (the word play on "sham" is appropriate) lets Pip believe that it is she who is his benefactor, but the real benefactor is actually the least likely person imaginable: Magwitch, the monstrous convict, who has made good in Australia and now returns to England (thereby breaking the rules of his sentence) in hopes that the boy he has "made" will return his devoted affection. Pip is horrified and disgusted: His money is contaminated. The lesson of love and human decency that he must learn comes very hard indeed. Yet he learns it: By the time poor Magwitch is reclaimed by justice, Pip is prepared to stand holding his hand in the public court. Thankfully, Magwitch dies in prison before he can be hanged. Pip himself now falls seriously ill and is nursed back to life by Joe. No one, however, can turn back the clock: The moment Pip is better, Joe (calling him "sir") retreats to the village. Pip's loneliness at the close seems mediated only by a vague promise that a chastened Estella may some day be his—a modification of the harsher original ending Dickens had intended.

Great Expectations is psychologically Dickens' most mature and realistic novel, although it works through his usual system of displacements and dark doublings: Loutish Orlick, Joe's other apprentice, for example, seems to function as Pip's alter ego when he attacks his uncaring sister, Mrs. Joe. It is also a novel that depicts the powerful influence of environment as well as of heredity: Magwitch, the convict, and bitter Miss Havisham were themselves both abused and lonely as children. For all of its somber coloring, however, the novel is also riotously funny, in the characteristically Dickensian mode of excess: Pontificating Uncle Pumblechook, a seed merchant who subjected the boy Pip to humiliation over Christmas dinner, gets his poetic comeuppance, Joe reports, when Orlick robs him, "stuff[ing] his mouth full of flowering annuals to perwent his crying out."

Summary

Charles Dickens did not create novels: He created a world. Since his death in 1870, a semantic slippage has taken place, whereby he has become identified with the Victorian age and with Englishness; this is not altogether inappropriate. His fictions have frustrated and inspired writers as different as Joseph Conrad, T. S. Eliot, and Graham Greene, to name but a few; they have also profoundly influenced early filmmakers and theorists such as D. W. Griffith and Sergei Eisenstein.

He is a well of creativity and joy in living. Nevertheless, through his erratic and eccentric fiction, he probes some of the mysteries of the human heart and human society; he allows readers to experience the world over again through the eyes of his child-narrators. As a result, Scrooge, Micawber, Pickwick, Fagin, Miss Havisham, and their companions have attained a life beyond the texts that gave them birth.

Bibliography

Ackroyd, Peter. *Dickens.* New York: HarperCollins, 1990.

Chesterton, G. K. *Charles Dickens.* New York: Dodd, Mead, 1906.

Collins, Philip. *Dickens and Crime.* Bloomington: Indiana University Press, 1968.

_____, ed. *Dickens: The Critical Heritage.* New York: Barnes & Noble Books, 1971.

House, Humphrey. *The Dickens World.* 2d ed. London: Oxford University Press, 1942.

Kaplan, Fred. *Dickens: A Biography.* New York: William Morrow, 1988.

Slater, Michael. *Dickens and Women.* Stanford, Calif.: Stanford University Press, 1983.

Stewart, Garrett. *Dickens and the Trials of Imagination.* Cambridge, Mass.: Harvard University Press, 1974.

Wall, Stephen, ed. *Charles Dickens: A Critical Anthology.* Harmondsworth, Middlesex, England: Penguin Books, 1970.

Wilson, Angus. *The World of Charles Dickens.* New York: Viking Press, 1970.

Joss Lutz Marsh

JOHN DONNE

Born: London, England
1572
Died: London, England
March 31, 1631

Principal Literary Achievement

Somewhat disparaged initially as a Metaphysical poet, Donne became known as one of the best poets of Renaissance England.

Biography

John Donne was born to prosperous parents in London, England, sometime in 1572. His father, also named John, was a successful iron merchant; his mother, Elizabeth, a descendant of Sir Thomas More and John Heywood, the dramatist. Both parents were devout Catholics. Their religion and especially his mother's literary background seem to have had a profound influence upon Donne. He would not always remain a Catholic; he eventually took orders in the Anglican church, but throughout his life, he retained a passionate interest in religion, and he was writing poetry before he was twenty-one. His parents sent him to Oxford, where he stayed for three years, but he left before he was sixteen and without a degree.

In 1590, he began his study of law at Lincoln's Inn, where he probably acquired most of his learning in law and where he entered the service of Sir Thomas Egerton, thereby establishing himself in a secular career. He took part in two military expeditions under the influence of Egerton, but they were uneventful for him; he wrote two poems based on them, "The Storm" and "The Calm."

While in Egerton's service in 1591, Donne met and in violation of Canon Law secretly married Ann Moore, Egerton's niece and the daughter of Sir George Moore, an event that profoundly affected Donne's career. As a consequence of the marriage, Egerton dismissed Donne from his employ, and Moore had him imprisoned briefly. Released after the Archbishop of Canterbury declared the marriage legal, Donne, now thirty, found himself with a wife and no prospects. Egerton refused to reinstate him, and Moore implacably refused to release Ann's dowry. Donne's marriage thus marks the end of one era of his life and the beginning of another.

During Donne's earlier era, he had begun to write poetry, including his *Songs and Sonnets*, his *Satires*, and his *Elegies*. These secular poems, early expressions of Donne's genius and typical of Renaissance poetry, were not originally printed but circulated

among friends. Each of the *Songs and Sonnets* is unique, each looking at one of the many possible perspectives of love, its glories and its failures. His *Satires*, all in the tradition of the seventeenth century, assault urban vice (his third satire deserves special note, for it reveals Donne's changing attitude toward religion as he moved away from Catholicism). The nineteen *Elegies* contributed especially to Donne's reputation as Jack Donne, a man-about-town and a frequenter of the ladies. All of these early poems reveal Donne's philosophical and scientific bent, his use of rugged, dramatic verse, his references to everyday experiences, his fondness for fantastic metaphors—qualities that identified him to the English writer and critic Samuel Johnson, at least, as a Metaphysical poet.

Following his release from prison, Donne moved from London to Pyrford and then to Mitchum, still searching for secular preferment. This period of Donne's life, characterized by fewer and different types of literary pieces, failed to produce a political appointment for him, but he did succeed in establishing himself with some worthy patrons. Among his patrons were Lady Magdalen Herbert, for whom he may have written the "La Corona" sonnet sequence and the "Autumnall," and Sir Robert Drury. When Drury's young daughter, Elizabeth, died, Donne wrote *An Anatomy of the World: The First Anniversary* (1611) and, subsequently, *Of the Progress of the Soule: The Second Anniversary* (1612), poems known today as the *Anniversaries*.

Also during this period, Donne began to establish himself as a writer of prose. His first important work was *Biathanatos* (1646), an argument justifying suicide and still of interest today because of what it reveals of Donne's erudition and of his state of mind at the time he wrote the work. His prose career further developed in the service of Thomas Morton, Dean of Gloucester, who retained Donne to write polemical prose against Catholics. Donne obliged with *Pseudo-Martyr* (1610), an attack against the Catholic church for teaching that to remain Catholic in defiance of British law was an act of martyrdom. This work also provides the best evidence up to 1610 that Donne had reconciled himself to the Anglican church. His most scathing attack upon Catholics was *Ignatius His Conclave* (1611), in which he has Ignatius, a Jesuit, depose Satan and become the sovereign of Hell.

In 1609, Sir George Moore relented and released Ann's dowry, an event that signaled a change in fortune for Donne. He never received the secular appointment he sought, but he decided instead to become a priest and took holy orders in the Anglican church in 1615. Close upon this appointment, his wife died in 1617 while giving birth to their twelfth child, and for the rest of his life Donne was, according to biographer Izaak Walton, "crucified to the world." Donne quickly established himself as the leading Anglican preacher of his day, and he was appointed dean of St. Paul's in 1621, a position he held for the remaining ten years of his life.

The last part of his life was devoted almost entirely to sermons, and although only six were published during his lifetime, one hundred fifty were published by the year 1700. His only important poetic accomplishments during this period were a few divine poems and hymns, including his *Devotions upon Emergent Occasions* (1624), written during a severe illness, and his "Hymn to God My God, in My Sickness," written, Walton concludes, only eight days before he died. He preached his last sermon before King Charles on February 15, 1631; he died on March 31, 1631, in London.

Analysis

Fewer than ten of Donne's poems were published during his lifetime, and he was better known as a preacher and a writer of prose, especially sermons. Donne himself seems not to have been sure of the value of the poetry he wrote before he became a priest. It was 1633 before his first collection of poetry was published.

Early response to his poetry was not entirely favorable. Even his friend Ben Jonson said that Donne "did not keep accent" and that he would perish for "being misunderstood." Samuel Johnson, calling him a Metaphysical poet, said that Donne's poetry was new but not natural, that it presented "heterogeneous ideas yoked by violence together." He did acknowledge that Donne demonstrated intensive and various knowledge. Johnson's critical views of Donne's poetry served as a standard for years, but in the twentieth century, largely through the influence of T. S. Eliot, who perceived Donne's images not as excesses but as significant examples of "sensuous apprehension of thought," Donne's reputation as a poet improved to the point that he is now regarded as a major English poet of the seventeenth century. He is still perceived as a Metaphysical poet, but the appreciation for such poetry has grown so that now Donne's Metaphysical qualities are not disparaged but admired.

Increasingly among moderns, Donne is seen as a product and spokesperson for his age, the Renaissance, a period characterized by new discoveries and intellectual advancements but also by the fragmentation of such institutions as feudalism and scholasticism, a time of separation of the secular and the spiritual, a turbulent, confusing world where truth could no longer be perceived as one. Thinkers such as Donne would have found themselves attracted to all the new worlds but detached from them. Donne said "the new philosophy puts all in doubt." To live in such a world invited either indifference or attempts, which Donne chose, to achieve a unified sensibility, of which his poetry becomes one of the finest statements of the period. As one might expect, unifying the fractured world of the seventeenth century proved to be a formidable task, and it is his poetic adaptations to this task that give Donne's poetry its original rhetoric and imagery.

Donne writes as a scholar, as a curious observer open to a wide range of experiences. He fills his writing with allusions to his wide reading: "A Valediction: Of the Booke" contains references to the Sybil, Homer, Platonism, national leaders, the Bible, alchemy, theology, astronomy, and languages; *Biathanatos* quotes more than one hundred authorities. His intellectuality shapes his rhetoric, for he crowds his ideas into his poetry. As if impatient of transition and connectives, Donne may construct a single line of poetry almost entirely of verbs: "I saw him I/ Assail'd, fight, taken, stabb'd, bleed, fall, and dye."

Well versed in casuistry and law, Donne writes analytically, dialectically, as opposed to reflectively. As one reads Donne's poetry, one senses an imagined conversation in which Donne constantly tries to convince, verbally pushing and shoving. His

sentences are more faithful to the form of conversation and logic than to poetic meter; thus, his poetry seems rugged and argumentive.

Yet Donne is not just a logical analyst; he is also a sensitive poet, and as he writes
in the chaos of his passion and thought, he creates some startling imagery. Thus, he
can write of the heart as the seat of the emotions, or he can write of the heart as a
butcher might think of it: "When I had ripp'd me, 'and search'd where hearts did
lye." He can also speak of bodies as temples of souls, or he can observe that "Rack't
carcasses make ill anatomies." Forcing such imagery into a poem can result in vivid
poetry, but it may also necessitate a vehicle to portray such sharply contrasting modes
of perception—what came to be known as one of the outstanding features of Donne's
poetry, the Metaphysical conceit.

It is particularly Donne's conceits, his extended metaphors, that have intrigued his
readers. Not that conceits are unique to him or even new. Previous poets such as Sir
Thomas Wyatt fully and carefully developed such images, but Donne pushes the conceit to startling new capacities for meaning, to extraordinary heights of association
blending quite disparate elements.

Essentially, the Metaphysical conceit joins two things not usually thought of as
being together, and in this fusion creates a new apprehension of truth. For example,
one may bring together flint and steel and produce fire. To understand how this analogy supports the notion of the Metaphysical conceit, it is important to see that when
one strikes the flint against the steel the result is not just flint or just steel, nor is it
some combination of the flint and steel; it is a new entity, fire. Similarly, Donne, in
one of his most famous conceits, brings together a compass and lovers. A compass
has no more to do with lovers than does flint with steel, but when Donne unites
them, a new concept emerges, a new way of looking at the relationship between
lovers. Again, Donne brings together a flea and an argument for seduction, and disparate as these elements are, once one sees how Donne fuses them in his poem "The
Flea," one can never think of seduction in the same way again.

Reading Donne's poetry is not always easy. It is the record of a passionate, analytical intellect at work. For him, no experience is ever complete. He constantly moves
ideas around, observes them from different perspectives, arranges them into new patterns of thought. Perhaps as much as anyone else, he captures the spirit of the Renaissance, and his poetry has become an embodiment of it.

A VALEDICTION: FORBIDDING MOURNING

First published: 1633
Type of work: Poem

In this moving poem containing Donne's most famous conceit, the compass, the poet gently argues against weeping when true lovers part.

"A Valediction: Forbidding Mourning," probably written to his wife in 1601 before Donne left on a trip to the Continent, has often been anthologized. It is not only one of Donne's most popular works but also one of his most representative.

The poem rests, as do most of Donne's love poems, in the tradition of Renassiance love poetry. There is, for example, the conventional analogy of dying and the parting of lovers; there are references to floods of tears, tempests of sighs, and the spiritualizing quality of love. The poem is not different in kind from other poetry of the period, but it is different in degree. Donne and his lover exceed the traditional model for lovers, for they have so spiritualized their love that to reveal it to common lovers by weeping at parting would profane it much as a mystic discussing his or her ecstatic union with God would cheapen that experience.

Further, the poem reveals Donne's awareness of and interest in Renaissance topics such as astronomy. For his own purposes in this poem, Donne takes the traditional view and derives his phrase "sublunary lovers" from the older Ptolemaic system, which argued that everything beneath the moon was imperfect and corruptible while all above the moon was perfect and incorruptible. Donne insists that ordinary love, being beneath the moon, is inferior to his love, which has been made perfect beyond the moon.

Typically, Donne pushes his argument to more complex levels of understanding and turns next to the notion of Platonic love, which he also compares with his own. The basic idea of Platonic love is the idea that, in another world, the Real World, there exist perfect ideals or archetypes for all particular things that exist in this, the actual world. Thus, all examples of love in human experience must be compared to the ideal of love in the Real World in order to determine their validity. In this framework, Donne argues that his love is the Platonic archetype. Unlike sublunary, inferior love, which is activated by the senses, Donne's love is nourished by the soul. Because of the superior love Donne and his lady enjoy, they should not behave as ordinary lovers and weep and sigh at parting.

Bringing to bear yet another argument against acting like inferior lovers, Donne next insists that his soul and the soul of his lover through a mystical union have become one. Thus, they do not experience a breach in parting but an expansion "like gold to ayery thinnesse beate." Actually, this argument is two-pronged, for it posits the superiority of Donne's love in that he compares it to gold, the costliest metal, and it offers further support that perfect love does not weep at parting, for it cannot admit absence.

The apex of Donne's argument is developed in the last four stanzas of the poem as he unfolds his famous compass conceit. The metaphor is relatively simple; its value lies primarily in its success in shocking the reader into new sensibilities. The lady is the fixed foot of the compass; Donne is the moving foot. The firmer the fixed foot (the truer the lady's love), the more just the circle of the moving foot.

This conceit, typical of Donne's best, represents an elaboration of a metaphor to the furthest stage intellect can pursue it. It unifies sensation and reason, description of things and feelings. Donne stresses the logic of his argument more than the beauty of his metaphor, and ultimately the reader is likely to be more impressed with the puzzle of the image, with the fact that it really works, than with its delineation of character or passion. Thus, the conceit serves as a fitting climax to a powerful but gentle argument that true lovers secure in the exaltation of their love disdain public shows of affection.

THE FLEA

First published: 1633
Type of work: Poem

This sardonic poem of seduction traces the mind of Donne at his argumentive best.

Perhaps interest in "The Flea" is, as the English scholar and writer C. S. Lewis has suggested, mostly accidental. Perhaps, as he says, if the flea had not acquired a reputation as an unpleasant pest, the poem would not be as striking as it is. On the other hand, possibly no conceit ever developed represents as well as Donne's flea a capacity for total meaning. Such a metaphor, coupled with the argumentive ingenuity of Donne, results in a remarkable poem.

It is impossible to say when the poem was written, but it was published among his *Songs and Sonnets*, which was included in *Poems by J. D.: With Elegies on the Authors Death* (1633). The poem's irreverent tone, its mocking challenge of traditional values, and its sardonic treatment of its subject matter mark it as one of Donne's earlier poems, when he was known as Jack Donne, "a frequenter of ladies and of plays." It is inconceivable that Donne could have written the poem after he became the dean of St. Paul's Church.

Told in the first person, the poem is a dramatic monologue, a form often used by Donne, wherein the narrator, who is a character in the poem, is speaking to someone who never replies. The drama of the poem evolves, however, through the narrator's response to events shared with the silent companion. In "The Flea," the narrator has clearly been attempting unsuccessfully to seduce a lady. She has rejected his advances, remonstrating that sex for them would be a sin, a shame, and, for her, a loss of virginity—strong traditional arguments in seventeenth century England. Yet her arguments, perhaps even more than the prospect of sex, inspire the narrator to new heights of argumentive persuasion couched in the conceit of the flea.

He begins with the assertion that sex between them would have no more effect than the bite of a flea, but then paradoxically argues for the significance of the flea he has just belittled. Now he claims that the flea represents the marriage bed, the ideal of sexuality; the Church, the sanctifier of marriage; and at least an earthly reflection of the Trinity, in that it represents three lives in one: the lives of Donne, the lady, and the flea. Why this paradoxical shift? Apart from Donne's love of paradox, he probably expects his argument to show that since all three of the impediments to sex—marriage, Church, and Trinity—can be summed up in a flea, they are not significant obstacles.

Donne next argues that he is concerned that she will, by killing the flea, commit the triple crime of his murder, her own suicide, and the destruction of their sexual union, crimes all possible because the bloods of Donne and the woman are mixed in the flea. He believes that the lady is capable of such murder because, by withholding her sexual favors from him, she constantly kills him.

Even as Donne speaks, the lady kills the flea and triumphantly declares that his fears are unfounded, for the death of the flea weakens neither her nor Donne. In a brilliant reversal, Donne turns her argument against her, pointing out that just as she insists that the blood lost in the death of the flea is nothing, so blood lost in her yielding to him would be equally insignificant.

The argument of the poem is well wrought, and as the conceit unfolds, its elements lose their identities in a new way of looking at sexual love. Significantly, even as Donne cajoles and teases the lady into accepting his conclusion, readers find themselves drawn into the argument, shocked perhaps by the appearance and function of the flea but pleased with the overall effect, thus proving the efficacy of Donne's conceit.

BATTER MY HEART, THREE PERSON'D GOD

First published: 1633
Type of work: Poem

In this intensely personal sonnet, Donne depicts in military and marital terms his ongoing struggle with God.

"Batter my heart, three person'd God" is one of nineteen sonnets that Donne wrote after taking orders in the Anglican church. Earlier in his life, before his marriage and ordination, he wrote some fifty-five poems published in *Songs and Sonnets*, but none of these is technically a sonnet. The latter nineteen sonnets that he wrote as an Anglican priest, however, are true sonnets, and they display Donne's continuing love of wit and paradoxes but also his deepening concern about his relationship to God.

"Batter my heart, three person'd God" is a fairly typical sonnet. It has fourteen lines, and the metrical scheme is iambic pentameter, five feet to a line; each foot contains an unstressed and a stressed syllable. The rhyme scheme is *abba, abba, cdcd, ee,* not the only sonnet rhyme sequence but a common one. The poem, typical of many sonnets, is made up of an octet: The first eight lines have the same rhyme scheme and develop a single image, in this poem, the image of a city under siege. The last six lines form a sestet, the first four lines having a consistent rhyme scheme and their own image, that of a marital relationship. The last two lines of the sestet form a couplet; they rhyme with each other and bring together the thought of the octet and the sestet.

As Donne matured and as his image changed from that of Jack Donne, man-about-town, to that of John Donne, dean of St. Paul's, his poetry also changed, as this poem shows. After he took Holy Orders, he directed his love poetry not to women but to God. He tempered the sardonic indifference of some of his earlier poetry with the submissiveness of faith, and the shocking conceits of his earlier writing soften. Yet his intellect remains as vigorous as ever, and his witty imagery and love of paradox still characterize his poetry.

The seemingly impatient, boundless energy of Donne's mind continues to erupt in his later poetry. Disdaining connectives and transition, it abruptly expresses itself in verb after strong verb. Thus, Donne complains in this poem that until now God has been content to "knocke, breathe, shine, and seeke to mend," but Donne desires God to "overthrow, and bend . . . to breake, blowe, burn, and make me new." These lines record a writer trying in his poetry to keep up with, to describe, somehow, the passionate, scintillating images that tumble from his mind.

The witty imagery of this poem, like much of Donne's work, is built upon paradox, not a surprising development when one couples Donne's seemingly innate love of paradox with the emphasis on paradox in the Christian tradition to which Donne turned. Donne's plea, for example, for God to overthrow him so he may stand, to enthrall him so he may be free, echoes the Christian ideas that the way up to God leads down, that one must lose one's self in order to find one's self, and that one must die to live. His appeal to God to ravish him so that he may be chaste recalls the paradox of Mary, the virgin Mother of God. Just as in the sex act the partner may aggressively surrender, so Donne "labors to admit" God. Ultimately, one finds in this poem a passionate yet reasoned attempt to resolve the Christian dilemma articulated by Saint Paul, who found himself doing not the good that he wanted to do but the evil that he did not want to do. Donne wants to be loved by God, but he finds himself "betroth'd" to God's enemy, Satan.

In this poem, however, unlike earlier poems, the metaphors do not shock; they are fairly standard in Christian writing in the seventeenth century. Nor is it Donne's argumentive wit, but perhaps the honesty of his depiction of the ongoing struggle between his body and his soul, that attracts. Vividly dramatized is his commitment to faith— his "captiv'd" reason is useless to him. The poem raises the question of whether the poetry of the dean of St. Paul's is as good as the poetry of Jack Donne, but it settles once and for all Donne's commitment to religion as a way of life.

HYMN TO GOD MY GOD, IN MY SICKNESS

First published: 1635
Type of work: Poem

In this poem, written perhaps as late as eight days before his death, Donne reflects upon his dying and his prospects of salvation.

"Hymn to God My God, in My Sickness" is perhaps the last poem that Donne ever wrote and thus serves as a good example of the poetic interests he maintained late in life after his wife's death and his ordination. Most critics divide Donne's career into at least two parts: an earlier, more productive period when he was known as a man-about-town and wrote primarily satires and witty treatments of love, and a later period after he accepted Holy Orders in the Anglican church. Clearly, "Hymn to God My God, in My Sickness" belongs to the latter period. As one might expect, there are similarities and dissimilarities between it and the poems of the earlier period. "Hymn to God My God, in My Sickness" reveals Donne's continuing wide intellectual interests and his ongoing talent for bringing these interests together in vivid, insightful metaphors; but it also shows a new, humbler concern for the welfare of his soul.

A cursory look at the poem reveals examples of Donne's intellectual interests. He raises the issue of cartography, the making of maps, popular in the Renaissance when discoveries of new lands constantly made news. Donne reveals his own interest in and knowledge of geography, referring to Jerusalem, Gibraltar, the Pacific Ocean, and the Bering Strait, which had become a hoped-for passage to Eastern riches.

His use of the phrase *"per fretum febris"* (through the straits of fever) does not establish him as a Latin scholar, though he probably was, but it is his thorough acquaintance with religious topics that is striking. Thus, he writes about how in Christianity the East symbolizes birth and resurrection, how the West symbolizes death, and how just as on a map East and West merge, so birth fades into death and death into resurrection. He refers to Shem, Ham, and Japheth, the sons of Noah, and the theory current in the seventeenth century that after the Deluge, these three sons repopulated the entire earth.

He shows his familiarity with the classical Christian notion that the Garden of Eden was located on the same spot where Jerusalem was later built and that the Tree of Knowledge of Good and Evil grew on the same site where Christ's cross stood, thus locating all four of these contrasting, contradicting symbols in the same place and creating a magnificently paradoxical image. Another paradox important to Donne and also indicative of his immersion in Christian theory is the paradox of the two Adams. As Donne points out, through the first Adam humankind fell from grace, forfeited the Garden of Eden, and was condemned to earn its bread with the sweat of physical labor. Through Christ, the second Adam, however, humanity is restored to grace, regains Paradise, and, instead of the pain of the first Adam's sweat, knows the balm, the saving efficacy, of the second Adam's blood.

In this poem, in one of his most vivid metaphors, Donne brings his knowledge of geography and religion together in a conceit wherein spiritual and physical cosmography unite in the body of Donne. Thus, his physicians become cosmographers, mapmakers, and Donne's body becomes their map. On this map, East, his birth, and West, his death, can be discerned. As surely as he began his journey in the East, he will conclude his journey in the West. Yet, asserts Donne, his West holds no fears for him, for as in all flat maps, and Donne's body is such a map, East and West meld into one, so Donne expects his death to merge into resurrection. Death will become life.

Reflecting on the poem to this point, one may discern several similarities between it and Donne's earlier poetry. It retains the same wittiness, love of learning, and penchant for striking comparisons as those earlier poems do. Yet there arises a difference in this poem. In previous poems, Donne flaunted his knowledge and used his wit to bully his opponents into submission. In this poem, Donne trusts not in his wit or argumentive acumen but in Christ's "purple" (His Lordship) to save him, and he concludes not with the original swaggering confidence that he has taught his opponent a lesson but with the humbler hope that he may learn from his own poem. Ultimately, his conceit of the map does not carry him to flights of fancy but to submission to his fate as he reflects upon the straits before him and the God who waits beyond them.

Summary

T. S. Eliot perceived John Donne's worldview as one of unified sensibility, as an attempt to hold together what Renaissance thought threatened to tear asunder; and a study of Donne's poetry confirms this view. Widely read, acquainted with all worlds but committed to none, able to bring together the most heterogeneous elements in convincing if shocking images, Donne stands out as a thinker capable of moving easily between absolutes and particulars, of probing potentialities, of heightening sensuality into philosophy, of thinking and feeling simultaneously, and of distilling all of these experiences into an intimate logic. His intensely personal record of the turbulent seventeenth century has meaning in modern humanity's chaotic world; his experimental Renassiance style of writing poetry has become characteristic of modern poetics.

Bibliography

Bald, R. C. *John Donne: A Life.* New York: Oxford University Press, 1970.

Bennett, Joan Frankau. *Five Metaphysical Poets: Donne, Herbert, Vaughan, Crashaw, Marvell.* Cambridge, England: Cambridge University Press, 1964.

Donne, John. *The Poems of John Donne.* Edited by Sir Herbert Grierson. 2 vols. London: Oxford University Press, 1912.

Eliot, T. S. "The Metaphysical Poets." In *Selected Essays.* New York: Harcourt, Brace & World, 1950.

Leishman, J. B. *The Metaphysical Poets: Donne, Herbert, Vaughan, Traherne.* New York: Russell & Russell, 1963.

Tuve, Rosamond. *Elizabethan and Metaphysical Imagery.* Chicago: University of Chicago Press, 1947.

Walton, Izaak. *The Lives of Doctor John Donne, Sir Henry Wotton Knight, Mr. Richard Hooker, Mr. George Herbert, and Doctor Robert Sanderson.* London: Oxford University Press, 1927.

Williamson, George. *The Donne Tradition: A Study in Elizabethan Poetry from Donne to the Death of Cowley.* New York: Octagon Books, 1973.

Ray G. Wright

FYODOR DOSTOEVSKI

Born: Moscow, Russia
November 11, 1821
Died: St. Petersburg, Russia
February 9, 1881

Principal Literary Achievement
Dostoevski is widely regarded as the leading practitioner of the psychological novel in the nineteenth century and as one of the greatest novelists of all time.

Biography

Fyodor Mikhailovich Dostoevski, novelist, journalist, religious polemicist, and political reformer, was born in Moscow, Russia, on November 11, 1821, the second child of Mikhail Andreevich Dostoevski and Marya Fedorovna Nechaeva. His father, a surgeon, had served for eight years in the army and, at Fyodor's birth, held a staff position at St. Mary's Hospital for the destitute of Moscow. An able and intelligent man who had succeeded in pulling himself out of generations of poverty, Dostoevski's father was nonetheless often violent, moody, and given to bouts of heavy drinking that frightened his children. His mother was an engaging and attractive woman, practical, efficient, and cheerful in running her household.

Dostoevski had seven brothers and sisters. He was closest to his older brother, Mikhail, and the third child in the family, his sister Varvara. These three seem to have formed a closer relationship to their father than the youngest five, whose lives were centered almost entirely on their mother. Mikhail, Fyodor, and Varvara shared intellectual and literary interests, and Fyodor's novels and stories reveal themes, types, and motifs closely linked to his lifetime experience with these two close siblings.

Dostoevski spent the first twelve years of his life at home, where he was schooled by his father and by private tutors. He finished his early education at the best boarding school in Moscow, an educational experience recorded in fictional alteration in his novel *Pedrostok* (1875; *A Raw Youth*, 1916). At sixteen, he entered the St. Petersburg military engineering school, where he was an indifferent student of soldierly science, spending much of his time at musical and theatrical performances, on nights out with fellow cadets, and especially in reading. Dostoevski was a voracious reader, working his way through the classics, being particularly fond of Homer and William Shakespeare. So taken was he with the greatness of these authors that he determined to master the literary craft in a way never before done in the Russian language. This

Ѳедоръ Михайловичъ
ДОСТОЕВСКІЙ

род. 30-го Октября 1821 г.
ум. 28-го Января 1881 г.

determination, coupled with his father's murder at the hands of the peasants on a small family estate and his mother's death by tuberculosis, led Dostoevski in 1844 to begin life anew. He resigned his engineering lieutenant's commission and became a full-time writer.

His first two literary attempts illustrate the power that he was to manifest throughout his career. First, he translated into Russian the French novelist Honoré de Balzac's *Eugénie Grandet* (1833; English translation, 1859). Balzac had recently been lionized on a visit to St. Petersburg, and Dostoevski saw his chance to create a success and make some money. Yet it is his choice of this particular work to translate that is important: *Eugénie Grandet* reveals motifs of criminality, the psychology of self-sacrifice, and the power of obsessive behavior that inform much of Dostoevski's later work. Second, he produced the short novel *Bednye lyudi* (1846; *Poor Folk*, 1887), which a friend gave to the great Russian literary critic Vissarion Belinsky to read. To Dostoevski's surprise and delight, Belinsky gave it high praise, recognizing the young author's uncommon and powerful insight into the tragic victimization of people caught in circumstances beyond their control. In this novel, Dostoevski reveals the ability to show from within a character's psychology, a new technique that caused the literary elite of his day to rank him immediately with Russia's greatest writers.

During the next six years, Dostoevski wrote many works showing an astonishing range of style and form. The most important of these is the novel *Dvoynik* (1846; *The Double*, 1917), in which a morbidly delicate clerk is shown progressively sinking into insanity, an almost clinical description underscored by the hero's encounters with beings in mirrors, on the street, in dreams, and so on, all of whom are embodiments of his worst pathological desires, and which portray the disease of advancing schizophrenia in a powerful new way.

In addition to his writing, Dostoevski participated in political discussions at the homes of leading radicals. The repressive Czar Nicholas I had arrested twenty-one of the participants in these discussions. All of them, including Dostoevski, were sentenced to be shot. He was saved at the last moment by the Czar's order to have him sent to prison in Siberia, to be followed by a stint in the army. The experience of a last-minute reprieve haunted him for the rest of his life, and the frightful conditions of the Siberian labor camp produced a changed man. During his imprisonment, he began to have sharp hallucinations, and this period marks the beginning of his bouts with epilepsy. Dostoevski emerged from prison and the army intensely spiritualized, so much so that he accepted his punishment as a just reward for his previous crimes, political and emotional. His intense prison experience also supplied him with material for the deeply penetrating psychological portraits that characterize the remainder of his literary output.

At the end of 1859, he was allowed to begin writing again. Returning to St. Petersburg, he found radicals against him because of his renewed interest in religion. Together with his older brother, he established the magazine *Vremya* (time) with the goal of drawing together into a cooperative stance the leading groups of Russian writers and intellectuals, a goal that was only partially met. In order to heal his emotional wounds and to gain breadth of experience, Dostoevski went in 1862 to Germany. While he was gone, the government banned the publication of *Vremya*, saying that it was unpatriotic. Undaunted, he returned and again, in partnership with Mikhail, began a new journal, *Epokha* (epoch).

The establishment of his new magazine in 1864 marks the beginning of Dostoevski's greatest writing period, the time in which he produced *Prestupleniye* (1866; *Crime and Punishment*, 1886), *Idiot* (1868; *The Idiot*, 1877), *Besy* (1871-1872; *The Possessed*, 1913; also known as *The Devils*), and *Bratya Karamazovy* (1879-1880; *The Brothers Karamazov*, 1912). His life was seldom happy: Problems caused by gambling and epilepsy continued to plague him, and marital peace eluded him until he met and wed Anna Grigorievna Snitkina, an unprepossessing but absolutely devoted stenographer who aided him greatly by bringing order to his emotional life and efficiency to his personal affairs. He had suffered from emphysema for years, and of that terrible disease he died in St. Petersburg on February 9, 1881, where he is buried.

Analysis

In a sense, all Dostoevski's works are psychological accounts of obsessive behavior. There is no epic sweep to the novels, even though they are very long, and no detailed "slice of life" observation on the part of the narrators. The manner in which his fiction differs from other work of his time is that Dostoevski uncovers for the reader the detailed psychological complexity of an act (such as murder) while avoiding complexity of motif and cleverness of rhetorical patterns. His work achieves a clinical economy of both subject and treatment. This economy, coupled with the reader's natural fascination with the bizarre obsessions that focus the stories, represents the creation of a new kind of serious fiction that is related to but rises above the psycho-thriller.

It would be a mistake, however, to assume that Dostoevski's novels and stories are easy reading. His real goal is to reveal the core of human nature. To do so, he typically subjects his characters to frightening situations, then gradually removes, one by one, the psychological props that they have used to keep themselves in balance, until, finally, they are left quite alone in their dilemmas. In this way, the reader is led into the depths of the human mind's darkest chasms. The reader's absorbtion in the question of what a human being will choose to do when left alone in the night of previously hidden obsessions is what creates the electric suspense of Dostoevski's stories. The chief manner by which he brings about this revelation is through the subtle manipulation of imagery.

First, almost all Dostoevski's works are set in the city, that soot-stained, chaotic collection of human souls crowded into a kind of heap. There is a certain protection in a city, but also an inevitable rubbing away of individual identity by too-close contact. Cities confine rather than liberate: Symbolically, they hide the self in a welter of interpersonal relations and complexities. Second, the novels and stories tend to focus on images of lower animal life (spiders, snakes, flies, lice, for example), providing for the reader the association of Dostoevski's obsessed characters with disease-carrying and filth-ridden loathsomeness. Finally, the use of dreams for symbolic purposes is omnipresent. There is usually a buildup of tension to the beginning of a dream, followed by a sequence that reveals a segment of a character's subconscious. Dostoevski accomplishes this very subtly, intermixing dreams as wish fulfillments, regressions, self-assertions, and foreshadowings.

The power of Dostoevski's art has been called "cruel" and even "sadistic," seeming to revel in the morbid and abnormal. Modern psychology, however, has provided a clinical understanding of mental and emotional abnormalities, so that it is now clear how the novels and stories anticipate and artistically present many of the discoveries made by social scientists. Dostoevski's art represents the first realistic view into areas of the psyche virtually unexplored before his time. Mental sicknesses now named by modern psychiatry are given life by his characters: manic depression, senile dementia, infantilism, and megalomania find form in Raskolnikov, Stavrogin, Natasha Filipovna, and Kiriilov.

In fact, Dostoevski's insistent use of dreams for symbolic purposes anticipates the most influential early psychological treatise in history, Sigmund Freud's *Die Traumdeutung* (1900; *The Interpretation of Dreams*, 1913). The dream that Svidrigailov (*Crime and Punishment*) has just prior to his suicide, in which he violates a child, is Freudian to the core. Stavrogin's (*The Possessed*) rape of a twelve-year-old girl is mirrored in his dream of the Lorraine painting, which comes to life and haunts him to the verge of insanity. Arkady (*A Raw Youth*) is aware that his dreams are the key to his identity, particularly the one in which a gruesome spider spins its web inside his bowels. Hippolyte (*The Idiot*) has a dream that perfectly reveals his split personality: A snake slithers off the wall of his bedroom and chases him around the house. It noiselessly follows him until, just as it touches his head, his dog (already dead for more than five years) runs up and bites the reptile in two. Hippolyte awakes as the leering dog stands in front of him with the two parts of the serpent still writhing in his mouth. Alyosha (*The Brothers Karamazov*) is spiritually transformed by the dream of his dead mentor's corpse being alive once again and present at the biblical marriage at Cana. Raskolnikov (*Crime and Punishment*) has a dream in which, as he is walking past a tavern with his father, he observes peasants beating a horse to death, a scene that he, upon waking, realizes represents his murder plan. The hero of "The Dream of a Ridiculous Man" eventually understands that dreams are always symbolic, always unreasonable, deeply embedded wish fulfillments. The use of dream imagery and dream analysis in Dostoevski's works has never been surpassed in Western literature and has been the most influential, along with Freud's writings, of any treatments of the idea.

In addition to Dostoevski's brilliance as a forerunner of psychoanalysis, his place as cocreator of the modern novel is secure. He produced his works while Gustave Flaubert, Leo Tolstoy, and Charles Dickens were creating theirs. Each of these writers attempted, in his own way, to describe realistically how human beings react to everyday life. Naturalistic views of heredity, environment, and human motivation are basic to the creation of the social types represented in the great nineteenth century novels, but Dostoevski treats these topics in a unique way. He is interested in throwing light on the primitive and raw elements of human nature, out of which social types may be understood. By showing characters in the grip of actual or potential crime and the consequences of these crimes, Dostoevski reveals that human ills and universal evil are not at all outside individuals: Rather, they rest squarely inside each individual.

NOTES FROM THE UNDERGROUND

First published: *Zapiski iz podpolya*, 1864 (English translation, 1913)
Type of work: Short story

A sick and spiteful man philosophizes about his irrationality, defending himself in advance against criticism of his negativism.

One of Dostoevski's most interesting and original works, *Notes from the Underground* represents the real beginning of his literary greatness, even though the earlier novel *Poor Folk* (1846) had already made him famous. Translated into many languages many times, this work is more widely read than perhaps any other late nineteenth century short story. The "underground man" has become a literary archetype, and numerous modern movements have claimed Dostoevski's creation as their spiritual progenitor. The story consists of two parts. In the first, the underground man gives a long monologue that encapsulates his philosophy, while in the second part, adventures from his life are recounted. Together, these halves form a whole psychological portrait, making a powerful statement against the possibility of rational social progress.

By noticing that the underground man tyrannizes everyone around him, one sees how easy it is for superficial and sentimental people to be corrupted by a strong personality. Thus, the story expresses a pessimistic vision of humankind as weak, too self-centered ever to experience joy, and prone to the agony of solipsism. The essence of the underground man's meaning lies in his assertion that, as far as he is concerned, the world can go to hell, just as long as he gets his tea. Moreover, *Notes from the Underground* is a political polemic aimed at reforming Russian society, with its endless wavering between Western European ideas and the "Russian soul." The recounted adventures in the second half of the story are symbolic representations of episodes from Russia's dislocated past and present. These recollections reveal that it is not really the underground man who has a problem with true identity: It is Russia itself. By extension, *Notes from the Underground* is also a renunciation of Dostoevski's own past. The author, through the narrator, derides his previously held optimism and joyful feelings, and he replaces them with pessimism, hopelessness, and despair. Something ugly had arisen in Dostoevski's spirit, and he felt compelled to give it expression, no matter how venomous it might be.

Above all, there seems little doubt that it is a full-blown attack on the particular positivist philosophy of Dostoevski's day, a philosophy holding that human beings are rational and capable of creating a better society for everyone through material progress. The underground man's spiritual isolation is the result of positivism's failure to make any material progress at all, and his self-disgust is an agonized cry of protest against it.

CRIME AND PUNISHMENT

First published: *Prestupleniye i nakazaniye*, 1866 (English translation, 1886)
Type of work: Novel

An intensely emotional intellectual, driven by poverty, comes to believe that he lives above common morality and commits a murder, only to find that his punishment is worse than he imagined it could be.

In *Crime and Punishment*, Dostoevski treats the problem of crime and the criminal mentality. He is not interested in the social aspects of criminal behavior, and there is little said in the novel about the legalities of crime. Dostoevski has an interior view of criminality, a conviction that crime and its inevitable punishment are deeply seated aspects of the human spirit.

Raskolnikov (the novel's hero) is presented from the inside. The reader knows what he did before knowing why he did it, and the story is told as a gradual revelation of the hero's motives. That accounts for the uncanny suspense of the first several chapters: The reader continually searches for the reason that Raskolnikov has murdered the pawnbroker. Intertwined with the reader's suspense is the slowly dawning realization that Raskolnikov himself does not know his motive. This "double suspense" creates a dense texture that gives the novel its complexity, a complexity laid over the relative simplicity of the plot.

As the novel progresses, Raskolnikov's possible motives become ever more bizarre. The consistent notion behind his behavior is revealed in his confession to the innocent prostitute, Sonia, after the crime, where he blurts out that he did it because he only wanted to see if he could go beyond a normal person's revulsion against such an act. This admission seems to suggest that Raskolnikov is an egotist, a self-styled superman who wants to see if he can get away with transgressing the law. The reader comes to find, however, that Raskolnikov's impulses go more deeply than that: Raskolnikov wants to see if he can overstep the limits of evil itself, if he can exert ultimate power over another person. That is what the murder means to him.

Dostoevski's brilliant unfolding of Raskolnikov's deepest motive really begins after the confession to Sonia. Before this point in the novel, the reader is puzzled by a welter of seemingly conflicting evidence about the hero's personality. Raskolnikov says he does not believe in God, and that there is no arbiter of absolute good and evil: Yet he is numb with self-doubt. In spite of his logical decision to commit murder, he is troubled and hesitant. His horrible dream of the peasants beating a horse to death causes him to awake trembling at the very thought that he himself might be so cruel. As he later walks along the banks of the Neva, his obsession with committing an evil act alternates with a loathing for the very idea. Then, after the deed has been done, something curious occurs that turns out to be the key to understanding his true motive and the rest of the novel. It becomes clear that Raskolnikov's response to having committed murder is merely puzzlement. In other words, he shows neither remorse nor joy. He realizes that he feels the same way that he has always felt.

Finally, the reader understands that the loathsome criminality of Raskolnikov's motive lies in its amorality. He had decided to murder the old woman pawnbroker on strictly logical grounds, but the unease that he continues to feel is not a guilty conscience stemming from a too-strict logicality. Had he murdered for money or out of anger and then been caught, his punishment would have been easier than that which comes to gnaw at him. Having made a cold-blooded sociopathic decision to assert himself at the expense of another's very identity, he finds his feelings locked into the conventional morality that his intellect so despises. He is thus caught in an emotional vacuum, the most inescapable kind of punishment. Raskolnikov has murdered an old woman, but the inability to have an authentically strong feeling about it has murdered him spiritually. In a dream, he tries to kill her repeatedly, slicing at her skull with an ax, but as he looks closely into her face he can see her laughing horribly. Raskolnikov has really killed himself with the ax of cold-blooded self-assertion. He has no clearly definable motive because he is a sociopathic personality.

In the end of the story, Dostoevski makes clear how problematic such a personality is for society. Once again, the author's meaning is revealed in a dream sequence. Raskolnikov is ill in Siberia and dreams that he and the rest of the world have been devastated by an infestation of highly intelligent germs. The infestation causes insanity. The infected believe themselves to be logical, scientific, progressive, and morally sound; Yet they get sick and go mad from the infection. Anarchy results, and human society disintegrates. Dostoevski's point is that sociopathic personalities are like these microbes, able to kill everything that they touch.

The sickness of cold-blooded amorality is shown against a background of conventional, commonsensical standards that define the boundaries of good and evil. The relationship between them is seen in the novel's other characters. Raskolnikov's sister, Dunya, is about to be married to Luzhin, a manipulative businessman, and the morally grotesque Svidrigailov hovers around them, while the prostitute, Sonya, and the policeman, Porfiry, attempt to maneuver the hero into a confession. Each relationship is flawed by the characters' tendency toward self-serving logicality, none more self-indulgent than that between Svidrigailov and Dunya, caused for the most part by Svidrigailov's profligacy. Years of cold philosophizing have left Svidrigailov with no heartfelt values, not even the common sense to distinguish between the most fundamental kinds of good and evil. In order to escape his emotional wretchedness, he fills his days with a sinister kind of debauchery. When his love for Dunya is rejected, he is able to shoot himself with a cool detachment. Sonia, although kindly and sensitive, is nevertheless a prostitute: Like the others, she has murdered herself by becoming a tool of the dissoluteness of other people. She, like the others, has defined herself by coolly deciding on a course of action that indulges others in their weaknesses. It is the ultimate punishment that results from sociopathic attitudes and behaviors: Like the crime, the punishment is cold, wretched, impersonal, and ultimately without any satisfaction.

THE POSSESSED

First published: *Besy,* 1871-1872 (English translation, 1913)
Type of work: Novel

In the troubled world of mid-nineteenth century Russia, a group of characters find that their interest in nihilism leads to disaster.

The Possessed is the most topical of Dostoevski's novels and stories. During the 1860's, the radical fringe of the Russian intelligentsia attempted to implant the ideology known as "nihilism" into the general revolutionary fervor caused by the recent abolition of serfdom. Nihilism (from the Latin *nihil,* meaning "nothing") was concerned more with destroying societal forms and traditions than with establishing something positive. The destructive anger of this group had been the topic of several novels already published, the most important of which was Ivan Turgenev's *Ottsy i deti* (1862; *Fathers and Sons,* 1867). *The Possessed,* therefore, is both an attack on nihilism, with sharp caricatures of contemporary revolutionaries, and an attempt to create the great antinihilist novel. Dostoevski's most important innovation to the antinihilist novel is the structural device of having two chief characters. These two, Pyotr Verkhovensky and Nikolai Stavrogin, embody the two sides of Dostoevski's political anger, his hatred of the Russian revolutionary left, and his violent distrust of the Russian aristocracy.

In addition to his key role in this novel, Stavrogin is a foreshadowing of characters to appear in Dostoevski's last novel, *The Brothers Karamazov* (1879-1880). In *The Possessed,* this character is obviously another version of Raskolnikov (*Crime and Punishment*), but whereas Raskolnikov is a weak man without values and direction, Stavrogin has a strong character but is still without values and goals. Through him, Dostoevski pictures the consequences of atheism, especially those destructive consequences particularly suffered by the strong and intelligent. Such persons begin in a vague moral drift, progress to a reliance on individual goals, develop from this a self-centeredness, and eventually come to a cosmic self-indulgence that forever separates the individual from moorings of universal truth, the only kind of truth that would bring meaning and significance to life. In his confession, Stavrogin reveals the obsession with which all amoral individuals are possessed, the need to punish themselves. He had considered shooting himself but decides instead to marry a completely unsuitable woman as a way of making his suffering last longer. Dostoevski's point is that masochism is the inevitable result of atheism, because atheism contains no transcendent value. That, then, means indifference, tedium, and ultimate self-annihilation.

Beyond the embodiment of individual, spiritual masochism, Stavrogin represents the social masochism of nihilism. He joins with the revolutionaries, those possessed with fanatical ideas, a possession compared by Dostoevski to the devils that drive the swine over the cliff in the New Testament. Stavrogin and the revolutionaries disrupt a provincial town with a series of spectacular scandals, but, in the end, Stavrogin finds that he is beyond caring about even the most wildly destructive of the radicals' plans. He has no spiritual center and can in the blink of an eye annihilate in his mind his interest in nihilism. That, then, is the basic flaw in the revolutionaries' doctrine: Its indifference to positive values is the seed of its own destruction. Nihilism cannot believe in anything, especially itself. It can only annihilate everything, including itself.

Pyotr Verkhovensky might be seen as the sadistic complement to Stavrogin's masochism. The son of a faded provincial liberal, Verkhovensky arrives in his family's town with grandiose plans for a revolution. He has a kind of genial charisma, and the radical group (formerly led by his father) quickly follows his lead. Their meanspiritedness results in ugly incidents, such as the desecration of an icon and the setting of fires. When a member of the group decides to leave as a result of a change of mind, Verkhovensky maneuvers the others into murdering him, after which he flees, leaving the rest to suffer the consequences.

Verkhovensky is modeled on the self-righteous dreamers who had infected Russian politics in Dostoevski's youth and who had been indicted thoroughly in *Fathers and Sons*. The significance of this portrait is that Verkhovensky is more than an example of Dostoevski's ability to create political satire. Verkhovensky is the culmination of Dostoevski's treatment of the interrelations of politics and religion, an embodiment of the idea that no social or political progress can be made without individual moral and spiritual regeneration. In using the disintegration of Verkhovensky's active participation in his home town to show how the political ideals of the Russian left are bankrupt, Dostoevski indicates that the real problem lies in the spiritual emptiness of the revolutionaries themselves.

Just as there are two main characters in the novel, so there are two stories. One is about the few days in August during which nasty events in a provincial town take place. The other is the past action of all the characters who people the present moment in that provincial town. There is a constant interplay of these stories, and events from one expand the meaning of the other. It is a very unique, complex, and artistically satisfying structural device and, along with the two-main-character strategy, makes *The Possessed* one of Dostoevski's greatest creations.

THE BROTHERS KARAMAZOV

First published: *Bratya Karamazovy*, 1879-1880 (English translation, 1912)
Type of work: Novel

The sons of an irresponsible provincial businessman return home and become involved in a complex series of events leading to tragedy and the family's destruction.

Like *Crime and Punishment*, *The Brothers Karamazov* revolves around a murder. Fyodor Karamazov, a corrupt provincial landowner and businessman, has fathered four sons: Dmitri, an army officer, by his first wife; Ivan, a teacher and scholar, by his second wife; Alyosha, a monk in training, also by his second wife; and Smerdyakov, an epileptic servant in his household and his illegitimate child, by a retarded local girl. Fyodor is murdered by Smerdyakov, but Dmitri's freewheeling anger and violence make him the suspect. After his arrest, a spectacular trial is held. The prosecution builds a solid case, and Dmitri is found guilty and sent to Siberia. Ivan learns that Smerdyakov is the real murderer, but, since nothing can be proved, Dmitri must suffer the consequences of the deed to the end. Ivan has a nervous breakdown, Smerdyakov commits suicide, and Alyosha goes to Siberia to offer what comfort he can to his brother.

The four brothers are symbolic of the basic causes of human spiritual isolation. Dmitri is a deeply sensual person, constantly involved in physical pleasures such as drink, sexual seduction, and material comfort; yet he is aware that his physical excesses are a grave weakness. Ivan is a self-aware intellectual whose arrogance isolates him from meaningful contact with common people. Alyosha has a narrow catechistic faith that imprisons him within the walls of religious naïveté. Smerdyakov represents the distorted drives of the classic passive manipulator. Gross sensuality, proud intellectualism, narrow religiosity, and scapegoating irresponsibility infect the entire series of relationships, not only between the brothers but also between them and the other characters, as well. The weaknesses of the brothers are projected as the fourfold nature of fallen humankind, the representation of spiritual failure and the legacy of Original Sin.

It is in the episode called "The Grand Inquisitor" that Dostoevski's philosophy of sin and redemption is distilled. Ivan tells the story to Alyosha in order to explain why he is so troubled by his inability to grasp the essence of religion intellectually. Set in sixteenth century Spain, the narrative portrays Christ's return to earth at a time when faith had been nearly eradicated by the Catholic Inquisition. Christ comforts the enemies of the Church, who are being burned at the stake, gives sight to the blind, weeps with those who mourn, and raises the dead. All who see Him know who He is. The Grand Inquisitor also recognizes Him and has Him arrested for performing acts contrary to the procedures of the Church. One evening, the old Inquisitor visits Christ in His vile prison in order to explain to Him why He must be burned at the stake. Christ must die, the old man insists, because His return would ruin the Church's centuries-old attempt to save humankind. Christ committed a grave error in rejecting Satan's three temptations in the wilderness, because those three temptations strike at the core of human weakness: Their eradication through Christ's power would mean human freedom, something that all of history proves is the root of disaster. Had Christ's example empowered human beings to happiness through freedom, the Church's work would be in vain. In any case, there is no evidence that humanity can handle freedom, so the Church, out of love for all people, establishes rules and indices to enslave them. In this way, the problems created by impossible freedom can be avoided. During this explanation, Christ slowly rises to His feet and finally kisses the old man gently. Deeply moved but clinging to his doctrine, the Grand Inquisitor warns Christ never to return and then releases Him.

This episode ties together the entire novel and shows *The Brothers Karamazov* to be a drama of the irony of the soul's choice. Mortality is defined by the necessity of choosing good over evil and creating freedom with those choices; yet such freedom is incompatible with human nature. Human beings might choose only the right through authority and spiritual coercion, and these motivations are the opposite of the example of Christ. The problem is that Christ Himself was perfect; that is, He embodied freedom and wanted it for all people. People, however, are not perfect and are not capable of disinterested righteousness, and that is why human beings will never choose freedom. The Grand Inquisitor's explanation of the world's future gives a vision of the problem: Human beings will whine and rebel until the age of reason and science brings about so much confusion and disturbance that they will begin to destroy each other. The very weakest will be left, and they will beg the Grand Inquisitor and his institutional religion to make their decisions for them. They will then be "happy" because they will be allowed no moral responsibility. The world will eventually be like a stern parent with many "happy" babies waiting to be coddled.

Summary

The novels and stories of Fyodor Dostoevski are explorations of human nature and the nature of the religious experience. His vision is ambivalent, verging on the cynically pessimistic, and burdened with the demons of human weakness. Yet, in the conflating design of their characterization and plot structures, the works provide a rich poetic texture of compelling truth about humankind's personal and religious values. His thought is radical and prophetic, and his art is confrontive. The novels are less an examination of religious ideology than a discernment of spirituality. Dostoevski asserts that life and art are meaningful: The nature of that meaning, however, is troubling, fraught with danger, and necessary to grasp.

Bibliography

Grossmann, Leonid. *Dostoevsky*. London: Allen Lane, 1974.

Leatherbarrow, William J. *Feodor Dostoevsky*. Boston: Twayne, 1981.

Mochulsky, Konstantin. *Dostoevsky: His Life and Work*. Princeton, N.J.: Princeton University Press, 1967.

Peace, Richard. *Dostoevsky: An Examination of the Major Novels*. Cambridge, England: Cambridge University Press, 1971.

Wasiolek, Edward. *Dostoevsky: The Major Fiction*. Cambridge, Mass.: MIT Press, 1964.

Wellek, René, ed. *Dostoevsky: A Collection of Critical Essays*. Englewood Cliffs, N.J.: Prentice-Hall, 1962.

Larry H. Peer

SIR ARTHUR CONAN DOYLE

Born: Edinburgh, Scotland
May 22, 1859
Died: Crowborough, Sussex, England
July 7, 1930

Principal Literary Achievement

Doyle created one of the first and most popular of fictional detectives, Sherlock Holmes.

Biography

Arthur Conan Doyle was born on May 22, 1859, into an artistic Catholic family living in Edinburgh, Scotland, and he grew up there. His father, Charles, was a public servant and artist who illustrated the first edition of *A Study in Scarlet* (1887), the first tale of Sherlock Holmes. Charles suffered from mental disease and alcoholism and was institutionalized from 1879 until his death in 1893. Arthur's mother, Mary Foley Doyle, reared seven children, of whom Arthur was the fourth. She oversaw Arthur's education, sending him to Jesuit schools at Stoneyhurst and at Feldkirch, Austria (despite the family's comparative poverty), and encouraging him to study medicine at the University of Edinburgh.

Doyle began his writing career soon after beginning medical study, publishing his first story, "The Mystery of Sasassa Valley," in 1879. At the university, he met two professors who became models for his most famous literary creations. Dr. Joseph Bell was the prototype for Sherlock Holmes; William Rutherford became the model for Professor Challenger of *The Lost World* (1912).

Before finishing his medical schooling, Doyle sought adventure, serving as ship's surgeon on two voyages. After completing his M.D. in 1885, he married Louise Hawkins. They had two children, Mary Louise and Alleyne Kingsley. A year after his marriage, he finished *A Study in Scarlet*.

Doyle thought of himself mainly as a historical novelist in the mode of Sir Walter Scott, whom he admired, but the public showed more interest in Sherlock Holmes. At the request of *Lippincott's Magazine*, Doyle produced *The Sign of Four* (1889). Relinquishing his medical practice in 1891, he turned to writing for his living. He then wrote a series of Holmes stories for *The Strand*, beginning with "A Scandal in

Bohemia." These were so popular that the editors asked for more. Before he had finished twelve of them (collected in *The Adventures of Sherlock Holmes*, 1892), he was tired of his characters and told his mother—who thought it a mistake—that he intended to kill Holmes in the last tale. He waited, however, until the next series, collected as *The Memoirs of Sherlock Holmes* (1894), to have Holmes die, in "The Adventure of the Final Problem." Having taken Louise to Switzerland after discovering her tuberculosis, Doyle was away from London when readers of *The Strand* were shocked by Holmes's death. Despite the sorrow and anger of Holmes's fans, Doyle published no more Holmes stories until *The Hound of the Baskervilles* (1902).

Between 1893 and 1901, Doyle continued writing popular stories for *The Strand*, the best about Étienne Gérard, a comic soldier in Napoleon's army. He also made a successful reading tour of the United States, sailed up the Nile River with Louise, and visited the Sudan as a war correspondent. Having been convinced that the climate of Surrey was good for tuberculosis patients, Doyle and Louise settled there in 1896. In 1897, he met and fell in love with Jean Leckie, then twenty-four. With typical loyalty and honor, Doyle maintained a platonic relationship with her until after Louise's death. He married Jean in 1907. They had three children, Denis, Adrian, and Lena Jean.

Before the outbreak of the Boer War in 1899, Doyle published story collections, novels, poetry, and drama. Too old for combat, he served under terrible conditions and without pay as a medical officer. His war experiences led to two books. In the second, *The War in South Africa: Its Cause and Conduct* (1902), he defended the British role in the war. For this service, he was knighted in 1902.

After running unsuccessfully for Parliament in 1900, Doyle visited Dartmoor. There he heard legends that became the inspiration for *The Hound of the Baskervilles*. While this novel was appearing in *The Strand*, William Gillette's play, *Sherlock Holmes* (1899), opened successfully in London, and American and British publishers offered Doyle about seventy-five hundred dollars per story to write more. He revived Holmes in "The Adventure of the Empty House" and continued to produce Holmes stories sporadically for the rest of his life.

Energetic, inquisitive, and ambitious, Doyle sought to influence public opinion in many ways during the last years of his life. He spoke out on political issues such as Irish home rule, ran again for Parliament, participated in an Anglo-German auto race, traveled widely in Europe and America, and was a war correspondent during World War I. In 1916, he became convinced that he had received a spirit message from the dead and proceeded to become a leader of the Spiritualist movement. He wrote several books on Spiritualism, including *The History of Spiritualism* (1926).

His best-remembered accomplishment in the last third of his life is the creation of Professor Challenger, the hero of *The Lost World*, a passionate scientist eager to explore unknown worlds. Like Holmes, Challenger eventually became a film hero. *The Lost World* also provided an outline for the classic film *King Kong* (1933).

Doyle fell ill with heart disease in 1929 and died on July 7, 1930, at his home, Windlesham, in Sussex, England, where he is buried.

Analysis

Doyle tended to think of his Sherlock Holmes stories as popular fiction, written primarily to maintain his income while he worked on more important works such as *The White Company* (1891). Though this historical novel in a medieval setting is thought to be one of his best books, and though his science-fiction novels about Professor Challenger are also well respected, the tales of Sherlock Holmes are still considered Doyle's best and most memorable work.

In Holmes and Dr. John Watson, Doyle created well-rounded, interesting characters. Holmes is the utter rationalist, understanding emotions almost exclusively as factors in the solution of interesting intellectual problems. He solves crimes by using keen observation, by building hypotheses based on established facts, and by testing those hypotheses. He is often amusing and entertaining when he and Watson play their game of inferring a character's habits or recent activities from the observation of details about their first appearance or possessions, such as an accidentally lost cane. Holmes is always superior at finding the correct way to arrange the clues into a meaningful order. Watson, though quite competent, is a more ordinary man, a doctor who eventually marries and lives a prosaic life except when he is with Holmes on a case. Then his life blossoms into adventure; and his loyalty, medical knowledge, physical strength, and energy serve Holmes well. Holmes is a creative genius, using a "scientific method" in an artistic manner to produce masterpieces of detection. Watson, as Holmes's Boswell, or biographer, turns these masterpieces into what Holmes often describes as trivial romances, more entertaining than instructive.

One factor that contributes to the enduring popularity of these tales is that readers have found the stories instructive as well as entertaining. Within the conventions of the classic detective story, Doyle tells stories that shed light upon interesting complexities of British Victorian society and upon some enduring social themes.

The classic detective story may be defined as taking place in a world where order is normal. In this way, it is distinct from the hard-boiled detective story, where disorder is the norm. The classic detective becomes necessary when criminals introduce disorder, threatening social and familial stability. In *The Hound of the Baskervilles*, a diabolical murderer attempts to kill the heirs of an estate to legitimize his more distant claim. In the process, he not only creates disorder in his family and among his immediate victims but also violates his own marriage and disrupts the good work in the community of the recently restored Baskerville family wealth. Furthermore, by making use of the old superstition of a vengeful hellhound that pursues the Baskerville heirs, the murderer undercuts the foundation of rationality upon which communal order rests. Critics have pointed out that Stapleton, the murderer, threatens to turn the whole community into an analog of the Grimpen Mire, an important symbolic setting of the novella, where people and animals can be lost and then sucked into the dangerous muddy pools at the slightest misstep. Holmes's function as a detective of rationality is to foil this villain and thereby protect society from disintegration. In contrast, a hard-boiled detective such as Raymond Chandler's Philip Marlowe in *The Big Sleep* (1939) works in a corrupt society to protect the innocent from its dangers, to salvage some order from the dominant chaos. The classic detective relies primarily upon mental work to sort out clues and discover the sources of disorder, while the hard-boiled detective relies more on violence to defend innocent victims. While the most common crime motive in the classic detective story is greed, the more common motive in hard-boiled detective fiction is power. Doyle may come closest to hard-boiled fiction in "The Adventure of the Final Problem" and "The Adventure of the Empty House," where Holmes encounters the organized crime of Professor Moriarty, a criminal for whom power and domination are more important than wealth.

Doyle's themes tend to concern family relations and their extensions into social and political relations. A number of these stories deal with corrupted relations between adults and children or between men and women, in which the physically weaker are endangered and abused because of their disadvantaged social position. Taken together, these tales provide not only exciting and suspenseful reading but also vivid portraits of Victorian life and insightful analyses of human nature and social life.

A SCANDAL IN BOHEMIA

First published: 1891
Type of work: Short story

Sherlock Holmes attempts to save the king of Bohemia from a scandal that would prevent his projected marriage.

As "A Scandal in Bohemia" begins, it is March of 1888. The recently married Dr. John Watson happens by his old bachelor quarters at 221B Baker Street and finds Sherlock Holmes pacing the floor in the brilliantly lit rooms. Since Watson has married and settled into domestic tranquillity, Holmes, for whom the life of the emotions would be grit in his machinery, has been alternating between cocaine-induced dreams and his fiercely energetic solutions of mysteries abandoned by the official police. On this evening, Holmes takes an unusual assignment, unlike those of the two previously published cases, *A Study in Scarlet* (1887) and *The Sign of Four* (1889). Indeed, Watson indicates that this is the first case in which Holmes fails, and his defeat comes at the hands of a woman, Irene Adler, an American singer, actress, and adventurer "of dubious and questionable memory," now deceased.

It may be because this is one of the earlier Holmes tales that it deviates so interestingly from the pattern of solution that later came to dominate these stories. This story strikingly resembles its great predecessor, Edgar Allan Poe's "The Purloined Letter," in which Auguste Dupin determines the hiding place of a woman who is apparently of the French royal family and then recovers a letter being used to blackmail her. Like Dupin in "The Murders in the Rue Morgue," Holmes surprises his friend early in the story with an accurate account of Watson's recent activities based on details about the condition of his shoes. Holmes's task is to locate and recover a photograph that shows Adler and the king of Bohemia together. Adler, a spurned lover, has threatened to deliver the photograph to Princess Clotilde, the king's intended, on the day their engagement is announced. Clotilde and her family would object so strongly to this proof of a previous sexual affair that the marriage would be canceled, disrupting international relations.

Holmes fairly easily determines that Adler, because she is an intelligent woman, would hide the photograph in her own home, but cleverly enough that ordinary burglars—who have already made two attempts—would not find it. In disguise, he observes her home and, by accident, witnesses her wedding to a lawyer. This event in itself might end her threat to the king, but Holmes wishes to make sure. He plots successfully to force her to show him the letter's hiding place. While assisting in this trick, Watson becomes less sure that he and Holmes are right to violate the privacy of the kind and beautiful Miss Adler, even to help the king.

Holmes and Watson have deliberately set out to break the law by stealing the photograph. Only as the story closes do they both realize that they have taken the side of a powerful man who has won Adler's love and then cast her aside for reasons of policy. Adler sees through Holmes's trick, flees with her husband and the photograph, and leaves behind a note for Holmes, saying she will not use the photograph to harm the king unless he threatens her further. She thus earns Holmes's and Watson's admiration, so that from then on Holmes refers to her as "the woman," and ceases to speak deprecatingly of women's intelligence. At the same time, the king earns their contempt for his failure to rise above the conventional demands of his rank to make such a magnificent woman his queen.

This story proves atypical in the Sherlock Holmes series because the detective is called upon to break the law in order to maintain a questionable idea of order. His love of mystery and his lack of respect for women help to draw him into this temptation, but his understanding of emotional values, despite his apparent freedom from the softer emotions, leads him to regret what he intended and to admire the woman whom he mistook for a criminal.

THE ADVENTURE OF THE SPECKLED BAND

First published: 1892
Type of work: Short story

Holmes aids a woman whose twin sister has died mysteriously upon the eve of her marriage and who fears that her stepfather may intend the same fate for her.

"The Adventure of the Speckled Band" is probably the most famous of Sherlock Holmes's cases, not only because of the diabolical plot of a stepfather to prevent his twin daughters from marrying and thereby diminishing his income from his deceased wife's estate but also because it so perfectly realizes the pattern of detection that became Holmes's trademark. Watson opens the story with the information that he has been freed to tell this story by the premature death of the client, Helen Stoner.

Helen comes to Holmes and Watson in April of 1883, terrified that she may meet the same fate as her sister, who died mysteriously two years earlier. Encouraged and reassured by Holmes, she recounts the reasons for her fears. Because of repairs on the house, she has had to move into the bedroom used by her sister when she died and has heard a low whistle in the night, just as her sister did on several nights before her death. Her sister died soon after announcing her engagement to be married, and Helen is now also engaged to marry. Furthermore, the stepfather, Dr. Grimesby Roylott of the Stoke Moran estate in Surrey, is well known as a violent and temperamental giant who brooks no interference with his will. Having married their mother in India, where his medical practice was successful until he murdered his Indian butler, he returned to England, where his wife died in a railway accident. He then retired with his young stepdaughters into virtual seclusion at Stoke Moran, where he gives some of his time to collecting exotic animals, such as a baboon and a cheetah—said to come from India—which he allows to roam free on his grounds. He also associates with bands of gypsies that he allows to camp on his grounds.

Summarized, these details about Roylott's life seem rather silly, but they work fairly effectively to account for Holmes's initial failure to discover how Helen's sister died and, therefore, what threat Helen must fear. This body of detail allows Holmes to develop two theories to explain the death, though he claims to have at least seven. The incorrect theory assumes that Roylott, with his clear motive for preventing his daughters from marrying, employs the gypsies by somehow making it possible for them to enter the woman's room at night and frighten her to death in some way. This theory would account for there being no signs of violence on her body, for the police having found no way of entering her room once she locked herself in, away from cheetahs and baboons, each night, and for her mysterious last words to Helen about a speckled band. When Holmes examines the scene, however, he makes several other pertinent discoveries, such as that there is a small opening at the ceiling between the woman's room and Dr. Roylott's room, that the bell rope that hangs down onto the bed is not functional, and that the bed is fastened to the floor and cannot be shifted. These and other details make the case clear to Holmes, but he must, of course, test it.

One of the great scenes in the Holmes's stories is the night that Watson and the detective spend in the absolutely dark room, waiting for something to happen. Only when the speckled band appears and reveals itself to be a poisonous snake do the two men fully realize that the evil doctor has trained an Indian swamp adder to descend through the opening, down the bell rope and onto the bed, and return. Holmes, now aware of what was supposed to happen, drives the dangerous snake back upon the doctor, catching the murderer in his own trap.

Though there are many interesting variations, this general pattern is usually recognized as the form of the classic Holmes story. A client gives the detective the unconnected clues that form a mystery. The detective invents structures that make sense of these clues and determines which one is correct. Usually this requires a personal inspection of the crime scene and some other research that uncovers unnoticed clues. The detective reaches a final conclusion by means of reasoning about this information, produces and tests the solution, and reveals the criminal. Though this process usually involves some action and danger, the central activity of the detective is solving the puzzle, and the reader's main pleasure is in attempting to reach the answer before or along with the detective. That is the general form one expects to encounter in the classical detective stories of such masters of the form as Dorothy Sayers and Agatha Christie.

This story also deals with Doyle's typical themes. Often, his client turns out to be a young woman who is, in some way, the victim of a powerful male—a relative, an employer, a former suitor. As is often the case, the motive here is to obtain money and property. All the Holmes stories emphasize the rationality of causes for mysterious events. This story especially—but not uniquely—underlines Holmes's wisdom. Like his famous contemporary, Sigmund Freud, Holmes is willing to listen to the problems of a nervous young woman, when even her future husband responds only with "soothing answers and averted eyes." Helen addresses Holmes as one who "can see deeply into the manifold wickedness of the human heart." That, however, is not true. Holmes is usually characterized as lacking insight into emotions beyond the common motives for crime. What he is really best at is developing and testing logical connections between seemingly unconnected events. Perhaps this apparent contradiction may be explained by Watson's assertion at the opening of the story that Holmes's rapid deductions were "swift as intuitions," suggesting that his logic is so fine an art that it may look like intuition or may mimic deep insight into the wickedness of the human heart.

THE ADVENTURE OF THE FINAL PROBLEM

First published: 1893
Type of work: Short story

Having trapped the evil master criminal, Professor Moriarty, Holmes tries but fails to evade Moriarity's attempts to kill the detective before being arrested.

In December of 1893, in the British magazine *The Strand* and the American magazine *McClure's*, readers were shocked to see Dr. Watson's melancholy account of the death of Holmes, who (according to Watson) was murdered two years earlier by Professor Moriarty, the Napoleon of crime. In writing "The Adventure of the Final Problem" and by introducing a new character of mythic proportions in Moriarty, however, Doyle probably effectively ensured that public pressure for more tales would increase rather than diminish.

"The Adventure of the Final Problem" is a tale not of detection but of rivalry and pursuit. Holmes comes to Watson's home in the night, when by good fortune Mrs. Watson is away on a visit and Watson is free to travel with Holmes to the continent to escape Moriarty. Moriarty is one of the first great leaders of organized crime in fiction. Doyle presents him as in every way Holmes's equal, except that Moriarty has inherited criminal tendencies that have made him diabolical. Moriarty has organized a crime network that is like a giant spider's web, with the professor as the spider at its center: "He is the organizer of half that is evil and of nearly all that is undetected in this great city." To counter the professor's web, Holmes has helped the police to construct a net in which those in Moriarty's gang, including the great spider himself, will be caught. He has not, however, been able to carry out this project without Moriarty's knowledge. On the day Holmes visits Watson, Moriarty has come to Holmes's rooms and promised that if Holmes destroys him, the professor will take Holmes with him. Holmes has refused to be intimidated and, as a result, has endured a series of murder attempts during the day.

Holmes requests Watson's company for a trip to Switzerland, the main purpose of which is to evade Moriarty until the arrests occur, which for unexplained reasons requires three days of waiting. Despite their elaborate measures, Moriarty is able to follow them. When his gang is arrested, Moriarty himself is not caught. The professor overtakes Holmes at the Reichenbach Falls in the Swiss Alps. When Watson returns to the scene he has been fooled into leaving, all the remaining evidence indicates that Holmes and Moriarty, locked in a final struggle, fell into the falls, from which their bodies cannot be recovered.

Repeatedly in this story, Holmes reflects to Watson that his career has reached a peak and, therefore, that he is willing to accept even death if this proves to be the only way to rid England of Moriarty. This fatalistic mood proves prophetic when it appears the two have died in an equal and apparently irresolvable struggle of wit and skill.

That Doyle had some reservations about killing his hero seems clear. While having the bodies lost may seem to annihilate Holmes utterly, it leaves quite open the possibility that Doyle later exploited: that Holmes in fact did not die but went underground to avoid the dangers of Moriarty's remaining friends. In "The Adventure of the Empty House," Holmes returns from three years of retreat to apprehend Moriarty's most dangerous remaining agents, among them Colonel Sebastian Moran. Of course, Doyle might have avoided reviving Holmes by "discovering" more of the many cases he solved before his death, as he did when he published *The Hound of the Baskervilles* (1902). Public pleasure at Holmes's "resurrection" greatly enhanced the detective's popularity and ensured a devoted readership for the many more tales Doyle wrote.

THE RING OF THOTH

First published: 1890
Type of work: Short Story

In this supernatural fantasy, an Egyptologist stumbles upon a four-thousand-year-old man, who tells him the story of how he came to live so long.

While Doyle is best known for his tales of Sherlock Holmes, he wrote a variety of other kinds of fiction, much of which is vigorous and entertaining. In interesting contrast to the Holmes stories, with their insistence upon rational explanation and natural order, are his stories of the supernatural. At the end of "Lot No. 249," one of his best supernatural tales, the narrator says, "But the wisdom of men is small, and the ways of Nature are strange, and who shall put a bound to the dark things which may be found by those who seek for them?" Doyle's tales of the supernatural also help to illustrate the wit and humor that, in fact, show up in many of his stories, for in these tales he often maintains an ironic narrative tone.

In "The Ring of Thoth," irony is directed at the central character, Mr. John Vansittart Smith, Fellow of the Royal Society. Though Smith is a highly talented scientist, he is also represented as a fickle fellow. The narrator opens the story with an extended metaphor of courtship. Smith "flirts" with zoology, chemistry, and Oriental studies, almost "marrying" each, but finally is "caught" by Egyptology. Then the metaphor turns real: "So struck was Mr. Smith that he straightway married an Egyptological young lady who had written upon the sixth dynasty, and having thus secured a sound base of operations he set himself to collect materials for a work which should unite the research of Lepsius and the ingenuity of Champollion." The humor continues as Smith journeys to Paris to study materials at the Louvre, where the narrator describes him as looking like a comic bird while he studies. When a pair of English tourists make disparaging comments about an attendant's appearance, Smith believes they are talking about him, making fun of his lack of physical beauty. Discovering his error, Smith notices that the attendant they are looking at really does look like an authentic ancient Egyptian.

Smith's curiosity is aroused, but when questioned, the attendant insists he is French. The ridiculous leads to the wondrous when, in the course of studying ancient documents, Smith falls asleep and remains unnoticed behind a door. He awakens in the early morning to discover the mysterious attendant unwrapping the mummy of a beautiful young girl, for whom the attendant expresses great affection. Then, in the course of searching among a collection of rings, the attendant spills some liquid and, in wiping it up, discovers Smith. As a result of this humorous series of accidents, Smith learns the story of Sosra.

Sosra, the attendant, is really an ancient Egyptian who developed an elixir of life.

He and his best friend, Parmes, the priest of Thoth, drank it and became immortal. Then they both fell in love with Princess Atma, who loved Sosra; she soon died of a plague, having been hesitant about taking the elixir herself. Parmes then discovered an antidote for the elixir, making it possible for him to die and join Atma in the afterlife, but he hid it from Sosra so that he and Atma would be separated forever. After four thousand years of searching, Sosra has finally found the Ring of Thoth, which contains the antidote. He tells Smith his story and, along the way, makes it clear that Smith knows litttle of value about ancient Egyptian culture, even though he is one of the best modern Egyptologists. Then he lets Smith out of the Louvre and goes to join his beloved.

This amusing and entertaining tale of the supernatural contrasts the fickle modern scientist with the dedicated ancient scientist, who by sixteen had mastered his craft, and who remained loyal to his first love for four millennia. On the other hand, Sosra's story contains a warning for Smith, who has given way to a passion for ancient knowledge that may lead him along a path parallel to Sosra's. The tale also casts an ironic light on the modern rationalist's faith that one can understand the past or master any area of knowledge, thus providing an implicit, though perhaps not very serious, critique of the world view espoused by Sherlock Holmes.

Summary

Sir Arthur Conan Doyle's biographers agree in describing him as typical of the late Victorian era. He remained confident throughout his life of the soundness of his own moral vision and in the basic goodness of British morality. As a public personage, he repeatedly took the lead, both in praising British principles and in criticizing particular policies. He is credited with helping to modernize British defense between the Boer War and World War I, especially the defensive gear of common soldiers. He twice played detective himself, investigating cases of people unjustly condemned to prison. One of these, the Edalji case in 1906, contributed to establishing a court of criminal appeal in 1907. Even his support of Spiritualism was a public crusade to effect the spiritual transformation of a nation he feared was in decline.

While his public services were many, Doyle will continue to be remembered mainly for the Sherlock Holmes stories. Holmes and Watson are indelible fixtures of Western culture, encountered in virtually every popular medium. These stories have influenced every important writer in the detective genre, from traditionalists such as Agatha Christie, Dorothy Sayers, and Ellery Queen, to hardboiled writers such as Raymond Chandler, Ross Macdonald, and P. D. James.

Bibliography

Carr, John Dickson. *The Life of Sir Arthur Conan Doyle*. New York: Harper, 1949.
Cox, Don Richard. *Arthur Conan Doyle*. New York: Frederick Ungar, 1985.
Doyle, Arthur Conan. *Memories and Adventures*. Boston: Little, Brown, 1924.

Edwards, Owen Dudley. *The Quest for Sherlock Holmes.* Totowa, N.J.: Barnes & Noble Books, 1983.

Hardwick, Michael. *The Complete Guide to Sherlock Holmes.* New York: St. Martin's Press, 1986.

Higham, Charles. *The Adventures of Conan Doyle.* New York: W. W. Norton, 1976.

Jaffe, Jacqueline. *Arthur Conan Doyle.* Boston: Twayne, 1987.

Nordon, Pierre. *Conan Doyle: A Biography.* Translated by Frances Partridge. New York: Holt, Rinehart and Winston, 1966.

Shreffler, Philip A., ed. *The Baker Street Reader.* Westport, Conn.: Greenwood Press, 1984.

Tracy, Jack. *The Encyclopedia Sherlockiana.* Garden City, N.Y.: Doubleday, 1977.

Terry Heller

MARGARET DRABBLE

Born: Sheffield, Yorkshire, England
June 5, 1939

Principal Literary Achievement
Drabble is a prolific novelist, one of the leading realists of British fiction in the second half of the twentieth century. She is also a noted scholar and critic.

Biography
Margaret Drabble was born on June 5, 1939, in Sheffield, Yorkshire, England, the daughter of a circuit court judge, John Frederick Drabble, and a teacher of English, Kathleen Bloor Drabble. Her older sister, Antonia, was to achieve a considerable reputation as a novelist under the name of A. S. Byatt; her younger sister, Helen, became an art critic; and a brother became an attorney. Drabble was educated at a Quaker boarding school in York and at Newnham College, Cambridge, where she concentrated in literature but spent much of her time in theater activities and was not involved with the literary set, dominated by the critic F. R. Leavis. After graduation from Cambridge in 1960, she spent a year as an actress with the Royal Shakespeare Company; in June, 1960, she married Clive Swift, an actor. She left acting when she became pregnant; her first three novels were written during her three pregnancies.

Her early novels, based closely on her own experiences as a young woman, were immediate critical successes. The first, *A Summer Bird-Cage* (1963), focused on choosing between marriage and a career; the second, *The Garrick Year* (1964), dealt with the apparent necessity for a young woman to choose between an acting career and her family. Drabble's conviction that motherhood and a career are not mutually exclusive led to *The Millstone* (1965; published in the United States as *Thank You All Very Much*, 1969), whose central figure pursues an academic career undeterred by the birth of her child. Drabble continued to write in a strictly realistic mode, focusing on characters of approximately her own age and, to a large extent, of her own station and condition in life. *Jerusalem the Golden* (1967) deals with a young woman less concerned with husband and children than with her desire to escape from a provincial town to the excitement of London. Social problems and dislocations as they affect individuals continued to occupy her attention through the novels of her later years: *The Needle's Eye* (1972), *The Realms of Gold* (1975), *The Ice Age* (1977), *The Middle Ground* (1980), *The Radiant Way* (1987), and *A Natural Curiosity* (1989).

While her primary reputation has been as a novelist, Drabble has achieved a con-

siderable reputation as a literary critic. Her thesis at Cambridge was a study of the fiction of Arnold Bennett, which led to a major book, *Arnold Bennett: A Biography* (1974). She wrote a brief study of a major Romantic poet, *Wordsworth: Literature in Perspective* (1966), and a broader study of the relationship of poetry and the environment, *A Writer's Britain: Landscape in Literature* (1979). She edited a collection of essays dealing with one of her favorite novelists, *The Genius of Thomas Hardy* (1975). She was chosen to edit a revised edition of *The Oxford Companion to English Literature*, which was published in 1985. For many years, she taught a course in literature at Morley College in London.

Drabble has received numerous awards, including the John Llewellyn Rhys Memorial Award in 1966, the James Tait Black Award in 1968, and the American Academy E. M. Forster Award in 1973. She received an honorary degree from Sheffield University in 1976. In 1980, she was named a Commander, Order of the British Empire. Drabble's marriage to Clive Swift ended in divorce in 1975; she married writer Michael Holroyd in 1982 and continued to live in London.

Analysis

Drabble admires the experimental methods of Doris Lessing's *The Golden Notebook* (1962), and Drabble's own prose occasionally owes something to the stream-of-consciousness methods pioneered by James Joyce and Virginia Woolf, but she has not been known as an experimenter in her own work. She prefers not to use chapter divisions, using spaces to indicate changes of location or action. The nearest thing to unconventional method occurs in the early novel, *The Waterfall* (1969): The novel opens with third-person narration but then switches to first-person narration by the central character; thereafter, the two methods alternate. On the whole, however, Drabble's fiction is in an older tradition. She has been compared to such sturdily realistic novelists as George Eliot, Charles Dickens, Arnold Bennett, and Henry James, among others. She has said that she would like to write the great English novel, a successor to George Eliot's *Middlemarch* (1871-1872).

Furthermore, she is sometimes seen as a feminist writer, since she is much concerned with the difficulties encountered by her female characters, but she rejects the description. In the past, she argued that feminism proposes oversimplified explanations for complex social and economic problems, which affect both sexes, although perhaps not equally. In this regard, she most closely resembles her admired predecessor Eliot.

Drabble's novels are straightforward descriptions of the events in the lives of people who are representative of their time and social position, although they could hardly be called average. She deliberately chooses to focus on characters whose ages and social positions are similar to her own at the time of writing, arguing that these would be the people whom she would know best and about whom she could therefore write with the greatest confidence. Because she herself had to contend with the complications of building a career while rearing several children, she presents a number of characters who must deal with this problem: It plays an important part in *The*

Garrick Year, in *The Millstone*, in *Jerusalem the Golden*, and in *The Realms of Gold*, all written while Drabble was wrestling with the same life choices that face her characters.

In her later novels, beginning with *Jerusalem the Golden*, Drabble abandons the first-person narrative that she had earlier been using in favor of an omniscient third-person narrator. Her usual method is to focus on a single figure or on two or more central characters and to describe in detail a day or an episode in the life of such characters. In the course of describing an incident, she uses flashbacks to convey whatever information she thinks is important about the childhood or youth of the character, interpolating commentary on specific actions or on more general social or economic activities of the time. Long narrative passages fill the gaps between the extended scenes that Drabble uses to convey critical episodes in the lives of her characters.

She occasionally addresses the reader directly, for example by introducing a character briefly, with a comment to the effect that he or she will appear later in a more important role. Near the end of *The Realms of Gold*, the narrator observes that all the surviving major characters are reasonably content and well off, and she tells the reader: "So there you are. Invent a more suitable ending if you can." Drabble is also willing, in what might be called an old-fashioned way, to insert comments on her own methods. At the beginning of the final section of *The Ice Age*, for example, she writes, "It ought now to be necessary to imagine a future for Anthony Keating. There is no need to worry about the other characters." At another point, in *The Realms of Gold*, while commenting about a coincidental meeting between characters, she mentions the coincidence but disarms criticism by saying that there will be less likely coincidences at other points in the book as there are in life.

Perhaps more important still, Drabble is never reluctant to comment on the social and economic situations in which she places her characters. The contemporary style is to ignore such matters or to leave them for the reader to deduce, but Drabble is outspoken in describing what seem to her the ills of society. In *The Ice Age*, in particular, she describes the laws and regulations that have made it possible for several of her principal characters first to make a considerable amount of money and later to be bankrupted or sent to jail. Since many of her major characters are women, she frequently makes pungent observations about the difficulties that women encounter in modern society. Her characters who try to be content with being housewives and mothers are never really satisfied, but those who choose careers along with motherhood encounter their own difficulties. Neither situation is anywhere close to ideal, although she never says anything critical of motherhood.

In other important ways, Drabble's methods run counter to those made popular by such modern novelists as Ernest Hemingway and F. Scott Fitzgerald. There are very few extended stretches of dialogue in Drabble's fiction. Instead, there are long narrative and descriptive sections informing the reader about characters, in the manner of Eliot or James. Dialogue is used only sparingly, to highlight special scenes; even when it is used, it is generally employed only as a counterpoint to a description of a conversation. Drabble is more interested in conveying the feelings and reactions of her characters than in trying to make accurate representations of how they speak, and she evidently believes that summaries with commentary are more effective for her purpose.

Furthermore, Drabble does not seem to be concerned that her readers will be bored by novels in which there is not much dramatic action. In some novels, crucial developments are precipitated by a shocking event. *The Waterfall* is unusual, in that the climactic action, a fatal automobile accident, is described directly; elsewhere, decisive events take place offstage. In *The Needle's Eye*, a divorced father kidnaps his three children and threatens to take them out of England; in *The Ice Age*, a young woman is involved in a fatal automobile accident in a Balkan country; in *The Realms of Gold*, an old woman dies of starvation. Yet none of these events is described directly. Rather, Drabble concentrates on the effects of such episodes on the characters who are at the center of the action.

Since violent action and snappy dialogue are not encountered frequently in Drabble's fiction, she must rely on style and characterization to hold the interest of her readers. Her style is unsensational but consistently interesting and fresh, at least in the long novels of her major period, including *The Realms of Gold* and *The Needle's Eye*. Her descriptions are detailed but seldom overly so, conveying a strong sense of what kinds of settings her characters inhabit, and her descriptions of characters are sharp and often witty.

More important, her characters are interesting. It is not Drabble's method to idealize these figures or make them grotesques. Instead, she provides them with a mixture of strengths and weaknesses so that they are recognizably human, generally admirable and entertaining without being boring. Frances Wingate, in *The Realms of Gold*, for example, is a successful archaeologist and an attractive and forceful woman, but she is also a careless mother, happy that her children no longer demand her attention, and she has foolishly broken off her affair with the man whom she genuinely loves for no reason at all other than that her life had temporarily become less than exciting. Rose Vassiliou, in *The Needle's Eye*, is a caring mother and a noble character in some ways, but she can also be dependent, annoying, and self-destructively moral.

Drabble's later novels—*The Ice Age, The Middle Ground, The Radiant Way*, and *A Natural Curiosity*—all received negative reviews. Critics argued that Drabble was more interested in depicting large social issues and commenting on those issues than in creating interesting and believable characters. Nevertheless, the respect with which her work is treated is a clear indication that she remains one of the major British novelists of the second half of the twentieth century.

THE WATERFALL

First published: 1969
Type of work: Novel

A young married Englishwoman, mother of two, falls in love for the first time and engages in a passionate affair with her cousin's husband.

In *The Waterfall*, Jane Gray is married to the successful guitarist Malcolm Gray, but she has driven him away with her indifference, her sloppy housekeeping, and her frigidity. When she gives birth to her second child, Bianca, she is looked after by her cousin and best friend, Lucy, and Lucy's husband, James Otford. She and James almost immediately fall in love, and when she has recovered from the aftereffects of childbirth they begin a passionate affair, keeping Lucy, the absent Malcolm, and both Jane and Malcolm's parents in ignorance.

For the first time, Jane is not only in love but also sexually passionate. The affair seems to be proceeding without difficulty until James suggests that they travel to Norway for a vacation with Jane's two children. She is reluctant at first but then agrees. At the beginning of the trip, however, they are involved in a terrible automobile accident. Both James and Jane have expected something like this to happen, since he is a very daring and bad driver, but ironically the accident is not his fault. Another driver is killed. Jane and the children are shaken but not injured, but James is thrown from the car and severely hurt; he remains in a coma for weeks.

Jane, pretending to be Mrs. Otford, remains near James and visits him every day, but Malcolm Gray eventually finds out where she is and tells Lucy. Lucy's reaction is to call and tell Jane that she wishes that both the lovers had been killed in the accident, but she soon relents and comes to join Jane in her hospital vigil. She reveals that her marriage was also going bad, that James was a lousy provider and had had other affairs before the one with Jane; the news is a severe shock to Jane. Lucy, it develops, is also having an affair, evidently not her first. When James recovers consciousness and begins to regain his strength and abilities, Jane leaves to return to her home. The affair, however, is not over; when James recovers, he and Jane manage to get together for brief trips that are the highlights of Jane's life.

Its narrow focus on the private lives of its characters makes this novel less socially concerned than most of Drabble's fiction. What keeps *The Waterfall* from being a conventionally tear-jerking romance is the technique that Drabble adopts of alternating chapters of third-person narration describing the romance with Jane's first-person comments, in which she admits lying about many things: her marriage, her blaming her parents for faults they did not have, and her describing the emotions other than passion that affected her during the affair. She feels no guilt, and at the end she has somehow managed to remain friendly with Lucy, but she recognizes that she is responsible for her own failings and her own decisions. Blaming fate, her parents, or others, as she had done in the earlier third-person segments, is no longer possible.

THE NEEDLE'S EYE

First published: 1972
Type of work: Novel

A man and a woman, both unhappy with their lives, form a friendship that never becomes romantic but that sustains both of them.

In *The Needle's Eye*, Simon Camish is a successful barrister who is profoundly unhappy in his marriage to Julie. Rose Vassiliou is a divorced mother of three children who lives in virtual poverty. The daughter of wealthy parents, she has renounced her family and donated a large inheritance to a charity, rather than accept money that she believes she does not deserve. When Simon and Rose meet, each recognizes in the other qualities that he or she lacks. The two are polar opposites. Simon devotes considerable energy to suppressing the emotions that Rose expresses openly and shamelessly. Simon has struggled all of his life to gain the money and social position that Rose has thrown away. He remains locked in a marriage to a woman who is concerned only with material things and who makes him unhappy, while Rose has divorced Christopher, the husband whom she married against her family's bitter opposition. Although he abused her physically and verbally, she feels guilty for separating Christopher from their children, whom he loves and misses. Ironically, Christopher, because he has become successful in business, is now closer to Rose's parents than she is.

As their friendship grows, Simon and Rose realize, separately, that they could be happy living together, even though there is no real sexual attraction between them. Yet Rose says nothing because she does not believe that she deserves happiness, and Simon cannot bring himself to speak of something so emotionally important to him. Christopher's kidnapping of his three children precipitates a confrontation involving himself, Rose, and Simon, an event that turns out to be quiet and undramatic. In the end, Rose takes Christopher back, Simon remains with Julie, and each continues to value and rely on the other's goodwill. Neither is truly happy, but both are more content than they had been.

The Needle's Eye combines social criticism with acute observations on the emotional difficulties of living in modern British society. Drabble disapproves of a society that values money and material objects highly and that does little to alleviate the conditions under which people without money have to live. Poverty, she observes, is not ennobling. Wealth is not ennobling either, but it makes the strains of life easier. The economic values of this society, however, are less damaging to the individual than are the social norms that require that a tight rein be kept on emotions and that pain and suffering should always be denied and minimized by the sufferer. Drabble also pokes holes in romantic ideas; Rose's youthful passion for Christopher brings her years of misery when the passion is spent, and her noble gesture of renouncing her inheritance leaves her miserably poor and puts Rose's children in the same condition.

Drabble does not suggest that society is entirely to blame for what happens to her characters. They make choices, and those choices go a long way toward determining what will happen in their lives. Among the minor characters are a few who have made choices that are better for them: Jeremy Alford, a lawyer, and his pregnant wife are quite happy, as is Miss Lindley, the teacher of one of Rose's children. Less happy are those, like Simon and Rose, whose choices have required them to struggle against their upbringing and early environment.

THE REALMS OF GOLD

First published: 1975
Type of work: Novel

A mature woman, a successful archaeologist, ends a happy relationship with her lover and tries to put her life back together.

The Realms of Gold is Drabble's most optimistic novel and the one in which she seems most relaxed as a writer. Her central figure, Frances Wingate, is about forty years old, a respected professional in the field of archaeology. Years before, she had correctly predicted the location of the ruins of an ancient trading center in the Sahara Desert and had led in its excavation, and consequently she has enjoyed a highly satisfying career. Her marriage to a wealthy man did not turn out well, but her children have become independent, and she is able to leave them for extended periods while she attends professional conferences and other meetings important to her.

The problem in Wingate's life is her broken relationship with Karel Schmidt, a lecturer at a small university, who had been her lover. Separated from him, Frances realizes that she had broken off their relationship for frivolous and foolish reasons. Her life, she believed when she made the break, had become too regular, too contented, and she needed change. The change that she manufactured has separated her from the only man she has loved, and she wants nothing more than to get him back. Very early in the novel, she sends him a postcard from an unnamed Mediterranean city, announcing that she misses him and loves him. She assumes that this will lead to a reconciliation, but when she does not hear from him she swallows her disappointment and determines to go on with her life. Because of a postal strike, the card does not reach Karel for weeks. In those weeks, the action of most of the novel takes place.

Frances travels to Africa for a conference, at which she becomes friendly with a cousin whom she had not known before, David Ollerenshaw. She enjoys flirting with a handsome Italian archaeologist and finds it satisfying to be an important figure among her contemporaries, but she also realizes that Karel is more important to her than this adulation and attention. Karel, having finally received her message, tries to join her in Africa but fails. After some comic errors, they are finally reunited in England.

Frances and Karel are sympathetic characters, but so are many of the others who populate this long book. Exceptions are Frances' parents. Like the parents in most Drabble novels, these characters are somewhat cold and distant; her father is head of a small university, while her mother, a lecturer on birth control and a sexual counselor, does not like sex. Her brother, Hugh, is an alcoholic who is successful in business but needs alcohol to dull his sensibilities. Hugh's son Stephen, a university student, has fathered a daughter and has become obsessed with the dangers that await her as she matures. Stephen's young wife has had a mental collapse and has had to be institutionalized. In the end, to avert the suffering that he believes is in store for her, he kills his daughter and himself. Frances' second cousin, Janet Bird, has no such fears. She tolerates a bad marriage and enjoys the company of Frances when fate brings them together, but she is not fearful for her child. In her quiet courage, she is like David Ollerenshaw, a geologist who the narrator says was intended for a large role but assumes only secondary importance.

Except for Stephen and his daughter, all the major characters in *The Realms of Gold* survive and, in varying degrees, find happiness. Even Karel's discontented wife finally finds her place in life and permits Karel and Frances to live together. She and Frances, although they do not like each other, learn to get along.

THE ICE AGE

First published: 1977
Type of work: Novel

Anthony Keating and the people associated with him are frustrated and unhappy during the economic depression in Britain during the 1970's.

After the relative contentment of the ending of *The Realms of Gold*, *The Ice Age* is like a cold shower. The later work begins the series of late novels in which Drabble adopts what critics have called a sociological approach in her fiction. These novels are concerned with the economic and social events in England during the years between 1973 and 1990, years in which a depression was followed by a period of recovery in some parts of the economy, fueled by the exploitation of North Sea oil. There is some justice in the critical complaint that Drabble became less interested in her characters than in how she could use the novel to address the current state of British affairs.

The structure of *The Ice Age* is unusual. As she often does, Drabble dispenses with chapter divisions, but this novel is divided into three parts; the first two move among five major characters and several minor ones. The final section focuses on only one of these characters. At the end, strong religious overtones are introduced, but it is unclear how seriously Drabble intends the religious motif to be taken.

Anthony Keating is at the center of attention and in the final section becomes the only important character. He is one of a group of middle-age men and women whose lives have been disrupted by financial and social upheavals. Anthony became involved in real estate speculation after finding several other careers boring. For a while, he and his partners were surprisingly successful, but an economic slump has hit them hard. Anthony has had a mild heart attack and is trying to recover, while wondering whether he is about to become bankrupt. His friend Max Friedmann has been killed by a bomb thrown into a London restaurant by the IRA (Irish Republican Army); Max's wife Kitty lost a foot in the incident and is trying to pretend that nothing bad happened. Anthony's lover, Alison Murray, is a onetime star actress who left the stage to look after her second daughter, Molly, born with cerebral palsy and somewhat retarded. Now Alison is desperately unhappy in the Iron Curtain country of Wallacia, where her disaffected daughter Jane is to be tried for vehicular homicide. Anthony looks after Molly. Len Wincobank, a very successful if piratical developer, crossed the legal lines and is in prison. His lover, Maureen Kirby, finds a new employer, who will become her new lover. Giles Peters, who got Anthony into the real estate business, is desperately looking for a way to salvage their investments.

The problems of these characters represent the problems of a sick and depressed society. The malaise is more spiritual than economic, for when better things begin to happen to at least some of the characters, they cannot believe in their good fortune and become even more depressed. When Alison returns to England from the dingy totalitarianism of Wallacia, she is extremely disappointed at what she finds and goes into a deep depression. Anthony's financial fortunes take a turn for the better, and he becomes solvent again, but he knows his good fortune cannot last, and it does not.

At the beginning of the third and final part of *The Ice Age*, Drabble dismisses most of the characters in a single paragraph and turns her attention to Anthony. He and Alison enjoy a brief period of contentment before he is called by a man in the British Foreign Office. Jane Murray, Alison's daughter, may be released from prison, he tells Anthony, but someone must go and get her. Anthony goes, somewhat reluctantly carrying secret messages from the Foreign Office. In Wallacia, Jane is released, and Anthony gets her to the airport, but as they are trying to get to their plane an uprising takes place. At Anthony's urging, Jane runs and is able to board the plane, but Anthony is left behind. After several months, his friends in England learn that he has been sent to prison for six years for espionage. The British ambassador in Wallacia realizes that his captors do not believe that Anthony was a spy; if they did, he would have been shot. Yet he will have to serve his term.

In prison, Anthony begins to write a book about the existence of God and the possibility of faith. In part, this is a reversion to his childhood as the son of a churchman, but it is also the only way in which he can try to understand what has happened to him. When he sees a bird that is far from its natural habitat, he takes it as a sign that he has not been forgotten by God. Recognizing that he believes this because he wants to, he cannot resist hope. Drabble, however, does not end on a hopeful note. Alison, living in England with Molly, has no hope, is neither alive nor dead. The doom-filled final sentence of the book is: "England will recover, but not Alison Murray."

Summary

Margaret Drabble belongs to the school of fiction that believes that novels can accurately depict the realities of life. Her intention is to show individuals trying to fashion satisfactory lives in a society that is or seems to be too often hostile. Her vision grows darker after 1977, but it is likely that her later works will be read as accurate guides to what life was like in the last four decades of the twentieth century.

Bibliography

Creighton, Joanne V. *Margaret Drabble*. London: Methuen, 1985.

Hannay, John. *The Intertextuality of Fate: A Study of Margaret Drabble*. Columbia: University of Missouri Press, 1986.

Moran, Mary Hurley. *Margaret Drabble: Existing Within Structures*. Carbondale: Southern Illinois University Press, 1983.

Packer, Joan Garrett. *Margaret Drabble: An Annotated Bibliography*. New York: Garland, 1988.

Rose, Ellen Cronan, ed. *Critical Essays on Margaret Drabble*. Boston: G. K. Hall, 1985.

_____. *The Novels of Margaret Drabble: Equivocal Figures*. Totowa, N.J.: Barnes & Noble Books, 1980.

Sadler, Lynn Veach. *Margaret Drabble*. Boston: Twayne, 1986.

John M. Muste

JOHN DRYDEN

Born: Aldwinckle, Northamptonshire, England
August 9, 1631
Died: London, England
May 1, 1700

Principal Literary Achievement

The leading literary figure of his day, Dryden elevated satiric poetry to a high art form and established the heroic couplet as the dominant stanza form for English verse.

Biography

John Dryden was born in the village of Aldwinckle, Northamptonshire, England, on August 9, 1631, the fourteenth child of Erasmus and Mary Pickering Dryden. His family were landowners in the area and were identified with the Puritan cause, which Dryden later rejected. Little is known about his childhood, since Dryden was reluctant to record events of his personal life. At about age fifteen, he was enrolled in Westminster School in London, an institution noted for its production of poets and bishops during the seventeenth century. The curriculum stressed not only classical learning but also original poetic composition in Latin and English. Following a thorough grounding in Latin classics under the headmaster, Dr. Richard Busby, he enrolled in Trinity College, Cambridge, completing the B.A. in 1654. After the death of his father brought him a modest income from family lands, he moved to London, where he held a minor clerical position in the government of Oliver Cromwell. Apart from infrequent visits to his native Northamptonshire, London was to be his place of residence for the remainder of his life.

Dryden began his career in literature relatively late, and his initial efforts showed little promise. He produced little poetry of merit before age thirty. An elegy on the death of Oliver Cromwell in 1658 was followed by a congratulatory poem, *Astraea Redux* (1660), on the Restoration of Charles II. Like most Englishmen of his day, Dryden welcomed the return of monarchical rule and fervently hoped that it would put an end to threats of civil disturbance and war that had characterized the Puritan Revolution. Following the Restoration, he determined to devote his life to literature, and in an age when authors had no copyright protection, he turned his attention to drama, which offered the surest rewards for a talented writer. His marriage in 1663 to Lady Elizabeth Howard, sister of the minor dramatist Sir Robert Howard, brought

him a generous dowry. Although the marriage was not entirely happy, Dryden was devoted to his three sons.

During the early 1660's, Dryden wrote a variety of plays, most notably heroic tragedies, which trained him to use the heroic couplet in dialogue. Later, he turned to the popular comedies of manners, tragicomedies, and even operas, which more resembled modern musical comedies than the grand operas of the nineteenth century. Following a precedent established by French poets, he became a literary critic by writing explanatory prefaces for his poems and dramas. In numerous occasional poems, he employed the couplet as an instrument for reasoning in verse.

In 1668, he was appointed poet laureate, a position that he held for twenty years. Although he received a generous annual stipend of two hundred pounds, the position identified him with the monarchy during a time of intense political conflict. During the late 1670's, when events surrounding the Popish Plot posed a threat to Charles II, Dryden turned his talent to political satire on behalf of the king. Initially, he succeeded in influencing a large portion of the public to support the king against the Whig Party. Continuing his efforts on behalf of the monarchy, Dryden translated obscure French prose works that held implied analogies to the political scene in England. Yet after the fall of James II in 1688, Dryden suffered the loss of both his political cause and his position as poet laureate. His declaration in 1686 that he had abandoned the Church of England for the Roman Catholic church increased his alienation. Dryden had seen the development of the two-party system in England and the triumph in 1688 of the parliamentary cause over the monarchy. Basically conservative by temperament, he never wavered in his mistaken belief that the fall of James II spelled ruin for the nation.

During the final decade of his life, Dryden found little success in writing for the theater, but he was able to undertake major translations of Juvenal, Persius, and Vergil, turning their classical Latin verses into popular English heroic couplets. His publisher Jacob Tonson was willing to pay generously for polished translations of major classical authors. He continued writing poems of praise (panegyrics) and verse epistles complimenting the work of younger contemporaries such as the playwright William Congreve. Though out of favor, Dryden was often surrounded by younger poets who admired his achievements. Ironically, some of his best poetry and prose was written during the final period of his life. He died in London on May 1, 1700, and was interred in the Poets' Corner of Westminster Abbey.

Analysis

Dryden experienced one of the most productive and varied literary careers in all of English literature. Sometimes called the first professional man of letters in England, he was motivated by the desire to re-create the classical excellence of Greece and Rome in vernacular literature. He dominated his age as no writer before or since has done, and indeed, the period 1660 to 1700 in English literature is designated by literary historians as the Age of Dryden. In poetry, translation, drama, and literary criticism, he was the leading author of his time. In addition, he produced biographies and anthologies of poetry. His literary career spanned four decades, one of the longest among English authors, and it is marked by a firm sense of literary genre and a lasting regard for classical principles.

Although his earliest productions were poetry, he established a reputation as a dramatist, beginning with the comedy *The Wild Gallant* (1663). His initial dramatic successes were heroic tragedies, highly artificial dramas featuring spectacular scenery, the love-honor hero, extravagant and bombastic speeches, splended costuming, and often exotic settings. They were written in heroic couplets, a pair of rhymed verses in iambic pentameter, a medium inspired by French rhymed tragedies. This dramatic genre, which endured into the 1670's, is seen at its best in Dryden's *The Indian Emperor: Or, The Conquest of Mexico by the Spaniards* (1665) and *The Conquest of Granada by the Spaniards, Parts I* and *II* (1670-1671). By the time Dryden wrote his most famous tragedy, *All for Love: Or, The World Well Lost* (1677), he had abandoned heroic couplets in favor of blank verse, the verse form used in most of his dramas after 1675. Dryden's efforts at comedy were mixed, for he was inclined to stress the licentious elements of the comedy of manners in plays such as *The Assignation: Or, Love in a Nunnery* (1672) and *The Kind Keeper: Or, Mr. Limberham* (1678). Yet one finds the sparkling wit of a comedy such as *Marriage à la Mode* (1672) comparable to that of more gifted contemporaries in the genre, such as Sir George Etherege and William Wycherley.

Despite their musical scores by Henry Purcell, Dryden's operas were not notably successful, yet his tragicomedies have drawn the admiration of critics. Among them, *Don Sebastian, King of Portugal* (1689) is highly regarded for its portrayal of characters and emotion and for its excellent blank verse.

As a literary critic, Dryden stands as one of the most important in English literature. Most of his essays are occasional; that is, they are attached to other works as prefaces or appendices. An important exception is *An Essay of Dramatic Poesy* (1668), Dryden's general assessment of the drama. The first systematic critic in English, he is a moderate neoclassicist. As a critic, Dryden attempts to explain the individual work and place it within the proper genre. He is noteworthy for defining important critical terms and genres, and his definitions of terms such as "wit," "drama," "satire," and "biography" are thoughtful and worthy of study. In addition to informing the reader about his own practices, Dryden includes responses to his detractors and opponents. His work is in large measure an outgrowth of the numerous critical controversies in which he engaged. Among these were the controversy with Thomas Shadwell over the nature of comedy, with numerous others over the use of heroic couplets in drama, with Thomas Rymer over the nature of tragedy, and with Jeremy Collier over the dramatist's ethical responsibility. These controversies helped shape his own critical views, which varied over his career.

In approaching an analysis, Dryden sought to ascertain the proper rules for the production of the type, a standard procedure with a neoclassic critic. Where rules and theories did not exist, he sought to discover and elucidate them. Turning to translation late in his career, Dryden developed his own theory, according the translator three approaches: metaphrase, paraphrase, and imitation. Metaphrase, or literal translation, he considered too limiting if translation is to be considered an art. Paraphrase, which Dryden preferred, permitted the poet to expand or contract the original passages and to modernize the use of names and allusions. The third, imitation, was only a loose rendition of the original, following its theme and organization. Dryden's ideal demanded that a translator replicate the poetic effects of the original for a modern audience of a different nation.

Since his theoretical approach was often ad hoc, Dryden maintains little consistency in his specific critical opinions; his consistency lies in his broadly neoclassic perspective. He is neither a rigid neoclassicist nor a slavish follower of precedent. For example, he argues that genius sometimes transcends the rules of art and produces superior aesthetic effects by violating the rules; he thus accepts the principle of poetic license. He points out how earlier geniuses such as William Shakespeare violated rules such as the classical unities and yet succeeded in drama, an indication that rules are not absolute.

The most significant passages from Dryden's critical works are those that record his judgments of other writers, for he possessed a keen appreciation for the merits of others and an unerring ability to discern them. His descriptions of the works of British authors, such as William Shakespeare, Ben Jonson, Francis Beaumont and John Fletcher, Geoffrey Chaucer, and Edmund Spenser, to name a few, are insightful and penetrating, and the list can be extended to include classical writers such as Homer, Ovid, Juvenal, Horace, and Vergil, among others. Some of the most important passages of this kind are to be found in *An Essay of Dramatic Poesy*, *A Discourse Concerning the Original and Progress of Satire* (1693), and "Preface to *The Fables*" (1700). Not only did he identify the great writers of his own nation; he also incorporated within his writings the basic concepts of English literary history, tracing the origin and development of a national literature.

Paradoxically, the most important feature of Dryden's criticism may be his supple, graceful, and idiomatic prose style. Dryden expressed his critical opinions in an elegant and fluent style that has marked him as a master of English prose.

Today, Dryden is most often remembered for his poetry. He produced more than two hundred poems in English, and for every original verse he wrote two others of translation. A poet of extraordinary versatility, Dryden employs numerous genres: odes, elegies, epigrams, panegyrics, prologues and epilogues, satires, verse epistles, and verse essays. His original poetry is often occasional—directed toward public events and prominent people of his own time—so that it mirrors upper-class English life of the late seventeenth century. In his panegyrics and verse epistles, he complimented important public figures of his time, often in an egregiously flattering tone. His satires and lyrics are rich in topical allusions relating to events of his day. Sometimes called journalistic, Dryden's poetry is also ratiocinative and argumentative, as if anticipating the Age of Reason. A master of reasoning in verse, he is better known for his epigrammatic wit and humor than for his portrayal of deep human emotions.

In addition to replicating classical poetic genres in English, Dryden established the heroic couplet as the dominant poetic form in England. While he wrote in a variety of meters, the rhymed iambic pentameter couplet is most frequent. Dryden polished the couplet by following grammatical order insofar as possible and by making the couplet a closed form, that is, normally having a full stop to conclude the second line. The heroic couplet proved an effective vehicle for developing reasoned discourse, for pointed epigrammatic wit, and for elegant, emphatic expression of ideas. Its major defects are that its polish seems artificial, notably in dialogue, and the stanza form calls attention to itself, inviting the reader to lose sight of the poem's organization. After dominating English literature for a century, the heroic couplet gave way to less rigid and restrictive verse forms.

AN ESSAY OF DRAMATIC POESY

First published: 1668
Type of work: Literary criticism

The rules of classical drama, while sound guides, may be ignored by modern writers if compensatory merits can be achieved.

An Essay of Dramatic Poesy, Dryden's only major critical essay to be published independently of any other work, is technically a Socratic dialogue introducing four characters, each with a different view of drama. Crites, who allegorically represents Dryden's brother-in-law Sir Robert Howard, defends the rules and practices of classical Greek and Roman dramatists. Lisideius, representing Sir Charles Sedley, defends the French neoclassic dramatists of the seventeenth century as most worthy of emulation. Eugenius, representing Charles Sackville, supports Elizabethan dramatists— William Shakespeare and Ben Jonson—as superior to all others. Neander, representing Dryden himself, suggests that the contemporary Restoration dramatists have in some ways surpassed the achievement of their predecessors. Each speaker in turn examines the qualities of plot, characterization, important themes, style, and diction in dramas of his chosen period. The word "essay" in the title suggests the tentative nature of Dryden's discourse, and throughout the speakers maintain a rational tone.

The discourse introduces the dichotomous approach frequently found in Dryden's poetry and prose, with terms juxtaposed and explored. This device is best demonstrated in Lisideius' definition of a play: "A just and lively image of human nature, representing its passions and humours, and the changes of fortune to which it is subject, for the delight and instruction of mankind." Contrastive terms such as "passion" (emotion) and "humour" (wit and eccentricity), "delight and instruction," and "just and lively" are hallmarks of neoclassic criticism. Dryden extends them to include contrastive authors such as Homer and Vergil, Shakespeare and Jonson.

Since Neander is the last to speak, the major emphasis of *An Essay of Dramatic Poesy* falls to his portion, and Dryden intends his points of view to prevail. Neander pays eloquent tribute to the genius of Shakespeare and Jonson, praising them as the two English predecessors who bear comparison with the ancient dramatists. Yet he defends contemporary drama by arguing that it depicts better manners than those of Elizabethan drama and that it has the added beauty of rhyme. In a lengthy analysis, Neander explains why rhyme should be considered superior to blank verse. The position on rhyme exposes both the tentative nature of *An Essay of Dramatic Poesy* and Dryden's tendency toward inconsistency in his critical opinions, for within less than a decade he reversed this position.

MARRIAGE À LA MODE

First produced: 1672 (first published, 1673)
Type of work: Play

The theme of rightful succession is developed through two plots centering on love—one an idealized version, the other sophisticated and cynical.

Dryden's most successful comedy, *Marriage à la Mode*, combines within its two distinct plots the conventions of romantic tragicomedy and the Restoration comedy of manners, a genre not fully developed when he produced his play. The tragicomic plot develops the theme of succession to the throne, perhaps Dryden's most important dramatic theme after the love-honor conflict. Having usurped the Sicilian throne, Polydamas discovers two young persons of gentle birth who have been living rustic lives under the care of Hermogenes, a former courtier. Hermogenes assures the usurper that one of them is his son Leonidas, though Leonidas is in reality the son of the king whom he had deposed. When Polydamas orders him to marry the daughter of his friend, Leonidas refuses, protesting his love for Palmyra, his companion under Hermogenes' care. When Polydamas seeks to banish her, Hermogenes identifies her as the king's daughter and claims Leonidas as his own son. Polydamas then seeks to force Palmyra to marry his friend Argaleon and banishes Leonidas under sentence of death. Faced with death, Leonidas wins over the tyrant's supporters, removes him from the throne, and pardons him as the father of his beloved Palmyra.

In the plot, the main elements of tragicomedy are prominent: the remote setting, the tyrannical usurper, the long-lost noble youth, the faithful servant, and idealized romantic love. Dryden's early debt to the tragicomedies of John Fletcher is apparent in his use of stock characters and situations.

In the subplot, the love theme reflects the cynicism of the comedy of manners. Two witty couples—Rhodophil and Doralice, Palamede and Melantha—express sophisticated and detached attitudes toward love and marriage. Before his marriage to Melantha, Palamede hopes to engage in an affair with Doralice, his friend Rhodophil's wife, while Rhodophil, disenchanted with marriage, seeks to make Melantha his mistress. Like characters of the comedy of manners, they satirize the Puritans, country folk, and romantic love. Love is to them merely a game of conquest. Disguises, masked balls, and assignations enliven the plot while witty repartee sparkles throughout the dialogue. The would-be rakes never realize their romantic goals because their plans go awry, and they remain friends at the end.

Though the two plots are loosely connected, both Rhodophil and Palamede support the right of Leonidas to the throne at the conclusion. Also, both plot lines reject the authority of parents to select the spouses of their children. For the most part, however, the two plots exist in separate worlds: the witty, sophisticated, urban milieu of the comedy of manners and the idealistic, sentimental world of the tragicomedy.

ABSALOM AND ACHITOPHEL

First published: 1681
Type of work: Poem

Political strife jeopardizes rights and long-established precedents, representing a threat to the nation.

Dryden's political satire *Absalom and Achitophel* reflects upon politics in England during the era of the Popish Plot (1679-1681), when the Whig Party, under the leadership of the earl of Shaftesbury, sought to prevent the legitimate succession of James, duke of York, because of his Catholicism. The Whigs supported a parliamentary bill that would have placed the illegitimate son of Charles II, James, Duke of Monmouth, on the throne. Alarmed by efforts to tamper with established monarchical power, Dryden employs the biblical revolt against David by his son Absalom as a parallel narrative to discredit the Whig cause.

The poem represents a mixed, or Varronian, kind of satire, for satiric passages exist alongside straightforward normative portions. The plot is both loose and inconclusive, the satiric elements being confined to the poem's first major section. Dryden narrates the origin and development of the supposed plot, which the Whigs had concocted to discredit the king's position. Each prominent Whig leader is the subject of an extended poetic character, ridiculing him as extremist and undermining his reputation. Though biblical names are used, readers of the time clearly recognized each object of Dryden's satiric thrusts. The efforts of Achitophel to tempt Absalom are partially successful. In the second section, Dryden outlines his theory of government, advocating established rights and powers and rejecting innovation. A second series of characters praises the king's supporters in Parliament, and the poem concludes with a speech by King David (Charles II) upholding his traditional rights, offering conciliation, but also indicating firmness.

In the poetic characters, Dryden's artistic skill is at its best. Using witty aphorisms and the stylistic conventions of the couplet—such as balance, antithesis, and chiasmus—Dryden succeeds in discrediting Whig leaders.

MAC FLECKNOE

First published: 1682
Type of work: Poem

An attack on false literary standards and poor literary achievement serves to advance desirable literary ideals.

Mac Flecknoe, a literary satire, employs the mock epic form to assail bad poets and poetry, represented by its victim, the dramatist Thomas Shadwell. Dryden establishes true literary norms through attacking inferior ones. The date of composition and occasion for the satire are uncertain, but it is generally thought that composition followed the death of Richard Flecknoe (c. 1678), an obscure poetaster. After the brief introduction, the satire introduces Flecknoe as a speaker deliberating his choice of a successor to the throne of Nonsense. Through the use of the convention of a mock coronation, Dryden gives the poem a narrative structure, a reflection of his view that satire is rightly a form of heroic (epic) poetry.

The introduction is a masterful passage combining irony and mock solemnity, contrasting the seriousness of succession with a throne epitomizing dullness. Sober aphorisms and allusions to Augustan Rome are deflated by allusions to the realm of Nonsense. Flecknoe selects Shadwell as the most fitting of all of his sons to occupy the throne of Nonsense and uphold dullness. Dryden incorporates numerous references to Shadwell's life and allusions to his dramas, with Flecknoe concluding: "All arguments, but most his plays persuade,/ That for anointed dulness he was made." Flecknoe chooses as the coronation site a run-down section of London near the Barbican, associated with inferior poets. The poem then describes the coronation, complete with procession, satiric description of Shadwell, the paraphernalia of office, and cheers of the assembled throng of hack writers and booksellers. Flecknoe urges his successor to find new ways to be dull, but to avoid boastful comparisons of himself with Ben Jonson and John Fletcher. Suggesting that Shadwell has been unsuccessful in all major literary genres, Flecknoe exhorts him to confine his talents to acrostics, pattern poems, and songs that can be sung to the lute. At the conclusion, as Flecknoe falls through a trap door, his mantle is borne aloft to settle on Shadwell.

The satire enables Dryden to develop at length one of his most congenial concepts, that of regal succession, though it gives an ironic twist to a theme that is usually serious. Monarchical allusions such as those to Augustan Rome, a distant ideal, serve to enhance the withering satire. Shadwell is ironically endowed with the name of a Roman successor, and Flecknoe is compared to Augustus Caesar, ironic elevations of the trivial that are characteristic of high burlesque. In the realm of literary succession, names of great dramatists and poets are used to deflate the pretensions of obscure poetasters, as in a passage describing the coronation site:

Great Fletcher never treads in buskins here,
Nor greater Jonson dares in socks appear;
But gentle Simkin just reception finds
Amidst this monument of vanish'd minds:
Pure clinches the suburbian Muse affords,
And Panton waging harmless war with words.

The major genres, such as Jonsonian comedy and the tragicomedies of John Fletcher, give way to punning and inferior wordplay as forms of entertainment. While the poem upholds important neoclassic principles, the overarching framework emerges from its narrative structure and from recurrent patterns of contrast: wit and dullness; sense and nonsense.

What provoked Dryden's mock attack on his literary rival remains unclear. As a poet, Shadwell produced only crude and inferior verses, but critics have found merit in his comedies, modeled after the comedies of humor produced by Jonson. Except for serious students of the period, they are now forgotten, and for most students of literature Shadwell's name survives through Dryden's satiric masterpiece.

TO MY DEAR FRIEND MR. CONGREVE

First published: 1694
Type of work: Poem

For his literary achievement at an early age, William Congreve is celebrated as a true successor to the throne of wit.

Although "To My Dear Friend Mr. Congreve, On His Comedy Call'd *The Double Dealer*" is formally a verse epistle, it is representative also of Dryden's numerous panegyrics, or poems of praise. Written during his final decade, it demonstrates his inclination to praise younger contemporaries and reflects Dryden's mastery of the heroic couplet. Readily divided into two sections, the epistle employs two of Dryden's most important poetic conventions: the conservative metaphor of the temple and the concept of succession, in this poem applied to the kingdom of letters.

In the first part, the poem praises Congreve by placing him within the context of English literary history. While Dryden grants the Elizabethan dramatists transcendent genius, he views their dramas as irregular and crude. The second great period of drama, the early Restoration, brought polish and refinement to the drama, or, in Dryden's words, better manners, yet this improvement had its price:

Our age was cultivated thus at length,
But what we gain'd in skill we lost in strength.
Our builders were with want of genius cursed;
The second temple was not like the first.

The elegant balance and aphoristic expression of the passage are succeeded by a bold chiasmus and further development of the temple metaphor, celebrating the achievement of a dramatist one generation younger than Dryden:

> Till you, the best Vitruvius, come at length;
> Our beauties equal, but excel our strength.
> Firm Doric pillars found your solid base;
> The fair Corinthian crowns the higher space:
> Thus all below is strength, and all above is grace.

Dryden endows the younger Congreve with the wit and genius of the Elizabethans and the polish and refinement of the Restoration dramatists. The comparison to the Roman architect Vitruvius is followed by another to the youthful Roman general Scipio Africanus to emphasize Congreve's early achievement.

Before renewing the panegyric in the poem's second part, Dryden becomes personal and speaks of his own career. Typically, he writes about himself with restraint; the numerous autobiographical passages in Dryden's poetry and prose reveal more about his reactions to events and less about the events themselves. In writing of himself, he couches his experience within the mythic context of literary succession; having been poet laureate, he had occupied a throne of letters. Writing of his loss of the laureateship, Dryden asserts that he could have been content had the office gone to Congreve. Instead, it went to his old enemy Thomas Shadwell. Despite this anomaly, he continues, Congreve's merits will elevate him to a throne in the kingdom of letters. Comparing Congreve with Shakespeare, he predicts a long and illustrious career for the youthful dramatist. Dryden, like a deposed monarch, recognizes that his own career is drawing to its close and asks Congreve to defend his memory against attacks that are certain to follow after his death.

The poem stands as an example of Dryden's generous praise, couched within a mythic context of his own invention. Ironically, Congreve retired from playwriting in 1700, and while his brilliant comedies remain alive today, his dramatic range was limited to the comedy of manners. He lived to fulfill Dryden's request, leaving a poignant memoir of the poet as a preface to the 1717 edition of Dryden's dramas.

ALEXANDER'S FEAST

First published: 1697
Type of work: Poem

Musical performances can so move the emotions, even of heroic individuals, that such individuals are influenced to undertake specific actions.

Alexander's Feast is Dryden's second ode honoring Saint Cecilia, the patron saint of music, and its theme, the power of music to move human emotions, is identical with that of "A Song for St. Cecilia's Day," written a decade earlier. Both odes are occasional, having been composed at the invitation of the London Musical Society. The second ode, however, is much more elaborate, for Dryden introduces characters and places them within a dramatic setting. The Greeks are celebrating their victory over the Persian King Darius, when the musician at the banquet, Timotheus, is called upon to perform.

With exalted strains, he creates within Alexander the Great a sense that he has become a deity. An alteration of tone changes his mood to a desire for pleasure, and following this a longing for love of his mistress Thaïs, who sits beside him. Somber strains evoke pity for the fallen Darius, but these are followed by strident tones calling for revenge on behalf of Greek soldiers who have perished. Alexander and his mistress and their company rush out, torches in hand, to burn the Persian city Persepolis. The poem concludes with a grand chorus, stressing the power of music to move emotions and contrasting the legend of Saint Cecilia with the power of Timotheus. Dryden recalls the story that after she had invented the organ, she played such beautiful music that an angel, mistaking the sounds for those of heaven, appeared as she played:

> Let old Timotheus yield the prize,
> Or both divide the crown:
> He rais'd a mortal to the skies;
> She drew an angel down.

The intricate form resembles the Pindaric ode in its lengthy and complicated irregular stanzas, yet its linear organization follows the tradition of Horace. Dryden achieves a complex, forceful, and energetic movement, and his use of historical events and characters contributes to a lively, dramatic expression of his theme.

Summary

John Dryden's amazingly varied literary production adapted the classical poetic genres to the England of his day. He sought to enrich the national literature and to serve as an instructor of manners and morals for his society. His appeal is primarily to reason, not to emotion.

His classical sense of polish enabled him to perfect the heroic couplet and make it the dominant verse form in English. His prose remains a model of lucid, idiomatic, and graceful writing.

Bibliography

Hoffman, Arthur. *John Dryden's Imagery.* Gainesville: University of Florida Press, 1962.

Hume, Robert D. *Dryden's Criticism.* Ithaca, N.Y.: Cornell University Press, 1970.

King, Bruce. *Dryden's Heroic Drama.* Princeton, N.J.: Princeton University Press, 1965.

McFadden, George. *Dryden: The Public Writer, 1660-1685*. Princeton, N.J.: Princeton University Press, 1978.

Miner, Earl. *Dryden's Poetry*. Bloomington: Indiana University Press, 1967.

Ramsey, Paul. *The Art of John Dryden*. Lexington: University Press of Kentucky, 1969.

Roper, Alan. *Dryden's Poetic Kingdoms*. London: Routledge & Kegan Paul, 1965.

Van Doren, Mark. *The Poetry of John Dryden*. New York: Harcourt Brace, 1921.

Ward, Charles E. *The Life of John Dryden*. Chapel Hill: University of North Carolina Press, 1961.

Winn, James A. *John Dryden and His World*. New Haven, Conn.: Yale University Press, 1987.

Stanley Archer

GEORGE ELIOT

Born: Chilvers Coton, Warwickshire, England
November 22, 1819
Died: London, England
December 22, 1880

Principal Literary Achievement

As an author who wrote in many different genres, Eliot is remembered primarily for her novels of social and psychological realism.

Biography

Mary Ann Evans was born on November 22, 1819, in Chilvers Coton, Warwickshire, England. (She changed her name in 1857 to George Eliot.) During her infancy, the family moved to Griff House, also on the seven-thousand-acre Arbury Estate near Coventry, which Robert Evans, Mary Ann's father, managed for the Newdigate family. Her mother's name was Christina Pearson. It was in this large, old farmhouse, with its wide lawns and mature trees, surrounded by fields, farmhouses, canals, and coach roads, that Mary Ann lived until she was twenty, gathering impressions that form much of the landscape of her fiction. She roamed the meadows with her brother Isaac and toured the estate with her father, waiting in farmhouse kitchens or the housekeeper's quarters of Arbury Hall or Astley Castle while her father conducted his business, and developing that sensitivity toward all social classes that informs her work. Persons, images, and events from these early years color her mature writing, notably *Scenes of Clerical Life* (1858), *Adam Bede* (1859), *The Mill on the Floss* (1860), *Silas Marner* (1861), *Middlemarch* (1871-1872), and the "Brother and Sister" sonnets (1874).

Besides her father and brother, a major influence on young Evans was Maria Lewis, a teacher at a boarding school Mary Ann attended during her ninth to thirteenth years. Miss Lewis' ardent evangelicalism appealed to her after the Evans family's attendance at "high and dry" Anglican services, unmarked by "enthusiastic" fervor or nineteenth century doctrinal questionings. (Long after she ceased to regard biblical writing as literally true, George Eliot created fictional contrasts between the less personal, old-fashioned religion of her father and the moral energy that she had experienced with evangelicalism.) At thirteen, she transferred to a Coventry school, where she learned drawing, painting, history, arithmetic, and etiquette; she cultivated English speech, excelling in French, music, and English composition. Her letters to

Miss Lewis indicate a religious austerity, and critic Gordon Haight finds evidence of a religious conversion within the evangelical party of the Church of England when she was fifteen.

After her mother's death in 1836, Evans became her father's housekeeper. Robert Evans left Griff House to Isaac and moved with Mary Ann to Bird Grove, a house just outside Coventry, where the intellectual leaders welcomed his mentally cultivated daughter. She became close friends with Charles and Cara Bray, sister of Charles Hennell, whose *Inquiry into the Origins of Christianity* (1838) had just appeared in a second edition. Evans' scientific reading had already weakened her earlier convictions; the emotional support of her new "free-thinking" friends influenced her to complete the break with Scripture-based Christianity and to undertake her first serious publication, *The Life of Jesus Critically Examined* (1846), a three-volume translation of David Friedrich Strauss's *Das Leben Jesu* (1835-1836). The fifteen hundred pages of German, with Latin, Greek, and Hebrew quotations, posed a two-year translation task. Published in 1846 without the translator's name, it was a major influence on the nineteenth century "crisis of faith" and identified Evans, for those who inquired, with the Higher Criticism, the scholarly examination of Scripture for its historical credibility.

Preoccupied with nursing her father until his death in 1849, Evans continued her reading, finding Jean-Jacques Rousseau and George Sand her favorite authors, and began translating Benedictus de Spinoza's *Tractatus Theologico-Politicus* (1670), which she never published. After Robert Evans died, the Brays took her to France and Italy, leaving her to spend the fall and winter in Geneva among political refugees from continental revolutions. She lived with the family of an artist, François D'Albert Durade, who painted her portrait, later translated some of her fiction, and became her lifelong friend. She enjoyed music, theater, mixing with celebrities, and making notes for fiction to come.

Returning to Coventry in 1850, Evans was asked to write for and help edit John Chapman's *Westminster Review*, the leading progressive quarterly in London. She was its de facto editor from 1851 to 1854, although Chapman received public acknowledgement. Through him, she continued to meet leading intellectual figures, among them Herbert Spencer and George Henry Lewes. Attracted at first to Spencer, she found Lewes to be the more enduring friend. Because Lewes had condoned the adultery of his wife Agnes, he was not permitted under English law to divorce her, but the marriage had clearly failed. He and Evans committed themselves to each other and lived together openly until his death in 1878, the royalties from her books continuing to support Agnes and her children.

In 1854, Chapman published Evans' translation of Ludwig Feuerbach's *Das Wesen des Christentums* (1841) as *The Essence of Christianity* (1854), and she left with Lewes for Germany to help with his biography of Johann Wolfgang von Goethe. On their return, he used his standing as essayist and reviewer to submit her early fiction without identifying her to the publisher John Blackwood. By the time that her identity was revealed, after *Adam Bede*'s publication, readers who objected to Evans' unconventional life could not take back their praise for George Eliot's fiction.

Virginia Woolf's view that the union with Lewes freed Eliot's creativity is supported by the record. With his encouragement and protection of her sensitivity to public criticism, she wrote her way past scandal and social ostracism into the hearts of her readers until many of the socially great, including royalty, sought her company. When Lewes died, after twenty-four years of devotion to her, she isolated herself for three months, despite pleas from friends, and completed the book he had begun.

In May, 1880, Eliot married John Walter Cross, twenty years her junior but a loving friend she and Lewes had known for several years. The marriage, though brief, was happy. She died in London on December 22, 1880, and is buried in Highgate Cemetery, London, near Lewes, the corners of the plots touching at one point.

Analysis

In a series of 1856 essays for the *Westminster Review*, George Eliot (the name she sent to Blackwood in 1857) formulates the theories of literary art that would shape the fiction she began writing in September of that year. Revealing the influence of Honoré de Balzac and French criticism, she explains "realism," a relatively new aesthetic concept to her English audience. The context is her praise for John Ruskin's *Modern Painters* (1843); it teaches "the truth of infinite value," or "realism—the doctrine that all truth and beauty" lie in art that represents "definite, substantial reality," not "vague forms, bred by imagination on the mists of feeling." She was to write instead of the "truth of feeling, as the only universal bond of union" between people. Although her contemporaries and later readers have been awed by her manifest intellectual depth and breadth, she considered what was "essentially human" far more important than cerebral analysis: "If Art does not enlarge men's sympathies, it does nothing morally."

Because Eliot believed that strife among people derived from lack of understanding of "what is apart from themselves," she defined the "sacred" task of the artist as awakening in self-enclosed people a knowledgeable, sympathetic understanding of "the perennial joys and struggles, the toil, the tragedy, and the humour" in the lives of others, particularly the laborers and artisans being misrepresented by writers who had not lived among them. For Eliot, all people of whatever social class were "struggling erring human creatures." Her purpose was not to argue the causes that made nineteenth century intellectual life controversial but to inform and cultivate her readers' moral imaginations away from self-centeredness and toward sympathy for others.

In an essay panning the falseness of those who would promote evangelical spirituality yet retain a fascination with the wealthy aristocracy, Eliot declared that the "real drama of Evangelicalism" lay "among the middle and lower classes," among those such as the farmers she had known on the Arbury Estate and the congregation she had met when attending chapel with Maria Lewis. She returned to the rural scenes and experiences of her youth for her first three books.

The three stories that constitute *Scenes of Clerical Life*—"The Sad Fortunes of the Reverend Amos Baron," "Mr. Gilfil's Love-Story," and "Janet's Repentance"—

were published serially in *Blackwood's Magazine* in 1857, then as a two-volume book in 1858. Stories of clerics, or churchmen, were popular at the time, but many were poor examples of literary art, because the authors idealized their characters into unreal, romantic heroes and made them spokespersons for partisan views in the doctrinal controversies of the mid-nineteenth century. Eliot's stories are about three quite different country parsons, fictional eleborations of actual people she had known. Her purpose is not to expound doctrine, however, but to show the relative effectiveness of each, according to his capacity for interpersonal sympathy. A subtler purpose, unrecognized by many readers in an age that accepted the subjection of women as natural and right, is to win sympathy for the sufferings of women, which have been caused by an insensitive and judgmental community, a too-rigid social caste system, the lack of economic opportunity, or a negligent—even brutal—husband.

Wanting to portray sympathetic characters with psychological realism despite her publisher's wish for heroes and heroines that were models of morally acceptable behavior, Eliot turned to the expanded form of the novel for her next book, *Adam Bede*, which became a best-seller before the year was over. She continued her success with *The Mill on the Floss*, the last of her early works based on the rural Midlands, and the most autobiographical. The Tulliver children, judgmental Tom and hoyden Maggie, are fictional variations on Isaac and Mary Ann Evans; The Dodson family's allegiance to custom-bound "respectability" reflects attitudes of the Pearsons, the author's mother's family. Maggie is Eliot's first major heroine, of several, who grow from an unconscious egoism to an awareness of another. She is also a tragic heroine developed by the classical formula: "a character essentially noble but liable to great error—error that is anguish to its own nobleness."

Romola (1862-1863), which Eliot interrupted to write *Silas Marner*, is among the least read of Eliot's books, but it was well received by the leading minds among her contemporaries, Henry James proclaiming it the "finest thing she wrote." Set in fifteenth century Florence, it develops the heroine from dependency and subjection to moral and spiritual autonomy and shows the author's increasing skill with mythic narrative techniques.

Felix Holt, the Radical (1866) repeats Eliot's theme of past influencing present, but presents the heroine, Esther Lyon, with a choice between entrapment in the tyranny of the past and the moral freedom of continuing to choose her commitments, a theme with added variations in *Middlemarch* and *Daniel Deronda* (1876). Her "political novel" is Eliot's first fully developed treatment of relatively contemporary England, but her imagery of entrapment is drawn from Dante Alighieri's description of hell. Set at the time of the first Reform Bill (1832), the novel's political part concerns issues current with the Reform Bill of 1867. Eliot favors a slow, organic cultural development, similar to Matthew Arnold's ideas, over political solutions attempted by legislation. The importance of sexual awareness, honesty, energy, and their intelligent commitment—always a theme in Eliot's work—receives more detailed treatment than in the first five books. Consequences of ill-considered sexual choices are seen not primarily as social disapprobation, but as the fugitive self-enclosure of Mrs. Transome, another tragic heroine as classically defined.

In the novel's more complex treatment of its milieu, the organic inclusion of the past in the present, and Esther's choice between creative or destructive acceptance of that past, *Felix Holt, the Radical* reveals the confidence of an established writer and anticipates the fuller treatment of similar ideas in *Middlemarch* and *Daniel Deronda*.

ADAM BEDE

First published: 1859
Type of work: Novel

As self-deception brings tragic consequences for Arthur, a young squire, and Hetty, a dairy maid, Adam, through suffering, learns tolerance for weakness.

In *Adam Bede*, Eliot again represents the humor and wit of the lower classes through their rural dialect and idiom, a skill that had captivated readers of "Amos Barton" and helped to establish her as a writer of humor, pathos, and social realism. Where the earlier work had divided such wit between a few characters and the narrator, however, the novel concentrates it in Mrs. Poyser, master of the colorful maxim, and leaves the narrator more distant than in the earlier story. Eliot interrupts the narrative, nevertheless, to instruct the reader in the aesthetic rules of realism. The well-known chapter 17 is often quoted as Eliot's artistic creed, favoring truthfulness over idealism, exhorting the reader to find beauty in "old women scraping carrots with their work-worn hands" as well as in "a face paled by the celestial light," and urging the reader to "tolerate, pity, and love" his "more or less ugly, stupid, inconsistent" fellow mortals.

For the germ of her story, Eliot recalled an episode recounted during her youth by her Methodist Aunt Samuel, who had visited in prison a young woman condemned to execution for the murder of her child, and who had wrought from her a penitential confession after the failure of others to do so. The novel goes far beyond the historical event, however, rendering it as art by the detailed fictional creation of Hetty Sorrel as childishly and unconsciously self-engrossed, hardly capable of any moral awareness that her acts could bring significant consequences, hardly able to distinguish fantasy from reality.

In a design of paired opposites found also in her other fiction, Eliot sharpens the delineation of Hetty's character by contrasting her with the selfless Dinah Morris, the young Methodist open-air preacher. Similarly, Eliot contrasts the title character, a village carpenter, to Arthur Donnithorne, heir to the estate and future landlord of the Hayslope community. They are compared primarily by their respective ways of expressing their love for Hetty, who is expected to marry Adam but whose aspirations to luxury and fashionable adornments make her susceptible to Arthur's admiring eye, as her fantasies enable him to seduce her, although he knows quite well that a young man of his class cannot marry a working girl.

Hetty's recognition of her limitations and errors is so slim that she can hardly be called a tragic character. Adam is the primary sufferer, since his love for Hetty has been genuine, if blind. Narrow and inflexible in his rectitude, he learns through his suffering to be more tolerant of weakness and, with his new "power of loving," to give and receive sympathy in the shared condition of fallibility. His moral growth is slow, in keeping with Eliot's psychological realism, but he softens in his judgment of others and awakens to the realization that Dinah, though not at all kittenish like Hetty, has her form of appeal too. In turn, Dinah reconsiders her resolution to follow an ascetic life, rechannels her ministering love in interpersonal directions, and comes to return Adam's love for her.

The misogynistic Bartle Massey claims his place in the community as he brings food and wine to the suffering Adam in an "upper room," one of the story's Christian images. Mr. Irwine, in his failure to sense Arthur's need for confession, is one of Eliot's recurrent churchmen who appear benevolent but prove ineffective.

Arthur, whose expected responsible leadership has represented hope to the community, can only leave Hayslope in shame. His departure signals the end of that older world, as the narrator regrets the loss of "Fine Old Leisure," but the novel ends optimistically, centered on Adam, Dinah, and their children.

SILAS MARNER

First published: 1861
Type of work: Novel

In a village of fairy-tale remoteness, a wronged and therefore bitter miser is redeemed, reborn, and restored to human fellowship through unselfish love.

In *Silas Marner*, George Eliot achieved some of her most successful symbolic narrative, a method that has been compared to Nathaniel Hawthorne's definition of "romance" with reference to this story. In this novel, Eliot's pervasive theme of spiritual renewal through the influence of human love and communal fellowship is embodied, as elsewhere, in realistic events, drama, and dialogue, with currents of symbolic meanings that suggest a mythic structure of concrete universals. Eliot called the story a "legendary tale" with a "realistic treatment."

The theme of spiritual rebirth is announced in chapter 1 by reference to Marner as "a dead man come to life again" and to his "inward life" as a "metamorphosis." The resolution is foreshadowed in the description of his catalepsy as "a mysterious rigidity and suspension of consciousness" that his former religious community has "mistaken for death." The rigidity of despair has driven him from his former home in a northern industrial city, the dimly lit Lantern Yard, where members of his "narrow religious sect" have believed him guilty of stealing church funds in the keeping of a dying man. Marner has been so stunned at being framed by the man he thought was his best friend, at being renounced by his fiancée, who soon married the guilty man, and at being believed guilty by his community, that he could only flee. Because he had believed that God would defend his innocence, he has felt utterly abandoned in his faith and has declared "there is no just God."

He chances among strangers in the isolated village of Raveloe and for fifteen years remains an alien at its fringes, immersed in his work as a linen weaver like "a spinning insect," loving only the gold he earns and hoards, with ties to neither past nor present. When his gold is stolen as the Christmas season begins, Marner announces his loss at the Rainbow (promise of hope) Tavern and, like Job, begins to receive "comforters," an interaction that slowly renews human feeling and consciousness of dependency. On New Year's Eve, as Marner longs for the return of his gold, he finds on his hearth instead a sleeping, golden-haired toddler, a baby girl who has wandered in while Marner held his door open during one of his cataleptic trances, leaving her laudanum-stupefied mother unconscious in the snow-filled lane. Marner can only think that "the gold had turned into the child," but then seeks the mother, goes for the authorities, and learns that the woman is dead.

Marner clings urgently to the child as his own and names her Eppie after his mother and sister, renewing his ties to his past. His conscientious fatherhood, under the good Dolly Winthrop's tutelage, brings him firmly into the community, including its church, making the ways of Raveloe no longer alien to him. As in *Adam Bede*, Eliot contrasts the Church of England as a vehicle of tradition with evangelicalism as awakening more fervent, personal religious feelings for some. She is not an advocate of either set of beliefs, however, but approves a religious sense that cultivates "a loving nature" with a Wordsworthian piety expressed in charitable acts and fortified by a nondoctrinal awareness of "Unseen Love." As Dinah the Methodist awakened this sense in Hetty, Dolly the Anglican awakens it in Marner, enabling him to ravel (weave or involve) himself into the "O"—to join the circle of fellowship. He is rewarded by Eppie's filial loyalty when her blood father offers to adopt her into his home of luxury and rank.

MIDDLEMARCH

First published: 1871-1872
Type of work: Novel

Personal destinies and vocational fulfillments are limited by chance, contingency, the social fabric, and inherited ideas, as well as flaws in the individual moral will.

Considered Eliot's masterpiece, *Middlemarch* develops a complex web of relationships in a provincial community shortly before the 1832 Reform Bill. The author's perspective from 1871 suggests that the hoped-for results from that legislation have not been achieved, just as the youthful hopes of her characters are not fully realized, perhaps for similar reasons lying with human limitations beyond correction by legislation.

Dorothea Brooke, a young heiress, is compared to Saint Theresa of Avila, whose "passionate, ideal nature demanded an epic life" and found it in reforming a religious order. For Dorothea, however, a "later-born" Theresa, philanthropic aspirations are "helped by no coherent social faith and order which could perform the function of knowledge for the ardently willing soul." Limited by narrow experience and Calvinistic education, with generous but vague impulses to do something grand, she marries Edward Casaubon, Rector of Lowick, a sterile and impotent pedant more than twice her age who needs a copyist to spare his eyes. Unable to see through his pretensions to scholarship or to suspect his poverty of soul, Dorothea believes she will grow by participating in his exalted research. Her ensuing joyless life, circumscribed by his fear that she will discover his fraudulent pose, as his young cousin Will Ladislaw has, is presented through imagery of entrapment in the Minotaur's labyrinth. Eliot satirizes property-based attitudes that find the marriage "a good match."

Tertius Lydgate, a young doctor aspiring to reform medical practice, is Dorothea's visionary counterpart. He has selected Middlemarch as a place to practice up-to-date medicine and pursue his research into "minute processes which prepare human misery and joy," but his intellectual ambition is weakened by irresolution and lack of self-knowledge. One of his weaknesses is his judgment concerning women, which brings him, after resolving to defer marriage, to propose to Rosamond Vincy, convinced that her "polished" and "docile" charm will be an adornment to his life. Once married, he does learn much of "human misery," as her egoistic vanity and drive for social status beyond Middlemarch force him to abandon his aspirations for a practice among the wealthy. Whereas Dorothea escapes her Minotaur by his death, Lydgate dies young himself, having compared Rosamond to a basil plant that "flourished wonderfully on a murdered man's brains."

Totally successful in achieving her goals, Rosamond is opposed dramatically to Dorothea, whose moral ardor (opposed to Rosamond's "neutrality") is noble but ineffective for choosing a husband, because she shortsightedly mistakes Casaubon's arid pedantry for spiritual breadth. As a product of Mrs. Lemon's school, Rosamond has learned to win admiration for her appearance, her parlor music, her sketches, and other typical "feminine achievements," such as getting out of a carriage gracefully. Eliot satirizes what passed for education to many Victorian ladies, leaving them with no higher aims than to marry well and please themselves in the stylish world. Rosy is awakened to her own humanity and that of others only once, in response to Dorothea's selfless act in her behalf when her indiscretion threatens her marriage.

Equally significant as obstacles to reform are the forces embodied in Casaubon and Nicholas Bulstrode, each representing a "religious" voice in England and each exposed as a pious fraud. Bulstrode's hypocritical evangelical pretensions oppress others and salve his own conscience for his shady appropriation, years earlier, of another's money. Eliot implies that the powerful use religion to maintain power and to thwart reforming efforts. Part of her artistic creed was to represent fully the medium in which her characters act. Therefore, voices of reform are frequently checked by a community afraid to set aside inherited customs and ideas. This point is most clearly made in the reference to Casaubon's will, which limits Dorothea's choices after his death as the "Dead Hand." The phrase alludes to Edmund Burke's claim that England would be saved from revolution by a mortmain, or dead hand, carrying a weight of tradition that innnovation could not displace.

A contrast with overreaching ambition is Caleb Garth, a man of integrity who concentrates on excellent performance of his work as land agent. His daughter Mary, with neither Dorothea's nor Rosamond's form of egoism, is solidly grounded in domestic and interpersonal values and will marry Fred Vincy only if he renounces his family's plan to place him in the Church, a step up in rank. Farebrother, a holdover from the older Low Church, demonstrates the religion of humanity that Eliot approves.

Will Ladislaw, who has sustained Dorothea as her respect for her husband turned to pity, brings light to the dark world of Lowick and a fresh, critical mind, educated on the Continent, to the stale parochialism of Middlemarch. His personal vitality restores Dorothea's energy as his aesthetic sensitivity awakens her undeveloped sense for beauty, and their marriage, though frowned upon in class-conscious and xenophobic Middlemarch, brings her a long-awaited proper channel for her reforming spirit as a helpmate to Will, who becomes a Member of Parliament on the reforming side.

DANIEL DERONDA

First published: 1876
Type of work: Novel

Egoistic cruelty and the will to power threaten far-reaching destruction, but compassion and a noble vocation energize conscience and the will to live worthily.

Daniel Deronda reaches beyond Eliot's other work in both form and ideas. The plot develops in two separate lines, one concerning the English upper classes and the other portraying a Jewish family living in the humbler part of East London. These lines converge in the title character, who has matured as the ward (and believes he is the illegitimate son) of Sir Hugo Mallinger, but discovers that he has a distinguished Jewish mother and grandfather. His discovery resolves dilemmas of identity and vocation, favorite themes of Eliot.

Deronda's alertness, compassion, and moral seriousness lead him to rescue two quite different maidens. One is Mirah, a despairing Jewess who tries to drown herself because she cannot find the mother and brother from whom she has become separated. As he aids her search, Deronda meets Mordecai, a visionary Jew who sees in

Daniel one who will complete his dream of perpetuating the Jewish cultural past in a coherent national future. The theme of inherited vision thus counterpoints the theme of inherited wealth.

The other maiden Deronda rescues is Gwendolen Harleth, a talented but ego-driven dilettante of limited experience and education. Deronda restores to her a necklace she has pawned to replace gambling losses; more significant, he awakens her conscience by disapproving of her reckless behavior. Later, after she has married Henleigh Grandcourt for money and power and is racked by guilt for having knowingly taken him from the woman who has borne his illegitimate children, she becomes dependent on the sympathetic, insightful Daniel to be her moral guide.

Eliot counterpoints the purposeless, property-absorbed, and morally vacuous daily trivia of the wealthy English, suggested in the name Mallinger, with the significant vocations of Mordacai and another Jew, Klesmer, a continental musician of excellent artistry. When Gwendolen suffers financial reverses and hopes to escape the humiliating oppression of a governess' life by successful acting and singing, Klesmer points out that in her world she has "not been called upon to be anything but a charming young lady, whom it is an impoliteness to find fault with." Lacking self-criticism or self-discipline, she is unprepared, he tells her, for "a life of arduous, unceasing work," suitable only to "natures framed to love perfection and to labour for it" and dreams only of "donning [an artist's] life as a livery," whereas its "honour comes from the inward vocation and the hard-won achievement." Klesmer's words dimly veil Eliot's judgment of the unproductive leisure class.

Again in this novel Eliot portrays marriage as bondage, but the unaware egoism of Rosamond and self-serving rationalizing of Casaubon, however deadly their effects, seem almost everyday evils compared with Grandcourt's calculated will to mastery. Accustomed to deference and regard as her due, Gwendolen has been favorably impressed by Grandcourt's polite but uninspired behavior and has found his lack of ardor pleasingly untroublesome. She marries him for money and power, driven by her own will to mastery and lacking the moral imagination to envision her life subjected to his unloving will. The torturous chemistry between them contrasts with the sympathetic meeting of souls in the marriages of Daniel and Mirah and of Klesmer and Catherine Arrowpoint. Eliot's repeated satire against marriage as an arrangement for the suitable inheritance of property is nowhere so stinging as in the Reverend Mr. Gascoigne's advice to Gwendolen that it is her "duty" to elevate her family by marrying rank, and in Mr. and Mrs. Arrowpoint's insistence to Catherine that her "duty" as an heiress lies in marrying the proper manager of their estate. The author's treatment of marital intimacy observes customary Victorian restraint but reveals evils of imposed brutality unusual in contemporary fiction. Her sensibility is represented in Klesmer's plea to Catherine: "don't give yourself for a meal to a minotaur."

This novel develops Eliot's most complex psychological explorations and moral implications of interpersonal action.

Summary

In its concern with human motives, especially unconscious ones, George Eliot's fiction is a major stage in the development of the psychological novel. Her treatment of sexual identity and relationships influenced the fiction of Henry James, D. H. Lawrence, and James Joyce. Depicting marriage as an inescapable trap, she treats both male and female characters with sympathy but is particularly concerned to expose and reform the suffering of subjugated women. Her analyses of Self and Other are often explained as deriving from the work of Ludwig Feuerbach, but there seems little doubt that Eliot's remarkable insight grew primarily from her own experience and imagination.

Bibliography

Adam, Ian. *Profiles in Literature: George Eliot.* New York: Humanities Press, 1969.

Beer, Gillian. *George Eliot.* Bloomington: Indiana University Press, 1986.

Haight, Gordon, ed. *A Century of George Eliot Criticism.* Boston: Houghton Mifflin, 1965.

Hardy, Barbara, ed. *Critical Essays on George Eliot.* Boston: Routledge & Kegan Paul, 1970.

————————. *The Novels of George Eliot: A Study in Form.* London: Athlone Press, 1959.

————————. *Particularities: Readings in George Eliot.* Athens: Ohio University Press, 1983.

Harvey, W. J. *The Art of George Eliot.* London: Chatto & Windus, 1961.

Kreeger, George R., ed. *George Eliot: A Collection of Critical Essays.* Englewood Cliffs, N.J.: Prentice-Hall, 1970.

Uglow, Jennifer. *George Eliot.* New York: Random House-Pantheon, 1987.

Willey, Basil. *Nineteenth-Century Studies: Coleridge to Matthew Arnold.* New York: Chatto & Windus, 1949.

Carolyn F. Dickinson

T. S. ELIOT

Born: St. Louis, Missouri
September 26, 1888
Died: London, England
January 4, 1965

Principal Literary Achievement

Accepted by most scholars as the most influential poet of the twentieth century, Eliot stood at the vanguard of a movement that reshaped the way poetry is written, and written about.

Biography

Thomas Stearns Eliot was born in St. Louis, Missouri, on September 26, 1888, the youngest child of a family with four daughters and a son. Eliot's grandfather, the Reverend William Greenleaf Eliot, arrived in St. Louis from Boston in 1834 and quickly rose to prominence. The Reverend Eliot made his mark not only as a Unitarian minister and abolitionist but also as an educator, becoming chancellor of Washington University in 1872. As a boy, Eliot was much influenced by his grandfather and by his family's New England heritage. His summers were usually spent in Gloucester, Massachusetts, where his father had built a vacation home. His mother, Charlotte Champe Sterns, herself a poet, also reinforced in Eliot a sense of his family's essentially New England outlook. As he matured, his sympathies shifted still farther east, to Great Britain. In his twenties, Eliot established permanent residence in England, eventually becoming a British citizen. The pull of these three very different places—the Midwest, New England, and Great Britain—is crucial to understanding Eliot both as a man and as a writer. His last great work, *Four Quartets* (1943), is in a sense an extended meditation on the way that history and geographical place had formed him.

Although his father, Henry Ware Eliot, was a business executive (president of the Hydraulic-Press Brick Company), Eliot was encouraged by his mother to pursue literary and scholarly interests. In fact, his early education was begun under her supervision, and her love of poetry very likely sparked his own. In 1898, Eliot began attending Smith Academy, St. Louis, and in 1906, he spent a year at Milton Academy, in Massachusetts, before entering Harvard. He received his B.A. in philosophy in 1909.

During this period, Harvard's department of philosophy was rich in stimulating and original thinkers, and Eliot studied under two important twentieth century philoso-

phers, George Santayana and Irving Babbitt. He began work on his master's at Harvard in the fall of 1909. He spent the following academic year, 1910-1911, studying in France, where he attended the lectures of another major modern philosopher, Henri Bergson. At the same time, however, Eliot became acquainted with the poetry of the nineteenth century French Symbolist poets, particularly Charles Baudelaire, Stéphane Mallarmé, and Jules Laforgue. Although he had written poetry throughout his adolescence and later at Harvard, the work of the Symbolists transformed him as a writer. His verse began to change radically, culminating four years later in the publication of "The Love Song of J. Alfred Prufrock" (1910-1911).

The year that Eliot spent in France, his biographers agree, altered him psychologically as well. He returned to Harvard deepened by his year abroad and less content with the narrow confines of scholarship. Nevertheless, he pursued graduate work until 1914, reading Indian philosophy and studying the work of F. H. Bradley, the subject of his dissertation.

By 1915, Eliot was living in London and becoming known in literary circles there: He had met another rising American poet, Ezra Pound, who was instrumental in seeing to it that "The Love Song of J. Alfred Prufrock" was published by Harriet Monroe in *Poetry* magazine (June, 1915). Pound also pushed forward the publication of Eliot's first book, *Prufrock and Other Observations* (1917).

Practical life in London was difficult for Eliot at first. He taught a variety of subjects at High Wycombe Grammar School and then at Highgate School. In 1917, he began work for Lloyds Bank as a clerk in the Colonial and Foreign Department. At the same time, he was steadily publishing reviews and criticism in a number of well-known English journals, thus strengthening his literary reputation. In 1919, *Poems* was published, and in 1920 a collection of essays, *The Sacred Wood*, assured his stature as a critic. Then in 1922 *The Waste Land* appeared. Thereafter, Eliot's position as one of the twentieth century's leading poets was no longer in doubt.

Yet this was also a period of severe personal stress for Eliot. He had married Vivien Haigh-Wood in 1915, and the marriage had been plagued with difficulties nearly from the outset. Both husband and wife were often ill with a variety of psychological and physical ailments (she was eventually institutionalized). In the fall and winter of 1921-1922, Eliot was on the verge of a nervous breakdown, and doctors prescribed travel and rest. It was during this period of recuperation that *The Waste Land* was composed.

Financial pressures also continued to weigh on Eliot, but these were relieved when, in 1922, he was given the editorship of *The Criterion*, a literary quarterly that Eliot managed until 1939. This position led in turn to his becoming a director of the publishing firm of Faber & Faber. He stayed with the firm until his retirement.

Throughout, his friend Pound continued to help him both in his personal life and in his literary career. *The Waste Land* had originally run to almost eight hundred lines, but Pound had cut the original nearly in half, tightening and focusing the work. Pound had also been a key figure in persuading Lady Rothermere, *The Criterion*'s financial backer, to hire Eliot as a fully salaried editor-in-chief. After World War II, when Pound's reputation was badly clouded, Eliot was quick to recognize his debt to "Uncle Ez." (It was Pound who gave Eliot his famous nickname "Possum.")

Eliot became an Anglo-Catholic in 1927. Throughout the remainder of his life, he was to explore the meaning of Christianity in his poetry, his essays, and his drama. In fact, his first substantial dramatic work, *The Rock: A Pageant Play* (pb. 1934), was intended to be staged within the church. Subsequent poetic dramas—especially *Murder in the Cathedral* (1935)—were animated by religious themes.

By 1940, Eliot was one of the most notable British literary figures, a key arbiter of taste and a keen critic of modern culture. *Four Quartets*, his last major nondramatic work, brought together the several threads of his life—personal, historic, religious—and capped his reputation as the foremost poet of his time. He was awarded the Nobel Prize in Literature in 1948.

The Nobel was only the chief distinction among dozens of awards and honors Eliot received during the last years of his life. He had become the English-speaking world's most distinguished man of letters, a role that he seemed to adopt easily. Yet like many of the earlier roles that he had played, that of the Great Man seemed to conceal the private Eliot, a true self that he rarely revealed to anyone. The one exception here may perhaps have been his second wife, Valerie Fletcher, whom he married in 1957. His last years with her, according to Eliot himself, may have been his happiest. He died in London on January 4, 1965.

Analysis

Writing about the poetry of Eliot is difficult for a number of reasons. One major difficulty is that Eliot himself helped dictate the rules for how critics interpret poetry in the twentieth century. He did this through his many influential essays on poetry, beginning with those in *The Sacred Wood*, and through the way he transformed the style of modern poetry. Every young poet writing in English after Eliot has had either to imitate or to reject him (often both).

Eliot as a thinker was profoundly interested in the role of literary tradition—the impact of earlier great writers on later ones. Yet he himself in a sense started from scratch. When Pound first read "The Love Song of J. Alfred Prufrock," he was astonished. Eliot, Pound wrote, "has actually trained himself and modernized himself on his own."

Sometime in the period from 1908 through 1910, Eliot managed to create a new poetic style in English. During this time, he had been reading the French Symbolist poets, who had flourished in the last half of the nineteenth century. Eliot was especially drawn to Laforgue, whose dramatic monologues contained a mixture of highly sophisticated irony and an original, difficult style. "The form in which I began to write," Eliot later commented, "was directly drawn from the study of Laforgue. . . . The kind of poetry that I needed, to teach me the use of my own voice, did not exist in English at all; it was only found in French."

The immediate result of this new style was "The Love Song of J. Alfred Prufrock," the first major modernist poem. Modernism was an artistic movement that lasted, in American and English literature, from about 1900 to 1940, although most literature since that time continues to be heavily influenced by modernist techiques. These techniques, first developed largely by Pound and Eliot, involved the use of free verse (poetry without regular meter and rhyme), multiple speakers (or personas) within one poem, and a disjointed, nonlinear style.

Another clear influence of French Symbolist poetry on "The Love Song of J. Alfred Prufrock" was Eliot's use of intensely urban imagery: Prufrock is a citizen of the modern city, an acute observer of its confusion, grime, and poignancy. The poem's opening lines were reminiscent of images that French readers had found in the work of Baudelaire. For English readers, however, the stark pictures of Eliot's poem were startling: "Let us go then, you and I,/ When the evening is spread out against the sky/ Like a patient etherized upon a table." When *Prufrock and Other Observations* appeared in 1917, readers knew that a new and powerful poetic movement was beginning to make itself felt. Eliot and Pound knew that they were creating a literary revolution: Both poets actively furthered the revolution through their essays, articles, and reviews. Two years later, in 1919, *Poems* was published. The volume included "Gerontion," a monologue spoken by an old man and cast in blank verse. Once again, the setting was bleakly urban and the sensibility of the speaker was distinctly modern, which meant that the speaker's viewpoint was ironic, detached, resigned.

The Sacred Wood, a collection of essays, appeared soon after the publication of *Poems*. Scholars still debate the impact on subsequent literature of these relatively short prose articles (most were writtten for literary magazines or newspapers). Students of modern English literature agree, however, that these essays, like the poems that preceded them, permanently altered the way readers assessed poetry. Eliot not only shaped readers' perceptions of modern poetry but also reevaluated the poetry of the past, the "tradition," as Eliot termed it.

Two essays from the collection are particularly important: "Tradition and the Individual Talent" and "Hamlet and His Problems." In the first, Eliot sets out two key critical ideas: the nature of the tradition and the "impersonal theory of poetry." For Eliot, the tradition of literature comprised a living body of works that both influenced contemporary writers and, at the same time, were somehow changed by the light cast on them by modern works. According to Eliot, the masterful poet, fully conscious of working within the tradition, is very much an instrument of the tradition: That is, he or she is in a way an impersonal medium for the common literary heritage. In "Hamlet and His Problems," Eliot introduced the theory of the "objective correlative," the idea that the words of literature should correspond exactly with things and with emotions:

One last key critical idea of this period (introduced in "The Metaphysical Poets" and "Andrew Marvell") was the "dissociation of sensibility." A practical effect of Eliot's emphasis on literary tradition was to give new importance to literary periods that had been neglected; one of these, in Eliot's view, was the era of the Metaphysical poets at the beginning of the seventeenth century. He believed that English poetry had declined in the period following the Metaphysical poets, such as John Donne and Andrew Marvell, and that the cause of this decline lay in a "dissociation of sensibility." In other words, thought and feeling in poems (sensibility) began to be severed (the dissociation). Poets were no longer able to join the intellect and the emotions to produce true masterworks.

These three ideas—the impersonal theory of poetry, the objective correlative, and the dissociation of sensibility—certainly changed the way American and British scholars studied poetry: Innovative critical schools, such as the American New Criticism of the late 1920's and 1930's, were the result, and university training in literature was also changed by these principles.

Easily as important, however, is the fact that Eliot's theories go a long way toward explaining what Eliot was trying to do in his poetry. In his next major poem, and his most famous, these ideas were given full play. *The Waste Land* is unquestionably one of the most important poems of the twentieth century. Its importance lies in its literary excellence—its insight and originality—and in its influence on other poets. Although Eliot said that he always wrote with his mind firmly on tradition, *The Waste Land* broke with the look, the sound, and the subject of most poetry written since the early nineteenth century. In the poem, allusions to myth, religion, Western and Eastern literature, and popular culture are almost constant; in fact, many stretches of the poem are direct, and unacknowledged, quotations from other sources. Because no one narrator appears to be speaking the poem, the work seems as impersonal as a crowded London street. The five sections of *The Waste Land* also constitute Eliot's "objective correlative," a chain of events that sparks a particular emotional mood. The mood is one of despair, loneliness, confusion—the central feelings, Eliot believed, of modern city dwellers.

During the early and mid-1920's, Eliot struggled to emerge from his own private wasteland. Many of the poems of this period, such as "The Hollow Men," reflect his desperation. At the same time, he was deeply immersed in the study of the great medieval poet Dante Alighieri, whose poetry and prose seemed to illuminate a way that a poet could approach religion and achieve serenity of spirit. Accordingly, at the end of the decade Eliot joined the Church of England; from then until the end of his life, he was a faithful to it. *Ash Wednesday* (1930) accurately describes the stage in Eliot's life that hovered between intellectual, nonbelieving despair and instinctive religious faith. In the poem, the speaker is far less impersonal than in earlier works: There is no reason to suppose, in fact, that the narrator is not Eliot himself, a man desperately seeking his God.

By 1930, Eliot was firmly established as an influential man of letters. Yet as his literary star continued to rise, his personal life became more difficult. By now, he had separated from Vivien, and in 1933, with the cooperation of her family, he had his wife committed to a mental institution. Thereafter, Eliot lived the life of a secular monk. He actually roomed in the households of celibate clergy throughout much of the 1930's.

Eliot had also become an even more prolific writer of reviews and essays. In fact, although he published a considerable amount of important criticism during the 1930's (including *The Use of Poetry and the Use of Criticism: Studies in the Relation of Criticism to Poetry in England*, 1933, and *After Strange Gods: A Primer of Modern Heresy*, 1934), his output of poetry had slowed to a trickle.

Not so his dramatic writing. Evidently, Eliot's creative drive had rechanneled itself toward the writing of plays, especially ones with strongly religious themes. His first full effort was *The Rock*, which was a modernized version of the traditional pageant play staged in a large church. The peak of his dramatic career, however, came with *Murder in the Cathedral*. In this play set in the Middle Ages, Eliot retells the story of the murder of Thomas à Becket by his former friend King Henry II. The work enjoyed much popular success in London and New York, and it has been repeatedly broadcast as a radio play. The widespread acceptance of *Murder in the Cathedral* led Eliot to believe that the time was ripe for a revival of poetic drama, although, as it turned out, he remained the only masterly practitioner of the form.

Eliot's last great poetic achievement came during the early 1940's, with the publication of *Four Quartets*. Written as Britain faced the threat of Adolf Hitler's armies, this long poem is strongly affirmative—a real departure, in many ways, from Eliot's previous work. Many critics argue, in fact, that this, and not *The Waste Land*, is his greatest poem. The *Four Quartets* consist of "Burnt Norton," "East Coker," "The Dry Salvages," and "Little Gidding" (three of which were published individually). In this sequence, Eliot has moved quite far from his earlier impersonality: The poem is nearly autobiographical, although much of it explores the relation of human beings generally to God. Each of the places named in the quartets had a deeply personal meaning to Eliot. East Coker, for example, is the town from which the Eliot family came to the New World, and the Dry Salvages are a group of small, rocky islands off the New England coast, where Eliot vacationed as a boy.

From World War II on, Eliot seemed increasingly to find the serenity for which he was searching. He continued to write plays, and these became more approachable, more popular, even more humorous.

Eliot definitely had his comic, whimsical side. Nowhere is this better displayed than in *Old Possum's Book of Practical Cats* (1939), the series of poems about extraordinary felines that went into the making of *Cats* (1981), the successful Broadway hit musical. It seems reasonable to suppose that Eliot would have appreciated his success on Broadway. One of the twentieth century's most difficult poets had at last found easy popular acclaim.

THE LOVE SONG OF
J. ALFRED PRUFROCK

First published: 1915
Type of work: Poem

A genteel, middle-aged speaker describes the emptiness and anxiety of a life lived in a grim twentieth century city.

"The Love Song of J. Alfred Prufrock" marks the beginning of the modernist movement in Anglo-American poetry. It is the first English-language poem in the twentieth century to employ free verse, startling juxtapositions of allusion and situation, an intensely self-conscious speaker (or "persona"), and a truly urban setting. The initial quotation is from Dante Alighieri's *La divina commedia* (c. 1320; *The Divine Comedy*), the great fourteenth century epic describing the author's descent into the Inferno and eventual ascent into Paradise. The lines (in Italian) are spoken by one of the damned souls to Dante as he journeys through Hell. Like souls in the Inferno, Prufrock exists in a kind of living death.

In the poem's opening lines, Prufrock invites the reader to accompany him as he walks through a modern city making his social rounds. Perhaps he assumes that they share his comfortable wealth and socially active life-style. As his proper, even prissy, name implies, Prufrock is neurotic, fearful, sensitive, and bored. His upper-class friends—the women who "come and go"—apparently lead arid and pointless lives. At any rate, what is evident right from the outset of the poem is that Prufrock is unhappy with his life. His unhappiness, he suspects, has something to do with the society in which he lives: There is, for example, the jarring clash between the grim cityscape through which he walks and the mindless tea-party conversation of his friends.

One important way in which this poem is different from the poetry of the century before it is the way in which the speaker describes nature. In the nineteenth century, poets described the natural world as the real home of God, as the fountain at which weary human beings could refresh themselves. A nineteenth century poet, such as William Wordsworth, might have described the coming of evening as being "gentle, like a nun." In contrast, Prufrock's evening is like a very sick person awaiting an operation; the dusk over the city is anesthetized and spread-eagled on an operating table. The urban images that follow this one are just as grim: Prufrock's city, which is perhaps Eliot's London, is a town of cheap hotels and bad restaurants. The streets appear sinister; they seem to threaten the people walking in them, bullying them with pointed questions. The urban landscape is made even more ominous by a "yellow fog" that, cat-like, "rubs" against windows and "licks" the "corners of the evening."

As night falls and the fog settles in, Prufrock describes another landscape—this time, a temporal one where time stretches to infinity. He knows, however, that he will not be able to use this time to advantage; as usual, he will be indecisive. "There will be time" enough, he says, but only for "a hundred indecisions."

Like the limitless streets outside his window, infinite time also threatens Prufrock. The more life he has left to live, the more he is left to wonder and to question. Wondering and questioning frighten him because the answers that they provoke might challenge the perfect, unchanging regularity of his tidy existence. He knows that time is dangerous, that "In a minute there is time/ For decisions and revisions which a minute will reverse." Nothing, in other words, is as settled as it seems. Yet nothing that has happened to Prufrock in his life is particularly comforting: He would like his life to change, but at the same time he fears change and the unexpected events that change might bring. He feels as though he already knows everything that is bound to happen to him. He especially knows the kinds of people whom he is likely to continue meeting—socialites who pin him down with their critical scrutiny.

Yet something besides these general, abstract worries bothers Prufrock. His chronic indecision blocks him from some important action. The reader never learns specifically what this thwarted act might be, but Prufrock seems to address a woman, perhaps one he loves. Their friends appear to gossip about them "among the porcelain" tea cups. Prufrock implies, however, that the woman would reject him if he could ever gather his courage and tell her how he feels. He pictures her sitting in her genteel drawing room, explaining that she had not meant to encourage him: "That is not what I meant at all," she tells him.

Prufrock knows, in any case, that he cannot be the hero of anyone's story; he cannot be Hamlet (despite Hamlet's similar bouts of indecision)—instead, he is only a bit player, even a Fool. He imagines himself growing old, unchanged, worrying about his health and the "risks" of eating a peach. Still, he faintly hears the mermaids of romance singing in his imagination, even though they are not singing to him. In a final imagined vision, he sees these nymphs of the sea, free and beautiful, calling him. Reality, however, intrudes in the form of "human voices," perhaps those of the art-chattering women, and he is "drowned" in his empty life.

TRADITION AND THE INDIVIDUAL TALENT

First published: 1920
Type of work: Essay

The writing of a poem is a living dynamic wherein the contemporary poet is shaped by literary tradition, while, at the same time, tradition is altered by the poet.

Only rarely in the history of English literature has a critical essay, such as "Tradition and the Individual Talent," so changed the way people understand poetry. Anyone who has any real interest in modern poetry—reader, critic, or poet—has had to confront this essay and decide for himself or herself its strengths and weaknesses.

One of the important ways that the essay has altered literary criticism has to do with the meaning of the title's key words, "tradition" and "individual talent." In the very first paragraph, Eliot indicates that, by "tradition," he does not mean what people usually mean in talking about literature; ordinarily, a "traditional" writer is perhaps an old-fashioned writer, one who uses tried-and-true plots and a steady, understandable style. Rather, Eliot uses "tradition" in a more objective and historical sense: His definition of tradition is paradoxical because he says that the historical sense of tradition is a keen understanding of both what is timeless and what is not. A true poet understands "not only the pastness of the past, but . . . its presence."

This is less confusing than it appears: Eliot simply means that, for a poet writing in the tradition—a poet who understands his or her heritage—all the great poetry of the past is alive. When the poet writes a poem, great poems of the past help to enliven the modern work. This dynamic relationship is not finished when the poem is written, however, because the new poem casts a new light on the poems that came before. In the same way that the tradition of great poetry helped shape a new, modern poem, the contemporary poem changes the way one looks at the poems that shaped it.

Another apparent contradiction lies in Eliot's use of "individual" in "individual talent." He says that a poet's true individuality lies in the ways he or she embodies the immortality of poetic "ancestors." In a sense, poets who know what they are doing "plug into" tradition; electrified by the greatness of the past, they achieve a sharper profile, a greater individuality.

It is important to stress that Eliot is not saying that good poets should simply copy the poetry of the past. In fact, he argues just the opposite: Good poets bring something new into the world—"novelty," he writes, "is better than repetition"—that makes an important advance on what has come before. To do this, the poet has to know what is truly new and different; a poet can do this only by having a thorough knowledge of the classic and traditional. To have this kind of knowledge means, in turn, that the poet needs to know not only about the poetry of his or her own language but also about the poetry of other nations and cultures.

In a crucial metaphor about midway in the essay, Eliot compares the poet to a catalyst in chemistry. He describes what happens when two gases are combined in the presence of a piece of platinum: A new compound is formed, but the platinum is unaffected. The platinum is the poet's mind, which uses tradition and personal experience (the two gases) to create a poem. In this kind of literary combustion, the poet remains "impersonal." That is, he or she manages to separate individual facts of life from the work of art that is being created. As Eliot says, "the poet has, not a 'personality' to express, but a particular medium," which is the medium of poetry.

In a third, concluding section of the essay, Eliot draws an important conclusion, one that has been crucial to the way poetry has been studied since the 1920's. The essay shifts the study of a poem from an emphasis on the poet as a person, to the study of the poem isolated from the poet. After reading this essay, critics would increasingly concentrate on the internal structure of poetry—the tropes, figures, and themes of the work. At the same time, critics would banish the life of the writer from the study of his or her writings; the poet's personality, as Eliot seemed to imply, was irrelevant to the artwork produced. The peak of this theory was reached with the New Critics and their successors in Britain and America from about 1930 through the 1950's. Later years, however, have seen a waning of the impersonal theory of poetry and a return of the poet to his or her work.

THE WASTE LAND

First published: 1922
Type of work: Poem

A complex tapestry of voices, cultures, and historical periods, the poem weaves a portrait of modern society in decay.

In order to understand *The Waste Land*—one of the most difficult poems in a difficult literary period—the reader might do well to envision the work as a much-spliced film or videotape, a montage of images and sounds. This imaginary film is, in a sense, a real-life documentary: There are no heroes or heroines, and there is no narrator telling readers what to think or how to feel. Instead, Eliot allows multiple voices to tell their individual stories. Many of the stories are contemporary and portray a sordid society without values; other stories are drawn from world culture and include, among other motifs, Elizabethan England, ancient Greek mythology, and Buddhist scriptures.

The poem is divided into five sections. In the first, "The Burial of the Dead," the speaker is an old Austro-Hungarian noblewoman reminiscing about the golden days of her youth before the disasters of World War I. The second section, "A Game of Chess," is set in the boudoir of a fashionable contemporary Englishwoman. The third, "The Fire Sermon," mixes images of Elizabeth's England, the Thames and Rhine rivers, and the legend of the Greek seer Tiresias. The fourth, "Death by Water," is a brief portrait of a drowned Phoenician sea-trader. The fifth, "What the Thunder Said," combines the above themes with that of religious peace. These parts combine in the poem's overall montage to create a meaning that encompasses all of them. Because the poem is so complex, that meaning must be left to the individual reader; but many students of the poem have suggested that, generally, Eliot shows his readers the collapse of Western culture in the aftermath of the war.

Part 1 is a natural beginning for his overall panorama because the speaker, Marie, describes her memories of a key period in modern history. Clearly, her life has been materially and culturally rich. Now in old age, thoughts of the past seem to embitter her, and she spends much of her time reading. The following stanzas describe the visions of the Sibyl (a prophetess in Greek mythology) and compare these to the bogus fortune-telling of a modern Sibyl, Madame Sosostris. The section's final stanza imagines a fog-shrouded London Bridge as a pathway in the Underworld, where souls fleetingly recognize one another.

In part 2, a narrator describes the sensual surroundings of a wealthy woman's bedroom—the ornate chair in which the woman sits, the room's marble floor and carved fireplace, her glittering jewels and heavy perfumes. She is bickering with a man, her husband or her lover, and complains that her "nerves are bad to-night." Then a contrasting setting appears: a London pub. Two women are gossiping in Cockney English about a friend's marriage gone bad.

A description of the River Thames begins part 3. The narrator juxtaposes the pretty stream that Renaissance poets saw with the garbage-filled canal of the twentieth century. Most of the section tells the story of an uninspired seduction. The speaker, ironically, is the Greek sage Tiresias, who, in legend, was changed from a man into a woman. In this androgynous mode, Tiresias can reflect on both the male and the female aspects of the modern-day affair between a seedy clerk and a tired typist. This section ends with snippets of past songs about the Thames and the Rhine.

The brief stanzas in part 4 picture Phlebas, a Middle-Eastern merchant from the late classical period. The tone is elegiac: The speaker imagines the bones of the young trader washed by the seas and advises the reader to consider the brevity of life.

The final section, part 5, is set in a barren landscape, perhaps the Waste Land itself, where heat lays its heavy hand on a group of anonymous speakers. They seem to be apostles of some sacrificed god, perhaps Christ himself. The opening stanza's description of confused "torchlight on sweaty faces" in a garden and an "agony in stony places" tends to suggest this Christian interpretation. Hope, however, has fled the holy man's followers, who wander through the desert listening to thunder that is never followed by rain. Nevertheless, the thunder holds some small promise. The poem shifts setting again. Now the thunder crashes over an Indian jungle while the speaker listens and "translates" the thunderclaps. The thunder speaks three words in Sanskrit, an ancient Indian language, which is also the language of Buddhist and Hindu scriptures. The first word is "Datta" ("given"); the second is "Dayadhvam" ("compassion"); the third is "Damyata" ("control"). In this three-part message from the natural world, which tells of God's gifts of compassion and self-control, the speaker finally finds cause for "peace"—the "shantih" of the closing line.

FOUR QUARTETS

First published: 1943
Type of work: Poem

The speaker meditates on his own life, the passing of time, and his own relation to God and to other human beings, living and dead.

Perhaps the best way to approach the *Four Quartets* is to view it as Eliot's spiritual autobiography. This long work is by far the poet's most personal poem. In it, he drops the many masks of his earlier verse—Prufrock or the multiple speakers of *The Waste Land*—and meditates on the meaning of life and God. The poem is divided into four sections, the "quartets" of the title: "Burnt Norton," the name of an English country house with a memorable garden; "East Coker," the village from which Eliot's English ancestors left for the New World; "The Dry Salvages," a group of small islands off the New England coast, to which Eliot would sail as a young man; and "Little Gidding," the name of a religious community led by Nicholas Ferrar, a seventeenth century Christian mystic.

Much of the language in this poem is undramatic, abstract, and philosophical. In fact, it is important to remember that Eliot was trained as a philosopher, so that when he uses common words such as "time" or "future," he has thought carefully about a very particular definition. As the poem makes clear, for Eliot "time" was not at all a vague concept.

"Burnt Norton" opens, as did *The Waste Land*, with a memory of childhood, although this time the memory is Eliot's own. He recalls a garden where children played hide-and-seek. The surroundings are calm, quiet, and lovely—like the memories themselves. The following parts of this first section approach the passage of time in different ways: the change of seasons as it is charted by the movement of constellations, the "still point" of religious illumination and its contrast with the "internal darkness" of worldly life, and the struggle to capture time and eternity in words (Eliot's own struggle as a poet).

Eliot imagines an older kind of time in "East Coker," the poem's second section. This is rural time, the cycle of the seasons in planting and harvest. Because the farming village of East Coker is also in Eliot's own past, as the place of his forebears, it represents historical time as well. In the section's third stanza, he pictures what an old country festival might have been like before the Eliots departed for America. When he looks at what his ancestors have bequeathed him, however, he feels deceived. He had hoped that their heritage would teach him how to grow old gracefully, but as he looks foward into old age, he sees only death—his own and that of others, no matter how powerful or famous. Thus he struggles to come to terms with the darkness. Words, he knows, cannot encompass death. He counsels himself to have patience, neither to hope nor to strive. Most of all, he realizes that he needs to put himself under the care of the "wounded surgeon," a figure for Christ. Dying repentant, Eliot believes, is the only true life.

"The Dry Salvages," section three, comprises two memories of Eliot's youth: the rhythm of the Mississippi River in his St. Louis boyhood and the sounds of the Atlantic Ocean near his family's summerhouse. The river and the sea are "gods," living beings that modern people have ignored—perhaps to their peril. His thoughts turn to New England fisherman, constantly fighting the elements, waiting to return to land. He draws a parallel between these men, cast on the harsh rhythms of the ocean, and his readers. They, too, are set on a voyage whose end cannot be known. They are not the same people who left port, for every moment they are changing. Like the sea, everything around the reader is unstable and flowing. Just as individuals are incessantly losing their past selves, so they are unable to see through the mists of the future. Memory remains their only reality, unless they attain the timelessness of the saint.

"Little Gidding," the last section, hints at an answer to Eliot's perplexity with the many kinds of time—human, natural, and divine. As he sits in a old English chapel, he hears a "Calling." Through Love, human beings are redeemed, and through death, they are mysteriously born again.

Summary

Many readers of modern poetry know the twentieth century as "The Age of Eliot." Be that as it may, T. S. Eliot's stature ranks him among the two or three great English-language poets of the last hundred years (the others being, perhaps, Ezra Pound and William Butler Yeats).

This is so for three reasons. First, as Pound pointed out, Eliot was the century's poetic forerunner: "The Love Song of J. Alfred Prufrock" stands at the threshold of the twentieth century's modernist tradition. Second, certain of Eliot's poems—especially *The Waste Land*—seem to convey the anonymity, confusion, and urbanity of the time better than those of any other poet. Third, Eliot was perhaps the last "Man of Letters" in the old English literary tradition; his views on literature and the canon held ultimate authority for many years and still have an astonishing influence throughout the English-speaking world.

Bibliography

Ackroyd, Peter. *T. S. Eliot: A Life.* New York: Simon & Schuster, 1984.

Frye, Northrop. *T. S. Eliot.* Edinburgh, Scotland: Oliver & Boyd, 1963.

Gallup, Donald. *T. S. Eliot: A Bibliography.* New ed. London: Faber, 1969.

Gardner, Helen Louise, Dame. *The Art of T. S. Eliot.* London: Cresset Press, 1949.

Gordon, Lyndall. *Eliot's Early Years.* Oxford, England: Oxford University Press, 1977.

Litz, A. Walton, comp. *Eliot in His Time.* Princeton; N.J.: Princeton University Press, 1973.

Newton-de Molina, David, ed. *The Literary Criticism of T. S. Eliot: New Essays.* London: Athlone Press, 1977.

Tate, Allen, ed. *T. S. Eliot: The Man and His Work.* New York: Delacorte Press, 1966.

John Steven Childs

EURIPIDES

Born: Phlya, Greece
c. 485 B.C.
Died: Macedonia, Greece
406 B.C.

Principal Literary Achievement

The youngest of the three great tragedians of Athens, Euripides reinterpreted the traditional myths of ancient Greece in light of the philosophy and psychological insights of his day.

Biography

Almost nothing is known for certain about the life of Euripides. While a number of ancient authors claim to supply information about his life or to comment upon his character, much of what these authors say has been based upon legends. At their worst, tales about Euripides have been corrupted by how the poet was depicted in ancient comedy and satire. Even at their best, these stories are often merely anecdotes misremembered or invented by the author's admirers long after his death.

Not even Euripides' birthplace is known for sure. Most ancient sources suggest that Euripides was born on Salamis, an island off the coast of Athens. Yet this tradition seems to be part of an ancient legend connecting each of the three major tragedians with the Battle of Salamis in 480 B.C. According to this legend, Aeschylus fought against the Persians in this battle, Sophocles sang in the chorus of youths that celebrated the Athenian victory, and Euripides was born on the island on the very day of the battle itself. The coincidence seems too incredible to be true. According to another tradition, which relates that Euripides was born at Phlya in central Attica, Greece, sometime in 485 B.C., may well be more accurate. His father's name was Mnesarchos, and his mother's name was Cleito.

The town of Phlya was famous for its temples, a detail that accords well with another story told about Euripides' youth. As a child, Euripides is said to have been a torchbearer and to have poured wine at festivals honoring the god Apollo. This privilege would probably have been reserved for the nobility, and it suggests that the family of Euripides was wealthy. Indeed, some ancient sources state that Euripides' mother, Cleito, was descended from a family of high social standing. A variant tradition stating that Euripides' mother was reduced to selling vegetables for a living appears to have been the invention of the comic poet Aristophanes.

Early in his life, Euripides moved with his family to Athens. There he received an education typical of many young Athenians of the fifth century B.C. He studied literature, art (especially painting), music, gymnastics, and philosophy. At that time, Greek philosophy was becoming a more important part of Athenian education than it had been for the poet's older contemporaries Aeschylus and Sophocles. As a result, Euripides would always be the most philosophical of the ancient tragedians. He was interested in evaluating new ideas and frequently assigned to his characters opinions attributable to philosophers alive at the time.

The Peloponnesian War, waged between Sparta and Athens, began in the year 431 B.C. and continued even after Euripides' death. This long struggle had a profound impact upon him. Initially a supporter of the war, Euripides presented the Athenians as glorious defenders of justice in *Hērakleidai* (c. 430 B.C.; *The Children of Heracles*). Nevertheless, after the Athenians committed atrocities on the island of Melos in 416 B.C., Euripides turned against the war and produced *Trōiades* (415 B.C.; *The Trojan Women*, 1783), a play that provided a critical commentary on war's cruelty against the innocent.

The comic poet Aristophanes, who included Euripides as a character in several of his plays, depicted the poet as a brooding intellectual who hated other people, especially women. Later authors took this depiction at face value and described Euripides as a hermit who lived in a cave on the island of Salamis. It is more likely, however, that Aristophanes' view of Euripides was intended to be satirical rather than realistic. Indeed, Euripides' reputation as a misogynist seems to be derived from his depictions of Medea, Phaedra, and Hecuba (as well as the belief that his own two marriages were unhappy) rather than from any attitude of the poet himself. While Euripides did, at times, include portraits of violent or threatening women in his plays, he also depicted women such as Alcestis, Iphigeneia, and Macaria in a more positive and sympathetic light.

Toward the end of Euripides' life, the poet retired from Athens and moved to the court of King Archelaus in Macedon. There he composed the *Bakchai* (405 B.C.; *The Bacchae*, 1781), a tragedy that was not performed until after his death. Stories abound concerning the death of Euripides. It is said that Euripides was attacked and killed by hunting dogs, perhaps intentionally released by the rival poets Arridaeus and Crateuas. This story of a violent death is too similar to that told about the death of Pentheus, the central character in *The Bacchae*, to be taken at face value. According to tradition, Euripides died in 406 B.C. in Macedonia, Greece.

Analysis

In *De poetica* (c. 334 B.C.-323 B.C.; *Poetics*, 1705), Aristotle quotes Sophocles as saying that he (Sophocles) presented individuals as they should be while Euripides presented them as they are. This concern for a realistic depiction of human character and motivation is one of the hallmarks of Euripidean tragedy. Rather than presenting action as the result of sweeping historical or religious forces, as did Aeschylus, or of noble and heroic individual choices, as did Sophocles, Euripides attributes actions in his plays to ordinary, and easily understandable, human emotions.

While the forces motivating the characters in Euripidean tragedy are frequently less edifying than those that Aeschylus or Sophocles attributed to their characters, this pessimism was central to Euripides' outlook upon the world. The horrors of the Peloponnesian War seem to have affected Euripides more deeply than his contemporaries, and he sought to depict those horrors upon the stage. Seeing few genuine heroes in his own society, Euripides was hesitant to assume that such heroes had existed in the remote past. His characters tend to be motivated by base emotions such as anger, greed, and lust rather than by the lofty piety and constancy that inspire such characters as Sophocles' Antigone.

Euripides was interested in the psychology of the characters who populate traditional Greek myths. He turns a skeptical eye toward the platitudes with which they justify their own actions and seeks to reveal a less flattering source of motivation. What was shocking to his contemporaries was that Euripides extended this psychological analysis even to the gods. He saw deities such as Aphrodite, Artemis, and Dionysus as symbols of emotions—lust, restraint, irrationality, for example—rather than as the anthropomorphic images worshipped in the temples.

Perhaps for this reason, Euripides was, in his lifetime, the least popular of the three Athenian tragedians. He won first prize in the annual poetic competition only four times and was awarded this prize one additional time after his death. Nevertheless, the ideas advanced by him became increasingly popular in the following centuries, and, for this reason, more of his works have survived than have the works of Aeschylus and Sophocles combined.

A Euripidean play will usually begin with an extended prologue that provides the audience with crucial information. The play will end with the appearance of a god who resolves the central conflict of the drama. The individual who delivers the prologue, known as the protatic character, may not even reappear in the rest of the drama. Nevertheless, protatic characters play an important role in determining how the audience views the action of the play. The god who appeared at the end of the drama was frequently lowered to the stage by means of a hoist, a turn of events called the *deus ex machina*.

This general structure of a Euripidean tragedy frequently gives the audience the impression that the action depicted on stage is predestined and thus inescapable. Yet it is important to remember that the determining factor in Euripidean drama is more frequently human emotion (and base emotion, at that) than divine will. Characters in a play by Euripides thus usually have little control over their actions. That is a result of the fact that they are victims of their own emotions, not pawns of some impersonal or cosmic Fate.

Euripides' view that emotions provoke much of human activity caused him to adopt a different focus in his tragedies from that of Aeschylus or Sophocles. Rather than depicting a world inhabited primarily by kings and the nobility, Euripides presents a more democratic universe. Not only do common people appear on stage more frequently in Euripidean tragedy than in the works of his predecessors, but they are also more central to the drama and tend to be more memorable. In Euripides' view of the world, human tragedy affects everyone; it is not merely the province of the aristocracy.

Euripides also was less constrained by traditional myths than were Aeschylus or Sophocles. He was free to change details of the plot, add characters, or incorporate elements from another story. This freedom often gives the Euripidean version of a myth a sense of greater realism. It also allows the author to criticize details of a myth that he regards as foolish or inconsistent.

MEDEA

First produced: *Mēdeia*, 431 B.C. (English translation, 1781)
Type of work: Play

A witch whose husband is about to leave her for another woman takes vengeance against him by killing his children.

The *Medea* illustrates many characteristic features of Euripidean tragedy. The play begins with a prologue in which the central conflict of the tragedy is revealed to the audience. This prologue is delivered, not by a god nor by any member of the nobility, but by a nurse, a character of relatively humble status. Yet the story that the nurse relates contains many fantastic elements and supernatural details: For example, she speaks of the Symplegades (the Clashing Rocks that destroyed ships attempting to sail through them), the Golden Fleece, and Jason's legendary ship, the Argo. Nevertheless, these mythological details will not be Euripides' central concern in this play. The poet will devote far more attention to human psychology and ordinary emotions (jealousy, anger, pride) than to the marvels of legend. Euripides' answer to the central question of this tragedy—What could lead a mother to kill her own children?—will not be the Golden Fleece or even a tragic curse, but a combination of spurned love, the desperate plight of women and exiles, and the individual nature of this particular mother.

Euripides quickly shifts attention away from the wonders of the prologue to the troubles that exist in Medea's marriage. For Medea, the predicament of a husband who intends to leave her is compounded by the low status of women in Greek society generally and by her further isolation as an exile. Medea speaks at length about the difficulties of women in ancient Greece (lines 231-251) and about the ill treatment accorded to foreigners (lines 252-258, 511-515). The audience observes that Medea has relatively few choices available to her. If Jason abandons her, Medea's life will be little better than that of a slave.

Furthermore, in Medea's debate with Jason (lines 465-519), the audience is reminded that Medea has used violence before when doing what she felt to be necessary. She had killed her brother, Apsyrtus, in order that Jason might escape from her father, Aeëtes. She had killed Jason's uncle, Pelias, in order that Jason's father might regain his throne. Thus, the audience begins to understand that Medea is a person who kills whenever she believes that she has no other choice. Because she is a woman and an exile in a world that is hostile to both, Medea's choices gradually diminish as the play continues.

In this way, Euripides has rewritten a traditional Greek fairy tale as a psychological study. He has brought his mythic characters down to the level of ordinary human beings and has shown that what motivated them were emotions that the audience could readily understand. By so doing, Euripides is able to make Medea seem a sympathetic character, despite her violent actions and the elements of fantasy traditionally found in her story.

HIPPOLYTUS

First produced: *Hippolytos*, 428 B.C. (English translation, 1781)
Type of work: Play

Phaedra, rejected by her son-in-law, Hippolytus, accuses him of rape.

The *Hippolytus* was part of only five trilogies for which Euripides was awarded first prize. One of the reasons for the success of this play may be that the *Hippolytus* is far more traditional in structure than many other Euripidean tragedies. For example, both Theseus and Hippolytus himself follow the pattern of the tragic hero described by Aristotle in *De poetica* (c. 334 B.C.-323 B.C.; *Poetics*, 1705): They are neither perfectly good nor purely evil but, while generally virtuous, suffer because of a flaw in character or by committing some mistake. Moreover, the play's emphasis upon the need for restraint in all human endeavor echoes the sentiment of the widely quoted Greek proverb, "Nothing too much." Theseus and Hippolytus are thus guilty of hubris (usually defined as excessive pride, insolence, and self-righteousness), which would have been regarded, even by the most conservative of Euripides' critics, as a fatal flaw of character.

Nevertheless, Euripides has made several important innovations in this work. First, his view of the gods is not at all the same as that found in traditional Greek religion. Aphrodite and Artemis, although they appear on stage in human form, are largely personifications of lust and chastity. It is the conflict between these competing forces that brings about the tragedy of Phaedra and Hippolytus; the inability of these characters to find a balance between the desires represented by Aphrodite and the goals represented by Artemis destroys them.

This image of the gods is not at all flattering. Aphrodite uses Phaedra as a pawn to achieve the vengeance that she desires against Hippolytus. Humankind is seen to be the plaything of the gods, subject to their whims and unable to escape the destiny that they have imposed. Yet since the gods are presented as human emotions in this drama, Euripides is not being fatalistic in the traditional sense. Rather, the poet is implying, even as the philosophers of his day had suggested, that humanity is the victim of its own passions and conflicting desires. In the end, it is human emotion, not destiny, which brings about suffering in the *Hippolytus*.

Phaedra's act of vengeance against Hippolytus, coupled with Medea's act of vengeance against Jason, helps to explain why Euripides so often was seen in antiquity as a hater of women. Yet Euripides added little to the depictions of these characters that could not be found elsewhere in their stories. Moreover, his depiction of men such as Jason and even, to a certain extent, Theseus is similarly unflattering, and he casts other women, such as Alcestis and Iphigenia, in a more positive light. For this reason, the violent acts of revenge committed by Phaedra and Medea result not from the author's misogyny but from his interpretation of their individual characters.

THE TROJAN WOMEN

First produced; *Trōiades*, 415 B.C. (English translation, 1783)
Type of work: Play

Shortly after the fall of Troy, Hecuba learns the fate of her children and grandchildren.

In 416 B.C., the Athenian empire, at war against Sparta, captured the neutral island of Melos in the Aegean Sea. Punishing the Melians for their resistance, the Athenians killed all the men who remained on the island and reduced the women and children to slavery. This act of unprovoked aggression turned Euripides against the Athenian cause in the Peloponnesian War, a cause that he had earlier supported. For example, his negative depiction of the Corinthians in the *Medea*, written during the first year of the war, may be traced in large part to the alliance that existed between Corinth and Sparta. Fifteen years later, however, Euripides has shifted from seeing the Spartans and their allies as the enemy to seeing war itself as the enemy.

The structure of *The Trojan Women* is episodic. That is to say, it does not so much tell a continuous story as depict a series of individual and discrete scenes. The sum total of the episodes is not a plot, as in standard narrative tragedy, but an impression. The impression that Euripides sought to convey in *The Trojan Women* is that war is unspeakably horrible. The author attempted in the various scenes of this tragedy to depict the suffering that war causes even for those innocents who do not fight in it, innocents such as women, children, and the elderly.

Unity is provided in the drama by the continual presence of Hecuba. In her person are represented all wives who have lost their husbands in war and all mothers who have lost their children. Each successive episode brings word of new sorrows to Hecuba. When she first appears to the audience, she is aware that she has lost her city, her position, and most members of her family. That seems tragic enough, but Euripides wanted to illustrate that war spares nothing for the innocent, not even their hopes. Hecuba must also endure seeing her daughter Cassandra apparently afflicted with madness. (The audience, however, which knew that the curse of Cassandra was to prophesy the truth but never to be believed, would have realized that her "madness" was really an accurate prediction of the future.) In the following episode, Hecuba learns that another daughter, Polyxena, had been sacrificed on the tomb of Achilles. Finally, Hecuba must endure the slaughter of Andromache's infant son, Astyanax, who is flung from the walls of Troy. Hecuba concludes (lines 1280-1283) that it is futile even to call upon the gods for help; the prayers of the innocent go unanswered.

The only consolation available to Hecuba is that her sufferings, and those of the other Trojans, were so severe that they will always be remembered (lines 1240-1250). Hecuba knows that, if it were not for their many sorrows, the Trojans would not become the subject of songs for generations yet unborn. This realization is cold comfort, indeed, but it is the only consolation that Euripides was willing to admit in this play. His goal was to see that later ages never forgot what the Trojans, like the Melians, had endured.

THE BACCHAE

First produced: *Bakchai*, 405 B.C. (English translation, 1781)
Type of work: Play

A king of Thebes is punished for resisting the cult of the god Dionysus.

In about 408 B.C., Euripides left Athens to accept the invitation of King Archelaus to write works for his court in Macedon. There Euripides died in 406 B.C. His final trilogy of plays, including both *The Bacchae* and *Iphigeneia ē en Taurois* (c. 414 B.C.; *Iphigenia in Tauris*), was produced in Athens by his son. Posthumously, he was awarded first prize for this trilogy, the fifth time that the poet had been so honored.

One of the reasons why *The Bacchae* may have been popular with its original audience was that it reflects a far more traditional view of humankind and the gods than do many of Euripides' plays. Dionysus in *The Bacchae* is still seen as a psychological force or as a state of mind (in this case, irrationality) like Aphrodite and Artemis in the *Hippolytus*. In this play, however, it is Pentheus, the "modern man" who uses reason to challenge the authority of the gods, who suffers most. At the end of the tragedy, Cadmus cites the fate of Pentheus as proof that the gods exist and that they punish those who resist them (lines 1325-1326).

The final words of *The Bacchae* are a restatement of the traditional Greek view that the gods act in ways that humankind does not expect and that human knowledge is therefore limited (lines 1388-1392). It is a conclusion that would be appropriate for nearly any Greek tragedy, and, indeed, it strongly resembles the endings of both Sophocles' *Antigonē* (441 B.C.; *Antigone*) and *Oidipous epi Kolōnōi* (401 B.C.; *Oedipus at Colonus*). This traditional Greek belief, that moderation is best because humankind's knowledge is limited, is central to the entire structure of *The Bacchae*. While Pentheus is punished for his stubborn resistance to the god Dionysus, his mother, Agave, who accepted the god, also suffers. For modern readers, this development is one of the most troubling aspects of the work; at the end of the play, Dionysus seems to be punishing both his enemies and his own followers. Yet it must be remembered that, for Euripides, Dionysus symbolizes irrationality. Those who exclude irrationality totally from their lives become stolid, unimaginative, and dull; when their carefully reasoned worlds collapse, they may be "torn apart" by irrationality, as literally happens to Pentheus in this play. Yet those who succumb to irrationality entirely are playing with madness, and they may eventually destroy what is most dear to them. With irrationality, as with everything, Euripides is saying, the middle way is best.

In dramatic terms, Euripides accomplishes a difficult task in *The Bacchae*. He manages to change the audience's opinion about both Dionysus and Pentheus as the drama unfolds. When Dionysus first appears, he wins the audience's favor: They are told that Pentheus is resisting the god unjustly and that Dionysus has come to Thebes in person to reward the just and to punish the guilty. By the end of the drama, however, Dionysus seems a fearful figure whose penalties are extreme and whose power destroys even those who embrace his cult. Pentheus, on the other hand, first appears as a brash, skeptical, and thoroughly unlikable individual. Yet by the end of the drama, the audience is likely to pity him because of the degree to which he has been punished. This ability to change an audience's perspective in such a short time is one of Euripides' finest accomplishments in this play.

Summary

In the works of Euripides, the traditional stories of Greek tragedy were reinterpreted in light of the philosophical theories current in the late fifth century B.C. Gods in Euripides' works usually personify human emotions and resemble only in outward form the highly anthropomorphic deities of Homer and Sophocles. Kings and nobles from the remote past speak in the language of the Athenian law courts. Ordinary people are also frequently introduced into Euripidean tragedy and are central to the plot.

Throughout the eighteen surviving plays of Euripides, it is possible to trace his evolution as an artist. Early works such as the *Medea* and the *Hippolytus* contain, despite their many innovations, the conventional view that the Athenians are a great and just people. This view declines in such works as *The Trojan Women*. Moreover, though his sense of disillusionment with the Athenian empire may have caused him to leave Athens in 408 B.C., his last works illustrate a return to a more traditional view of humanity and the gods.

Bibliography

Barlow, Shirley A. *The Imagery of Euripides*. London: Methuen, 1971.
Bates, William Nickerson. *Euripides: A Student of Human Nature*. New York: Barnes & Noble Books, 1961.

Conacher, D. J. *Euripidean Drama: Myth, Theme and Structure*. Toronto: University of Toronto Press, 1967.

Michelini, Ann Norris. *Euripides and the Tragic Tradition*. Madison: University of Wisconsin Press, 1987.

Murray, Gilbert. *Euripides and His Age*. New York: Henry Holt, 1913.

Vellacott, Philip. *Ironic Drama: A Study of Euripides' Method and Meaning*. Cambridge, England: Cambridge University Press, 1975.

Jeffrey L. Buller

HENRY FIELDING

Born: Sharpham Park, Somersetshire, England
April 22, 1707
Died: Lisbon, Portugal
October 8, 1754

Principal Literary Achievement

Fielding's greatest achievement lay in his contributions to the development of the novel, eclipsing his multifaceted career as a dramatist, a journalist, and a lawyer and magistrate deeply involved with the problems of his society.

Biography

Henry Fielding was born at Sharpham Park, his maternal grandfather's estate near Glastonbury, in Somersetshire, England, on April 22, 1707, the first child in a family of five. His father, Edmund Fielding, was a lieutenant who fought under the duke of Marlborough against the forces of Louis XIV of France. His mother, Sarah, was the granddaughter of Sir Henry Gould, Baron of the Exchequer; her family had been considered gentry for several generations. Yet Henry Fielding himself was not fully included among this upper class; with his family being considered "poor relations," he was déclassé. This situation, perhaps, was the genesis of his later contemptuous attitude toward many of the upper class, an attitude exhibited particularly in his novels.

During his childhood, Fielding lived in the village of East Stour, Dorsetshire. He was educated at home during his early years. His mother died when he was eleven, and he was then sent to the home of a cantankerous maternal aunt, who encouraged his impudence when his father remarried when Henry was thirteen, this time to a "Papist" Italian. For this impudence, he was sent to school at Eton. Consequently, his father and the family servants saw him in a very unflattering light. He discovered firsthand the malicious misjudgments others could make, a realization that he used later in *The History of Tom Jones, a Foundling* (1749; more popularly known as *Tom Jones*). At Eton, however, he found lifelong friends, as well as enjoyment of his studies. There, he developed deep friendships with George Lyttleton and with William Pitt the Elder. After an unsuccessful elopement when he was nineteen, he then settled in London. In time, he began to see the city, with the numerous temptations available, as a great corrupter of the susceptible, another realization that he put to use in his novels.

Fielding's literary career began early, before he was twenty-one. His first publica-

tion, "The Masquerade," a verse satire, appeared in late January, 1728, and weeks later, his first play, *Love in Several Masques*, a light comedy, was produced. In spite of finding it somewhat difficult to judge what audiences wanted, Fielding became the leading playwright of the period between 1730 and 1737. During these years, his dramatic skill in great demand, he produced a number of comedies, numerous skits, and farces, including his best farce, *Tom Thumb: A Tragedy* (1730; revised as *The Tragedy of Tragedies: Or, The Life and Death of Tom Thumb the Great* (1731). *The Historical Register for the Year 1736* (1737) was a vicious attack on the contemporary political corruption. The stage—and his dramas—had become a part of the political background of his time. Fielding, chief among the attackers, satirized the Walpole government through his farces. The government, however, finally struck back. The Theatrical Licensing Act of June 21, 1737, shut down this criticism, including Fielding's. With drama now severely restricted and future dramas to be censored by a powerful Lord Chamberlain, Fielding was thus effectively denied the stage.

Fielding was not through. With the closing of the theaters, he turned to law, studying at the Middle Temple and qualifying in 1740. In 1734, he married Charlotte Cradock. They became the parents of two daughters. With her ill health and his own health deteriorating, Fielding found it difficult to maintain his law career. Partly because of his own improvidence, he endured some long periods of "considerable poverty," but, assisted by a longtime friend, Ralph Allen of Bath, along with his wealthy Eton friend, Lyttleton, he was able to continue. (Allen and Lyttleton he used as models for Squire Allworthy in *Tom Jones*. His wife became the model for Sophia Western in *Tom Jones* and for the heroine in his last novel.) When his wife died in 1744, he was too devastated to write much for more than a year afterward.

More by circumstance, Fielding became enmeshed in the writing of novels. In the fall of 1740, Samuel Richardson had developed the series of model letters for newly educated young ladies into a connected whole that became his first novel, *Pamela: Or, Virtue Rewarded* (1740-1741). The book was immensely popular. Fielding, however, had found Richardson's heroine "too passive" and regarded Richardson himself as a "milksop and a straitlaced preacher out of his pulpit." Five months later, *An Apology for the Life of Mrs. Shamela Andrews* (1741) appeared, clearly a parody, showing in a savage satire a money-grubbing, lusty wench, decidedly the opposite of Richardson's chaste heroine. That book, also in epistolary form, was published under a pseudonym. This parody has been ascribed to Fielding, but whether he actually produced it is debatable: A number of Fielding's biographers do not include it among his accomplishments.

Fielding's *The History of the Adventures of Joseph Andrews, and of His Friend Mr. Abraham Adams* (1742; more commonly known as *Joseph Andrews*) is more often acknowledged as his first novel. He followed this with the heavily satirical, fictionalized *The History of the Life of the Late Mr. Jonathan Wild the Great* (1743, 1754), based on an actual highwayman of the same name, using this new genre to criticize Walpole again. He followed with *Tom Jones*, considered to be his masterpiece, and finally with *Amelia* (1751).

In 1747, Fielding remarried, this time to his wife's maid and friend, Mary Daniel. This marriage, though it raised some scandal in class-conscious England, was quite happy. Five children were born of it.

In 1748, with Lyttleton's aid, Fielding was appointed police magistrate, or justice of the peace, for Westminster in London. He had long been disturbed by the various corruptions that he had observed in the courts; once powerless to intervene, he was able now to battle from within against this corruption, including the "trading justices" who had been padding their incomes by imposing and embezzling fines. In 1749, his jurisdiction was to include the whole county of Middlesex; he also was chairman of the quarter sessions court at Westminster, in addition to a court at Bow Street. Together, with his blind half brother, John Fielding, also a magistrate, he established new standards of honesty and competence on the bench. To do this, he wrote a number of legal inquiries and pamphlets, including a proposal for banning public hangings and for organizing the Bow Street Runners, a pioneer group established to detect crime. In 1753, in spite of increasingly ill health, he wrote an exhaustive and humane "A Proposal for Making an Effectual Provision for the Poor." That same year, he both organized and established a plan for breaking up the criminal gangs then flourishing in London. His often sympathetic treatment of the lower classes in his novels is evident. Unlike many of his contemporaries, he recognized the existence of the "deserving poor."

Since 1741, Fielding's health had been gradually deteriorating. In 1754, he resigned his magistracy and, with his wife and a daughter, sailed to Lisbon, Portugal, where, he felt, the milder climate could possibly help him. In that city on October 8, however, only two months after his arrival, he died. He left a nonfiction journal, *The Journal of a Voyage to Lisbon*, published posthumously in 1755.

Analysis

Fielding, a man of his eighteenth century society, was naturally class-conscious, perhaps opinionated, and possibly a bit self-righteous; like many of his contemporaries, he was "conservative, consistent, and orthodox" in his beliefs. His view of a stratified society was hardly unusual, for almost everyone felt that "all government was based on the principle of subordination and the duty of all classes of men is to contribute to the good of the whole." To Fielding, the homes of the high-placed were no more than prisons: "Newgate [Prison] with the mask on." He displayed caustic attitudes toward this group in both *Joseph Andrews* and *Tom Jones*. His own religious beliefs were integral to his very being. As a magistrate he acted upon these beliefs; he was sympathetic toward his impoverished clients and also accepted a smaller salary. Fielding's scrupulously honest efforts in time reduced the questionable practices that he had seen. He carried this same honesty into his novels.

Yet Fielding was his own man, a truly independent thinker. Not entirely in sympathy with his contemporary world, he was hypercritical of the mores of every class, satirizing the various, odious behaviors of his world in the persons of numerous characters in *Joseph Andrews* and *Tom Jones*, particularly those that exemplified hypocrisy, which he deemed "an ungenerous behavior," whatever the class of the person. The upper class provided numerous examples. In *Joseph Andrews*, he satirizes Lady Booby's attempt to seduce her much younger, chaste footman, Joseph, an act not only reprehensible but also ludicrous. In *Tom Jones*, he shows a lady by position as actually no more than a high-born prostitute or pimp.

Fielding did not spare the middle class, either. In *Joseph Andrews*, he depicted the un-Christian behavior of Parson Trulliber, who laughed at Parson Adams' swine- and mud-stained clothes, constantly berated his own wife, regardless of who was present, and then spurned Parson Adams' need of a loan, though he could have spared much more money than what had been requested. The latter was the essence, Fielding thought, of "faith without works," in his mind typical of a then-current popular religious leader whose ideas Fielding especially detested. Innkeepers, doctors, lawyers, maids, tutors—these became the targets of Fielding's strong disapproval. "Money called the tune" at the time, an idea Fielding could not support.

The lower class, also, came under Fielding's satire. While he could be compassionate toward many of this class, he could still deplore their flaws. A "practical idealist," he gave to the needy, supported the Foundling and Lying-In Hospitals, established subscriptions for old men, and shared his scant income and his plenteous writing talents where he could, even up to the few months before his death. Moreover, unlike his contemporaries, he recognized the dualities of human nature, the constructive-destructive natures of human beings. The basically admirable Squire Western and Squire Allworthy, in *Tom Jones*, he shows as each having the human blemishes of class consciousness. Tom Jones himself he shows as a basically decent young man but one who still must learn prudence through a number devastating experiences, which he eventually surmounts, gaining the necessary wisdom. Even Parson Adams, in *Joseph Andrews*, shares this duality of nature.

Fielding, then, was indignant at the world that he knew. This feeling led to his satiric view of this world, an irony he reiterated repeatedly on stage, in journals, and in his novels in order to correct and redress the awfulness of existing conditions, high and low. He became, then, in his novels especially, "the most faithful representative of his age: he gave its coarsenesses, its brutalities, and sometimes with too little consciousness of their evils, though no one ever satirized more powerfully the worst abuses of the time." He found that his witty but serious approach with his "sure and just sense of values" could and did make dents in the general attitudes and behavior.

Fielding also "represents the strong, healthy common sense and stubborn honesty of the sound English nature" in his particular way, with his object "to give a faithful picture of human nature." Thus, he usually created the illusion of reality, using all ranges of humor—slapstick, situational (based on characters in situations), and the practical joke—to show the various behaviors in his characters that needed correcting. His world appreciated humor in whatever form, and Fielding knew his world very well.

JOSEPH ANDREWS

First published: 1742
Type of work: Novel

A parody in the first ten chapters, this novel tells of the adventures of a young man, although centering more on his traveling companion.

Many critics say *Joseph Andrews* is Fielding's first novel, discounting *An Apology for the Life of Mrs. Shamela Andrews* (1741; commonly known as *Shamela*). *Joseph Andrews*, however, though a parody of *Pamela: Or, Virtue Rewarded* (1740-1741; commonly known as *Pamela*) in its first ten chapters, is "more refined and truly comic" than *Shamela*. Joseph is the "newly invented" brother of Richardson's heroine, and Squire Booby and Lady Booby the counterparts of *Pamela*'s Mr. B. When Fielding had achieved his purpose, his novel soon moved on into an almost picaresque tale centered more on Parson Adams, who, from the eleventh chapter on, dominates the novel.

The full title is typically eighteenth century: *The History of the Adventures of Joseph Andrews, and of His Friend Mr. Abraham Adams, Written in Imitation of the Manner of Cervantes.* The novel was published anonymously in 1742 and did not achieve the immediate acclaim that *Pamela* had, though a new edition came six months later. Fielding was not part of the literary mainstream, a situation true generally of the other early novelists. Individuals "of taste and intellect" liked Fielding's book, finding *Joseph Andrews* truer, more real, "not a tissue of silly make-believe." Fielding—and Richardson—thus validated this new form of fiction.

Joseph Andrews could be called a picaresque novel in structure, for its plot line is similar to the one-line structure of picaresque fiction, much like Miguel de Cervantes' *Don Quixote de la Mancha* (1605, 1615), Fielding's mentor's book. The plot of the novel progresses by "shuttling," moving forward by "small oscillations of emotion," which, in the larger, all-over design, are small parts of a unified whole, episodic in nature. At times, events seem like reversals, followed by forward movement.

In the novel, Fielding employed ironies, unmaskings, conflicts, and reversals. He used coincidences, too, but credibly, indicating one should trust in Divine Providence, the basis of his own creed. One of these coincidences is the peddler, as a burlesque of *Oedipus Tyrannus* (c. 429 B.C.), acting as a messenger in the novel: He arrives just as he is needed, and he happens to know the rights of the births of the two young people, the very information that is needed then. Fielding himself acted as a superior observer, writing in the third person (rather than using Richardson's first person of the epistolary form). Though there are realistic situations and characterizations in *Joseph Andrews,* Fielding did not strive for complete authenticity.

By reversing the sexes of the two main figures of *Pamela* in his own novel, Fielding showed more clearly, he felt, the silliness, the ludicrousness of the "sentimentality and improbability" prevalent in much of his contemporary world. His title character becomes Joseph because he acts like the biblical Joseph, who rejected Potiphar's wife. With his engagement to Fanny, Joseph, at first almost a paragon, becomes more like a normal human being, more real, rather than an improbable "cardboard" character.

In the general plot, Joseph rises from a low rank to become a footman in the London house of a baronet (actually the lowest rank of gentry), Sir Thomas Booby, who dies early in the novel. Not long after, Joseph is inappropriately importuned by the newly widowed Lady Booby and then by Mrs. Slipslop, Lady Booby's horrendous waitingwoman. In the meantime, Fanny Goodwill, Joseph's eventual "intended," is dismissed for her "immorality" (as Slipslop terms her behavior), but principally so because she is attractive. A virtuous, chaste young woman, though naïve, she exists to be rescued. She is sent home to Somersetshire, on the Booby's country estate. Joseph, too, has now been dismissed and has headed for the same destination.

Parson Adams, who was Joseph and Fanny's tutor en route to London, happens upon Joseph in an inn just outside London. The Parson reverses his route and, with Joseph, makes his way back to Joseph's country home, encountering numerous characters and adventures on the way, including rescuing Fanny from a dire situation. At home comes the denouement: the revelation of Fanny and Joseph's true parentages, a seeming reversal, and a hilarious nighttime bedroom scene at Lady Booby's. After all the reversals and seeming conflicts, Joseph and Fanny overcome their difficulties.

Fielding, in this novel, followed "the quixotic pattern of master and Man meeting on the road," much as Cervantes did. Yet he used his previously developed theater skills, too, for the last book of *Joseph Andrews*, the "musical bed" situation, showed quite surely "excessive stagecraft in Fielding's art." In other places, too, he evidently utilized this previous experience, adapting it to this new genre.

Looking at Fielding's cast of characters in *Joseph Andrews*, one sees that the psychology of the characters stands out more so than Fielding's "puppet-like manipulation" of them. Fanny and Joseph, while humanized, are hardly more than conventional young lovers. Parson Adams, however, is a "living human being," both aggressive and humble, a mixture of strong and yet unsophisticated sentiments, comic and yet maddening, but lovable in his unselfish kindness, his unwavering goodness, and his thoroughly honest nature. He is the epitome of naïve virtue, probably Fielding's finest conception.

In *Joseph Andrews*, Fielding utilizes his characters to expose eighteenth century mores: the class consciousness, the easy willingness to admit a formerly lower-class person into a higher class, when circumstances rectify situations. Two incidents illustrate this last point. The Boobys readily admit Fanny, a former serving maid, into their upper-class family, having learned that Fanny is by birth really Pamela's sister, and Mr. Wilson, formerly an outcast rake of London absorbed in the "bright lights," is readily reaccepted once he becomes a respectable country gentleman.

Joseph Andrews, however, is not merely a didactic novel. It is that, true, but the didacticism is masked with the overlay of irony and humor. Fielding's characters are part of a plot replete with ludicrous but essentially serious undertakings and reversals. It is a plot carried out by psychologically realistic characters in humorous yet realistic situations. Fielding's didacticism is, therefore, effective.

TOM JONES

First published: 1749
Type of work: Novel

In this pseudo-autobiographical novel, a thoroughly good young man, through a series of adventures, evolves from innocence to maturity.

Fielding's best-plotted novel, his masterpiece, *The History of Tom Jones, a Foundling*, probably was begun in 1746. When the novel finally appeared, it was "enthusiastically received" by the general public, though not by two groups, the Tory journalists, who strongly disliked Fielding for supporting the House of Hanover, and Richardson and his group, who saw Fielding as a "filthy and immoral writer," even to the point of slandering Fielding himself, particularly for "marrying his cook."

This novel can be labeled pseudoautobiographical: Tom Jones, the main character and hero, is to a large degree, a fictionalized version of his creator's own boyhood experiences, as well as Fielding's own psychological responses to those experiences. The narrative structure moves, through the journey to London that Tom makes, from innocence to experience. Fielding, in this novel, used a central plan, interspersed with seemingly peripheral incidents or subplots, all of which helped the central plot to move steadily toward a desired terminal objective. These peripheral episodes thus fit into the main plot—seeming detours, but all part of the route that Tom must take on his road to knowledge. Using the tight construction of a well-made play, Fielding produced in *Tom Jones* one of the best-plotted novels in English.

Fielding himself called *Tom Jones* a "comic epic poem in prose," though others say it is "essentially a comic romance." Yet Fielding does include some parts that parody the effects of heroic poetry, particularly the digressions. Like other eighteenth century writers, Fielding felt that it was his duty to try to change his society. Thus, he headed each of the eighteen books of *Tom Jones* with an introductory essay, each of which elaborates on an idea that he wished to promote, much like the Greek chorus in a tragedy. The digressions that he interjected only briefly divert the plot, which continues inexorably on to its conclusion.

The structure of *Tom Jones* shows three major parts, each six books in length. The first third of the novel is set in the Paradise Hall of Squire Allworthy in Somersetshire. Here, Tom's infancy and early years to age twenty need only the first three books to be told; the beginning of his twenty-first year and his break with the Squire highlight the next three books. The second third, books 7 through 12, take but weeks to complete, recounting Tom's adventures on the road to London. The third part, books 13 through 18, is set in London, taking only days to completion. Yet the tone is grimmer, not the comical rowdy, farcical adventures Tom has hitherto met on the road but ugly involvements: prostitution, incest, and the like, similar to what Fielding had seen of London himself.

Tom, as a seeming orphan, is an antihero (part of the picaresque tradition.) As such, he is in a sense isolated from his society, which does not know what a truly good person is; as such, he does not fit in. Fielding shows this in numerous scenes. Tom is the essentially good person, though he does sometimes do things that result in harmful outcomes. After Tom's foolishness results in Black George being fired, Tom tries, typically, to atone by giving financial assistance to Black George's family and obtaining another job for him. Nothing Tom does deeply harms another person— more often, Tom harms himself. He is even able to forgive Thwackum's vicious beatings. Throughout the novel, Tom's adventures illustrate his good impulses, his desire to do the right thing each time. Fielding does not see virtue without fault—one has to achieve it by experience, taking it as one goes, the good with the bad. The good-natured will survive, as Tom does.

Blifil, Tom's foil, is quite evidently Tom's mirror side. Fielding shows the reader Blifil's toadying in the presence of the tutors, his freeing Sophia's bird and giving a glib, rationalized excuse to Squire Allworthy—"the bird wanted to be free"—and his remembering Tom's trespasses and relating them to the Squire in the worst light, so that Tom is dismissed from Paradise Hall. There, Blifil is the snake, so to speak, "cold, calculating, selfish, ambitious," eager to supplant his good-natured opposite by manipulation. The two have the same mother, the same environment, the same education, but totally different natures, again illustrating Fielding's fascination with determinism, or predestination (fate). The other characters in *Tom Jones* may be additional old stock types, with each of the four humors represented. The Man of the Mountain can be said to represent the melancholy; Partridge, Tom's putative father, the sanguine; with others representing the choleric and phlegmatic humors.

A mentor character, Squire Allworthy, Fielding's mouthpiece, is never shown as a "pompous fool." Having been modeled on two of Fielding's good friends, Squire Allworthy is shown as a good man, though not all wise. Fielding would have been ashamed to mock these friends. Like many good people, Allworthy is not able to imagine what some others would think or do; he is thus all too susceptible to the villains' manipulations. As a result, he puts Tom out of Paradise Hall and onto the road. He is an honorable man, who, when finally presented with the deeds of his nephews, Tom and Blifil, is able to recognize his own shortcomings, restoring Tom to grace and Blifil to his own hell. As a mentor character, his purpose is to put the author's ideas into practice; like other such characters, he is not especially well-developed but remains wooden and static.

Squire Western is an example of the Tory independent landowners who generally favored the Stuarts. He, like his society, hated the German Hanoverians, who, in his view, were foisted upon the English. (Fielding himself favored the Hanoverians.) Decidedly Church of England (as Fielding was), he is hostile to central government, preferring peace rather than the upset of war, especially internecine, or civil, war.

Squire Western's sister, having been immersed in the Hanoverian court, is therefore suspect at home, not only for her political-social leanings but also as a model for Squire Western's daughter Sophia, who is of marriageable age. Never having been married herself, she is finally discredited as a suitable role model. *How could she know?* seems to have been both the Squire and Sophia's attitudes.

The tutors, modeled after two Salisbury acquaintances, are foils to Tom. Thwackum, the principal tutor, represents violent authority; he rationalizes his vicious beatings of Tom, having no concern with goodness or charity. Fielding shows Thwackum to be an outraged, morally bankrupt hypocrite; when the tutor learns that Squire Allworthy plans on leaving one thousand pounds to him, Thwackum laments that it is only that. Another hyprocrite is the other tutor, the deist Square, who on the surface upholds the "natural beauty of virtue" but finds no qualms in sneaking out to Molly Seagrim's for a sexual tryst, where Tom discovers him. Square represents rational persuasion, but both he and Thwackum vitiate the principles they have espoused as teachers. Of the two, though, Square does grow as a character.

Summary

Henry Fielding was the second of the early novelists. As such, he was an "innovating master of the first order." In *Joseph Andrews* and *Tom Jones*, as in his other novels, he discarded his predecessor's epistolary method, calling his own books " 'comic epics in prose' "—in effect, the first modern novels, the development of which influenced Charles Dickens and William Makepeace Thackeray in the nineteenth century. Though he is hardly an "exalted moralist" or a philosopher, his opinions do shape his novels, in part or in whole, in various episodes. *Joseph Andrews* and *Tom Jones* show him to be one of the most thoughtful of novelists. Though satiric, he maintained a somewhat realistic outlook; he is the first novelist to give the impression of frankly and fully recording normal behavior: His characters are "real people" who could step off Fielding's pages into real life, thus sidestepping the encroachment of the then prevalent sentimentality.

Bibliography

Baugh, Albert C. *A Literary History of England*. New York: Appleton-Century-Crofts, 1948.

Ehrenpreis, Irvin. Afterword to *The History and Adventures of Joseph Andrews*, by Henry Fielding. New York: New American Library, 1979.

Sherburn, George. "Fielding's Social Outlook." In *Eighteenth Century English Literature: Modern Essays in Criticism*. Edited by James L. Clifford. London: Oxford University Press, 1959.

Sherwood, Irma Z. "The Novelists as Commentators." In *The Age of Johnson: Es-

says Presented to Chauncey Brewster Tinker. Edited by Frederick W. Hilles. New Haven, Conn.: Yale University Press, 1949.

Stephen, Leslie, Sir. *History of English Thought in the Eighteenth Century.* 2 vols. New York: Harcourt, Brace & World, 1962.

Stevenson, Lionel. *The English Novel: A Panorama.* Boston: Houghton Mifflin, 1960.

Watt, Ian. *The Rise of the Novel: Studies in Defoe, Richardson, and Fielding.* Berkeley: University of California Press, 1962.

Mary Beale Wright

GUSTAVE FLAUBERT

Born: Rouen, France
December 12, 1821
Died: Croisset, France
May 8, 1880

Principal Literary Achievement

Flaubert is recognized as one of the world's greatest novelists. His novel *Madame Bovary* is particularly acclaimed as a masterpiece of world literature and an example of realism.

Biography

Gustave Flaubert was born in the historic Normandy city of Rouen, in northern France, on December 12, 1821. His father, Dr. Achille Cléophas Flaubert, was a surgeon in Rouen, where Gustave went to school. Gustave was one of six children, only three of whom survived to adulthood. Among them was his older brother Achille, who became a doctor like his father. Gustave was a good student, winning prizes for history and earning his *baccalauréat* in 1840.

Between 1840 and 1843, Flaubert studied law in Paris but failed his examinations. In 1844, he began to suffer from strange fits identified as epilepsy. The first attack rendered him an invalid for several months and led to the family's moving to Croisset, outside Rouen. A second consequence of the illness was that Flaubert's family came to accept that he would not pursue a career and allowed him to devote himself to his writing. Certain critics, among them the French existentialist Jean-Paul Sartre, have commented extensively on the role of Flaubert's debilitating illness on his subsequent literary career.

In 1846, Flaubert's father died, a loss quickly followed by the death of his sister Caroline in childbirth. Flaubert remained with his mother, Caroline Fleuriot (she did not die until 1872), and his infant niece, and he began to develop his literary ideas. His first draft of *La Tentation de Saint Antoine* (*The Temptation of Saint Anthony*, 1895), the final version of which was not published until 1874, was read to friends at this time, and the seeds of the novel that would become *Madame Bovary* (1857; English translation, 1886) were sown. While working, Flaubert lived a hermit-like existence at the family's country house at Croisset. This reclusive regime did not prevent Flaubert from visiting Paris as well as more distant and exotic sites. In October, 1849, Flaubert left France with his friend Maxime du Camp for a journey to the Middle

East that lasted until May of 1851.

Both during and after this journey, Flaubert kept in touch through letters, and his correspondence, edited and published after his death, survives as an important record of his thoughts and ideas, as his extensive correspondence with the novelist George Sand illustrates. During the period when Flaubert was working intensively on *Madame Bovary* (1851-1853), he also wrote to Louise Colet, herself a writer; she was his mistress and, some have argued, one of the models for the character Emma Bovary.

Flaubert did not publish his first novel, *Madame Bovary*, until 1856, when it began to appear in serial form in the *Revue de Paris*. The following year, the novel became the subject of a trial. The agents of the repressive Second Empire regime unsuccessfully prosecuted the novel for obscenity, claiming that the depiction of adultery would corrupt public morals. Flaubert was eventually acquitted of the charges, and the novel appeared in book form. Even without the publicity of the trial, the novel became famous, in part thanks to Flaubert's now-famous style (Flaubert was extraordinarily demanding of himself and was constantly revising until he found *le mot juste*) and his development of "free indirect style," a form of reported speech in which it becomes increasingly difficult to distinguish between the voice of the narrator and the interior monologue of the protagonist.

After the turbulence of the trial, Flaubert took another trip that lasted from April to June of 1858. This time he travelled to Tunisia to collect information for a book he was planning, to be set in Carthage. This novel, entitled *Salammbô* (English translation, 1886), was subsequently published in 1862 and marked a new trend in Flaubert's work. His eye for detail was every bit as keen, and the novel boasts lush passages of description that illustrate Flaubert's romantic tendencies, but his choosing to set the novel in the distant past has been seen by many critics as significant.

Flaubert returned to a contemporary setting in his next novel, *L'Éducation sentimentale* (*A Sentimental Education*, 1898). The book was first published in France in 1869, near the end of the Second Empire; its description of the 1848 revolution added to Flaubert's reputation as a realist, thanks to his meticulous documentation of contemporary life. Flaubert's career was interrupted by the political events of 1870, when France went to war with Prussia, a confrontation that quickly brought about the end of the Second Empire. Flaubert continued to suffer from nervous illness but served in the National Guard. The interruptions to his work were not only political, however, for on April 6, 1872, his mother died. Flaubert persevered with his writing despite the setbacks. He dabbled briefly in theater, but his play *Le Candidat* (*The Candidate*, 1904) ran for only four performances in 1874 before being canceled. Flaubert had more success with his novel *The Temptation of Saint Anthony*, an idea on which he had been working since the 1840's. The novel was finally published in 1874.

During the remaining years of his life, Flaubert worked alternately on two projects: *Trois Contes* (1877; *Three Tales*, 1903) and *Bouvard et Pécuchet* (1881; *Bouvard and Pécuchet*, 1896). These works required prodigious quantities of documentation, and progress was slow. In addition, Flaubert was beset by health problems as well as financial worries. When the husband of his niece Caroline, Ernest Commanville, went bankrupt, Flaubert helped out financially to avoid bringing dishonor on the family, but the cost was great. He himself was ruined financially, forced to sell many family heirlooms that he was reluctant to part with, and he faced the prospect of relying on his writing to bring in an income. *Three Tales* was eventually published in 1877, and Flaubert could finally give his undivided attention to *Bouvard and Pécuchet*, but it was too late. He died on May 8, 1880, in Croisset, his last work still unfinished. It was published nevertheless, despite its incompletion, in 1881, the year following Flaubert's death.

Analysis

Flaubert has been hailed as a realist, thanks mainly to his masterpiece *Madame Bovary*; he has also been claimed as a precursor of decadence, but Flaubert cared little for labels. He did not affiliate himself with any particular school of literature, and his main concern was with style. His works alternate between works of realism and exoticism. His first novel, *Madame Bovary*, his most celebrated accomplishment, was followed by *Salammbô*, a work set in the distant past. Flaubert returned to the recent past and the politically charged years of the 1848 revolution with *A Sentimental Education* but again departed from this realistic approach in *The Temptation of Saint Anthony*.

Despite this alternation, all of Flaubert's works share certain features: They are meticulously researched, stylistically rich, and exhaustively rewritten. His letters are a valuable complement to his prose fiction works, documenting his struggles with style and recounting how, for example, he would declaim his work aloud in order to find exactly the right word to fit not just the meaning of the sentence but its formal structure and poetic cadence as well. Flaubert's style became legendary, and admirers could recite typical passages. One favorite example was the opening sentence of *Salammbô*, whose tripartite structure was typical of Flaubert's style.

Although the name of Flaubert is often associated with the realist school, his works were influential in a number of other ways. The themes of mysticism, sadism, and the femme fatale, a pattern in Flaubert's work already discernible in Salammbô but accentuated by *The Temptation of Saint Anthony* and by the short story "Hérodias" (published in Flaubert's collection *Three Tales*), were recognized in the 1880's as important precursors to the decadent movement in literature.

Flaubert's interest in realism was also a reflection of his preoccupation with the power of the cliché to obscure meaning even as it appears to make meaning possible. Throughout his life, Flaubert was fascinated by what he came to call "received ideas"— ideas that on the surface seem meaningful but, when examined, reveal lack of critical thought and mediocrity. The first illustration of this theme occurs in the character of Homais, the chemist in *Madame Bovary*. Homais has an opinion about everything, but his pronouncements are usually unoriginal, pompous, and complacent.

Flaubert was still preoccupied by this idea at the end of his life, in *Bouvard and Pécuchet*. Although unfinished, it is nevertheless a masterpiece (like most, if not all of Flaubert's published works). The result, once again, of meticulous research, the novel illustrates Flaubert's mockery of bourgeois complacency through the figures of two middle-class clerks who, meeting by chance, decide that they are soul brothers based on the (to them) portentous realization that they have the same ideas. Flaubert undercuts this spiritual affinity by revealing that their uncanny sympathy is proven (in their estimation) by the fact that each had had the brilliant idea of writing his name inside his hat. The banality of this initial point of commonality sets the tone for their joint story. They retire from their menial jobs and buy a farm in Normandy, determined to devote themselves to a great communal project that will realize their ambitions and ideals. They sink their fortunes into a series of fads, each sillier than the next (landscape gardening, fertilizer experimentation, social reform, and the study of phallic symbolism), in which their total lack of talent or inspiration brings failure after failure. While Flaubert created characters who become mouthpieces for received ideas, he also collected examples of received ideas and compiled them into a sort of dictionary arranged alphabetically by theme and titled *Dictionnaire des idées reçues* (1910, 1913; *Dictionary of Accepted Ideas*, 1954).

Flaubert's relentless mockery of middle-class self-satisfaction is extremely humorous but relies heavily on irony for its effect, and the reader must be constantly vigilant in order to perceive the disjunction between the high tone of the speeches of various characters and its inappropriateness. Flaubert seldom intrudes as narrator to point out these juxtapositions; indeed, his famous style of free indirect mode obscures the role of the narrator. This style lies somewhere between interior monologue (presenting things the way they are perceived by a given character) and indirect (or reported) speech presented by a third-person narrator or observer. The narrator does not tell the reader what to think but presents narrative events colored by the perceptions of individual participants, which the reader must then evaluate. Thus, a famous scene in *Madame Bovary* depicts a troubled Emma seeking to unburden herself to the priest Bournisien. Emma catches him at a bad moment, when he is distracted by the more temporal concerns of controlling an unruly group of boys. His attention is only half on Emma, a problem compounded by his own lack of spiritual vision and understanding. The best comfort he can offer is to suggest her problem may be due to something she has eaten.

MADAME BOVARY

First published: 1857 (English translation, 1886)
Type of work: Novel

A young woman, unable to reconcile her idealistic vision of life with reality, commits suicide after a series of adulterous affairs.

Madame Bovary, Flaubert's first published novel, is arguably his greatest. Emma Bovary has become one of the most famous characters in world literature, and critics continue to debate and interpret her life, which, in its depiction of the conflict between idealism and reality, remains every bit as relevant today as it did when first published.

Formally divided into three parts, each one corresponding to a stage in Emma's life, the novel opens with Charles Bovary's youth and ends after Emma's death, making Charles, as it were, a set of parentheses that enclose Emma's life. Each section corresponds to an important stage in the narrative. The first part ends with the move to Yonville and the news that Emma is pregnant, thus presenting optimism at the prospect of change. As the reader suspects, however, the change does not bring happiness, and Emma quickly becomes dissatisfied once again. In her search for happiness, she turns to adultery with the rakish and unabashedly exploitative Rodolphe, whom Emma persists in seeing as a romantic hero. Emma plans to elope with him, but he balks at the last minute, and Emma is thrust into a depression that ends the second part of the novel. In the final section, Emma engages in yet another adulterous affair, this time with Léon, using the pretext of music lessons as the cover for her regular visits to nearby Rouen. The affair quickly becomes a routine, however, and a typical day sees Emma lying ever more blatantly to cover her tracks, selling property to pay the mounting bills, juggling the money problems, and taking less and less trouble to be discreet about the affair. For once, Emma is getting what she wants—excitement, romance, luxuries—and is forced to confront the fact that these are not the things that bring happiness. Unable to extricate herself from the financial problems that are ruining the family, and now irrevocably disillusioned about the possibility of finding happiness, she concludes that the only alternative is suicide.

Her dissatisfactions are highlighted by the contrast between her ideals and her uninspiring husband. The novel opens with the description of Charles Bovary as a schoolboy, a rather bumbling and boorish figure who provokes derision and mockery in his new classmates. It has often been noted that the name "Bovary," derived from the Latin for "ox," symbolizes Charles's bovine character: slow, coarse and unrefined, rather dull-witted. Charles's unfortunate start in life does not prevent him from becoming a doctor with a modest country practice and marrying for the second time for love, not for money. He marries Emma, the daughter of one of his farmer-patients, who then takes over as the central character of the narrative. Charles is an "officier de santé," a phrase often simply translated as "country doctor," but it is important, especially for contemporary readers, to remember that this was a second-class kind of doctor. Thus, although Charles is associated with the prestigious field of medicine, he is presented as one of its less-skilled practitioners. His was a modestly paid and extremely unglamorous occupation, which consisted mainly of contact with the most distasteful aspects of human malaise.

Flaubert describes in detail Emma's background and education, for the fact that her outlook has been conditioned by reading novels is important in understanding her subsequent disappointments in life. She has high expectations of marriage and looks to it to fulfill all her dreams and ideals. When reality does not live up to these hopes, she is quickly dissatisfied. She imagines that satisfaction can be found in motherhood, romantic affairs, religion, material possessions, and any number of other fads that temporarily inspire her enthusiasm, but she is disappointed every time. At the end of the novel, when she despairs of finding happiness and realizes that she has ruined her family's life through the debts she has incurred, she poisons herself with arsenic, turning her disillusionment inward in a self-destructive gesture of defeat.

Critics have disagreed over how Emma's character should be interpreted. According to some, her idealism is seen as destructive and unrealistic, an example of the negative forces unleashed by romantic and indulgent imagination or, more reductively, as the folly of a materialistic and acquisitive woman who brings about the downfall of her family through her unbounded and selfish desires. A more sympathetic reading has also emerged based on a different understanding of the role of gender in the novel, a reading that sees Emma less as a silly woman, and more as a character in search of a deeper meaning to life but trapped by circumstances. These differences of interpretation are highlighted by different interpretations of the title of the work, which stresses that the heroine is not Emma, but *Madame.* Does the title, symbolizing Emma's married, public identity, call attention to what she betrays, or to the situation that entraps her?

A SENTIMENTAL EDUCATION

First published: *L'Éducation sentimentale*, 1869; (English translation, 1898)
Type of work: Novel

The idealistic young Frédéric Moreau falls in love with an inaccessible woman and, over the course of a lifetime, gradually loses his ideals.

A Sentimental Education, Flaubert's third novel, furthered the author's reputation for realism through its depiction of the recent past, specifically the events of 1848. The novel also had another realistic twist in its autobiographical underpinnings: The basis for Frédéric's infatuation with Madame Arnoux is Flaubert's idealization of Madame Maurice Schlésinger (Elisa Foucault), whom he had met while on vacation at Trouville, when he was only fourteen. Madame Schlésinger, the wife of a music editor and then twenty-six years old, became for Flaubert the model of an ideal but distant woman.

A Sentimental Education follows its hero Frédéric Moreau over a period of many years, from his youth and its romantic aspirations through a series of lessons in life in which Frédéric is exposed to the decidedly unromantic side of a number of lifestyles. Political idealism, brotherhood, high society, finance, and the art world are all demystified as Frédéric learns more about each segment of society. Gradually, his ideals are eroded, leaving him only with disillusionment. When he gets together with his old childhood friend, Deslauriers, at the end of the novel, they relive their schoolboy days, and one incident in particular when they went to a brothel. In the closing words of the novel, the two men decide that these were the best times they had ever had. The nostalgia for their lost youth and innocence is poignant, yet at the same time the reader is left wondering. If a botched visit to a brothel is the highlight of their youth and the best that they remember, this fact alone speaks volumes about the many disappointments their lives contain.

A constant theme weaving together Frédéric's lessons in life is his love for Madame Arnoux. He meets her for the first time by chance when she is a fellow traveler on the ferry he is taking home to Nogent, and it is love at first sight for him. He is only eighteen years old at the time, but this idealized love quickly becomes the dominant passion of his life. Frédéric befriends the expansive and genial Monsieur Arnoux, Marie's husband, and becomes more deeply involved in his fortunes than he (Frédéric) would otherwise prefer, all in an attempt to retain his proximity to Arnoux's wife. Frédéric loans money and becomes implicated in Arnoux's affairs with mistresses, all to retain some contact with the family. Each time he resolves to take action, a twist of events thwarts him at the last minute (or are these merely pretexts to disguise his own ambivalence?), and Flaubert's talents are fully deployed in creating dramatic irony that constantly defers resolution of the plot.

The most significant example of this irony comes when Frédéric finally has a chance to consummate his relationship with Madame Arnoux. They arrange a rendezvous, for which Frédéric even arrives early, but his anticipation gradually turns to disappointment as he waits and waits. Finally, after five hours, he leaves. This disappointment precipitates Frédéric's next action, for he goes to see Arnoux's mistress Rosanette in order to get his revenge. Thus, by the time he learns the real reason for Madame Arnoux's failure to appear (her child had fallen ill), he had already judged the situation and engaged himself in another course of action (with Rosanette).

While preserving his ideal love, unconsummated, for Madame Arnoux, Frédéric enters a number of liaisons with other women that highlight in various ways the primary relationship. The relationship with Rosanette, for example, serves to contrast carnal love with the ideal and spiritual qualities with which Frédéric endows his love for Madame Arnoux. Similarly, his relationship with Louise underscores the role of inaccessibility in the development of the plot. Louise is ultimately uninteresting to Frédéric because she is accessible, and this paradox (wanting only what one cannot have) provides the key to understanding the failure of Frédéric's relationship with Madame Arnoux: The moment that he thinks that she has finally become accessible to him is the moment that he starts looking elsewhere.

Frédéric Moreau is a male counterpart to Emma Bovary (indeed, the poet Charles Baudelaire once remarked that Emma Bovary had a man's soul in a woman's body), both characters trying to break out of the human condition of frustrated desire. Superficially, both characters can be read as weak and misguided individuals who suffer from the illusion that the grass is always greener somewhere else. Yet Flaubert treats this theme with indulgence for his characters' weakness and suggests that their dissatisfactions also possess a metaphysical dimension.

THREE TALES

First published: *Trois Contes*, 1877 (English translation, 1903)
Type of work: Short stories

The life story of an obscure country servant is followed by the medieval story of Saint Julien and complemented by a reworking of the biblical story of Herodias.

Three Tales consists of three short stories: "Un Cœur simple" ("A Simple Heart"), "La Légende de Saint Julien l'Hospitalier" ("The Legend of St. Julian, Hospitaler), and "Hérodias." Taken together, these three stories reflect Flaubert's thematic concerns and artistic style. "A Simple Heart" tells the story of Félicité, a simpleminded and religious family servant. Set in contemporary, provincial France, this short story became an exercise in realism and narrative style. "The Legend of Saint Julian, Hospitaler" reactivates Flaubert's interest in historical settings and the lives of saints (with a fantastic twist), while "Hérodias" shares some of these features (the historical setting) while also incorporating the themes of exoticism and the femme fatale, a theme frequently explored by nineteenth century writers through the story of Salomé, which enjoyed a particular vogue in literature and painting at the turn of the century. Despite these different settings and themes, the three stories present a certain unity through recurrent motifs and patterns.

Stylistically, these stories reveal Flaubert's mature writing skills, and the minimal use of dialogue gives Flaubert ample room to develop his narrative techniques. Félicité, whose name ironically means "felicity" or "happiness," is shown through a third-person narrator whose voice blends imperceptibly into a more articulate version of her own inner voice. It is the story of an obscure and overlooked life, told in five carefully structured parts. Félicité lives vicariously through the children of her mistress Madame Aubain, through a nephew, and finally even through a parrot. Just when she seems most unwanted herself, she adopts an unwanted parrot, Loulou, who becomes her companion. When the parrot dies, she has it stuffed, and at the moment of her own death she confuses the sight of Loulou with a vision of the Holy Ghost descending from heaven.

Flaubert stated that his intentions in "A Simple Heart" were not to be ironic but to evoke pity. He relied heavily on autobiographical details for the background materials and even brought home a stuffed parrot that he kept on his desk as inspiration during the writing of the story. It was not pity for himself he wished to evoke, even though his recent financial ruin was still a source of pain. Instead, he was responding to a challenge from the novelist George Sand, who had reproached him for being unable to depict simple goodness. Sand died before she was able to see her challenge bear fruit in this story.

This rather muted story stands in contrast to the two historical panels of this triptych, a structure echoing the alternation in Flaubert's work between contemporary and exotic works. In the companion panels, the reader finds the story of Saint Julian, which invokes the bright colors of a gothic stained-glass window, and the equally colorful, but more barbaric, story of Hérodias, also with a saintly figure, that of John the Baptist.

The story of Saint Julian focuses on the fulfillment of three predictions. Julian's birth is accompanied by two divine prophecies. The first, that he will be a saint, is delivered to his mother, while the second, predicting military glory, is told to his father. Julian himself receives a third, and more troubling, prophecy. The young Julian is an avid hunter, but when one of his targets, a stag, addresses him in a human voice to tell him he (Julian) will kill his parents, he leaves home to avoid his fate.

The second part of the story sees Julian fulfilling the prophecy of military glory, where he continues to indulge his bloodlust. Like his more familiar counterpart Oedipus, Julian nevertheless cannot escape his destiny, and the narrative leads the reader to the inexorable fulfillment of the stag's curse. Leaving his palace one night to hunt, Julian returns to find two people in his bed. Supposing them to be his wife and a lover, he kills them in a rage, only to discover that the couple was his own parents, on a pilgrimage, to whom his wife had given up the bed.

To complete the cycle of prophecies, the third segment takes up the prediction of sainthood. Julian has become an outcast to atone for his sins and lives a poor and hermit-like existence. One night, during a storm, a leper asks to be ferried across the river. Julian complies and also grants the leper's requests for food and shelter. The leper eventually requests that Julian warm him with his own body, and when Julian does this, the leper is miraculously transformed into Jesus, who transports Julian with him to heaven.

Here, Flaubert does not focus on the inner thoughts and perceptions of characters, choosing instead to present them like the naive characters of the cathedral window that inspired them and to show the workings of tragedy. Julian is a tragic character, doomed by his own love of pointless killing but redeemed by charity and humility. The twin themes of fate and faith link all three stories in this series.

The final panel of the triptych is also similar to the story of Saint Julian by also being depicted on Rouen cathedral, in Flaubert's hometown, though this time in the form of a stone carving rather than a stained-glass window. "Hérodias" throws the reader into the midst of the narrative at a crucial time, precisely when the actors in a tragic drama can yet intervene to change the course of events. In the opening scene of "Hérodias," Herod Antipas is up before dawn, agitated, contemplating the need for decision and action. The timing of the action (it occupies twenty-four hours, from dawn to dawn—gives the story a classical form. Herod must decide how best to use his prisoner John the Baptist (Iaokanann) in his quest to control Jerusalem.

Herod's situation is precarious. He is planning to celebrate his birthday, and a number of powerful Romans have been invited to attend, but at the same time he is being attacked by the King of the Arabs. Once again, prophecy has a role to play, for it has been predicted that someone important will die in the citadel that day. Herod's problem is that there are so many important people around, it is not clear who the victim will be. The irony is that Iaokanann is not on his list of possibilities, since he fails to consider him important.

A Roman inspection of the citadel is the pretext for a lavish description of the visiting dignitaries, the fortress, and of Iaokanann himself, setting the tone of intrigue and excitement that dominates. The description, reminiscent of Flaubert's earlier novel *Salammbô*, continues with the evening feast, which also serves to illustrate the clash of cultures and to air the growing rumors concerning Iaokanann's role in a new religious movement.

The climax of the evening is Salomé's dance. Salomé is the puppet of her scheming mother Hérodias, who uses her daughter's seductive charm to manipulate the powerful men around her. Flaubert maintained that the interest of "Hérodias" lay not in the religious theme but in the figure of Hérodias as a kind of Cleopatra figure, that is, a study in power and seduction. Herod is particularly smitten by Salomé because of her resemblance to Hérodias (Salomé is her daughter by an earlier marriage) and offers her any reward she chooses. Salomé asks for the head of Iaokanann, which is brought to her on a platter.

Summary

Gustave Flaubert's reputation as a master of prose fiction is based on a number of long novels, as well as some shorter fiction, that sustain the quality of his best moments.

His style, innovative in its use of an ambiguous narrative voice and the result of much care and labor, has contributed to his standing as a major writer. His psychological insight, and, more recently, an appreciation of his experiments in the control of narrative perspective make him one of the first modern novelists and one of the greatest of all time.

Bibliography

Bart, Benjamin F. *Flaubert.* Syracuse, N.Y.: Syracuse University Press, 1967.

Brombert, Victor. *The Novels of Flaubert: A Study of Themes and Techniques.* Princeton, N.J.: Princeton University Press, 1966.

Culler, Jonathan. *Flaubert: The Uses of Uncertainty.* Ithaca, N.Y.: Cornell University Press, 1974.

Fairlie, Alison. *Flaubert: Madame Bovary.* London: Edward Arnold, 1962.

Giraud, Raymond Dorner. *Flaubert: A Collection of Critical Essays.* Englewood Cliffs, N.J.: Prentice-Hall, 1964.

Haig, Stirling. *Flaubert and the Gift of Speech: Dialogue and Discourse in Four "Modern" Novels.* New York: Cambridge University Press, 1986.

La Capra, Dominick. *"Madame Bovary" On Trial.* Ithaca, N.Y.: Cornell University Press, 1982.

Lloyd, Rosemary. *Madame Bovary.* Boston: Unwin Hyman, 1990.

Sherrington, R. *Three Novels by Flaubert: A Study of Techniques.* Oxford, England: Clarendon Press, 1970.

Starkie, Enid. *Flaubert: The Making of the Master.* New York: Atheneum, 1967.

Melanie Hawthorne

FORD MADOX FORD

Born: Merton, Surrey, England
December 17, 1873
Died: Deauville, France
June 26, 1939

Principal Literary Achievement
One of the most productive writers of the modernist period, Ford was a stylistic innovator, an invaluable editor and collaborator, and a great novelist.

Biography

Ford Madox Ford was born Ford Hermann Hueffer in Merton, Surrey, a suburb of London, England, on December 17, 1873, the eldest son of Francis Hueffer, a musicologist and critic, and Catherine Brown Hueffer, daughter of the renowned painter Ford Madox Brown. He was given the upbringing appropriate to the scion of an artistic family; lessons in languages, in music, and in painting preceded entry into an experimental school, Praetorius. There he remained until his father died in 1889, leaving the family penniless; they had to be taken in by Ford's grandfather.

Fordie, as he was known to his friends, roamed the streets of London for the next few years, associating with aesthetes and decadents, anarchists and artists. Aided by his grandfather, he published three books of fairy tales by the time he turned twenty-one and began working on a serious novel; these accomplishments emboldened him to elope with Elsie Martindale, whom he had met years before at Praetorius, in 1894.

After two very uncomfortable years, Elsie's parents forgave their daughter and agreed to help support the young couple; by that time, Ford's own career was progressing with the publication of *Ford Madox Brown* (1896) the official biography of his late grandfather, and his introduction to Joseph Conrad, the Polish-born novelist, with whom Ford would be connected for the next decade. Although the value of this relationship has been much debated, it is undeniable that Ford (who was by now calling himself Ford Madox Hueffer) provided Conrad with vital information about English idioms and customs, in addition to psychological support during the latter's frequent bouts of despondency. Nevertheless, the products of this collaboration—*The Inheritors* (1901), *Romance* (1903), and *The Nature of a Crime* (serial, 1909; 1924)—are markedly inferior to the works each wrote on his own during this period, such as Conrad's *Lord Jim* and Ford's *Fifth Queen* trilogy.

During the first decade of the twentieth century, Ford was best known as a writer

Janice Biala and Ford Madox Ford

of nonfiction. His study of the English Channel towns, *The Cinque Ports*, appeared in 1900; *The Soul of London* appeared in 1905, and two further books on English country life followed in 1906 and 1907. Interspersed with these were collections of fairy tales, biographies of artists such as Hans Holbein, and a weekly newspaper column. Though these works made little money for Ford, they kept his name before the public; meanwhile, he was preparing his brilliant re-creation of the life of Katherine Howard, fifth queen of King Henry VIII, published as *The Fifth Queen* (1906), *Privy Seal* (1907), and *The Fifth Queen Crowned* (1908). In this trilogy, Ford for the first time successfully fused his lifelong learning about England with his growing knowledge of contemporary human psychology; in Ford's hands, Henry VIII's fifth queen, actually executed for fornication, becomes a champion of conscience framed for her efforts to restore Catholicism to England.

Unfortunately, none of these books ever sold more than a few thousand copies. In fact, Ford's career up to the outbreak of World War I was marked by outright failures, interspersed with a few half-successes, such as *Mr. Apollo* (1908), *Ladies Whose Bright Eyes* (1911), and *The New Humpty-Dumpty* (1912). Perhaps his greatest fame stemmed from the *English Review*, which Ford edited from its first issue in December, 1908, until the middle of 1910. This journal, like Ford's later magazine *Transatlantic Review*, gave voice to an entire generation of literary artists, from established writers such as H. G. Wells and Henry James to new voices such as those of Wyndham Lewis, Ezra Pound, and D. H. Lawrence. It also lost nearly £500 an issue; within two years, Ford had been forced out. It was perhaps in response to this lack of critical and financial success that Ford began an affair with Violet Hunt, who had had five previous liaisons, including one with the writer W. Somerset Maugham. Ford's wife refused a divorce, took him to court, and ultimately forced him to leave England for most of the next two years. Such shows of force could not persuade Ford to return to his wife, and though Elsie never admitted to a divorce, she finally allowed him to advertise his mistress as his wife, making Ford and Violet acceptable once more in polite society. Ironically, these ugly years of struggle provided Ford with material for his greatest work, *The Good Soldier* (1915).

By the time this novel appeared, England was at war with Germany. Ford wrote two books of propaganda, then enlisted in the army as a junior officer. Although he was never directly in the front lines, he spent several weeks under continual artillery fire, received a concussion, and was sent home in March of 1917. Ford's experiences in World War I would serve as the raw material for his other great work of fiction, *Parade's End* (1924-1928, 1950). Still suffering from the effects of shell shock, Ford moved to a cottage in Sussex, where he was joined by Stella Bowen, a young Australian painter whom he had met through Ezra Pound; to prevent a repetition of his earlier legal difficulties, he changed his name at this time to the familiar Ford Madox Ford. His shell shock might explain the frequent lapses from factuality that fill the pages of *Thus to Revisit* (1921), the first of several books of memoirs and recollections Ford would write, which also include *Return to Yesterday* (1931) and *Portraits from Life*, (1937). These works are characterized by incisive description of events that

never took place; their inaccuracies and outright fantasies have haunted Ford's reputation ever since.

The last twenty years of Ford's life were spent alternately in France and the United
States, where a new generation admired him as a teacher and father figure. He began
The Transatlantic Review, which he edited with Ernest Hemingway, publishing works
by writers as disparate as James Joyce and Gertrude Stein. He went on a long U.S.
lecture tour in 1926 and 1927, returned to France, ended his liaison with Stella Bowen,
and sailed back for another American tour in 1928. In the spring of 1930, he was back
in Paris, where he met the woman with whom he would pass the rest of his life,
Janice Biala; in 1931, he published his last first-rate work, a collection of poems about
Janice called *Buckshee*.

The onset of the Depression made the life of a writer even harder, and Ford was
pushed into a series of works designed simply to pay the bills that inexorably mounted
around him; by the end of his career, he had returned to that nonfictional form with
which he had begun, perhaps the best example of which is *Provence* (1935). Still
dreaming of critical respectability, he finished a comprehensive literary history entitled *The March of Literature* in 1938. The accumulated effects of forty years' over-
indulgence in food and wine, however, finally caught up with him; on June 26, 1939,
in Deauville, France, he died of uremia and heart failure.

Analysis

Ford is best known for his leadership of the modernist movement in literature, a
movement famous for its experiments in form and style but equally important for its
revolution in subject matter. The Victorians, for example, had turned to fantasy as a
way of escaping the evils of urbanization and industrialization; the modernists, in
contrast, used the fantastic as a way of confronting human beings' deepest psychological reactions to extreme situations. These writers thought of themselves as discovering new planes of existence, or (in a famous image invented by the novelist
Virginia Woolf) exposing the buried connections among the isolated, alienated inhabitants of the times. Such efforts were underscored by the scientific discoveries of
the time, such as Sigmund Freud's psychoanalytical theory, Henri-Louis Bergson's
theory of temporality, and Albert Einstein's theory of relativity, all of which were
published between 1895 and 1905.

Throughout his career, Ford insisted that literature must confront the main issues of
contemporary life, even though its outward subject might be a tale five centuries old
(the Fifth Queen Trilogy), or might involve actions considered physically impossible
(*Henry for Hugh*, 1934). Ford even wrote a series of satires on contemporary life—
The Simple Life Limited (1911), *The New Humpty-Dumpty* (1912), and *Mr. Fleight*
(1913)—though he lacked sufficient courage to publish them under his own name,
using the pseudonym "Daniel Chaucer" for the first two titles. The *Parade's End*
novels contain the most vivid re-creation of wartime experience in the history of
English literature.

Most of Ford's serious analysis of the social and political changes that characterized the early twentieth century remains unacknowledged by contemporary readers, however, because of Ford's striking stylistic experimentation. Ford often used a point of view that is mistakenly called the "interior monologue," but he was one of the first to recognize that people do not, as a rule, make speeches to themselves. In place of the unrealistic "monologue," Ford offered a succession of fragments, each one arising into consciousness but quickly succeeded by other, seemingly unrelated, fragments. His work can thus be called the first truly realistic work in literary history.

Ford's technique offered a second advantage as well. Since Samuel Richardson wrote *Pamela: Or, Virtue Rewarded* as a series of letters in 1740, writers have striven to record action that takes place in the immediate present accurately yet effectively, but all that they have created is a series of acceptable conventions for interpreting retellings of past events as if they were happening in the present. James Joyce in *Ulysses* (1922) and Ford in novels from *The Fifth Queen* (1906) to *The Last Post* (1928) created a sense that what was taking place for the character was being immediately transcribed for the reader. Ford's name for this new technique was "Impressionism," a term he borrowed from the painters among whom he had grown up during the 1890's.

The method of literary Impressionism has not proven to be as historically important as pictorial Impressionism was. Both techniques seemed unnatural and chaotic at first, demanding a wholesale reeducation of the audience. Yet where Impressionism in art ultimately allowed audiences to appreciate the beauty of painted surfaces as well as the beauty of pictured scenes, literary Impressionism could not offer an equivalent alternative form of satisfaction. Works written in this style remain notoriously difficult to read; for full understanding, they must be enacted, not merely scanned. Those who are willing to give the work this extra attention, however, will find that they have enlarged their experience along with their understanding.

The primacy of memories and impressions is the greatest strength of Ford's fiction, but it is simultaneously the gravest weakness in his nonfiction. To be plain about it, Ford was a liar—but a liar out of art, not malice. Each time Ford wrote a fictitious anecdote about one of his more famous contemporaries, he would convince himself that the incident was true in every detail; each time such an anecdote was called into question, the entire memoir became suspect. Soon, no one believed anything Ford wrote. The real culprit was, in fact, Ford's commitment to literary Impressionism. At the time he wrote the lie he thought it was true; the lie had first appeared, and subsequently taken shape, in his mind, and therefore it must be thought of as a truthful image, if not an image of the truth. If only Ford could be granted his stylistic premise, the lapses from factuality of his books would no longer be grounds for condemnation.

Nevertheless, Ford's made-up memories caused him to alienate one old friend after another. As an example, when Joseph Conrad died in 1924, Ford published a long appreciation of his old friend, receiving high praise for the way in which he had brought a literary giant to vibrant, breathing life—that is, until those who had known

Conrad best began to protest over the "vast differences," as Conrad's widow put it, between the incidents they had witnessed and those which Ford now described. In turn, Ford defended his approach, calling the book "a novel, not a monograph; a portrait, not a narration."

THE GOOD SOLDIER

First published: 1915
Type of work: Novel

A widower reveals the corruption and depravity hidden beneath the polite surface of a longtime relationship.

The Good Soldier is several novels at once. It is a romantic comedy of manners that turns sour; it is a social satire that offers no normative way of life; it is a true confession by a consummate liar; it is a profound psychological study of people one can never quite understand; it is a modernist tour de force. Most tellingly, it is Ford's masterwork.

The image one must keep in mind when reading *The Good Soldier* is the onion. It is composed of layer upon layer; cutting into it at any point brings tears to one's eyes, and when one has peeled away the final layer there is absolutely nothing left for one's efforts—no kernel, no pith, no ultimate moral. Ford wanted to call it "The Saddest Story," and only his publisher's insistence that no one would buy a book with such a depressing title in the middle of the Great War led him to change it.

The novel is a first-person narrative, covering a little more than ten years in the life of John Dowell. Dowell is a member of that privileged class whose names echo through history. His "farm," as he calls it, occupies several blocks of downtown Philadelphia. In 1901, drifting through a life of gentlemanly idleness, he meets and marries Florence Hurlbird of Stamford, Connecticut; they sail to Europe for their honeymoon, only to discover that Florence has a heart ailment that prevents her from ever returning to America. Thus they drift from one resort to the next, following the social calendar; in one of these resorts, Bad Nauheim, they meet Edward and Leonora Ashburnham, whose lives will intertwine with theirs in disastrous fashion.

For nine years life seems perfect; the two couples meet at Nauheim, spend an idyllic summer, and part the best of friends. Underneath that immaculate surface, however, deadly currents seethe—lust and greed disguised as sentiment and prudence. Florence and Edward are lovers; Leonora, to whom Edward has turned over management of his estate, does not dare to speak out for fear of scandal and financial ruination. Then Florence discovers that she has been supplanted in Edward's heart by Nancy Rufford, Leonora's young ward, and that same evening, an old acquaintance spots Florence and reveals Florence's lurid sexual history; her veils of deceit stripped away, she poisons herself. Edward and Leonora return to England, where Leonora informs her ward about Edward's growing love; the resulting complex emotions drive Nancy to a breakdown. Leonora asks John to come keep Edward company, while she ships Nancy out to India in the hope that a change of scene will help her. Faced with this second loss, Edward kills himself. Within months, Leonora has remarried and started a new family. John, who also loves Nancy, resumes his old role of nursemaid.

It is a plot worthy of a soap opera, but it is only half the story. The other half is made up of the revelation of John's character and his associated revelations about the idle rich—and these are far more profound than the melodramatic incidents of the surface. Readers have never succeeded in understanding John Dowell. His dry wit belies his pose as "an ignorant fool." His ability to contrast the problems that arise from "keeping a shut mouth to the world" with the "hell" that results from Florence's and Leonora's compulsive talking shows that he is in fact a consummate reader of character. Yet he is himself a connoisseur of talk. He deliberately obscures his story with flashbacks and digressions, he presents statements as truths that he later labels lies, and he invites the reader to admire his closest friends, only to sentence them to death, insanity, and "intense solitude." Does he hate his wife for the twelve years of lies she imposed on him? At one point, he claims that he "hates her with the hatred of the adder," but later in his narrative he claims not to think about her at all. Does he admire Leonora for her efforts to save her marriage, her faith, and finally herself? Again a reader can only answer, "sometimes."

The Good Soldier is thus a triumph of literary Impressionism. It is a melodrama without a hero, a psychological study conducted by a dolt, and a confession (made up as the narrator goes along) by the only character who has not been guilty of a crime. It is, in other words, terrifyingly like real life. Moreover, most readers will conclude, if real life is like *The Good Soldier*, then they had better beware.

PARADE'S END

First published: 1924-1928, 1950; includes *Some Do Not . . .* , 1924; *No More Parades*, 1925; *A Man Could Stand Up*, 1926; *The Last Post*, 1928

Type of work: Novels

An unlikely hero survives desertion by his friends, calumny by his wife, and the terrors of the Great War, finding happiness at last with the woman he loves.

Parade's End is a series of four novels depicting the meeting, courtship, and ultimate fulfillment of two modern heroes, Christopher Tietjens and Valentine Wannop, despite social condemnation, personal travails, and World War I. Into these novels Ford poured his own experiences as a writer, as a lover, and as a soldier; he used the techniques of literary Impressionism to transform them into an utterly believable narrative. Some people have felt that, taken as a whole, these four novels constitute the best record available of the revolution in English society caused by the Great War.

The first novel of the sequence, *Some Do Not . . .* , begins just before the outbreak of World War I and records the creation of an emotional bond between Christopher and Valentine during a police pursuit, a breakfast party, and a fog-shrouded late-night carriage ride. Ford presents his hero and heroine as two of the last moral human beings left in Western society; while all around them friends, relatives, and nations succumb to their passions, Christopher and Valentine, as the title puts it, do not. At the same time, they are being judged according to these others' standards, and thus their fornication is presumed on all sides. As a result, acquaintances will cut them, employers will demote them, and even their parents will endure bitter disappointment; and because *Parade's End* is not a fairy tale, these reactions will never be wholly resolved.

The second novel of the sequence, *No More Parades*, finds Christopher with the army in France. His efforts are going unrewarded, his wife is raising a scandal about him, and his love for Valentine Wannop has been buried deep under layers of responsibility. At the climax of the novel, he must undergo an extended interrogation to avoid a court-martial on charges of striking a superior officer (who had stormed into his hotel room late at night without identifying himself); that same morning, his command is to be subjected to a formal inspection. The resulting interior monologue invites comparison with Molly Bloom's final monologue in James Joyce's *Ulysses* (1922). In *A Man Could Stand Up*, the third volume, Christopher has been moved up to the front lines, where he must survive a last-ditch enemy barrage. Shortly thereafter, the war finally ends; it is at last time for his love to surface from under four years of military repression. When Valentine's name does pop into his conscious mind, he is astonished: "What! Is *that* still there?" Ford finally grants his lovers their first embrace, though not until the very conclusion of the novel: "They were dancing! . . . They were setting out."

Later in life, Ford claimed that these three novels formed a perfect whole; the addition of *The Last Post*, he felt, broke the unity of time and place created by the frame of World War I and the dual themes of battles in the trenches and battles between the sexes. Most readers, however, find this final novel emotionally necessary, for in it Christopher's wife, Sylvia, finally ends her private war and agrees to a divorce; the "curse" on the Tietjens family, which has been a recurring subtheme, is ended with the cutting down of Groby Great Tree; and Valentine gives birth to the first undisputed Tietjens. In addition, Ford provides another culminating monologue, this time the dying thoughts of Christopher's brother Mark; confronting his impassive presence, even Sylvia falls silent.

Finally, Ford's introduction of this final theme, a reprise of his earlier concern in *The Good Soldier*, gives *Parade's End* a larger significance. In this tetralogy, Ford has examined the profound crises that he, and England, had recently faced, and has found not the mere accommodation of "peace in our time" but the dawning of a final resolution, the acknowledgement that "you must have a pattern to interpret things by." It is not itself a statement of the pattern, but it will have to do.

Summary

Had Ford Madox Ford written only half a dozen novels, served as editor of only one great literary magazine, and encouraged only a few writers and artists to embrace the principles of modernism, he would still be remembered as a great man and a great artist. He drank too deeply from the cup of life, writing too many words, loving too many women, and leaving behind too many disappointed expectations. Only now, when his personal and artistic imperfections have faded, can one perceive the real and lasting power of Ford's vision and the truth of his impressions.

Bibliography

Harvey, David Dow. *Ford Madox Ford: A Bibliography of Works and Criticism.* Princeton: N.J.: Princeton University Press, 1962.

Judd, Alan. *Ford Madox Ford.* Cambridge, Mass.: Harvard University Press, 1991.

Lid, R. W. *Ford Madox Ford: The Essence of His Art.* Berkeley: University of California Press, 1964.

Mizener, Arthur. *The Saddest Story: A Biography of Ford Madox Ford.* New York: World Publishing, 1971.

Snitow, Ann Barr. *Ford Madox Ford and the Voice of Uncertainty.* Baton Rouge: Louisiana State University Press, 1984.

Stang, Sondra J., ed. *The Presence of Ford Madox Ford.* Philadelphia: University of Pennsylvania Press, 1981.

Hartley S. Spatt

E. M. FORSTER

Born: London, England
January 1, 1879
Died: Coventry, England
June 7, 1970

Principal Literary Achievement

Forster was a prominent English novelist, essayist, and short-story writer. His works display an enormous depth of insight into the human condition.

Biography

Edward Morgan Forster was born in London, England, on January 1, 1879, the only son of Edward Morgan Llewellyn Forster, a descendant of prominent members of the Clapham Sect, an evangelical group of social activists, and Alice Clara (Lily) Whichelo Forster. His father, an architect who had studied with Sir Arthur Blomfield (Thomas Hardy's mentor), died unexpectedly in 1880. That left the one-year-old Edward Forster in the care of his mother, his maternal grandmother, Louisa Whichelo, and his paternal great-aunt and godmother, Marianne Thornton, who financed his education and became his benefactress. In 1893, Forster and his mother moved to Tonbridge, and he attended Tonbridge School, where he was very unhappy, from 1893 to 1897. In 1897, he went to King's College, Cambridge, and developed a number of personal relationships that had a profound influence on his work. In his last year at Cambridge, Forster became a member of the Apostles society, which later evolved into the Bloomsbury Group. This group was a literary, artistic, and intellectual society, active in the Bloomsbury area of London, and comprising such notable figures as Virginia Woolf, the novelist; Lytton Strachey, the biographer; Clive Bell, the art critic; Roger Fry, the artist and critic; John Maynard Keynes, the influential economist; Victoria Sackville-West, the poet and writer; and others. After Forster left Cambridge, he took an extended tour of Italy and Greece with his mother. This travel provided the setting and material for his early novels, which satirize English tourists abroad. His literary career began in 1903 with his contributions to *The Independent Review*, a Bloomsbury Group periodical of liberal anti-imperialist sympathies.

In 1905, Forster tutored the children of the Countess von Arnim in Germany and returned to England for the publication of his first novel, *Where Angels Fear to Tread* (1905). He taught Latin at the Working Men's College and lectured on Italian art and history for the Cambridge Local Lectures Board. In 1906, Forster became a tutor and

developed a strong relationship with Syed Ross Masood, an Indian Muslim patriot. *The Longest Journey*, Forster's second novel, published in 1907, *A Room with a View*, published in 1908, and *Howards End*, published in 1910, established Forster as one of England's leading novelists.

Forster visited India between 1912 and 1921, and during World War I he spent three years in Egypt. He published three minor works: *The Government of Egypt* (1921), *Alexandria: A History and a Guide* (1922), and *Pharos and Pharillon* (1923). In 1924, Forster published *A Passage to India*, his final and most critically acclaimed novel. He began the work in 1913, and after an extensive hiatus, Forster completed the novel in England after his return from India.

After inheriting a house from his aunt in West Hackhurst, near Dorset, Forster lived there with his mother until her death in 1945. He gave the Clark Lectures at Cambridge and published them as *Aspects of the Novel* (1927). In 1936, he published his first collection of essays, *Abinger Harvest—A Miscellany*, which was an attack on the hypocrisy and self-righteousness that he attributed to the British mentality. After being evicted from his West Hackhurst apartment in 1947, Forster visited America and lectured at Harvard and Hamilton College. Forster wrote two biographies, *Goldsworthy Lowes Dickinson* (1934) and *Marianne Thornton* (1956), collaborated with Benjamin Britten and Eric Crozier on the libretto for the opera *Billy Budd* (1951), and published his second collection of essays, *Two Cheers for Democracy* (1951), and an uneven collection of his letters and experiences from India in *The Hill of Devi* (1953).

Forster received significant recognition for his literary achievements. Queen Elizabeth II awarded him membership in the Order of Companions of Honour to the Queen (1953). In 1960, Santha Rama Rau adapted *A Passage to India* (pb. 1961) for the stage. After playing in London for a year, the play opened on Broadway and ran for 110 performances. Most critics believed that the play was inferior to the novel; however, Forster was pleased with the adaptation. On June 7, 1970, he died in Coventry, England, at the home of Bob and May Buckingham. He had two works published posthumously, *Maurice* (1971), written in 1913 but not released until the public disclosure of his homosexuality, and *The Life to Come and Other Stories* (1972), fourteen stories that reveal much about his private inner life.

Analysis

Critics generally agree that Forster's finest achievements were his novels, in which plot is overshadowed by the conflict of ideas and development of character. Forster achieves objectivity in many of his novels by utilizing the figure of the outsider as narrator. His narrative style is straightforward, with events progressing in logical order. Much of Forster's work is a study of personal relationships. Personal emotion is elevated above social convention in most of his novels, and Forster utilizes the recurring theme of society's oppression of the individual's characteristically generous and sensitive inclinations. The heart/conscience conflict as illustrated in Mark Twain's *The Adventures of Huckleberry Finn* (1884) is a major concern in many of Forster's works. He consistently expresses opposition to racism and prejudice among individuals.

A *Passage to India* is generally considered to be Forster's artistic masterpiece; it was his last novel. This work is a sympathetic rendering of the assumption that, once human beings are prisoners of mythology, it is very difficult to change their thinking. They must transcend the elements of culture that imprison them in order to reach out to humanity. The title of Forster's novel comes from Walt Whitman's poem but is its thematic antithesis. Whitman envisions the total unity and spiritual connections of all people, and Forster suggests that this is not possible. As a humanistic novel, *A Passage to India* illustrates the indifference of nature and humanity's compulsion toward order. "The inarticulate world is closer at hand and readier to resume control as soon as men are tired."

His subsequent works took the form of literary criticism, general essays, and biography. Perhaps his most well-known and influential volume of nonfiction is *Aspects of the Novel*. Forster posits a theory of characterization coupled with a "pattern and rhythm" for the novel. He suggests that characters in a novel are either round, able to surprise the audience, or flat, stereotypes or caricatures.

Many of Forster's works utilize music and art as basic tools of communicating meaning. It was his belief that music is the deepest of the arts and that music, more so than language, "would civilize the barbarian." In *A Room with a View*, Reverend Arthur Beebe understands the nature of Lucy Honeychurch by the way that she plays Beethoven. He is aware of the depths of her passion and observes that, if she lived the way she plays, her life would truly be exciting. The *Howards End* passage explores the reaction of the audience to Ludwig van Beethoven's Fifth Symphony and ironically makes clear the ineffability of a musical experience. A sensitive or intuitive person might have insights into realities communicated via the medium of music, since word symbols or language is an inadequate tool for expressing life. Music has a way of transcending and displays an integrating power. It plays a powerful and evocative tool in five of Forster's works.

In *E. M. Forster* (1971), Martial Rose observes Forster's ironic temper. He pigeonholes Forster as an acute observer and disinterested craftsman who rarely allowed an indulgence of personal passions to ruin the pattern of a work of order. Forster admired the work of Voltaire, praising him for his critical genius and humanity. He applauded Voltaire for his concern for truth, belief in tolerance, pity for the oppressed, and ability to "drive his ideas home."

The ethical impulse characterizes the whole of Forster's writing. This quality constrained his writing in aesthetic terms. He was oftentimes locked into a defensive and contradictory position. Often, he insisted on the separation of the creative and critical faculties, and other times he felt that they were inextricable.

A ROOM WITH A VIEW

First published: 1908
Type of work: Novel

Italy provides the landscape and the freedom to abandon English boundaries and to experience life passionately.

A Room with a View may be considered in two parts, part 1 taking place in Italy and representing the Greek world and its Dionysiac element, and part 2 taking place in England and representing the medieval or ascetic. A synthesis of the views or divisions will provide a balanced perspective.

Miss Lucy Honeychurch, a young Englishwoman, and Miss Charlotte Bartlett, her cousin and chaperon, arrive at the Pension Bertolini and are disappointed to find that they have been misled about their rooms. They are not south, but north, and neither has a view. During dinner, Mr. Emerson and his son, George, generously offer to exchange their rooms, which do have a view. Emerson believes that women like looking at a view; men do not. He does not care what he sees outside; his view is within. Charlotte and Lucy are startled by the so-called tactlessness and indelicateness of their offer. They see Reverend Arthur Beebe, who assures the ladies that some niceties go against the grain. He agrees to act as an intermediary and makes arrangements with the Emersons to switch rooms. Charlotte is careful not to give Lucy the room formerly occupied by the young Mr. Emerson. She believes that, in a small way, she is a woman of the world and knows where some things can lead.

Later, Reverend Beebe hears Lucy Honeychurch playing the piano and asks if he can say something daring. He tells Miss Honeychurch that, if she could live in the way that she plays Beethoven, it would be very exciting for everyone. Music provides the one outlet for Miss Honeychurch's enormous passion and is indeed a force that will eventually lead her to a more vital and spontaneous existence.

Miss Honeychurch later decides to go for a walk alone. She sees Mr. Emerson at Santa Croce Church. He is clearly a nonconformist and guides her through the Giotto frescoes. Miss Honeychurch finds that she is very comfortable with him, but she is confused over why he is so concerned about his son. Meanwhile Miss Eleanor Lavish, a novelist, and Miss Bartlett are wandering about Italy alone. Miss Lavish believes that only by exploring the unknown does one get to know a country. She tells Miss Bartlett that she has her eye on Miss Honeychurch. She believes that Lucy Honeychurch is open to the physical sensations and can be transfigured in Italy.

Miss Honeychurch walks through the Piazza Signoria and passes two men arguing over a debt. She faints at the sight of the ensuing street brawl as a stabbed man, bleeding from the mouth, dies at her feet. George Emerson is there to retrieve her. After he revives her, she asks him to get the photographs that she dropped during the chaos. Because they have blood on them, George throws them away. The Italian's death brings them close together. Lucy asks that George not tell anyone about the incident.

Traveling with a number of guests from the pension, Lucy Honeychurch and Miss Bartlett drive to Fiesole. The group disperses, and Lucy asks to be taken to speak with Reverend Beebe. The driver mistakenly leads her to George Emerson, who is standing at the end of a beautiful pathway covered with violets. Captivated by the moment, George embraces Lucy Honeychurch. Their kiss is interrupted by Miss Bartlett, who rushes Lucy away. Miss Bartlett is afraid that George will talk about the kiss and tells Lucy that he is obviously accustomed to stealing kisses. Cutting their visit short, Miss Bartlett and Miss Honeychurch take the train to Rome.

Lucy Honeychurch returns home to Surrey and promises to marry Cecil Vyse, a decadent dilettante who revels in material possessions. Reverend Beebe visits Mrs. Honeychurch and comments on how promising Lucy seems to be. He notes that she plays Beethoven passionately and lives so quietly. Beebe suspects that one day music and life will mingle and that Lucy Honeychurch will be wonderful at both. Cecil Vyse startles Reverend Beebe with the announcement of his plans to marry her. While traveling in Rome, Cecil meets the Emersons and convinces them to lease a villa in Surrey from Sir Harry Otway. The local residents had hoped that a certain class of residents would move into the villas, and Cecil encourages the Emersons to move in to disrupt the social order.

Reverend Beebe takes Freddy Honeychurch (Lucy's brother) to meet the Emersons, and Freddy encourages George and Beebe to "go for a bath" at the pond. Lucy Honeychurch, Cecil, and her mother encounter the frolicking swimmers while walking through the grounds. Lucy is shocked to learn that the Emersons have taken the Otway villa. Cousin Charlotte Bartlett comes to visit and is concerned that the Emersons are in Surrey. George, Freddy, Lucy, and a friend invite Cecil to play tennis with them, and he sneeringly declines. After the tennis game, Cecil reads "Under the Loggia" by Eleanor Lavish aloud to George and Lucy, who recognize the description of their kiss. On the way into the house, George kisses her again. Lucy scolds Miss Bartlett for telling Miss Lavish about the kiss.

Lucy lies to George about her feelings for him. She implores him to leave and never return. George tells her that Cecil is incapable of loving her as a woman and can only love her as a possession. He tells Lucy that he loves her and that Cecil does not. George reluctantly leaves. Symbolically, George Emerson can be seen as a protagonist of life, Cecil Vyse of material possessions (art), and Charlotte Bartlett of order and decorum (antilife). If Miss Honeychurch marries Cecil (who thinks of her as a work of art, not as a woman), she would be denying her own happiness. At this point, however, she is ashamed of her passionate attraction for George. Denying her love for George, Lucy breaks her engagement to Cecil and makes plans to meet Teresa and Catherine Alan in Athens. Charlotte Bartlett arranges a meeting between the elder Mr. Emerson and Lucy. Lucy lies to George, Cecil, Mr. Beebe, and Mr. Emerson about her feelings. She finally abandons her plans to go to Greece, marries

George against the wishes of her mother, and returns to Italy with George to their room with a view.

In *The Achievement of E. M. Forster* (1962), J. B. Beer posits the notion of the importance and symbolism of the "view" in a conversation between Miss Honeychurch and Cecil Vyse:

> "I had got an idea—I dare say wrongly—that
> you feel more at home with me in a room."
> "A room?" she echoed, hopelessly bewildered.
> "Yes. Or at the most, in a garden, or on a road.
> Never in the real country like this.". . .
> "I connect you with a view—a certain type of
> view. . . . When I think of you it's always as
> in a room.". . .
> To her surprise, he seemed annoyed.
> "A drawing-room, pray? With no view?"
> "Yes, with no view, I fancy. Why not?"

Significantly, the novel begins and ends with the same view in the pension in Italy. The reticent Lucy Honeychurch is finally victorious over the repressive urgings of conformity and accepts her call of life. She is a different person now and has opted for life rather than antilife. The union of George Emerson and Miss Honeychurch represents a comingling of intellect and heart.

A PASSAGE TO INDIA

First published: 1924
Type of work: Novel

> The domination of the Indian people by the forces of British imperialism suggests the impossibility of bridging the gulf of antipathy between the races.

A Passage to India has a tripartite structure labeled mosque, caves, and temple. Each section serves as a symbolic signpost and corresponds to the seasons of the Indian year.

After being summoned to the house of Major Callendar, Dr. Aziz, a Moslem doctor at the Government Hospital, discovers that the major has gone and that he must walk back to his house because two English women departed in his hired tonga (two-wheeled vehicle). While stopping at a mosque on his way back to Chandrapore, Dr. Aziz meets Mrs. Moore, the mother of Ronald Heaslop, the City Magistrate. Aziz and Mrs. Moore seem to "connect" with each other and share a common understanding of life. Under the racially fragmented system of British colonialism, however, neither the British nor the Indians can speak publicly of this kind of communication. The elderly Mrs. Moore invites Dr. Aziz to walk back to the club with her and introduces him to Adela Quested, newly arrived from England and the fiancée of her son. Although *A Passage to India* clearly addresses social and political issues, the major theme is the plight of the human race. The fact that the characters struggle unsuccessfully to "connect" in the novel indicates Forster's pessimism, yet he portrays a desire on the part of Aziz, Fielding, Mrs. Moore, and Miss Quested to understand and to establish meaningful relationships with each other.

Mrs. Moore and Miss Quested want to see the real India and complain about the colonialized India that they have seen. Turton, a member of the British club, holds a bridge party for them and invites a few native Indian guests. The party is a failure, in that the Indians separate into groups apart from the British and the situation is uncomfortable. Mr. Fielding, the Government College principal who associates freely with the Indians, invites the ladies to tea at his home. Miss Quested persuades him to include Dr. Aziz and Professor Godbole, a Hindu teacher and associate of Mr. Fielding. At the tea, Miss Quested and Mrs. Moore have a refreshing conversation with Dr. Aziz and Professor Godbole. Aziz is overjoyed by the interaction of the group members and invites all of them to visit the Marabar Caves. Mrs. Moore and Adela Quested accept the invitation, and Aziz plans an elaborate outing.

Heaslop arrives to escort his mother and his fiancée to a game of polo and is very rude to Dr. Aziz. The incident causes Adela and Heaslop to quarrel, and she breaks off their engagement. The couple then goes for a ride, and after striking an unidentified animal on the road, Adela changes her mind, and they are reconciled.

Unfortunately, Professor Godbole and Mr. Fielding miss their train and Aziz must escort the British ladies to the Marabar Caves alone. Mrs. Moore is frightened by a loud booming echo in the first cave and stops to rest. Considering the gulf between the British and Indians, Mrs. Moore sees the futility of her Christian and moralistic ideas about life echoed in this hollow sound. Mrs. Moore declines to continue their explorations, and Dr. Aziz, a guide, and Adela proceed along. Adela upsets Dr. Aziz by inquiring whether he has more than one wife. Aziz leaves her briefly to regain his composure, and Adela wanders into a cave and claims that she is almost assaulted by Aziz. She stumbles down a hill, where she meets Nancy Derek, who has brought Fielding to the caves. Nancy takes Adela back to Chandrapore.

The Marabar Caves section of the novel is one of the most puzzling. Goldsworthy Lowes Dickinson and a number of readers and other reviewers of Forster's works objected to the mystery of the Caves scene. In a June 26, 1924, letter to Dickinson, Forster wrote the following:

> In the cave it is either a man, or the supernatural, or an illusion. And even if I know! My writing mind therefore is a blur here—i.e. I will it to remain a blur, and to be uncertain, as I am of many facts in daily life. . . . It sprang straight from my subject matter.

Mrs. Moore is at once devastated and terrified by the hollow, booming echo from the caves. Her revelation suggests that perhaps the gulf that lies between the British and

Indians cannot be bridged and that her Christianity is no match for the inexplicable. She has no answer for the confusion at the caves and realizes that all the British can do is to "muddle."

Aziz meets Fielding at the caves, and neither knows what has happened. They assume that Adela decided to leave with Nancy. Dr. Aziz and Fielding return by train, and Aziz is met by the police inspector and arrested. Fielding and Mrs. Moore alienate themselves from the British by siding with Dr. Aziz. Realizing his mother's position about the matter, Heaslop arranges passage for Mrs. Moore to return to England, and she dies at sea. During the trial, one of Aziz's friends accuses Heaslop of smuggling his mother out of India so that she cannot testify in defense of Dr. Aziz. The Indian spectators loudly begin calling for Mrs. Moore. Then, Adela exonerates Aziz with her testimony and is publicly ostracized by the British. Fielding rescues Adela, encourages Aziz not to file a damage suit against her, and she returns to England.

Two years later, Dr. Aziz is the personal physician to the Rajah of Mau, a Hindu state in India, and Professor Godbole is the minister of education. Aziz has become totally disillusioned with the British, including Fielding. He has not accepted any letters from Fielding because he assumes that Fielding has married Adela Quested. Aziz is angered to learn that Fielding is visiting Mau as a part of his official duties. When Dr. Aziz meets Fielding again, he discovers that the former Stella Moore, daughter of Mrs. Moore, has married Fielding. Because of the distance between them, Dr. Aziz and Fielding cannot renew their friendship. The floods in Mau prevent the Moores from leaving immediately.

Before Fielding and his family make their departure from India, he and Dr. Aziz decide to go horseback riding together and begin rather amicably discussing the British/Indian problem. Sensing the end of their association, Aziz and Fielding attempt to swear eternal friendship but are forced down separate paths by rocks presenting narrow pathways for the horses. This symbolizes their inability to bridge the gulf between their races and indicates that a friendship between them is not yet possible.

The Indian setting is very important in *A Passage to India* and is an antagonistic agent to the British colonialists. The landscape attempts to expel the British, and some critics pinpoint the correspondence of the three sections of the novel to three divisions of the Indian year: cool spring, hot summer, wet monsoon. The caves are elemental, and the narrative begins with extensive references and descriptions of the physical setting. The nothingness of the caves should convince people to accept the irrational and emphasizes their relative insignificance. The British experience in India suggests that humanity must not oppose the natural rhythms of the earth and attempt to impose order on the "chaos" that is India.

HOWARDS END

First published: 1910
Type of work: Novel

The manor house is a symbol of personal freedom and offers hope to a disordered society.

Howards End, sometimes proclaimed as Forster's most mature novel, uses the country house as a symbol of cultural unity. On the title page of the early editions is the phrase "Only connect." Forster admonishes humankind that its most significant failure is the reluctance to establish relationships with each other and eliminate the obstacles of prejudice that divide and subjugate individuals. The Schlegels and the Wilcoxes represent two different ways of life. The Schlegels signify culture ("sweetness and light"), and the Wilcoxes represent materialism (acquisitiveness and power). The threat of the "machine in the garden" or the growing materialism in Edwardian England challenges the order of traditional English society. Although the mood of the novel is social comedy, it exhibits the trappings of a novel of manners, and the serious subject of social and political upheaval is implied.

The narrative begins with Helen Schlegel's letter to her sister Margaret. She writes from Howards End, where she is a guest of the Wilcox family. The Wilcox family had met the Schlegels while both families were vacationing in Germany. Both sisters had been invited to Howards End, but Margaret stays with Tibby, their brother, who is ill. Helen Schlegel falls in love with Paul Wilcox and the Wilcox family, but both families are opposed to the match. In a rather indelicate manner, Helen breaks off her relationship with Paul. In a bumbling rescue by her aunt, Mrs. Munt, Helen returns home. Mrs. Munt breaks every rule of decorum and embarrasses Helen and herself. Soon the Wilcox family rents a flat across the street from the Schlegel home. The Schlegel home is a leasehold property, inherited from their father. At the expiration of the lease, they will have to move. Mrs. Ruth Wilcox and Margaret Schlegel become good friends.

Helen Schlegel accidentally takes an umbrella from Leonard Bast at a concert. This working-class young man intrigues the Schlegel sisters, who do not know of his attachment to Jacky, a woman some years older than Leonard and soon to become his wife.

Shortly after Ruth Wilcox and Margaret Schlegel become friends, Ruth dies. She leaves Howards End to Margaret, much to the dismay of her husband and son. No one tells Margaret of her inheritance since it is not part of the official will. After several years, Helen and Margaret meet Henry Wilcox in the park. Wilcox deliberately misleads them about the stability of the firm for which Leonard Bast works. Wilcox is attracted to Margaret and sees Bast as a possible rival. Unaware of that, the two women advise Bast to change jobs, and he does so.

When the long-term lease on the Schlegel home expires, Margaret receives a letter from Mr. Wilcox offering to lease them his house in London. Margaret goes with him to look at the house, and he proposes marriage. In spite of the joint disapproval from the Wilcox and Schlegel families, Margaret accepts his proposal. There is the hope that a union between Henry and Margaret will form a vital bond and facilitate the coalescence of the two different ways of life. Forster writes the following:

> Mature as he was, she might yet be able to help him to the building of the rainbow bridge that should connect the prose in us with the passion. Without it we are meaningless fragments, half monks, half beasts, unconnected arches that have never joined into a man.

Deprived of experiencing the power of true love, Margaret has expectations that she might be able to bring him to her way of thinking.

After learning that Leonard Bast lost everything he had following the bad advice that Helen and Margaret had given him, Helen believes that Henry Wilcox should compensate Bast. Margaret learns that Jacky Bast had been a mistress to Wilcox and thinks it unnecessary and in poor taste to assist the Basts. Helen falls in love with Leonard Bast, spends part of a night with him, and offers him £5,000, which he refuses. Helen remorsefully leaves England. Unaware of the relationship between Helen and Bast, Margaret marries Henry Wilcox, and Helen does not return for the ceremonies. Several months pass and Helen finally returns to England. She avoids Margaret and Wilcox but wants to retrieve some books that she had stored at Howards End. When Margaret sees Helen, she discovers that Helen is pregnant. Helen asks to spend a night with her sister, but Henry forbids it.

Margaret disobeys her husband and spends the night at Howards End with Helen. Charles Wilcox comes the next morning to get them out of the house. He meets Leonard Bast, who has come to try to get funds from Margaret. Seeing Bast, Charles seizes a saber and strikes him several times. Bast dies suddenly. Charles is sentenced to three years in prison for murdering Bast. Publicly disgraced by the manslaughter verdict and imprisonment of his son, Henry Wilcox becomes an invalid and unfortunately is unable to connect and form the bridge between his own and Margaret's divergent life-styles. Margaret takes care of Henry out of kindness rather than love. Margaret, Henry, and Helen move into the house at Howards End.

Helen and Leonard have a son, and Henry develops a deep attachment to this child. Finally following the wishes of his former wife, Henry makes a new will that gives Howards End to Margaret. Upon her death, the house will go to the illegitimate child of Leonard Bast. Ironically, this child will be the inheritor of all that Henry Wilcox and his son had been trying to keep. Helen and Leonard's offspring represents the epitome of human diversity and the future of England.

Summary

E. M. Forster writes: "As a rule, if a writer has a romantic temperament, he will find relationships beautiful." This statement encapsulates the optimistic truths that Forster asserts in his literature about the nature of humanity. Considered by some critics to be one of the greatest moralists of his time, Forster directs his attention to character flaws that cause temporary disharmony in personal relationships.

In "E. M. Forster as Victorian and Modern: *Howards End* and *A Passage to India*," Malcolm Bradbury contends that Forster demands a personal connection between inner and outer worlds and demands that both society and humankind be whole. This explains the fact that Forster's works focus on individual redemptions and personal relationships, while, at the same time, they are very social novels.

Bibliography

Arlott, John. *Aspects of E. M. Forster.* New York: Harcourt, Brace & World, 1969.

Beer, John. *The Achievement of E. M. Forster.* London: Chatto & Windus, 1962.

Bradbury, Malcolm, ed. *A Passage to India: A Selection of Critical Essays.* Englewood Cliffs, N.J.: Prentice-Hall, 1966.

Colmer, John. *E. M. Forster: The Personal Voice.* Boston: Routledge & Kegan Paul, 1975.

Crews, Frederick, *E. M. Forster: The Perils of Humanism.* Princeton, N.J.: Princeton University Press, 1962.

Furbank, P. N. *E. M. Forster: A Life.* New York: Harcourt Brace Jovanovich, 1978.

Godfrey, Denis, *E. M. Forster's Other Kingdom.* London: Oliver & Boyd, 1968.

McDowell, Frederick. *E. M. Forster.* Boston: Twayne, 1987.

Summers, Claude J. *E. M. Forster.* New York: Frederick Ungar, 1983.

Trilling, Lionel. *E. M. Forster.* 2d ed. New York: New Directions, 1965.

Wilde, Alan. *Art and Order: Critical Essays on E. M. Forster.* Boston: G. K. Hall, 1985.

Charlene Taylor Evans

JOHN FOWLES

Born: Leigh-on-Sea, Essex, England
March 31, 1926

Principal Literary Achievement

Fowles has been both critically and popularly received for his first four novels—*The Collector, The Magus, The French Lieutenant's Woman*, and *Daniel Martin*—three of which have been made into films.

Biography

John Fowles was born in Leigh-on-Sea, Essex, England, on March 31, 1926. It was during World War II that his family was evacuated to the more remote town of Ippeplen, South Devon; there Fowles discovered the beauty of the countryside that figures so prominently in his fiction. In these early years, he developed a love of nature, patterning Frederick Clegg's butterfly-collecting obsession in his novel *The Collector* (1963) after his own. It was not until later that he learned to love nature for itself.

As a student at the Bedford School, Fowles studied German and French literature and eventually rose to the powerful position of head boy. At Bedford, he learned to love literature and power. Only later did he learn to hate the latter. He then went into military service and spent six months at the University of Edinburgh, completing training as a lieutenant in the merchant marine right as the war was ending. Following the war, he continued his education in German and, more particularly, French literature at New College, Oxford, from where he was graduated with a B.A. with honors in 1950. His fiction owes much to his study of French literature, particularly his early interest in existentialism and his continuing interest in the Celtic romance, from which stems his express belief that all literature has its roots in the theme of the quest.

After graduation, Fowles taught English at the University of Poitiers. A year later, he took a job teaching English on a Greek island, which provided the grist for his first written (but not his first published) novel, *The Magus* (1965, 1977). It was also there that he met Elizabeth Whitton, whom he married three years later. Having begun writing, he continued to teach in and around London until the success of his first published novel, *The Collector*, allowed him to quit teaching to become a full-time writer. Two years later, *The Magus* was published following twelve years of writing and revision. (Still not happy with it despite its good reception, Fowles revised and republished it in 1977.)

In 1966, he and Elizabeth moved to Lyme Regis in Dorset. Their first residence was a farm at the edge of the Undercliff; subsequently, they moved to an eighteenth century house overlooking Lyme Bay. The town and the farmhouse figure prominently in *The French Lieutenant's Woman* (1969), both the book and the film (1981). He is perhaps best known for this novel, for which he won two awards: the Silver Pen Award from the International Association of Poets, Playwrights, Editors, Essayists, and Novelists (PEN) in 1969 and the W. H. Smith and Son Literary Award in 1970. Fowles himself is most pleased with the film adaptation of the novel, the only one of his books that has achieved popular success as a film.

The Ebony Tower (1974), Fowles's short-story collection, was written in the midst of writing his next novel. In 1986, the title story in the collection was made into a film in England. Three years later, *Daniel Martin* (1977) was published and marked the high point of his popular success.

The novels that have followed have not been as well received, by either the critics or the public, because of their increasingly experimental nature. These include *Mantissa* (1982), which takes place inside the head of a writer with amnesia, and *A Maggot* (1985), a historical novel, set in the eighteenth century, about the mysterious disappearance of a duke's son and the various versions of the story told by those who knew him.

While principally known for his fiction, Fowles also wrote a volume of poetry, *Poems* (1973); a philosophical work, *The Aristos: A Self-Portrait in Ideas* (1964, 1966, 1968); and a historical work, *A Short History of Lyme Regis* (1982). He also wrote a number of essays accompanied by photographs, including *Shipwreck* (1977), *Islands* (1978), *The Tree* (1980), *The Enigma of Stonehenge* (1980) and the foreword to an illustrated volume, *The Undercliff* (1989).

A mild stroke in 1988 limited his output. After his wife, Elizabeth, died in March, 1990, from stomach cancer, Fowles continued to live and work in Lyme Regis.

Analysis

Fowles's fiction has one main theme: the quest of the protagonists for self-knowledge or wholeness. In each of the novels, as well as in the short stories, the protagonist is faced with learning how to quest in a world in which the contemporary quester is cut off from the traditions and rituals of the past that once gave questers of old (exemplified by heroes such as Lancelot, King Arthur, and the Knights of the Round Table) purpose and direction.

What separates the journey of the Fowlesian hero from the journey of the medieval hero is that much of it has become internalized. Where the quester of old battled dragons, monsters, and mysterious knights, the modern quester has no such obvious obstacles. For the modern quester, the battles are largely inward, as the quester must struggle against ignorance and inertia. The modern journey can thus be seen in psychological terms with the results measured by the quester's ability to attain self-knowledge or wholeness, which is often characterized in Fowles's fiction as the ability of the hero to know love.

In this respect, Fowles sees his fiction as having a social dimension in its capacity to help alter people's view of life. While he claims to pay little attention to what the critics write, he has always paid serious attention to the opinions of his readers. From the many thousands of letters he has received, he feels that his fiction has moved readers to think and act differently as they identify with the struggles of his questers. His main social concern is with the condition of human beings, trapped like potential fossils in a receding sea (an image that figures prominently in *The French Lieutenant's Woman*).

Likewise, Fowles is concerned with nature, in the sense of the "natural man" who must be discovered by the protagonists on the quest, as well as with humanity's respect for nature. Many of the pivotal scenes in his fiction are set in natural landscapes: the Undercliff in *The French Lieutenant's Woman* or Thorncombe in *Daniel Martin*, to name but two examples. The antiheroes are often those who fail to understand or respect nature, an example most succinctly portrayed in the character of Frederick Clegg in *The Collector*.

His short-story collection, *The Ebony Tower*, was originally called "Variations" because Fowles saw the stories as variations on the themes of his longer fiction. These same variations are evident within the long fiction, making the whole body of Fowles's fiction subject to examination under one central theme—that of quest and discovery—with variations.

Its clearest statement is made in Fowles's first written, later rewritten, novel, *The Magus*. About its conception, he once said, "I only knew the basic idea of a secret world, whose penetration involved ordeal and whose final reward was self-knowledge, obsessed me." To look briefly at the basic idea of this secret world and the ordeal and reward that await the successful protagonist is to understand the basis of Fowles's fiction in its many variations.

In the story, Nicholas Urfe, well educated and in the prime of life, nonetheless wants to kill himself because he does not see sufficient reason to live. Embarrassed by his lack of commitment even to death, which prevents him from pulling the trigger on the gun, he soon stumbles into the land of adventure provided by his guide on the quest, Conchis, who represents the mythic wise old man. Within this secret realm, always described as an otherworldly place, Nicholas experiences all the challenges of the quest: danger, love, temptation, and moments of clear vision. Finally ejected from the mythic landscape, he returns to London with enough understanding to know that it is Alison, the woman whose love he earlier rejected, for whom he must now wait and of whom he must prove himself worthy. The final scene, cast in the garden of Regents Park, does not answer the question of whether they ultimately reunite because it is not as important as the evidence of the self-knowledge Nicholas has attained. For Fowles, this ambiguous ending, made more so in the revised version, is a way of leaving the story "unconcluded," a device he varies in subsequent novels, with multiple endings in *The French Lieutenant's Woman* and no ending in *A Maggot*. It is only in *Daniel Martin* that the happy ending is achieved, and then only after much struggle on the part of the protagonist-author. It comes as no surprise that the novel following *Daniel Martin* leaves reality behind altogether, as the protagonist-author of *Mantissa* creates a fiction inside his head. There the ending is circular, returning to its unclear beginning.

While many of his questers are successful to the extent that they gain self-knowledge and come to know and experience love, not all succeed. Most poignantly a failure is Frederick Clegg in *The Collector*. In this novel there are no winners, for Clegg, who longs for love and thinks he understands nature, is in fact as trapped as the butterflies he traps and kills. Likewise, he traps and kills Miranda, the girl he thinks he loves, because he does not know how to journey and cannot learn from the signs and signals presented to him. His fear keeps him trapped in a downward spiral of worsening experience. Following Miranda's death, it is inevitable that he will trap again and that the inevitable cycle will repeat itself.

Other questers fail, particularly those presented in the short-story collection, *The Ebony Tower*. There, the variations are largely those of the dark side of the quest: what happens when the protagonists, for a variety of reasons, cannot choose to respond to the call to the quest. From the ebony tower of the first story to the dark cloud of the last in the collection, the stories are increasingly dark portrayals of the failure of the questers to break out of their molds. In *A Maggot*, Bartholomew may succeed in breaking free, but the mystery of his disappearance is never fully determined. The woman he leaves behind can free herself only by removing herself completely from society to join a new religious order and give birth to its future leader.

Throughout all of these variations, however, the central theme persists: Can we choose, and, if so, how do we choose? These ideas concern Fowles, not only for his characters but also for himself as a novelist and a human being.

THE COLLECTOR

First published: 1963
Type of work: Novel

A butterfly collector wins the lottery and, with the money, buys a house in the country and captures the girl of his dreams.

The Collector, Fowles's first published novel, was an instant hit. While the British viewed it as criminal fiction, Americans liked it for its psychological exploration of a troubled character. Written from a split viewpoint, it tells the story first from Clegg's point of view, then repeats the same story from Miranda's diary, and finally returns to Clegg's describing the inevitable ending and his plans for the future. In the telling, the marked differences separating the two characters is evident. Clegg's narrative is halting, formal, and nearly inarticulate in places. Miranda's narrative is free-flowing, alive with feeling, expressive, and natural. Their two tales, divided as they are by language and background, reflect the vast differences that separate them.

Echoing many of the same ideas expressed in his philosophical work *The Aristos: A Self-Portrait in Ideas* (1964), Fowles examines his social concerns over the split between "the Many," which Clegg represents, and "the Few," which Miranda represents. Clegg, who suddenly finds himself wealthy as a result of winning money in the football pools, is given the money of "the Few" without any of the education to appreciate it or to use it wisely. He is freed to quest, but he does not have the inner or outer knowledge to understand what confronts him and what he can choose. Thus, he fails not only for himself; his failure also causes Miranda to die. For Clegg, Miranda remains nothing more than his most prized specimen, better than even his most beautiful butterflies.

Miranda, too, has lived in a world isolated from the Many, and it is only as a result of being Clegg's prisoner that she is forced to think about the world he inhabits. As a result of her entrapment, she takes the journey of inward discovery that her diary later reveals. She knows that she will be a better person for her experience if she survives the imprisonment. To her credit, she comes to understand Clegg and to have sympathy for him. Still, even with all of her education and class superiority, she cannot humanize him.

Clegg's only emotion is that concerning the loss of his ideal. He has admired Miranda from afar and idealized her to be all that woman should be in his view. When her reality, her vitality, clouds the picture, his admiration turns to disgust and gives him "permission" to treat her as a specimen to be chloroformed and photographed to suit his perverted tastes. In most of the photos, he cuts off her head, symbolic of his repressed desire to see her merely as a beautiful body, without her willful intelligence.

Miranda's diary breaks off with the words. "Do not let me die." Clegg's account picks up after that, first as a rationalization of his failure to prevent her from dying, which is also an unrealized admission of his inability to accept the call to the quest. When he goes to the doctor's office, it is crowded with people and he does not have the courage to go straight in to see the doctor. Unnerved by the people and the look of the doctor, he flees; the result is that Miranda dies. At first it bothers him terribly, and he romantically imagines killing himself so that the two can lie together forever. Even this notion soon, however, passes, as he begins to find fault with her, eventually blaming her for her own death.

His final chilling thoughts of his next victim, a girl he has already identified specifically to avoid making the mistake he made with Miranda of "aiming too high," demonstrate the repetition of the cycle that will be Clegg's life: Unable to quest toward self-understanding, he is doomed to repeat himself.

THE MAGUS

First published: 1965
Type of work: Novel

A young man journeys to a small Greek island, where he experiences many adventures under the watchful eye of his guide, Maurice Conchis.

The Magus was the first novel Fowles wrote, although not the first that he published. After working on it for many years, he finally released it for publication in 1965. Despite its success, Fowles remained dissatisfied with the novel and subsequently revised it for republication in 1977. It is an important work for its portrayal of the protagonist trapped in a meaningless world who must learn to choose life and love, and for its use of myth and mystery to define what is lacking in the protagonist's life. The Greek island setting is important as the other world in which the journey takes place; likewise, it was important to Fowles as the place where his journey as a writer began.

Nicholas Urfe is the protagonist who becomes the quester. Fleeing England and the love of Alison, he journeys to Greece to find adventure and to escape his commitments. Adventure he does find, but not in the form he expected. He seeks mystery with a small *m*; what he finds is Mystery with a capital *M*: the mystery of himself, which he learns as he quests.

His guide for the journey is Maurice Conchis, who has already taken the journey of self-discovery and who has knowledge to impart to others. As in all of Fowles's fiction, one of the central themes of this novel is that of unmasking. Each person hides behind many masks; the question is one of knowing which is the real person. Conchis wears many masks as part of the "godgame" he prepares and presents for Nicholas' education. Various characters are unmasked, leading up to the unmasking of Nicholas in the central trial scene and the announcement that he is now one of the "elect." Nicholas knows that he has been exposed and feels changed, but he does not fully comprehend the extent of the change. Thus, as he is evicted from the realm of myth and returned to the real world of London, he comes slowly to understand that the final challenge of the quest will be a reunion with Alison, whom he had earlier rejected.

Since so much of Fowles's fiction measures the success of the quester in terms of the ability to know and experience love, Nicholas is given the opportunity to demonstrate his changed relationship toward women and to continue to learn from several women: Lily de Seitas, the mother of the twins who play such an important role in the Greek island adventure; Jojo, the young waif he takes in and who falls in love with him; and Kemp, the crusty landlady who is actually one of his guides on the quest. Finally, with the breaking of the plate, the gift that Mrs. de Seitas has given him, and an almos ...arful scene involving Nicholas that subsequently and inexplicably occurs, Kemp knows that Nicholas is ready to receive Alison again, and she arranges it.

Whether they reunite or separate is not important to Fowles (although it continues to remain important to his readers). What matters in terms of Nicholas' quest is how far he has come in his ability to know and want love and in his ability to share. His journey will continue, with Alison or perhaps with someone else.

What may make this novel such a perennial favorite on college campuses are the techniques Fowles uses to present the tale. The story is told in a first-person narrative by Nicholas after the events have taken place; he nonetheless reveals only what he knew at any given point in the story. Readers tend to want to decipher the truth or mystery of the events just as Nicholas does. They share Nicholas' surprise, shock, and fear at the strange twists and turns of events. Thus, as Fowles hopes his fiction will do, the book has the potential to change readers. When Nicholas does not tell the new American quester, Briggs, what he will really experience on the island of Bourani, so, too, the reader is as likely not to tell a friend what he or she will experience when reading this book. The adventure awaits each reader.

THE FRENCH LIEUTENANT'S WOMAN

First published: 1969
Type of work: Novel

A nineteenth century gentleman abandons the woman to whom he is engaged in order to pursue "the French lieutenant's woman," who, meanwhile, has mysteriously fled.

Charles Smithson, the protagonist of *The French Lieutenant's Woman*, is very much like Nicholas Urfe of *The Magus*. He is well-born and well-bred and should be in an excellent position to enjoy the fruits of life, but he finds himself vaguely dissatisfied. Thinking that marriage to the clever Ernestina Freeman will provide the sense of fulfillment his life lacks, he is quickly dissuaded of this notion upon his instant attraction to Sarah Woodruff, the "French lieutenant's woman."

She is Mystery with a capital *M*, and her separate world, which she has created for herself with her fabricated tale of sexual encounter with the French lieutenant, gives her the freedom the nineteenth century setting and her circumstances would not otherwise provide. She and the Undercliff that she frequents become the mythic landscape, the otherworld that Charles enters in search of adventure, even as Nicholas enters Bourani in *The Magus*.

Both Charles and Sarah are trapped into roles that neither wants. Sarah has the education of a well-bred lady but her lower social standing keeps her in the working class. Charles is a gentleman, but he chafes at the rigid world he inhabits. Unknown to him is his longing to break free. His hobby is the study of fossils trapped by the receding seas when the world changed. Likewise, his place in history is at a turning point in the world, at the end of the Victorian era. The question that the novel poses is whether Charles, like his echinoderm fossils, will be trapped as the world changes, or whether he can break free.

Commerce is on the rise, and even while Charles does not expect that he will have to work to earn a living, he is surprised to find that his uncle, from whom he has expected to receive a handsome inheritance, has remarried, dimming Charles's chances of living the life of perpetual ease. Even so, he declines an offer by Mr. Freeman, Ernestina's father, to come into the world of business, feeling ill-suited for this endeavor.

Charles believes in a Darwinian view of the world and enjoys arguing about this new scientific view with Dr. Grogan; but the scientific pursuit of knowledge does not fully satisfy him, which explains why he is so easily and surprisingly taken by the mysterious woman he first sees at the end of the quay in Lyme Regis. The pursuit of Sarah becomes his obsession. In discovering the "Sarah" within him, he discovers his ability to feel love. As is true of so many Fowles characters, this is the mark of his progress on the journey. Charles chooses, as the questing hero must, to give up certainty and reputation (marriage to Ernestina) to pursue the unknown (Sarah) and all that it might hold.

Freedom of choice, freedom for the individual, is a major concern in this novel as well as in others by Fowles. What is particularly compelling in *The French Lieutenant's Woman* is Fowles's use of the Victorian setting and the form of the Victorian novel, complete with intrusions by the author to comment on the action and even change the ending. The first "ending" comes in the middle of the novel, so it comes as no surprise that this is not really the ending but rather a device to show what the traditional Victorian ending to the tale would be: Charles's decision to avoid the temptation of Sarah and to marry Ernestina and live out his lot in life.

Having dispensed with the traditional Victorian ending, Fowles steps in to inform the reader that it was a myth. So saying, he returns Charles to the pivotal moment of choice, and this time Charles chooses to get off the train in Exeter to go find Sarah, who he knows is there. They do meet in a brief sexual encounter, but when Charles learns that she has fabricated a turned ankle to get him into her room, he flees her in disgust. Later, realizing that he has been rash and determining to break off his engagement to Ernestina (something a gentleman does not do) to marry Sarah, he finds, on his return, that Sarah has mysteriously left. The rest of the novel focuses on Charles's growing awareness of his feelings, which his desire for Sarah represents.

Two more endings conclude the novel. In both, Charles and Sarah meet each other once again, just as Nicholas and Alison meet again in the conclusion to *The Magus*. In the first ending, the couple are reunited through the intercession of the child born of that brief sexual encounter. In the second and final ending, the one Fowles hoped readers would accept as the most real, the clock is turned back and Charles and Sarah are again reunited, only to part. As Charles once again flees from Sarah, he knows that he must begin again, as though reborn. Yet he knows that he is not a trapped echinoderm but a man who has broken free into a new world of choices. Although Sarah cannot be the object of his love, he now has found "an atom of faith in himself," and the future, with all of its potential, awaits him.

DANIEL MARTIN

First published: 1977
Type of work: Novel

A middle-aged screenwriter living in Hollywood is called back to England to his dying friend's bedside and there returns to his first love, the man's wife.

In his fourth novel, *Daniel Martin*, Fowles writes his first happy ending. The protagonist, Daniel Martin, a writer and alter ego for Fowles, struggles throughout the novel with the concept of the happy ending and whether the late twentieth century world can accept it. He finally decides, as his own life reveals to him, that the happy ending is possible. The route to that decision forms the action of the novel. At the same time, Daniel's story becomes *Daniel Martin*, the novel Daniel has wanted to write.

The quester has now come of age; in fact, he is middle-aged. His dilemma is like that of the questers of the earlier novels whose stories were of younger men confronting issues of choice and freedom. Once again, the protagonist is a man who seems to have everything. In this case, his "everything" is a successful life as a playwright and now screenwriter in Hollywood and a beautiful young actress for a lover. Yet the same longing and sense of incompleteness are within him, just as they are within Nicholas and Charles in Fowles's previous novels. For Daniel, the call to the quest comes in the form of a phone call that returns him to the bedside of his former best friend, who is now dying. Returning to England, he is faced with the unfinished business of his life. With Anthony's suicide, the way is cleared for him to become reunited with Jane, his true love and now Anthony's widow. Daniel sees his opportunity to come alive again; Jane resists.

To know where they began, Fowles takes the action back to their college days at Oxford and to the deep bond of friendship among four friends: Anthony, Jane, Jane's sister, and Daniel. Although Daniel and Jane come to realize that they love each other, Daniel makes the "correct" choice (the same choice Fowles presents in the first ending of *The French Lieutenant's Woman*) and marries the one he is "supposed" to marry, not the one he loves. That marriage ends in divorce, and although Jane stays married to Anthony until his death, their marriage does not provide the true depth of feeling that she might have had with Daniel.

Once Daniel has rediscovered the significant moments and sacred places in his past, he longs to find these places and moments again. Thus, the journey moves into the present and the future with Daniel's invitation to Jane to take a trip with him. Fittingly, the trip is a journey up the Nile, which symbolizes lost worlds as well as the potential for a future world with Jane. From that journey, in which he explores much about his feelings for Jane and his own feelings, he persuades Jane to continue with him to Palmyra, an ancient city of wealth and prosperity now in ruins. Again the symbolism of place is apparent: Their arrival in the wasteland of Palmyra can symbolize either what they will become or the potential to turn their own wasteland into a garden if they can escape the bonds that separate them. They do the latter in Jane's symbolic burial of her wedding ring in the sands of the desert. Thus, with her ties to the past severed and with their earlier ties to each other revived, they journey together into the future. The only unfinished business for Daniel is to let Jenny, his Hollywood lover, gently go. The last scene of this first novel with a happy ending places Daniel and Jane in the kitchen together, the quintessential picture of home, talking about the novel Daniel can now write—which is in fact the one the reader has just read.

Summary

The whole body of John Fowles's fiction can be seen as variations on the theme of quest as discovery, which Fowles sees as at the heart of literature dating back to the twelfth century. Fowles gives that theme a distinctly modern twist with his psychological examination of characters in search of meaning in a meaningless world. The successful questers learn to choose freely; the unsuccessful ones remain trapped in roles they merely play out over the course of their lives.

The freedom of choice is more important to Fowles than any specific choices his characters make, which is why he tries to give his characters so much choice. It is also why he writes open endings and multiple endings in some of his novels. Not only are his characters left to choose for themselves, but so, too, are his readers.

Bibliography

Barnum, Carol M. *The Fiction of John Fowles: A Myth for Our Time*. Greenwood, Fla.: Penkevill, 1988.

Beebe, Maurice, ed. "John Fowles Special Number." *Journal of Modern Literature* 8, no. 2 (1980/1981).

Conradi, Peter. *John Fowles*. New York: Methuen, 1982.

Ellen Pifer, ed. *Critical Essays on John Fowles*. Boston: G. K. Hall, 1986.

Huffaker, Robert. *John Fowles*. Boston: Twayne, 1980.

Olshen, Barry N., and Toni A. Olshen. *John Fowles: A Reference Guide*. Boston: G. K. Hall, 1980.

Onega, Susana. *Form and Meaning in the Novels of John Fowles*. Ann Arbor: University of Michigan Press, 1989.

Palmer, William J., ed. "Special Issue: John Fowles." *Modern Fiction Studies* 31 (Spring, 1985).

Carol M. Barnum

CARLOS FUENTES

Born: Panama City, Panama
November 11, 1928

Principal Literary Achievement

Aside from affirming a powerful Mexican identity in his writing, Fuentes introduced innovative language and experimental narrative techniques into mainstream Latin American fiction.

Biography

Carlos Fuentes was born on November 11, 1928, in Panama City, Panama, into a Mexican family that he later characterized as typically petit bourgeois. As the son of a career diplomat, Rafael Fuentes, and Berta Macias Rivas, Carlos Fuentes traveled frequently, attending the best schools in several of the major capitals of the Americas. He learned English at the age of four while his family was living in Washington, D.C. He was graduated from high school in Mexico City then studied law at the National University and the Institut des Hautes Études Internationales in Geneva.

Upon his return to Mexico, he became assistant head of the press section of the Ministry of Foreign Affairs in 1954. While he was head of the department of cultural relations at the Ministry of Foreign Affairs, he also founded and edited *Revista mexicana de literatura* (Mexican review of literature). He later edited or coedited the leftist journals *El espectador*, *Siempre*, and *Política*.

In 1954, Fuentes published a collection of short stories entitled *Los días enmascarados* (the masked days), his first book. He also began to devote himself to writing full-time—novels, book reviews, political essays, film scripts (for Luis Buñuel, among others), and plays.

Fuentes' next two novels reflect his social and artistic concerns at the time. *La región más transparente* (1958; *Where the Air Is Clear*, 1960) deals with Mexico's social, political, and cultural problems from a loosely Marxist perspective. The book was widely read, became controversial, and established Fuentes as the leading young novelist of Mexico. *Las buenas conciencias* (1959; *The Good Conscience*, 1961) is a portrait of a bourgeois family in the provincial town of Guanajuato.

The innovative techniques of Fuentes' first novel, *Where the Air Is Clear*, are more fully developed in *La muerte de Artemio Cruz* (1962; *The Death of Artemio Cruz*, 1964). That novel portrays the Mexican Revolution and its betrayal in modern Mexican society through the memories of Cruz as he lies dying. Generally considered to

be Fuentes' most successful novel, it has been translated into fifteen languages.

With his novella *Aura* (English translation, 1965), a psychological fantasy published also in 1962, Fuentes begins to turn away slightly from his earlier focus on social issues and toward Magical Realism. His next work, a collection of short stories, *Cantar de ciegos* (1964; songs of the blind), focuses on the secret and often bizarre lives of individuals, in a more realistic vein.

For the next several years, Fuentes lived primarily in Paris, although he returned frequently to Mexico City. Much of his next two novels, *Cambio de piel* (1967; *A Change of Skin*, 1968) and *Zona sagrada* (1967; *Holy Place*, 1972), was written in Paris. Fuentes moved back to Mexico in 1969 and published what was to become a famous essay on Latin American literature, *La nueva novela hispanoamericana*. His second novella, *Cumpleaños* (1969), appeared the same year. Two plays followed the next year.

From 1975 to 1977, Fuentes served as Mexico's ambassador to France. Following completion of *Terra nostra* (1975; English translation, 1976) and *La cabeza de la hidra* (1978; *The Hydra Head*, 1978), he returned to his investigation of the European scene in *Una familia lejana* (1980; *Distant Relations*, 1982). *Cristóbal nonato* (1987; *Christopher Unborn*, 1989), a novel, as well as a collection of short stories, *Constancia y otras novelas para vírgenes* (*Constancia and Other Stories for Virgins*, 1989), were published in 1989.

Analysis

Fuentes' overriding literary concern is with establishing a viable Mexican identity, both as an autonomous entity and in relation to the outside world. Myth, legend, and history often intertwine in Fuentes' work. Fuentes turns to Mexico's past—the Aztec culture, the Christian faith imposed by the Spanish conquistadors, and the failed hopes of the Mexican Revolution—and uses it thematically and symbolically to comment on contemporary concerns and to project his own vision of Mexico's future. In portraying Aztec civilization, Fuentes contrasts the superhuman Mexican gods with the classical deities who do resemble mortals. The Mexican gods are "the other, a separate reality," according to Fuentes. This separation incites a paradoxical encounter between what cannot be affected by humans (the sacred) and the human, physical, and imaginative construction of those sacred spaces and times.

The Cuban novelist Alejo Carpentier has argued in his famous essay "Lo real maravilloso" (the marvelous real) that indigenous American culture and nature provide its writers with a wealth of startling images. They constitute a spontaneous, native type of surrealism that contrasts with the artificial variety practiced by European surrealists. In this kind of Magical Realism, supernatural events appear to grow out of the environment rather than descending upon it from beyond. Fuentes uses Magical Realism in two distinct but related capacities: to underline extreme psychological power and to suggest the presence of ancient cosmic forces drawn from Mexican mythology. The juxtaposition of seemingly incompatible images in his fiction often results from the proximity of two different cultures, from the intrusion of ancient beliefs or figures into modern life.

Cultural layering in Fuentes' fiction often manifests itself in character "doubling," or the confusion of identities. Often the characters in Fuentes' work are psychologically or socially deviant. Many are misfits, while others do not tolerate ways of life that differ from their own.

THE DEATH OF ARTEMIO CRUZ

First published: *La muerte de Artemio Cruz*, 1962 (English translation, 1964)
Type of work: Novel

Through the deathbed meditations of one individual, Artemio Cruz, the novel explores how the Mexican Revolution has affected Mexican society at large.

In *The Death of Artemio Cruz*, Fuentes' most widely known novel, Cruz uses his memory to fight against death; Fuentes uses his novel to fight for the memory of the original ideals of the Mexican Revolution, subsequently forgotten and betrayed. The text that Artemio Cruz narrates during the final twelve hours of his life is perhaps his final attempt at domination before he is conquered by death. Struggles for power, however, pervade not only individual relations within the novel but also social relations. The hunger for power consumes not only Cruz as an individual but also society at large. During the Mexican Revolution, the original impetus of the struggle was fragmented, its spirit weakened by the power struggles of its generals; in the years following the revolution, the disruptive desire for power persists, in Fuentes' view.

Private power struggles, fragmenting and disintegrating intimate relations, are most fully developed in the war between Artemio and his wife, Catalina. The tension between the couple is only one manifestation of the continual play of opposing forces in the novel. Like Cruz, who is divided between past and present, body and mind, love and domination, Mexico is divided between the rich and the poor, Spanish and Indian heritages, modern buildings and ancient ruins, revolutionary ideals and mundane compromises. Compressed into the mind of one man, as he lies dying, these divisions take on urgency and universal significance.

The confrontation between memory and death continues throughout the novel. It motivates the most striking aspect of the novel—the division of the text into three different modes of narration and three different verb tenses. The interest of the novel depends to a large extent on the carefully orchestrated interplay between the different voices of Cruz.

With few exceptions, Artemio narrates the entire book. His sickness and imminent death are recounted in the first person and present tense; his meditations and desires in the second person and the future tense; and the events of his past life in the third person and the past tense. While the persons and tenses of the voices are clear, the perspectives of the voices preclude precise descriptions, since they share many images and ideas. They are often described as three distinct parts of the mind: the conscious, the subconscious, and the unconscious. These three different voices demonstrate the coexistence of Cruz's separate selves.

The novel reveals a continual interplay of historical and individual forces. Fuentes' technique is to alternate the three voices in brief sections rather than to present three long narratives, a technique that heightens the tension that the reader experiences between sympathy for and condemnation of Cruz. The shifting perspectives make the choice difficult.

From the novel's central focus on the conflicts within Cruz, the reader moves outward to the conflicts that divide Mexican society as a whole, particularly to the problems posed by the Mexican Revolution. Fuentes has compressed approximately 150 years of Mexican history into the novel. As in Cruz's personal story, so in the historical panorama of Mexico the narrative moves backward in search of origins.

Through the figure of Cruz's paternal grandmother, Ludivinia Menchaca, the historical narrative begins in 1810, the year of her birth and the year of the first revolution, the war of independence from Spain. Cruz's grandmother embodies the old order, the landed aristocracy, which resisted reform movements even back in the mid-nineteenth century. Artemio Cruz is born on her family's land but denied its heritage. Although he fights in the revolution against the order upheld by families such as the Mechacas, he ends up in virtually the same position as his grandmother, denying a voice to later revolutionaries.

Ludivinia's vision of the "green-eyed child," Artemio Cruz, outside her window, forms the link between the tumultuous period through which she lived and the later revolution. In between came the years of Porfirio Díaz, who originally rose to power when he opposed the reelection of the former president, Benito Juárez, in 1870. In order to strengthen Mexico financially, the Díaz regime allowed many foreign concessions to enter Mexico, gave away huge amounts of land taken from the Indians, and denied freedom to the press. The second revolution began in 1910, when Francisco Madero opposed the reelection of Díaz. Madero became president in 1911, but his government became weakened by continued fighting. Victoriano Huerta took over in 1913 and Madero was killed by Huerta's forces. These acts provoked Venustiano Carranza and Álvaro Obregón to rise against Huerta and to uphold the original constitution against Huerta's politics of personal power. Carranza and Obregón were supported intermittently by the forces under Pancho Villa and Emiliano Zapata.

In 1913, when the reader first sees Cruz in the revolution, he is fighting with the forces of Carranza against Huerta. When forced to choose sides between Carranza and Obregón, he chooses Obregón, who later becomes president. Fuentes suggests that, early in the revolution, leaders concentrated too heavily on ideology and ignored practical concerns of the common people, including land reform. The betrayal of the revolution by Cruz evokes Fuentes' own revolutionary perspective. Four specific failings of postrevolutionary Mexican society are echoed throughout the novel: class domination, Americanization, financial corruption, and failure of land reform.

TERRA NOSTRA

First published: 1975 (English translation, 1976)
Type of work: Novel

Using European history to investigate the origin of Latin American culture, Fuentes' novel explores the continuing dynamics of cultural colonialism and independence.

Terra Nostra opens amidst chaotic scenes in Paris: Repentant sinners converge on the church of Saint Germain de Pres and hundreds of women give birth along the banks of the Seine. A man named Pollo Phoibee meets a young woman with grey eyes and tattooed lips, called Celestina, who wants him to explain all these strange events to her. Pollo slips and falls into the Seine. Symbolically echoing *The Fall of Icarus*, the painting by sixteenth-century Dutch artist Pieter Bruegel, the Elder, Pollo—and the reader—fall into the temporal realm of art. There, historical events are shifted out of their traditional sequence and combined with fantastic events. In the next chapter, Pollo, now nameless, has fallen back into sixteenth century Spain. He is discovered on a beach and taken to a palace by the queen of the land, La Señora. This occasion is the first of many instances in the novel in which water serves as a linking device between distant places and times.

The first section of *Terra Nostra*, called "The Old World," concerns the activities of La Señora's husband, El Señor, and his court. El Señor, an imaginary version of Philip II of Spain, is obsessed with the task of building an elaborate palace (the Escorial, to function primarily as a royal mausoleum) and by the prospect of his own death. By sacrificing his life to the building of the magnificent monument, with statues of his ancestors, he hopes to arrest time, to attain eternal life.

El Señor's religious passion ultimately causes him to neglect and mistreat his queen. She recounts a bizarre scene in which she falls on her back in the palace courtyard and cannot get up by herself because of her heavy iron hoopskirts. Everyone abandons her to the elements for days because only the king is allowed to touch her. Mold grows on her, her skin burns and peels, and she is so lonely that she welcomes the mouse that crawls under her skirts. When El Señor finally appears and has a mirror held before her, La Señora screams at seeing her now-unrecognizable face. She believes that her husband has caused her to fall and to rot, so that their appearances would be equally repulsive. La Señora finally realizes, however, that it is not her husband's evil nature that has caused his cruelty; his extreme Christian fervor has caused him not to touch her. She decides then that she will choose the Devil to combat him, and henceforth she will follow her own desires.

"The Old World" section of the novel ends with Celestina's companion, the pilgrim, as he begins to tell a tale to El Señor, the tale that constitutes his adventures in

"The New World," the second and briefest section of the novel. At first, the visions of the New World are idyllic. Ultimately, however, the pilgrim and his friend, an old man named Pedro, are cast upon a beach covered with pearls. Pedro stakes out a claim and is killed defending it from the natives. The natives believe that the earth is divine and cannot be possessed by any person. Pedro has been destroyed by his need for private property in a society that seems to practice a kind of cosmic socialism. He has violated the native utopian tradition that Fuentes (in his essays) hopes will resurface in Mexico.

The society's anticipation and acceptance of the pilgrim as one of their original princes naturally recalls the Aztec belief that the arrival of Hernán Cortés constituted the long-awaited reappearance of the plumbed serpent-god Quetzacoatl. In each case, the conquest of the New World by the Old is facilitated by the incorporation of an Old World explorer into the New World religion. Earlier, the Spaniards killed the Indians with guns; now, the pilgrim offers them a mirror as a gift, but it is no less fatal. The ancient views himself and dies of terror. The people then claim the pilgrim as their chieftain and founder. He finally sees his aged reflection in a mirror, however, as the original ancient had done. (The mirror might also suggest a variety of external or internal conflicts—between two cultures, two people, two parts of the self.)

Finally, before returning to the Old World, the pilgrim again meets the original ancient, who explains to him that he has killed his own hostile brother (part of himself). The ancient says that this continual struggle between opposing forces is necessary for life. This life cycle is precisely what El Señor is trying so desperately to avoid by his plan for eternal fixity within the Escorial.

It is also why, at the beginning of the third part of the novel, El Señor resists the discovery of the New World. This section of the novel is called "The Next World." El Señor is overwhelmed by the knowledge of the New World and also by the philosophy of the ancient, who proclaims that the essence of life is change. El Señor wishes to hide these things from his people so that they will not envision a system other than the one by which he rules them. Most of all, he fears the pilgrim himself, whose task is to achieve freedom. Near the end of the novel, presumably after El Señor dies, he climbs a stairway in his palace, where "on each step the world offered the temptation to choose anew . . . but always in the same, if transfigured place: this land, land of Vespers, Spain, Terra Nostra." Yet Terra Nostra is the known world on old maps, and El Señor has remained there, never venturing to explore his new domains across the sea.

The last chapter of the novel reiterates the opening scene in Paris, where Pollo and Celestina meet in a final embrace. They are fused into one androgynous being that can possess itself continuously in an ecstasy of love. Power struggles are abolished; this act of love abolishes the difference between the self and the other. Their embrace is a wedding that reverses time, since its single self-fertilizing being resembles the figure of Uroboros, an undifferentiated unity imagined in many ancient mythologies to precede humankind's division into individual creatures of different sexes.

This apocalyptic end, is a vision, not a confirmation, of paradise and represents the hope that the "next world" will succeed the known world. Love triumphs here, but it cannot abolish the cruel cycles of history. Thus, at the end of the novel, the reader is left balanced between two visions: unity versus diversity, "ours" versus "yours" or "mine," love versus power, satisfaction versus frustration.

Summary

In his fiction, Carlos Fuentes confronts the problems of Mexican identity through the presence of ancestral voices and indigenous mythologies. His is a view of humankind molded by history yet morally responsible for individual actions, situated in time yet responsive to eternal values. The fictional mode that he uses to express his view is Magical (symbolic) Realism, a realism that can be comprehended only through symbols.

Bibliography

Brody, Robert, and Charles Rossman, eds. *Carlos Fuentes: A Critical View*. Austin: University of Texas Press, 1982.

Brushwood, John S. *Mexico in Its Novel*. Austin: University of Texas Press, 1966.

Duran, Gloria. *The Archetypes of Carlos Fuentes: From Witch to Androgyne*. Hamden, Conn.: Archon Books, 1980.

Faris, Wendy B. *Carlos Fuentes*. New York: Frederick Ungar, 1983.

Guzman, Daniel de. *Carlos Fuentes*. New York: Twayne, 1972.

Genevieve Slomski

FEDERICO GARCÍA LORCA

Born: Fuentevaqueros, Spain
June 5, 1898
Died: Víznar, Spain
August 19, 1936

Principal Literary Achievement

Considered the most important Spanish dramatist in the twentieth century, as well as an outstanding poet, Lorca made a major contribution to the poetical theater of his time.

Biography

The son of a well-to-do landholder, Federico García Rodríguez, and a former school teacher, Vicenta Lorca, Federico García Lorca was born in the small village of Fuentevaqueros near the Andalusian city of Granada on June 5, 1898. Legend has it that Lorca was a slow walker and talker, but his mother and brother remembered that he was normal in his development. He did, however, display at an early age a vivid imagination and a strong creative flair. He was fond of staging puppet shows written and costumed by him for an audience composed of the family servants. He also liked to play the role of priest at impromptu masses. These childhood interests foretold his success as a playwright, director, and actor, and they underscore the importance of religious ritual in his life.

The years spent as a child in a rural Spanish village left an indelible imprint on his mind and inspired the many metaphors and symbols from the natural world that characterize his poetry and plays. He himself emphasized this influence:

I love the countryside. I feel myself linked to it in all my emotions. My oldest childhood memories have the flavour of the earth. . . . Were this not so I could not have written *Blood Wedding*.

Lorca's first love was music. He played the piano extremely well and hoped that his parents would send him to Paris for lessons leading to a career as a concert pianist. They refused to grant his wish, and he turned to writing instead. Music's loss was literature's gain. He published his first book, *Impresiones y paisajes* (1918; *Impressions and Landscapes*, 1987), a series of prose vignettes about his travels in central

700

Spain with a student group, followed by his first book of poetry, *Libro de poemas* (1921; book of poems). In these poems, fanciful and deft though they are, he has yet to find his own voice and is much influenced by the Nicaraguan poet Rubén Darío and two older Spanish poets, Juan Ramón Jiménez and Antonio Machado.

Although he finally managed to earn a law degree at the University of Granada, Lorca was an indifferent student bent on becoming a poet despite his father's skepticism. In 1918, he went to Madrid and took lodgings at the Residencia de Estudiantes, a private residence for students attending the University of Madrid. The Residencia was a center for liberal intellectual life in the capital. Many of its residents, such as Lorca, went on to become internationally known. Two of them were the painter Salvador Dalí, who was then especially close to Lorca, and the film director Luis Buñuel.

The publication of *Romancero gitano* (1928; *The Gypsy Ballads of García Lorca*, 1951, 1953) catapulted its author into the limelight. Using the form of the Spanish ballad, Lorca created a modern mythology for his gypsy protagonists. They are subject to the forces of nature (a malevolent female moon kidnaps a gypsy boy; an erotic wind chases a gypsy girl) and are persecuted by the guardians of society, the infamous Spanish Civil Guard. Sensual, provocative, and dazzling, *The Gypsy Ballads of García Lorca* became a best-seller overnight and branded its author as a poet interested only in Andalusian folklore, a label that Lorca resented.

Seeking a change of environment and a new direction for his poetry, Lorca went to New York City in June, 1929, enrolled in a class in English at Columbia University, made friends, and walked the streets of the metropolis. A few months after his arrival, Wall Street crashed, and he witnessed the hysteria provoked by this event. He responded to the vitality of the blacks and viewed them as victims of society, like the gypsies in his own country. New York's "cruel geometry," its heartlessness, the concrete wasteland, the canyons formed by skyscrapers were overwhelming. Reading in translation the poetry of Walt Whitman and T. S. Eliot helped suggest new ways that his own poetry might take. He returned to Spain, via Cuba, in March, 1930, with the manuscript of *Poeta en Nueva York* (1940; *Poet in New York*, 1940, 1955), in which a strong poetic voice denounces in surrealistic imagery the inhumanity of capitalism's prototypical city.

In 1934, the bullfighter Ignacio Sánchez Mejías, a friend and fellow writer, was fatally gored in the bull ring. *Llanto por Ignacio Sánchez Mejías* (1935; *Lament for Ignacio Sánchez Mejías*, 1937; also known as *Lament for the Death of a Bullfighter*), written a short while after the tragedy, is generally considered to be one of the finest of modern elegies.

Lorca's interest in the theater goes back to his childhood. His first efforts as a playwright met with dismal failure in Madrid in the 1920's. While in New York, he made a vow to return to writing plays. In a letter to his family, he said, "One must think of the theater of the future." Once more in Spain, he became a popular lecturer and also organized a student theater group known as La Barraca, which toured the provinces with a repertoire of classical and modern Spanish plays. Lorca served as director, actor, and set designer. *Bodas de Sangre* (*Blood Wedding*, 1939), the first of what was to become a trilogy on the frustration and repression of women in rural Spain, opened to an enthusiastic Madrid audience in 1933. It was followed in 1934 with the premiere of *Yerma* (English translation, 1941). Posthumously, *La casa de Bernarda Alba* (*The House of Bernarda Alba*, 1947) opened in Buenos Aires in 1945. These three plays are still presented around the world and are known equally well in Russia, China, and Japan. *Blood Wedding* and *Yerma* represent some of the most successful examples of poetry written for the stage in the twentieth century.

Lorca's fame, his friendship with left-wing figures, his proclamations of sympathy for the workers and the poor, and his homosexuality made him an object of loathing on the part of the Fascists. He was in Granada when the Spanish Civil War broke out in July, 1936. It was a period of anarchy in which many old scores were settled. Denounced to the Fascist military commander of Granada, Lorca was summarily executed on August 19 of that year, in Víznar, Spain. His body lies in a mass grave along with many other victims of this tragic episode in Spanish history.

Analysis

Humor, irony, whimsy, the prime ingredients of Lorca's early poetry, set the tone for the pervasive theme of his first books. His had been a relatively happy childhood, spent at play in a small village bathed in Mediterranean light, close to nature, where he busily observed animals and reacted to the mixture of the young, old, and infirm that naturally surrounded him. Many of his unpublished stories written as a teenager reveal a strong sense of compassion for those less fortunate than he, and this moral sense was to make itself especially felt in *Poet in New York*, as he witnessed the plight of the blacks and the poor in New York. In *Book of Poems*, Lorca sought the language of flowers and stones, playfully described an old lizard moving along the path like a nearsighted philosopher, or celebrated the cicada's endless need to sing. When he grew older, he realized that his childhood had been a kind of Eden, and its loss frequently provided him with poignant metaphors.

Andalusia also suggested a style and a theme for his first mature poetry. Flamenco singing (*el cante jondo*, the deep song) had come to Spain probably from Africa. Its long, monotonous wail was the province of the gypsy. In *Poema del cante jondo* (1931; *Poem of the Gypsy Seguidilla*, 1967), Lorca attempts to imitate this emotional chant and, through metaphor, to describe some of its effects upon the listener. When he writes that "The wail imprints in the wind, the shadow of the cypress," he shows the power of the deep song to permeate everywhere and the tragic pitch reached by its feelings (the cypress is associated with death).

From the poems inspired by the *cante jondo*, it was a short step to *The Gypsy Ballads of García Lorca*, where Lorca's gift for metaphor first astounded a large public. In primitive mythology, no dividing line exists between the natural and supernatural world. Elements of nature are personified and interact with humans, and the gods quarrel and make love among themselves and the inhabitants of the earth. That is the world that Lorca attempts to re-create in his gypsy ballads. The moon hypnotizes a gypsy girl, the wind snarls at the roof of a house in which another gypsy girl has taken refuge. Other elements of nature (trees, water) react in sympathy to the plight of the gypsies. Sex, violence, and a strange beauty of language combine to explain the attraction of these ballads.

The poet formed by a rural agrarian society found himself horrified and offended by New York. The moon loses its mythical magic and becomes a fat woman wetting the streets. Prevalent adjectives such as "hollow" (perhaps an echo of T. S. Eliot's "hollow men") and "empty" express the sense of alienation that Lorca felt. *Poet in New York*'s rage and despair speak not only for Lorca's loneliness in this alien land but also for his outrage at the poverty and the treatment of the blacks. "Ode to Harlem" depicts the blacks as victims of white civilization and proposes to show as early as 1929 that "black is beautiful," and that whiteness, whether bleached or in the blush of apples, must be abolished so that the blacks can have their freedom of expression. "I denounce everyone/ Who ignores the other half," he wrote in a poem about New York's offices. Moral outrage controls the pell-mell rush of imagery and keeps the surrealistic tendency from getting out of hand. The poet, condemning the mindless slaughter of animals, mourning for the lost Eden of his childhood, and evoking a dance of death through Wall Street, has written a classic book on the alienation and despair produced by the urban landscape.

Reading Walt Whitman and meeting the American poet Hart Crane helped Lorca come to terms with his homosexuality. His "Ode to Walt Whitman," written in New York, idealizes a pure homosexual love in contrast with that of male prostitution. He began work on two obscure and difficult plays in which he explored homosexuality and its relation to all forms of love, *Así que pasen cinco años* (pb. 1937; *When Five Years Pass*, 1941) and *El público* (pb. 1976; *The Audience*, 1958).

As a child, Lorca was deeply Catholic, and some of his unpublished pieces show how closely he identified with the figure of Jesus Christ. Letters from New York to the family recount his disillusion with the coldness of Protestant churches and their lack of ritual. Even in his most pagan moments, he expresses himself from a Spanish Catholic experience, and his images often come from church icons, the history of the saints, and the Bible. His religion is also a source of his strong moral feelings in the face of economic suffering and racial prejudice.

Lorca's dramatic trilogy, *Blood Wedding, Yerma*, and *The House of Bernarda Alba*, promises to be an enduring monument. Each play addresses the ultimately tragic oppression by society on the freedom of individuals. In *Blood Wedding*, a marriage of convenience is violently subverted when Leonardo, who is already married but has always longed for the bride, carries her off into the forest. He is killed by the outraged villagers, and the bride is excoriated by the bridegroom's mother. In *Yerma*, the protagonist is a childless woman (*yerma* means "barren") who does not love her husband but cannot leave him because society forbids it. In a fit of anger and frustration, she strangles her husband, thus killing her only legitimate chance of having a child. Bernarda Alba suffocates her daughters' desires and rules like a cruel despot in *The House of Bernarda Alba*. She determines that the eldest should marry first, even though the youngest is the most attractive. The suitor Pepe el Romano courts

Angustias but has an affair with Adela. When Bernarda discovers what has been occurring, Adela commits suicide, but the undaunted matriarch shouts that her youngest has died a virgin, thus continuing to impose her will.

Lorca's work is an outcry against oppression of all kinds (sexual, social, racial). Individuals need to be free to express themselves, and silence is a form of death.

THE GUITAR

First published: "La guitarra," 1931 (English translation, 1938)
Type of work: Poem

The all-powerful guitar evokes a strange, magic world.

"The Guitar" typifies Lorca's purpose in the *cante jondo*: to approximate in print something of the auditory experience in hearing the music. Two characteristics are notable. The sound of the guitar is like a wail (*llanto*), the same word that refers to the flamenco singing. "The lament of the guitar begins," is the opening line of the poem, and it is repeated two lines later. The guitar's lament is monotonous and repetitious (like the wind and the rain), and Lorca achieves this effect through further repetition. Three times he writes the phrase, "It is impossible to silence it." Meanwhile, the strength of the guitar's sound is sufficient to break the wine cups of dawn. Flamenco players sing and dance all night, and their revelry persists until daybreak.

For what does the guitar wail? Why is its sound so heartbreaking and haunting? In a series of brilliant metaphors, Lorca supplies some answers, summarized in the simple lines, "It weeps for/ things far away." "Sand of the warm south/ asking for white camellias" associates the guitar with Andalusia, situated on the Mediterranean Sea with its beaches and flowers. "It weeps arrow without target/ evening without morning." Arrows without targets, evenings without mornings are metaphors of disorientation. Another cause for its grief is "The first dead bird/ upon the branch," a reference to the loss of innocence, a theme that appears often in Lorca's verse.

Finally, this instrument that evokes so many poignant feelings itself becomes a metaphor: "Oh, guitar!/ Heart grievously wounded/ by five swords." It is a splendid example of a Lorca metaphor. The body of a guitar roughly approximates the shape of a heart, which is wounded by the five fingers of the person playing it. Yet the image also evokes the common household religious print of the Sacred Heart of Jesus, wounded by the grief of the world.

RIDER'S SONG

First published: "Canción de jinete," 1927 (English translation, 1937)
Type of work: Poem

A horseman has set out on a journey to the Andalusian city of Córdoba; even though he knows the way, he will never reach his destination.

In "Rider's Song," one of his most popular short poems, Lorca has written a parable about the unattainability of goals. The refrain that frames the poem, "Córdoba/ Far away and alone," indicates in somber tones the rider's destination. Córdoba in the eleventh century was the capital of Arabic Spain and the richest city in Europe, and for a modern traveler it is still a city of great cultural wealth.

Mounted on a valiant black pony, olives in his saddlebag, the moon lighting his way, conditions seem optimum for the rider. Yet the moon is usually a malevolent figure in Lorca's poetry, and it soon turns red, the color of violence and blood. "Although I know the roads/ I'll never reach Córdoba," exclaims the narrator, and the reader discovers why: "Death is looking at me/ From the towers of Córdoba." The road seems suddenly long, and the poem ends the way that it began: "Córdoba./ Far away and alone." The poem takes on special meaning for the reader who knows that Lorca greatly feared death and was executed at the age of thirty-eight in the midst of a brilliant career.

BALLAD OF THE MOON, MOON

First published: "Romance de la luna, luna," 1928 (English translation, 1937)
Type of work: Poem

Dressed as a woman, the moon descends to earth and, by means of her dance, casts a spell on a gypsy boy and carries him off with her.

Since it is the first poem in *Romancero gitano* (1928; *The Gypsy Ballads of García Lorca*, 1951, 1953), "Ballad of the Moon, Moon" sets the tone and also signals the role of the moon and other natural elements in the book. The moon appears in the smithy (gypsies were often blacksmiths) dressed as a woman, wearing a bustle of white lilies (suggested by the moon's whiteness), and she begins a lascivious dance in front of a little boy left in the shop by his parents. Lorca renders the spell cast on the boy through rhyme and repetition: "The boy stares and stares at her./ The boy keeps staring hard." Captivated, the boy warns the moon that she must flee before the gypsies return or they will chop her up for necklaces and silver rings, typical gypsy jewelry. The words that he uses to caution the moon are incantatory, "Run away, moon, run away, moon."

But the moon refuses to be frightened and answers the boy with her own prediction: When the gypsies come, they will find you on the anvil with your tiny eyes shut. Enthralled, the boy draws near. A rider is heard galloping across the plain, and in the smithy the boy's eyes are shut. The moon gives way to the sound of dry hooves pounding on the ground, which suggests death.

The gypsies return through the olive groves, their bronze faces also under the spell of the moon. A barn owl hoots, and through the sky goes the moon, taking a boy by the hand. The boy's body lies inside the smithy, but his spirit has gone with the moon. The gypsies, upon discovering their loss, commence to wail and shout. Outside, the air, this time a sympathetic element of nature, watches over them.

There are many stories in Greek and Roman mythology of the moon descending to the earth to capture a young man and take him away. The most famous case is the handsome Greek shepherd Endymion, whom the moon goddess found irresistible. Thus did Lorca create a modern mythology for his gypsies, weaving strands of ancient tales and local Andalusian culture.

LAMENT FOR IGNACIO SÁNCHEZ MEJÍAS

First published: *Llanto por Ignacio Sánchez Mejías*, 1935 (English translation, 1937)

Type of work: Poem

Lorca mourns the death of his friend, fellow poet, and famous bullfighter in terms that remind the reader of the mythical and religious source of bullfighting.

Lament for Ignacio Sánchez Mejías grows out of a series of facts that help explain some of the poem's allusions. Ignacio Sánchez Mejías (1891-1934), the son of a Seville doctor, was a member of Lorca's generation, a patron of the arts, a writer admired for his plays, and a nationally known bullfighter who had learned his art from the great García y Belmonte. Sánchez Mejías retired from bullfighting in 1922 but allowed himself to return to the ring in 1934, close to the age of forty-three. He was gored on August 11, 1934. Taken to a clinic in Madrid, gangrene set in, and he suffered a painful end, writhing on his bed. He died on August 13. The next day, his body was placed on a train to take him for burial to Seville, and a Madrid newspaper in bold headlines announced the time of the train's departure: AT FIVE O'CLOCK IN THE AFTERNOON.

Lorca had strong thoughts on the origin and nature of the bullfight, and it is these convictions that help explain the rhetoric of the elegy on the death of his friend. The sport, if it may be called that, was connected to the Spanish character. As Lorca noted, "Spain [was]·the only country where death is the national spectacle." Ancient Near Eastern religions deified the cow, and many primitive religions required the annual sacrifice of an animal to ensure the fertility of the crops. Bulls were bred in Spain in Roman times, and the modern art of bullfighting began in the eighteenth century. Lorca viewed the bullfighter as priest, the struggle with the animal as a ritual, and the entire spectacle as a primordial pagan rite. The bull's bellow in the ring, the blood that is shed before the roaring crowd, the entwined movement of man and animal originate, Lorca believed, in primitive spectacles from the Mediterranean region of Europe.

The poem consists of 220 lines divided into four parts. Part 1, "The Goring and the Death," creates the turmoil that surrounded Ignacio's accident and the agony of his death. With a dirgelike effect, every other line reads "At five o'clock in the afternoon." Attributes of the goring and the clinic are strewn between each of these funereal lines: the winding sheet, the basket of lime to be thrown on the spilled blood in the ring, cotton and oxide, the operating table ("a coffin with wheels"), groups of silent men on the corners awaiting the news, and the metaphor that announces the gangrene: "death laid eggs in the wound." The gored flesh burns like the sun, and it is five o'clock on all the clocks!

Part 2, "The Spilt Blood," starts with an anguished shout, "I do not want to see it" (Ignacio's blood on the sand). The poet cries out to his old friend the moon to rush to the scene and sends for jasmines so that their whiteness will cover the blood.

Lines 67 to 74 incorporate for the first time mythical elements. The cow of the old world licking up the generations of blood spilled on the sand alludes to the primitive cow goddess. The bulls of Guisando are standing stone statues not far from Madrid, erected as part of a bull cult. With this device, Lorca turns the personal tragedy of Ignacio's death into an event with mythic proportions, a millennial sacrifice. Ignacio did not flinch when he saw the horns near, but the "terrible mothers/ lifted their heads," for they scented once more the sacrificial blood. These terrible mothers contain, as is so often the case in Lorca's poetry, several layers of allusion: the fates of Greek mythology and the baleful female goddesses in different religions.

The elegy demands a recitation of the deceased's qualities, and Lorca waxes eloquent. Ignacio is a prince, his strength a river of lions, his laughter as white as a lily, his countenance a blend of Rome and Andalusia. He knew how to fight, but he was also an artist "soft with the ears of corn." Now, however, his blood ("nightingale of his veins") soaks into the earth, to form part of a pool of agony that stretches to the stars. No chalice can contain it, no song can smother it. The poet shouts once more: "I do not want to see it!!"

Part 3, "Body Laid Out," presents a series of complex images evoked by the thought of Ignacio's body awaiting its transport to Seville to be buried. He is stone cold, defenseless (rain penetrates his mouth); mourners crowd around the body, creasing the shroud. The scene needs men with hard voices to accompany this captain bound by death. Finally, the poet releases the body: "Go, Ignacio: do not feel the hot bellow./ Sleep, fly, rest: the sea also dies!"

After the preceding torrent of grief, part 4, "Absent Soul," has a haunting, quiet sadness, a final acceptance. The loneliness of the dead and their eventual disappearance into oblivion form its basic themes. The bull, the fig tree, the child no longer know Ignacio, because he has died forever. Autumn will come and go, death will continue. Only art will preserve Ignacio, and thus Lorca returns to the purpose of all elegies, to erect a verbal monument in words to the departed individual. Many readers think that Lorca wrote his own epitaph in the final stanza: "Not for a long time will there be born, if indeed he is born,/ an Andalusian so famous, so rich in adventure."

BLOOD WEDDING

First produced: *Bodas de sangre*, 1933 (first published, 1935; English translation, 1939)
Type of work: Play

Lorca's first hit, *Blood Wedding*, using prose and poetry, recounts the story of a rural wedding in southern Spain that ends in violence.

Blood Wedding bestowed fame and fortune overnight on its author. In 1928, Lorca read a newspaper account of a wedding that ended in tragic circumstances near Almería (southern Spain). He clipped the article, reread it five years later, and in a week finished his play, which became a hit in Madrid, Barcelona, and Buenos Aires. In *Blood Wedding*, Lorca forcefully presents the theme of his three tragedies: Love that is unfulfilled because of the need to preserve honor and appearances results in death. A good-natured, hardworking young man contracts matrimony with a woman. The bridegroom is the only surviving member of a family that has been involved in a feud with the Felixes, and his mother is still overcome with a mixture of rage and fear that her only surviving son will meet the same fate. In rural Spain, where there were no secrets, it was known that the bride had been seeing someone else before the engagement. She is still madly in love with Leonardo (of the Felix family), who is married and the father of a boy. While the wedding celebration continues with singing and dancing, Leonardo rides away with the new bride. He is pursued by the groom, and the two men kill each other, thus causing the mother's forebodings to come true.

This simple plot summary does little to account for the sharp visual and verbal impact of the drama. Lorca assigned a different color to each one of the scenes and characters. The groom's house has yellow walls, a pink cross accents the bride's dwelling, and the scene of the wedding has shades of whites, grays, and cool blues. Flowers are assigned to each character, carnations to the groom, a crown of orange blossoms to the bride. Folk lullabies are used for their musical effect and to advance the plot, folk dances enliven the foreground of the wedding, while in the background the passions of Leonardo and the bride impel them to a tragic conclusion.

Signs of the care with which this play was crafted are the various clues at the outset as to the fate that will befall the characters. The mother, still grieving over the murder of her husband and first son, curses all knives and sharp-edged weapons. Leonardo's first speech reveals that he has had to put new shoes on his horse, suggesting that he is riding his stallion to death by making nightly visits to the bride-to-be. Even the lullabies contain portents. Leonardo's mother-in-law sings to her grandchild about a giant horse (Leonardo) that refuses to drink water (conform to custom) and rides with a silver dagger (death) in his eyes, through the gray valleys where the mare (the bride) awaits.

Vintage Lorca is the blend of fantasy and symbolism in the first scene of act 3. Leonardo and the bride take refuge in the forest from the groom, and in this section of the play Lorca exercises his talent for magic and mystery that marked *The Gypsy Ballads of García Lorca*. He sets the stage carefully: "A forest at night with great moist tree trunks and a murky atmosphere. Two violins are playing." The moon emerges in the guise of a young white-faced woodcutter and recites a poetic monologue about her mythical powers. She wants no shadows and will shine on the groom's white vest and point the way for the daggers. A barefoot beggar woman appears, her face hardly visible under the dark-green folds of her garment. Representing death, she directs the moon to throw lots of light, for they cannot escape.

The vengeful, unforgiving figure of the mother is plain. Her grief is monumental, and she scorns the bride's passion. The fact that the bride in the final scene proclaims that she is still a virgin seems beneath contempt as far as the groom's mother is concerned.

As Leonardo and the bride cling to each other in the forest and await the groom and his men, they are portrayed as if in the grips of a force much stronger than they. "I love you, but leave me," cries the bride, torn between her passion and her honor. Leonardo replies that the blame is not his, "The blame belongs to the earth,/ And to the smell that comes/ From your breasts and your braids." It is this powerful passion in conflict with tradition and honor that creates the tragic conclusions of Lorca's three plays.

Summary

Readers of Federico García Lorca's poetry and plays encounter an intense, shattering emotion, one that occasionally hovers on the edge of melodrama but that frequently stirs deep feelings. Lovers of metaphor are fascinated by the play of his imagination and keep discovering new interpretations as they read his verse. Yet Lorca is not a difficult poet, for he believed in keeping firm control, obeying what he called the logic of the poem.

After he was executed by the Fascists in 1936, he became a symbol of the poet as a victim of repression. His reputation outside Spain grew accordingly. Now, with the history of the Spanish Civil War long past, it is a testimony to his talent that he continues to be probably the best known of modern Spanish writers.

Bibliography

Craige, Betty Jean. *Lorca's "Poet in New York": The Fall into Consciousness*. Lexington: University Press of Kentucky, 1977.

Cobb, Carl. *Federico García Lorca*. Boston: Twayne, 1967.

Gibson, Ian. *Federico García Lorca: A Life*. New York: Pantheon, 1989.

Honig, Edwin. *García Lorca*. Norfolk, Conn.: New Directions, 1963.

Lima, Robert. *The Theatre of García Lorca*. New York: Las Américas, 1963.

Young, Howard. *The Victorious Expression*. Madison: University of Wisconsin Press, 1964.

Howard Young

GABRIEL GARCÍA MÁRQUEZ

Born: Aracataca, Colombia
March 6, 1928

Principal Literary Achievement
One of the most admired writers of Latin American fiction, Nobel laureate García Márquez has brought worldwide recognition to the contributions of Latin American authors in contemporary world literature.

Biography

On March 6, 1928, Gabriel José García Márquez was born in Aracataca, Colombia. The oldest of twelve children of Luisa Santiaga Márquez Iguarán and Gabriel Eligio García, the boy was reared by his grandparents. He refers to his grandfather, a retired colonel, as the "guardian angel" of his "infancy." The old man instilled in him a love for the past, especially the Colombian Civil Wars of 1899 to 1903. García Márquez also grew up hearing his grandmother and aunts tell stories of local myths and legends.

After graduation from the National Secondary School near Bogotá in 1946, García Márquez entered the National University of Colombia to study law. While there, he also read poetry avidly and began to write short stories. In 1948, an assassination in Bogotá triggered a civil war that politicized García Márquez and caused the closing of the National University. When he resumed his studies at the University of Cartagena, García Márquez studied journalism. In 1950, he went to work as a columnist for *El Heraldo* in Barranquila. He also spent considerable time reading and discussing fiction with other journalists and writers in local cafes and bookstores. That is how García Márquez first became acquainted with the European and North American authors who particularly influenced his work, including William Faulkner, Ernest Hemingway, James Joyce, Franz Kafka, and Joseph Conrad.

In 1954, García Márquez returned to Bogotá as a film critic and reporter for *El Espectador* and, in his spare time, wrote short stories. He published the first novel, *La hojarasca* (*Leaf Storm*, 1972) in 1955. In addition to fiction, García Márquez also wrote a true account of the shipwreck of a Colombian naval destroyer, which *El Espectador* published anonymously. This story included material about illegal government activity and stirred so much controversy that the editor of *El Espectador* sent

García Márquez abroad to work as a foreign correspondent. When the Colombian government eventually shut down *El Espectador* altogether, García Márquez remained in Paris. The two political novels that he wrote during this time were well received in literary circles: *La mala hora* (1962; revised, 1966; *In Evil Hour*, 1979) and *El coronel no tiene quien le escriba* (1961; *No One Writes to the Colonel and Other Stories*, 1968). Yet his fiction did not attract significant public attention until his surprise bestseller *Cien años de soledad* (1967; *One Hundred Years of Solitude*, 1970).

In 1958, García Márquez left Europe to work for the newspaper *Momento* in Caracas, Venezuela. That same year, he married Mercedes Barcha and continued to write stories. From 1959 to 1965, however, García Márquez—who, like most Latin American intellectuals, supported the Cuban Revolution—concentrated fully on journalism and political issues. His return to fiction resulted in *One Hundred Years of Solitude*, considered one of the major novels of the twentieth century. Because of the financial security that it brought, García Márquez was able to support his wife and two sons and still devote himself full-time to writing. He also began to travel widely, denouncing political dictatorship and speaking in support of human rights. In 1971, he received an honorary doctorate from Columbia University, and, in 1972, he won the prestigious Rómulo Gallegos Prize in Venezuela and the Neustadt International Prize for Literature. After publication of additional novels and a collection of short stories, García Márquez was awarded the Nobel Prize in Literature in 1982.

In 1985, García Márquez published *El amor en los tiempos del cólera* (*Love in the Time of Cholera*, 1988), another major work of fiction that received laudatory reviews. A subsequent novel, *El general en su laberinto* (1989; *The General in His Labyrinth*, 1990), challenged the image of Simón Bolívar—generally considered to be Latin America's greatest hero—and sparked great controversy in Latin America. Returning to Colombia early in 1990 after thirty years of living in political exile, García Márquez continued to commute with his wife among homes in Mexico, Cuba, and Colombia. In addition to fiction and some journalism, he continued to write scripts for television and to prepare his memoirs.

Analysis

Latin American fiction flourished in the 1960's and became appreciated as a powerful force in contemporary literature. Along with fellow Latin American authors Julio Cortázar, Ernesto Sabato, Mario Vargas Llosa, and Carlos Fuentes, García Márquez is one of the most significant influences in this period (called The Boom). His fiction presents a reality quite unlike the novels of the previous generation. Blending history, folktales, and imagination, García Márquez creates an expanded vision of life. Literary critics have coined a term for this bold interweaving of imagination and reality: Magical Realism.

The bulk of García Márquez's fiction, which includes social and political issues and commentary, is set between the early 1800's and the early 1900's in the mythical village of Macondo, which resembles his childhood village of Aracataca. García Márquez researches details of daily life in the nineteenth century for use in his fiction.

Yet he also considers himself "quite disrespectful of real time and space" and, thus, free to build relationships between different worlds and eras. Because he has "no desire to change a detail" that he likes "just to make the chronology function properly," García Márquez writes stories that free readers from space/time boundaries and encourage them to take a fresh look at the world. Nothing is impossible, García Márquez seems to suggest.

Through rich and luxurious language, García Márquez characteristically offers detailed images of persons, places, and things. He even offers his readers mathematical precision. In *One Hundred Years of Solitude*, for example, a breakfast consists of exactly eight quarts of coffee, thirty eggs, and juice from forty oranges. Rain falls in Macondo for precisely four years, eleven months, and two days. Such concrete specificity within myth and legend helps to create the stimulating interplay between reality and fantasy for which García Márquez is best known.

Thematically, García Márquez is interested in things that upset the established order in people's lives. A recurring image is a plague that comes and changes all that it touches. García Márquez once said that the only subject about which he writes is solitude, and it is certainly a recurring theme. He also said that all of his books are about love, and that also seems to be true. Frequently, he investigates the relationship among love, solitude, and power, especially with an eye toward uncovering an individual's relationship to his or her fate or destiny.

Death is another characteristic theme, although the gloomy perspective prior to 1959 contrasts sharply with García Márquez's more mature work. García Márquez also writes frequently about both the humor and pathos of aging, from his first two books, *Leaf Storm* and *No One Writes to the Colonel and Other Stories*, to his more recent *Love in the Time of Cholera* and *The General in His Labyrinth*. He cites his grandparents as the models for most of the people in his fiction. Other influences from García Márquez's childhood also abound: old houses, ancient matriarchs, a sense of nostalgia, civil wars, colonels, and banana companies, among other things.

Although García Márquez's work shows thematic consistency, his tone and style have undergone considerable changes. His early work was generally most concerned with communicating content through a precise, controlled style. An exception was his elaborate, dense first novel, *Leaf Storm*. In the late 1950's, however, García Márquez's approach became more allegorical, and he entered into a period of literary crisis, a period of severe self-criticism and dissatisfaction with previous work. Caught between his old sparse style and the growing mythical approach, with its flowing language, supernatural occurrences, and hyperbole, García Márquez wrote no fiction until 1965. Then, while he was driving from Mexico City to Acapulco, García Márquez had a vision of how he could, at last, tell the story of his childhood, and he immediately returned home to write in seclusion, sometimes for fourteen hours a day. Writing constantly for one and a half years, he produced the masterpiece *One Hundred Years of Solitude*, in which his Magical Realism blossomed fully. Some critics have been disappointed that, since this novel, García Márquez has not extended Magical Realism more. Yet García Márquez explains that his work as a whole is founded on "a geographic and historical reality" that is not that of "magical realism and all those other things which people talk about." He takes a different path in every book, he says, because "style is determined by subject, by the mood of the times."

García Márquez's more recent fiction continues to display his wide-ranging and considerable literary skills. *Love in the Time of Cholera*, although written about an octogenarian and in the author's own maturity, offers an almost childlike delight in the powerful discovery that old age can be a time of love, joy, and passion. *The General in His Labyrinth*, in contrast, presents an almost humorless investigation of García Márquez's ever-present themes of solitude, love, and destiny. Yet both reflect the author's own vibrant energy and enthusiasm for life. Although death is a major theme in his work, García Márquez has said that he does not pay much attention to it because it distracts him from the most important thing in life: what one does. By interacting with the worlds that García Márquez creates, his readers become better able to reflect upon their own worlds—the realities that they themselves create—and embrace more of the field of all possibilities in their own daily lives.

ONE HUNDRED YEARS OF SOLITUDE

First published: *Cien años de soledad*, 1967 (English translation, 1970)
Type of work: Novel

Six generations of the founding family of Macondo are chronicled in this comic masterpiece.

One Hundred Years of Solitude traces the Buendía family dynasty through six generations of chaotic decline. Family patriarch José Arcadio Buendía founds the almost-perfect town of Macondo with three hundred inhabitants, all under age thirty. A man of "unbridled imagination" who always goes "beyond the genius of nature and even beyond miracles and magic," José Arcadio devotes his life to the quest for knowledge but is finally overwhelmed by the intensity of his own pursuit and spends his last days chained to a chestnut tree, preaching in Latin against the existence of God.

José Arcadio's son, Colonel Aureliano, shepherds Macondo into a period of political rebellion and conflict. A giant American fruit company develops the town, but worker exploitation erupts in a violent strike, and thousands are killed in a secret massacre. Úrsula, matriarch of the family and José Arcadio's wife, struggles to save the family from an evil destiny for more than 130 years. Her death, however, signals the demise of the family and of Macondo. At the end, the two surviving Buendías together conceive a child, who is born with the prophesied curly tail of a pig. Both the child and his mother die, leaving the father alone.

The novel seems to be written from the perspective of an omniscient author until the final pages. At the conclusion, the reader learns that the story has been the unfoldment of the prophecy made by the old gypsy Melquíades, who had long ago recorded the history of the Buendías family in Sanskrit. As his final act, the sole survivor of the family, as well as of the town of Macondo, the father deciphers the parchments of Melquíades. He begins to read of the very instant that he is living, *William Tell* "prophesying himself in the act of deciphering the last pages of the parchments, as if he were looking into a speaking mirror." He realizes that at the precise instant that he finishes reading, the entire story will be wiped from the memory of humankind and that it will never be repeated, because "races condemned to one hundred years of solitude did not have a second opportunity on earth."

Thus, the novel becomes a world that both gives birth to, and consumes, itself. The main theme is solitude, humankind's destiny in a universe that it can never completely comprehend or control, and the novel has been interpreted as a family saga, as a history in microcosm of Colombia, and even as an epic myth of the human experience moving from the paradise of Eden to the apocalypse. With majestic irony and magic, García Márquez interweaves details of everyday life with the fantastic to create such memorable images as a plague of insomnia that afflicts the whole town, Remedios the Beauty, who rises to heaven still clutching the bed sheets that she was hanging out to dry, and a cloud of yellow butterflies, which follow Mauricio Babilonia everywhere that he goes. Although grounded in Latin American history, this work manipulates the facts and figures to suit poetic purposes, for example, expanding the number of people who actually died in the United Fruit Company strike of 1928 from seventeen to more than three thousand because García Márquez wanted enough bodies to fill a train.

This novel circles and recircles. García Márquez describes José Arcadio Buendía as one with enough lucidity to sense that time can stumble and have accidents, and therefore splinter and leave an "eternalized fragment" in a room. In this novel, darting back and forth between visions and memories of generations, García Márquez bends both time and space to create his own eternalized fragment of reality. Critics worldwide have hailed this comic masterpiece as Magical Realism at its best.

LOVE IN THE TIME OF CHOLERA

First published: *El amor en los tiempos del cólera*, 1985 (English translation, 1988)
Type of work: Novel

An octogenarian renews his courtship of a woman who spurned him more than fifty years ago, and this time love triumphs.

Love in the Time of Cholera is a celebration of life over death, love over despair, health over sickness. It is the story of Florentino Ariza, who was rejected by Fermina

Daza in his youth. He maintains a silent vigil of unrequited love for fifty-one years, nine months, and four days, until he meets Fermina again at her husband's wake and renews his suit. The novel spans a period from the late 1870's to the early 1930's, and it is set in a South American community, besieged by civil wars and plagues, that is modeled after Cartagena, Colombia.

Florentino, an eighteen-year-old apprentice telegraph operator, sees thirteen-year-old Fermina and falls madly in love. Fermina's father finds out and sends his daughter on an extended trip to remove her from temptation. She returns years later, rejects Florentino, and accepts the proposal of a cultured physician and cholera specialist, Dr. Juvenal Urbino. Although Florentino continues to love Fermina throughout the years, he also continues his own social relationships—engaging in 622 long-term liaisons, which he records in a series of notebooks—and becomes president of a river boat company. Then Florentino learns that eighty-one-year-old Juvenal has died, falling off a ladder trying to capture a condescending, bilingual parrot. Although *Love in the Time of Cholera* does not have the extended fantasy of *One Hundred Years of Solitude*, touches of unexpected, delightful humor—like the parrot—abound. In the midst of careful detailing, it is almost as if García Márquez winks and turns his head to tell the reader a private joke.

When Florentino attends Juvenal's wake at the Urbino home, Fermina orders him to leave. Undaunted, he launches an almost-teenage courtship and eventually triumphs, consummating his passion on a riverboat during a trip on the Magdalena River. The ship is unable to dock because of an outbreak of cholera on board, and the crew and passengers are running low on supplies. Yet Florentino is focused on life, not death. At the end of the novel, the captain asks Florentino how long he thinks they can keep going up and down the river, and Florentino responds, "Forever."

This novel differs considerably from much of García Márquez's previous fiction. It is a more precise and simple story, in contrast to his often complicated, multiple narratives. Except for a brief section in the beginning, the plot proceeds chronologically. And although reality and fantasy intermingle, the fantastic in this novel is not as fantastic as in other works, and the line between the two is less blurred. Critics have suggested that *Love in the Time of Cholera* reads like a nineteenth century novel of the majestic, narrative tradition.

García Márquez still focuses on love and destiny, two of his most enduring themes, but this novel is an optimistic celebration of life. Evil and negativity are present, and this time his characteristic plague is cholera. In this novel, however, such situations make people want to live more, not less. García Márquez has explained that Fermina's and Florentino's romance—which is based on the relationship of his father and mother—was sparked by an image that he once saw: an elderly couple, very much in love, dancing on the deck of a ship. García Márquez told an interviewer that he could not have written *Love in the Time of Cholera* when he was younger because it includes points of view that he did not have before. García Márquez continued, "I think that aging has made me realize that feelings and sentiments, what happens in the heart, are ultimately the most important."

Summary

The fiction of Gabriel García Márquez is an investigation of what has been called poetic truth. Most of his work presents pictures of nineteenth century Latin American life that are recognizable in many respects, but García Márquez also deals with deeper truths and investigates more universal patterns. To do so, he blends fantasy and realism in what critics have called Magical Realism, creating works that have earned him not only the Nobel Prize in Literature but also the kind of recognition that he says he has always desired: people reading and talking about his books "not with admiration or enthusiasm but with affection."

Bibliography

Bloom, Harold, ed. *Gabriel García Márquez*. New York: Chelsea House, 1989.

Fau, Margaret Eustella. *Bibliographic Guide to Gabriel García Márquez, 1979-1985*, Westport, Conn.: Greenwood Press, 1986.

──────────. *Gabriel García Márquez: An Annotated Bibliography, 1947-1979*. Westport, Conn.: Greenwood Press, 1980.

McMurray, George R., ed. *Critical Essays on Gabriel García Márquez*. Boston: G. K. Hall, 1987.

Williams, Raymond L. *Gabriel García Márquez*. Boston: Twayne, 1984.

Wood, Michael. *García Márquez: "One Hundred Years of Solitude."* Cambridge, England: Cambridge University Press, 1990.

Jean C. Fulton

ANDRÉ GIDE

Born: Paris, France
November 22, 1869
Died: Paris, France
February 19, 1951

Principal Literary Achievement
Following World War I, Gide emerged as a leading spokesperson for rebellious youth seeking to lead spontaneous and "sincere" lives in opposition to conventional morality.

Biography
André Paul Guillaume Gide was born on November 22, 1869, in Paris, France, the only child of Juliette Rondeaux and Paul Gide. Both parents were Huguenots in Roman Catholic France and believed in a strict Protestant upbringing for their son. Gide's father died when André was only eleven years old. This loss, combined with a somewhat nervous temperament, turned Gide into a difficult and unhappy young man plagued by psychosomatic illness. At an early age he developed an almost obsessive infatuation for his cousin, Madeleine Rondeaux, whom he worshiped as an idealized epitome of pious and pure young womanhood. They saw each other at family gatherings and corresponded regularly for several years; both families, however, apparently opposed the two of them getting married, and they had to wait until the death of Gide's mother in 1895.

Gide's relationship with Madeleine was a platonic and spiritual one throughout their married lives. Though he was unfaithful to her, he continued to place Madeleine on a pedestal and to find in her the inspiration for much of his best work. Madeleine served as the model for Marceline in *L'Immoraliste* (1902; *The Immoralist*, 1930) and for Alissa in *La Porte étroite* (1909; *Strait Is the Gate*, 1924), both female exemplars of Christian morality and piety.

The major crisis in their marriage occurred in 1918, when Gide returned from one of his jaunts to Switzerland with his lover, Marc Allegret, to learn that Madeleine had burned all of his letters to her. Gide was profoundly distressed by the destruction of what he believed to be the expression of the most noble side of his nature; he was also forced to recognize, perhaps for the first time, the very real pain his duplicitous life was causing her. Following Madeleine's death in 1938, Gide privately published a small volume, *Et nunc manet in te* (1947, 1951; *Madeline*, 1952), which attempted to

justify his unorthodox marital relationship and to express remorse at having forced his wife to lead a life of loneliness and isolation.

With hindsight, it is easy to identify a moral continuum in the influence of Gide's mother and wife on his own sense of self. Together, they represent the forces of Protestantism, spirituality, and the highest standards of morality; they also represent the forces of repression and denial, against which Gide would find himself struggling his entire life. As a timid and shy young man, Gide was uncomfortable with his peers. He was embarrassed by his own sheltered existence and lack of exposure to the male initiation rites of his generation. The turning point of his life occurred on a trip to Africa in the summer of 1893, following the publication of his first few books and his acceptance into the literary circles of Paris. He and Paul Laurens, the son of a well-known painter, set out with the express goal of finding opportunities for their first sexual adventures. Both quickly became involved with a young Arab dancing girl, and Gide began what was to become the first of a series of relationships with young Arab boys. Gide saw his new life as a kind of rebirth marked by health, joy, and sensuality. These experiences, then, became the basis for the natural, unfettered existence he would preach in such works as *Les Nourritures terrestres* (1897; *Fruits of the Earth*, 1949).

Gide continued to write prolifically throughout his life. He often worked on several books at the same time, almost as if the warring aspects of his personality needed to find expression in separate ways. In the 1930's, he also began to play a more active political role, speaking out throughout Europe against the dangers of Fascism. As a precursor to the postwar existentialists, Gide is famous for the credo most clearly articulated by Bernard in *Les Faux-monnayeurs* (1925; *The Counterfeiters*, 1927), a belief that individuals must find their own law for living within themselves and then use it as their guide. In a sense, Bernard represents a restatement of Gide's youthful credo that one can only learn to live by living, in this case more maturely understood to include the sense of responsibility and social awareness lacking in *Fruits of the Earth*.

In 1947, Gide was awarded the Nobel Prize in Literature. The presentation address acknowledged the controversy surrounding the apparent immorality of Gide's work: "The work of André Gide contains pages which provoke with almost confessional audacity. . . . One must always remember that this manner of acting is a form of the impassioned love of truth. . . . Through all the phases of his evolution, Gide has appeared as a true defender of literary integrity, founded on the personality's right and duty to present all its problems resolutely and honestly." Andre Gide died on February 19, 1951, in Paris, after a long and rich literary life that included the publication of more than eighty volumes of stories, novels, memoirs, and literary essays.

Analysis

Gide's earliest works were influenced by symbolism and decadence. *Le Voyage d'Urien* (1893; *Urien's Voyage*, 1964), for example, takes the reader on a highly ironic journey to a series of perpetually changing landscapes. Gide's sensual language and playful exploration of consciousness and perception in this work has been compared to the poetry of Edgar Allan Poe and Arthur Rimbaud. Gide later rejected what he termed the German mysticism of such early works in favor of a crisper, more precise style that he felt better suited the French language.

Gide's first work, *Les Cahiers d'André Walter* (1891; *The Notebooks of André Walter*, 1968), though published anonymously, brought him into the literary circle of the famous French Symbolist poet, Stéphane Mallarmé. Gide became acquainted with the major writers of his time, including Paul Valéry, with whom he maintained a literary correspondence throughout his life. In *Paludes* (1895; *Marshlands*, 1953), however, Gide satirized the artificiality of Mallarmé's artistic credo and called for an art based on spontaneity rather than an abstract concept of artistic purity. *Fruits of the Earth* was Gide's most successful attempt to put his new artistic beliefs into practice; it is a work that reads like a series of unrelated personal experiences; sensual language replaces metaphor and symbol. It was also the first work by Gide demonstrating the influence of Johann Wolfgang von Goethe and Friedrich Wilhelm Nietzsche, the great German apostles of titanic individualism. Though only five hundred copies of *Fruits of the Earth* were sold in the first ten years following its publication, the post-World War I generation embraced its call for an honest and spontaneous life and its apparent condemnation of conventional morality.

With the publication of *The Immoralist* in 1902, Gide's works became increasingly psychological, almost appearing to be case studies of the nature of individualism confronting a series of polarities—sickness and health, asceticism and sensualism, relationship and independence, puritanism and paganism, Europe and Africa. *The Immoralist* tells the story of a young academic who revolts against repression and conformity as he strives to achieve what he believes to be a healthy, sensual, unfettered existence. It is often compared to two other tales, *Strait Is the Gate* and *La Symphonie pastorale* (1919; *The Pastoral Symphony*, 1931), written in similarly concentrated, journalistic styles with the same thematic polarities at their center. *Strait Is the Gate* tells the story of a young woman as excessive in her piety as Michel in his immorality. She literally tries to destroy herself in renunciation of the love she craves and out of fear that she might resemble the adulterous mother whom she despises. *The Pastoral Symphony* tells the story of a self-deluded Calvinist minister who falls in love with an innocent, blind child whom he has rescued from poverty. As a mature, married man who should be a model of morality for his community, he cannot at first admit the sexual nature of his feelings for her.

Together, these three tales portray a complex erotic drama performed against a backdrop of Puritan repression and self-denial. The stories of all three are variations on experiences from Gide's own life—in particular, the repressiveness of his Protestant upbringing, his unconsummated marriage to his cousin Madeleine, his extensive travels in Africa, and his struggle to accept his homosexuality. All three are tightly structured; the second half of *The Immoralist*, for example, repeats the journey of the first half in reverse. In his *Journal* (1939-1950, 1954; *The Journals of André Gide, 1889-1949*, 1947-1951), Gide complained that all three were misread; middle-class

French men and women failed to note the irony in Gide's use of unreliable narrators. They condemned *The Immoralist* for its pagan hedonism and praised *Strait Is the Gate* for its Christian values, in both cases missing Gide's critique of excessive behavior.

The last period of Gide's long and rich literary life was dominated by the writing of his *Journal* and of *The Counterfeiters*, his most complex and ambitious work, the only one he called a novel. *Si le grain ne meurt* (1926; *If It Die . . .* , 1935), Gide's chronicle of his youth and sexual initiation in North Africa, is, in effect, the preface to the *Journal*. With its publication, Gide's contemporaries began to understand the close relationship between his life and his fiction. He himself spoke of his characters as representing possibilities within himself that might have become monstrous if left unchecked by the little bit of common sense he possessed.

In writing his one novel, Gide acknowledged his growing awareness of the individual's relationship to a larger society and gave vent to his own fears about the impact of Fascist thinking on all aspects of French life. *The Counterfeiters* takes almost all of the themes and characters found in earlier works and weaves them into a comprehensive study of French literary circles and middle-class life. It is, in a sense, a serious sequel to *Les Caves du Vatican* (1914; *The Vatican Swindle*, 1925; better known as *Lafcadio's Adventures*, 1927), a farcical tale filled with complex plots and amusing coincidences. Lafcadio, its flippant young hero, who kills a complete stranger for no good reason other than the exercise of pure freedom, becomes (as Bernard) the most positive of Gide's protagonists. Bernard is ultimately the only one of Gide's characters who seems capable of both true individualism and social responsibility, and whose authenticity allows him to be faithful both to himself and to others.

Gide spent six years writing *The Counterfeiters*; it was the last major fiction of his career. For the remaining twenty-five years of his life, he continued to work on his journals, a variety of short stories, literary essays, and even political exposés of French colonial practices in Africa. At his death, he was honored as one of the great moral voices of the twentieth century; a year later the Holy Office of the Vatican ordered that his entire work be placed on the index of prohibited books. Corrupter of youth or model of sincerity and authenticity? The paradox is appropriate; no writer has ever been more aware of the contradictions within himself and his world.

THE IMMORALIST

First published: *L'Immoraliste*, 1902 (English translation, 1930)
Type of work: Novel

A young anthropologist journeys from sickness to health to debauchery in rebellion against his repressive Protestant upringing.

The Immoralist was the first of Gide's famous series of quasi-autobiographical, psychological tales. It is narrated as if it is a confession made to three friends of the protagonist, Michel. He has summoned them together to hear his story, not to pass judgment, but simply to listen. Strangely, he wishes that their friendship may "resist" the accounting of his life that he is about to make. In the end, however, the friends believe that they have been unwittingly turned into "accomplices," that Michel's confession is a veiled attempt to legitimize his "immorality" rather than to express remorse at the pain and suffering he has caused.

The framing context of the story is significant in that it helps the reader appreciate Gide's irony. The novel has been misread as a call for a Nietzschean individualism that revels in its own freedom. The only clue to an action's propriety, according to such a philosophy, would be the pleasure the individual takes in it irrespective of its impact on others. Ménalque, the Nietzschean apostle of pure freedom in the novel, mocks the "man of principles" as "the most detestable kind of person in the world" and warns Michel that as a married man with responsibilities he must choose between his freedom and his happiness. In attempting to heed Ménalque's advice and to satisfy his own sensual desires, Michel proves at least indirectly responsible for the declining health and ultimate death of his wife, Marcéline. As he concludes his story, Michel begins to wonder if his nights of debauchery were as freely chosen as he wants to believe or if he had, in fact, become the victim of the "brutality of passion." His friends are "struck dumb" in the end by the confession they have just heard. Gide must have expected that his readers would feel the same; "Drag me away from here," Michel begs, "I can't leave of my own accord."

This novel, like most of Gide's work, is highly structured. It divides neatly into five sections. The first and last sections take place in Africa, the setting for Michel's recovery from tuberculosis and Marceline's ultimate death from it. The second and fourth sections are set in Normandy, where Michel first involves himself in the management of his inherited property and then later almost consciously sets out to destroy it. The middle section is set in Paris, where Michel presents lectures on his new philosophy, exalting the savagery of the Goths and condemning Latin culture as antithetical to life. It is there that Michel feels most attracted to Ménalque, who alone seems to understand why Michel is now "burning what he once worshipped."

Perhaps the most striking example of the tale's conscious symmetry is the contrast between two highly symbolic scenes. Early in the novel Michel experiences the healing power of sensuality as he delights in "the circumspect call of turtledoves" and the sight of a naked child tending a herd of goats. Toward the end, Michel goes to sleep among a group of young boys lying in the open air and wakes up covered with vermin. This second "baptism" marks the final stage of Michel's journey, which has taken him from sickness to health, from impotence to debauchery, and from a passive observer of the immorality of others to an active participant in the seamiest of existences.

THE COUNTERFEITERS

First published: *Les Faux-monnayeurs*, 1925 (English translation, 1927)
Type of work: Novel

The Counterfeiters juxtaposes several complexly interwoven plots with the journals of a would-be novelist.

The Counterfeiters is Gide's most complex and ambitious work, the only one he called a novel. There are at least a dozen characters and almost as many subplots surrounding a group of families, some of whose children are involved in a ring of counterfeiters. On its most coherent level *The Counterfeiters* is a study of adolescents attempting to discover who they really are and how they may achieve authentic, "sincere" lives in the face of all the false, counterfeit attitudes and social forms that dominate their middle-class lives.

The two major characters, Olivier and Bernard, share a love of literature and an enthusiasm for life. Bernard, however, is by far the stronger of the two; he alone is capable of true authenticity, of discovering his own internal law and living by it. In terms of one of the novel's major metaphors, Bernard is the fish who sees with his own light; Olivier is the fish who becomes the prey of others because he swims either too high or too low. Olivier at his best is capable of true lyricism; at his most vulnerable he falls under the influence of Robert de Passavant, a literary counterfeiter who is guilty of claiming the ideas of others as his own.

Olivier is ultimately rescued from Passavant's pernicious influence by his uncle Édouard, whom he has always adored but whom he has been too shy to approach. Édouard functions in a sense as the center of the novel. His notebooks are juxtaposed with Bernard's and Olivier's narratives; they provide most of the key subplots and a running commentary on the nature of the novel viewed in terms of the same problem of authenticity at work in the lives of the main characters. Édouard is not the implied author of the novel but rather a character in his own right understood to represent the opposite of Passavant. He would like his art to be absolutely "true," "unedited," and "original." His particular dilemma is how to move beyond observation and journal writing without falsifying his material, a dilemma Gide sees as endemic to the novel, the "freest" of literary genres.

The novel turns on the passing of Édouard's mentorship from Bernard to Olivier, Édouard's nephew and lover. This transfer of influence occurs the night of the Argonaut dinner, one of the major set pieces of the novel in which key characters both real and fictional, and key plots from both the narrative proper and the journals, all intersect. For Passavant, it is a night of celebration turned to ridicule. For both Bernard and Olivier, the night brings a coming of age. Bernard's sexual initiation marks his growing independence; Olivier's encounter is followed by a failed suicide attempt proving his continued vulnerability.

By this point in the novel Bernard emerges as one of Gide's true heroes, the only character in *The Counterfeiters* strong enough to live a potentially productive life, both free of hypocrisy and morally good. Bernard's story is a variation on the classic pattern of the hero's journey: He progresses from the discovery that he is a "natural" child, hence free from the genetic curse of following in his father's footsteps, to the influence of a sympathetic surrogate father (Édouard) under whose wing he experiences both pure and spiritual love, to the passing of his *baccalauréat* examination (a required rite of passage for French schoolboys), to a return home in recognition of the true love that the father he rejected has always felt for him.

In one of the most explicit message chapters of the novel, "Bernard and the Angel," Bernard longs "for dedication, for sacrifice," for some noble cause outside of himself to which he could offer his newly won freedom. Unfortunately, most of the ready-made causes he sees around him strike false notes. As he struggles with his Angel, Bernard wonders if it is possible to live without a goal and still not coast aimlessly through life. (Christopher) Columbus, he thinks, did not know where he was going when he discovered America: "His goal was to go ahead. . . . Himself was his goal." Bernard fears that without a goal he may live badly. Gide clearly believes that it is a risk worth taking.

Summary

André Gide's ultimate literary achievement is that of a moralist in the great French tradition. Though he proved an innovator in his experimental works, *The Counterfeiters* and *The Vatican Swindle*, he was most influential as a proponent of individualism and what he called, "sincerity." Gide's moral philosophy was a product of both his times and his own personal experience. Gide managed to reconcile the post-World War I yearning for excitement and adventure with his own profound belief in moral goodness. The distance between Michel's obsessive pursuit of his own sensual pleasures in the name of freedom and Bernard's return home in acknowledgment of his responsibility to others marks the distance between the romantic individualism of the 1890's and the existentialism of the 1950's. It is the same distance Gide traveled in his own life and work.

Bibliography

André Gide: 1869-1951. Yale French Studies 7. New York: Kraus Reprint Corporation, 1965.

Brée, Germaine. *Gide*. New Brunswick, N.J.: Rutgers University Press, 1963.

Cordle, Thomas. *André Gide*. Boston: Twayne, 1969.

Fowlie, Wallace. *André Gide: His Life and Art*. New York: Macmillan, 1965.

Freedman, Ralph. *The Lyrical Novel: Studies in Hermann Hesse, André Gide and Virginia Woolf*. Princeton, N.J.: Princeton University Press, 1963.

Guerard, Albert J. *André Gide*. Cambridge, Mass.: Harvard University Press, 1951.

Heller, Erich, ed. *Three Studies in Modern French Literature: Marcel Proust, André Gide, François Mauriac.* New Haven, Conn.: Yale University Press, 1960.
O'Brien, Justin. *Portrait of André Gide: A Critical Biography.* New York: Alfred A. Knopf, 1953.

Jane Missner Barstow

JOHANN WOLFGANG VON GOETHE

Born: Frankfurt am Main, Germany
August 28, 1749
Died: Weimar, Germany
March 22, 1832

Principal Literary Achievement

Widely recognized as one of Germany's greatest lyric poets, Goethe is most famous for his very personal, autobiographical verse and his profound understanding of human individuality in relationship to nature, history, and society.

Biography

Johann Wolfgang von Goethe was born in Frankfurt am Main, Germany, on August 28, 1749, the eldest son of Johann Kaspar and Katharina Elisabeth Goethe. He was educated at home by his lawyer father before attending the University of Leipzig to study law in 1765. Goethe acknowledges his parents' influence in his autobiography, indicating that from his father he inherited his stature and the serious conduct of his life, and from his "dear mother" he acquired the gaiety of spirit and his love of storytelling.

As a student in Leipzig, a leading cultural center of eighteenth century Europe, Goethe developed an interest in literature and art and became acquainted with the dramatic works of his contemporaries Friedrich Gottlieb Klopstock, German Romantic poet, and Gotthold Ephraim Lessing, German literary critic. Their influence and Goethe's affection for Anna Katharina Schönkopf, daughter of a Leipzig tavern owner, is reflected in his early poetry and dramatic works, especially in the one-act comedy in verse *Die Laune des Verliebten* (pb. 1806; *The Wayward Lover*, 1879). Illness caused Goethe to return to Frankfurt in 1768. During his convalescence, he studied religious mysticism, astrology, and alchemy. His familiarity in these areas becomes evident in his best-known work, *Faust* (part 1, 1829; part 2, 1854; English translation, part 1, 1823; English translation, part 2, 1838).

Goethe received his law degree in 1771 from the University of Strasbourg and returned to Frankfurt to practice law with his father for four years. In Strasbourg, Goethe made the acquaintance of the German philosopher and literary critic Johann Gottfried Herder, a leader in the German Romantic movement known as *Sturm und Drang*

(Storm and Stress). Herder introduced Goethe to the works of William Sha
and consequently, Goethe patterned his first dramatic tragedy on Shakespea
matic style. He received his first literary acclaim with *Götz von Berlichingen n   ...er
eisernen Hand* (1773; *Götz von Berlichingen with the Iron Hand*, 1799), the fictionalized story of a German knight whose exploits stimulated a national German revolt
against the authority of the emperor and the Church early in the sixteenth century.

In 1774, Goethe's reputation as an author of international fame was established
with the sensational success of *Die Leiden des jungen Werthers* (1774; *The Sorrows
of Young Werther*, 1779), a sentimental and psychological novel in letter form, inspired by his infatuation with Charlotte ("Lotte") Buff, the fiancée of his friend G. C.
Kestner.

Goethe's influence as a writer spread throughout Germany and was enhanced by
his association with Duke Karl August, who invited him to live and work at the ducal
court in Saxe-Weimar. Goethe moved to Weimar in 1775 and, except for a two-year
sojourn to Italy, lived in Weimar until his death in 1832. At the court of Karl August,
Goethe assumed a wide variety of governmental duties. He became a member and,
later, head of the duke's cabinet. As a minister of the state, he managed state fi-
nances, military recruiting, and social activities. He also pursued his personal interest
in science, spending years studying horticulture, geology, botany, and biology.

The governmental duties that Goethe had accepted consumed much of his time in
the first ten years at Weimar and significantly limited his literary activities. Except for
some notable poems, such as the lyric "Wanderer's Nachtlied" ("Wanderer's Night
Song"), and the ballad "Erlkönig" ("The Erlking"), he wrote little during the period
between 1775 and 1785. At this time, his primary intellectual stimulation came from
correspondence with Charlotte von Stein, the wife of a Weimar official. Frau von
Stein, a woman of refined literary taste and culture, was seven years his senior and the
mother of seven children. She dominated Goethe's intellectual and romantic interests
for twelve years, until his journey to Italy in 1786. He remained there until 1788.

In Italy, Goethe found new vitality. He had become weary of life at the Weimar
court and of his relationship with Charlotte von Stein. His study of ancient Greek
and Roman literature, art, and architecture and its influence on the Renaissance provided him with new inspiration. The products of his Italian stay include the classical
dramas *Iphigenie auf Tauris* (1779; *Iphigenia in Taurus*, 1793) and *Torquato Tasso*
(1790; English translation, 1827). These works introduced the classical period in German literature with their focus on ideas and form.

Goethe's return to Weimar proved difficult and disappointing. His new literary principles met with considerable opposition, and his decision to live with young Christiane Vulpius offended court circles and aroused the enmity of Charlotte von Stein.
Christiane gave birth to his son in 1789; to legitimize the child, Goethe married Christiane in 1806. For some time, Goethe reabsorbed himself in his scientific interests,
publishing *Beyträge zur Optik* (1791, 1792) and *Zur Farbenlehre* (1810; *Theory of Colors*, 1840). Goethe also spent much of his time in nearby Jena, where he met Friedrich Schiller, German poet, dramatist, philosopher, and historian.

Beginning in 1794, a close friendship developed between Goethe and Schiller that proved inspiring to both men. Their intellectual partnership caused them to be viewed, then and now, as the two leading figures in German literature. The friendship, with its stimulating daily discussions and collaborations on various projects, proved rehabilitating to Goethe's literary interests. When Schiller died in 1805, Goethe buried his grief in an intense study of Oriental literature, drawing parallels between his personal experiences and elements of Oriental culture. His study culminated in a collection of love poems, rich in Oriental imagery, published under the title *West-östlicher Divan* (1819, *West-Eastern Divan*, 1877).

Goethe remained productive until his death in Weimar on March 22, 1832. His writings in the period betwen 1805 and 1832 include the novel, *Die Wahlverwandtschaften* (1809; *Elective Affinities*, 1849); an account of his Italian journey, *Wilhelm Meisters Lehrjahre* (1795-1796; *Wilhelm Meister's Apprenticeship*, 1824); his autobiography in four volumes, *Aus meinem Leben: Dichtung und Wahrheit* (1811-1814, 1833; *The Autobiography of Goethe*, 1824); and the second part of his most famous dramatic poem, *Faust*, published posthumously in 1833.

Analysis

Goethe is recognized as one of the greatest and most versatile European writers and thinkers of modern times. He profoundly influenced the growth of German Romanticism. His first novel, *The Sorrows of Young Werther*, was one of the literary sensations of the eighteenth century. A psychological unfolding in letter form, it brings new focus to the epistolary novel. With *Elective Affinities*, Goethe created a new type of fiction. Instead of concentrating on one individual character, Goethe builds this novel around social concerns, the complications of human relationships, and divorce.

Many of Goethe's works are autobiographical. The subtitle and tone of the first volume of his autobiography sets a new standard for autobiographical writings. Because Goethe defines his own writings as fragments of a grand confession, it is important to study his life in order to understand his work. That is especially true of his poetry, which is characteristically extremely personal and private. With his autobiographical writings, Goethe himself makes the most important contributions to the understanding of his own literature.

The lyrical poetry of his early days brought Goethe into the foreground of the German literary arena. Collecting folk songs with his friend Johann Gottfried Herder inspired him to write numerous poems in the folk song style. Some of these became popular favorites among the German people, such as "Heidenröslein" ("Little Rose of the Heath") and "The Erlking." In both poems, Goethe explores the themes of love, alienation, and death. In "Little Rose of the Heath," the love is that of a young man, and in "The Erlking," it is the love of a father for a young child. Both poems are reflective of the passions of Goethe's Storm and Stress period, during which the focus was on depth of emotions and on the individual.

While Goethe's initial fame comes from his lyric poetry, it is his dramatic poem *Faust* that is considered the crowning achievement of his long life and one of the masterpieces of world literature. In style, theme, and point of view, it delineates Goethe's impressive range of development from the early, rebellious Storm and Stress days to the calm classicism and realistic vision of his later years. The themes of the individual's right to negotiate his own destiny, to strive for knowledge and power, and to cross the threshold into the supernatural all contribute to making *Faust* a landmark as the first major work in the spirit of modern individualism.

FAUST

First produced: *Faust: Eine Tragödie*, part 1, 1829 (first published, 1808; English translation, 1823); *Faust: Eine Tragödie, zweiter Teil*, part 2, 1854 (first published, 1833; English translation, 1838)

Type of work: Play

A medieval scholar turns to supernatural forces in his quest for knowledge and sells his soul to the Devil.

Goethe began his most famous work, *Faust*, while he was in his twenties. He published the first part of *Faust* in 1808 and completed the second part two months before his death. The Faust story is based on the legend of the Renaissance scholar, Dr. Faustus, who quested after universal knowledge by means of alchemy and magic. The real Johannes Faustus lived from 1480 to 1540. His legendary adventures became the subject for innumerable puppet shows and popular folk dramas throughout the seventeenth and eighteenth centuries in Germany. Thus, Goethe was familiar with the Faust myth since childhood, and from the time that he was twenty, until he died at eighty-two, the theme never left his imagination.

The theme of Goethe's *Faust* befits both the Romantic fascination with the supernatural, as well as the theme of justice and good and evil that have occupied literature since biblical times. Yet Goethe takes the theme of good and evil beyond the traditional Christian concept embodied in God and the Devil. Influenced by the study of Oriental literature, Goethe sees the world as a totality composed of opposing forces: light and dark, good and evil, male and female, yin and yang, physical and spiritual, natural and supernatural. God and the Devil (whom Goethe calls Mephistopheles, which means "without light") are representative of these opposing forces on a larger, as well as a smaller, scale: within the macrocosm (the universe) and the microcosm (humanity). There exists on all levels a constant struggle between the opposing forces, with each side striving to overcome the other. It is this striving that is key to understanding of Goethe's work. The redeeming factor of Faust is that he continues to strive. To Goethe, the ideal man, the Faustian man, never gives up striving.

The story of the Faust drama (sometimes referred to as the Gretchen tragedy) begins in Heaven. In "The Prologue in Heaven"—a modern enactment of the Job story—the Devil, Mephistopheles, complains that God's creation, man, is so pitiful and corrupt that it is no more fun to torture him. God asks Mephistopheles if he knows the good man Faust. The Devil laughs and offers God a bet: "What do you wager? You will lose him yet." God accepts Mephistopheles' bet for Faust's soul and points out that as long as man strives, he will make mistakes, but that he is basically good.

Despite Mephistopheles' gleefully wicked intent to make Faust "eat dust" like his cousin the Snake, God tells Mephistopheles that He never hated him or those like him, but instead, he considers him necessary to provoke humankind to action. These lines embody the key to understanding the theme of the Faust story and the Faustian striving:

> I have never hated the likes of you.
> Of all the spirits of denial
> The joker is the last that I eschew.
> Man finds relaxation too attractive—
> Too fond too soon of unconditional rest;
> Which is why I am pleased to give him a companion
> Who lures and thrusts and must, as devil, be active.

Goethe depicts the Devil not as the customary embodiment of fear-filled threat and wickedness but rather as a jovial but serious mischief maker. When the curtain closes after the prologue and Mephistopheles is left alone on stage, he humorously observes that God is not all that bad, saying, "I like to see the Old One now and then."

The first part of the tragedy begins with Faust alone in his study. Dr. Faust is a professor, doctor, lawyer, and theologian. He has studied all that there is to study but bemoans the fact that he still knows nothing. He teaches, but he feels that he is merely leading his students by the nose, since they could read for themselves and know all that he knows. He would like to be able to teach something that would improve humankind.

There is one subject, though, of which Faust knows virtually nothing: the world of the spirits. He opens a book on mystic art by Nostradamus and sees the sign of the Macrocosm and then of the Earth Spirit. Inspired to venture into this mystic world, he calls forth the Earth Spirit. In a flash of red flame, the Spirit appears before him then vanishes as Faust is unable to detain it. Feeling dejected, Faust decides that there is only one way to experience the world of the spirits, and that is to go through the door to death. He considers crossing that threshold and reaches for a vial of poison. As he lifts the poison to his lips, Faust hears the church bells outside ringing in Easter morning (symbolic, of course, of rebirth). He puts the poison down, decides to delay his quest for now, and takes a walk in the village with Wagner, his student.

A black poodle joins Faust and Wagner on their walk and follows Faust back to his study. The poodle fidgets nervously as Faust reaches for the Bible and begins to read: "In the Beginning was the Word." Faust ponders the biblical text then writes what he considers to be a correction: "In the beginning was the Deed." The squirming poodle distracts Faust. Then Faust realizes that this dog is not an ordinary one. Suddenly, mist fills the small room, and from behind the stove, Mephistopheles steps forward, dressed like a traveling scholar.

When Faust asks the name of his guest, Mephistopheles identifies himself as the dark side of Totality, the evil side of good, the power that negates, but in negating creates "A part of that Power/ Which always wills evil, always procures good . . . I am a part of the Part which in the beginning was all/ A part of the darkness which gave birth to light." The image of Mephistopheles as a part of the Greater Whole, as that force that destroys (negates), but in destroying the old creates the new, is essential to the theme of the play. Believing that he can still Faust's unrest and continuous striving, Mephistopheles challenges Faust to a wager. He agrees to be Faust's servant and to do or show him anything that he wants. If Faust ever says that he is totally satisfied, that the moment is so perfect that he wants it to last forever, then he will die and Mephistopheles will possess his soul.

The Devil and Faust sign their bet in blood. Before they begin their quest. Mephistopheles takes Faust to the Witch's Kitchen for a youth potion. The witch, startled to find two traveling scholars in her kitchen, does not recognize the Devil. He chastises her and tells her that the Devil must go along with the times. The time for cloven feet, pitch forks, and traditional views of Satan is over: "Satan has long been a myth without sense or sinew. . . . They are quit of the Evil One but the evil ones remain./ You may call me Noble Baron, that should do; I am a cavalier among other cavaliers."

On leaving the Witch's kitchen, Faust and Mephistopheles begin their adventures. In their sojourns, Faust falls in love with a young girl, Margaret—usually referred to as Gretchen. Gretchen is the embodiment of innocence. She falls in love with Faust but is uneasy around Mephistopheles. Since Gretchen lives with her mother, consummating their love is a problem, until Mephistopheles secures a sleeping potion. Unfortunately, the sleeping potion is too strong, and Gretchen's mother dies. Gretchen's brother, Valentine, appears and challenges Faust to a duel. Faust, with Mephistopheles at his side, kills Valentine. Faust is then ushered away by Mephistopheles to a witches' celebration, the Walpurgis Night. In the meantime, Gretchen has discovered that she is pregnant. She gives birth then kills her illegitimate child and goes to prison.

In the midst of the bizarre activities of the Walpurgis Night, Faust is distracted by a mirror image of Gretchen in jail. He confronts Mephistopheles with what he (the Devil) has done. Mephistopheles, however, reminds Faust that he is merely his servant, and that Faust, alone, is responsible for his actions. In other words, the Devil did not make him do it; he simply facilitated the act.

Faust goes to Gretchen and, with Mephistopheles' help, wants to get her out of prison. Gretchen at first rejoices at seeing Faust, but when she realizes that Mephistopheles is behind him, she turns away from Faust and bids him farewell. All she wants is to die and be punished for her sins. After Faust and Mephistopheles leave, a heavenly voice calls out that Gretchen's soul is saved, she having been an innocent victim of circumstance. Thus ends *Faust*, part 1.

At the beginning of *Faust*, part 2, Faust awakens, again on Easter morning (a new rebirth), to continue his adventures with Mephistopheles. Faust has learned that personal gratifications do not satisfy him and now sets out on an expedition to do something for humankind. He encounters a king who is out of money, and Mephistopheles suggests issuing paper money.

Faust, part 2 is considerably longer than *Faust*, part 1 and is usually considered too cumbersome for stage productions with its intricate network of details. A familiarization with the major themes, however, is important in understanding the Faust story in its entirety. One of the themes that occupied much of Goethe's later works is classical mythology. In the second part of the tragedy, Faust falls in love with Helen of Troy and asks Mephistopheles to conjure up the famous heroine. He marries Helen and has a son with her, whom he calls Euphorion. When Euphorion (who is thought to be a symbol for the English poet Lord Byron) is seven years of age, he tries to fly from the top of a ledge and crashes to the ground. With the death of Euphorion, Helen of Troy returns to the underworld, and Faust is left to continue his quest for satisfaction.

Goethe filled *Faust*, part 2 with extensive symbolism, revealing his increasing interest in the more restrained and structured classics, contrasting his earlier fascination with the Romantic extremism. The union of Faust and Helen represents the union of Romantic emotionalism and classic restraint. Their offspring is euphoria (Euphorion), but euphoria is short lived.

Tragedy and failure do not prevent Faust from his striving. In the hope of doing something of value for humankind, he seeks to reclaim land from the sea to convert it into a public housing project. By the end of *Faust*, part 2, Faust is a hundred years old and blind. He hears digging outside and thinks that Mephistopheles is finally working on the housing project. Overjoyed at the thought that finally something will be done for humankind, Faust makes his way outside to let Mephistopheles know that this moment is the one for which he has been waiting. He dies reflecting that he has never found a moment so beautiful, so pleasant, that he wanted it to linger. The digging sound that Faust heard was Mephistopheles preparing Faust's grave. In the final scene of part 2, the soul of Faust is carried to Heaven, saved because the moment that he had found most beautiful was a moment that he thought would benefit humankind.

In contrast to the traditional Christian concept of good and evil, Goethe depicts the two forces not as mutually exclusive but as part of the greater Totality, as intricate parts of the Whole, of which all are a part. In portraying the opposing forces as existing in the macrocosm (the universe) and the microcosm (humankind), Goethe indicates that both forces exist on every level, that all humankind has an inherent goodness that is sometimes challenged by the inherent bad.

Goethe's perspective is directly influenced by Oriental thought. Western interest in Oriental literature began to spread in Europe at the end of the eighteenth century with the Romantic fascination for the exotic and reached a high point during the nineteenth century.

THE SORROWS OF YOUNG WERTHER

First published: *Die Leiden des jungen Werthers*, 1774 (English translation, 1779)
Type of work: Novel

An artistic and intellectual young man, tormented by hopeless love for a young married woman, ends his anguish with a gunshot to his head.

The first great popular success of Goethe's career was *The Sorrows of Young Werther*. It is a sentimental and psychological novel in letter form, influenced by Samuel Richardson, an eighteenth century English novelist famous for his epistolary novels. The letter-writing style is a natural genre for Goethe, whose writings are filled with biographical and autobiographical elements.

The character, Lotte, to whom the protagonist, Werther, is irrevocably drawn, was inspired by Goethe's unhappy infatuation with Charlotte ("Lotte") Buff, the fiancée of his friend G. C. Kestner. Goethe met Lotte during his summer stay in Wetzlar in 1772. The end of the novel, with Werther pulling the trigger of the gun pointed at his head, was most probably prompted by the tragic fate of Karl Wilhelm Jerusalem, secretary of the Brunswick ambassador, who committed suicide in October of 1772 after a public reprimand and the subsequent ostracism from aristocratic circles for his infatuation with the wife of a colleague.

In the letters to his friend, Goethe's character, Werther, describes the joy and agony of his love for Lotte. She also feels the attraction but is betrothed to Albert, whom she subsequently marries. Werther befriends Lotte's husband but is convinced that Albert's love for Lotte is not as deep as his own. After a passionate embrace with his beloved, the chaos and excruciating turmoil in his heart becomes unbearable for Werther. He asks Lotte to let him borrow Albert's pistols for safety on a journey that he never takes. Instead, in an ironic twist, the weapons of protection provide Werther with the means to end his suffering.

Goethe's sentimental novel stands for more than the fate of Werther. It becomes the creed of a whole generation protesting the oversimplified and optimistic rationalism of the Enlightenment, with its emphasis on reason and its disregard for emotions. *The Sorrows of Young Werther* met with enthusiastic response from its readers and was soon translated into most of the European languages.

Its popularity produced a kind of Werther fever, with imitations of Werther behavior, which unfortunately led to a series of suicides. For a brief time, the publication of the novel was stopped and its sale banned. The reverberations of the effect of *The Sorrows of Young Werther* reached into the twentieth century, with psychologists referring to a rash of suicides among young people as the "Werther syndrome." The popularity of this novel testifies to Goethe's success in directing into a single channel the many currents of sentimentalism that were so prevalent during the German Romantic period.

THE ERLKING

First published: "Erlkönig," 1782 (English translation, 1799)
Type of work: Poem

A father on horseback, clutching tightly his fevering and hallucinating child, rushes in vain to get his son home before he dies.

The theme, setting, and mood of Goethe's "The Erlking" capture the spirit of the Romantic period of the late eighteenth century. Characteristics of Romanticism include a love for nature, a fascination with the supernatural, and the recurring theme of love and death, all of which are contained in Goethe's poem.

"The Erlking" begins with a narrator describing a father's frantic ride home on horseback, through the woods, holding tightly his fevering child. The child begins to hallucinate and tells his father that he sees the Erlking:

> "O father, see yonder!" he says;
> "My boy, on what do you so fearfully gaze?"
> "O, 'tis the Erlking with his crown and shroud."
> "No, my son, it is but a dark wreath of cloud."

The father's rational explanation of what his son sees remains unheeded. The fevering child describes the luring of the Erlking, who invites him to come with him, promising toys and playmates. The fearful child hesitates, but the Erlking persists and finally takes him by force. At the end of the poem, the father arrives home with his son dead in his arms.

The Erlking symbolizes death, which is to the Romantic not only a source of fear but also a source of attraction to the unknown and the supernatural. Goethe's poem embodies the universal theme of the loss of innocence. In this perspective, the Erlking becomes the monstrous maturity, which lures youth but destroys its innocence. The fatalistic tone of the poem suggests that innocence inevitably succumbs to, and is destroyed by, the socialization of adulthood.

Goethe's poem reflects the Romantics' view of society as the culprit in the destruction of innocence. They believed in the natural goodness of humankind and emphasized the expression of feelings, which they considered more important than intellect. In eighteenth century Germany, emotionalism burst forth in violent form in the Storm and Stress literary movement, of which Goethe was an integral part.

WANDERER'S NIGHT SONG

First published: "Wanderers Nachtlied," 1776 (English translation, 1799)
Type of work: Poem
   Addressed to the creator, the poem is an appeal for freedom from the torment of the soul and the bustle of life.

"Wanderer's Night Song" is representative of the poems written by the young Goethe at the height of his Storm and Stress years. It is indicative of his love of nature and his view of nature as the creator of all things. "Wanderer's Night Song" exemplifies Goethe's pantheistic ideas and sentiments, which he developed out of his study of the seventeenth century Dutch philosopher Baruch Spinoza and the eighteenth century French philosopher Jean-Jacques Rousseau. The poem is an appeal to nature to allow the sweet freedom (symbolic of death) to enter the chest, suggesting the stopping of the heartbeat. This poem, like "The Erlking" and *The Sorrows of Young Werther*, yearns for freedom from emotional agonies, a freedom attainable only by crossing the final threshold of physical existence.

Summary
   Johann Wolfgang von Goethe, as a poet, dramatist, and novelist, made a major contribution to world literature. His themes of individuality and social concerns reflect a profound understanding of human interrelationships. With his lyric poetry, his novels and dramas, and his vast correspondence with his contemporaries, Goethe influenced writers and thinkers of his own time and helped shape the literary movements of the nineteenth century. Goethe is widely considered to be one of the most versatile and prolific figures in all world literature.

Bibliography
Bennett, Benjamin. *Goethe's Theory of Poetry*. Ithaca, N.Y.: Cornell University Press, 1986.
Brown, Jane K. *Goethe's "Faust": The German Tragedy*. Ithaca, N.Y.: Cornell University Press, 1986.
Fiedler, Hermann G. *Textual Studies of Goethe's "Faust."* Oxford, England: Basil Blackwell, 1946.
Lange, Victor, ed. *Goethe: A Collection of Critical Essays*. Englewood Cliffs, N.J.: Prentice-Hall, 1968.
Robertson, John. G. *The Life and Work of Goethe, 1749-1832*. 1932. Reprint. Freeport, N.Y.: Books for Libraries, 1971.
Staiger, Emil. *Goethe*. 3 vols. Zurich: Atlantis Verlag, 1952-1959.

Elisabeth Stein

NIKOLAI GOGOL

Born: Sorochintsy, Ukraine
March 31, 1809
Died: Moscow, Russia
March 4, 1852

Principal Literary Achievement

Russia's greatest writer of serious comedy, Gogol penned novels, short stories, and dramas that add human pathos to hilarity and stretch portrayals of reality from the ordinary to the eccentric and the grotesque. His work profoundly influenced future literary pieces of psychological focus or of the absurd.

Biography

Nikolai Vasilyevich Gogol was born in the village of Sorochintsy, near the town of Dikanka in the Poltava Province of Ukraine, on March 31, 1809. Gogol was the first surviving child of Vasily Afanasievich Gogol-Yanovsky, a landowner of dubious claim to Polish nobility who owned 150 to 200 serfs and was given to arranging plays and pageants for the amusement of the local gentry, and Maria Ivanovna Kosiarovsky, the niece of the wealthy local patriarch, Dmitri Prokofeyevich Troschinsky. At the time that her marriage was arranged, Maria was barely fourteen years old. She was herself a child in a household that she was expected to fill with other children. Maria was an extremely doting mother whose children, especially her oldest son, Nikolai, could do no wrong. She was given to fantasy and, when extolling her children, did not let truth or reality interpose. Later, after Gogol's death, she gave interviews in which she claimed that her son had invented the steam engine and designed the network of railroads then spreading across the country.

Gogol began his education in the district school at Poltava. He was enrolled there in the same class with Ivan, his younger brother and closest companion. Ivan's sudden death during the summer vacation of 1819 had a lasting impact on Gogol. He was a lifelong hypochondriac who lived in particular fear of death's caprice. He later told acquaintances that his continual seeking of medical treatment was attributable to distress caused by his stomach being in an upside-down position. Dmitri Troschinsky agreed to pay for his transfer to the boarding school in Nezhin, which he attended from 1821 to 1828. While there, he participated with a number of future literary contributors in school dramas. His schoolmates called him the "mysterious dwarf" because of his aloofness and his physical appearance and posture. It was in the school

at Nezhin that Gogol began to write literary works of his own and to plan his move to the capital of St. Petersburg, where he was sure that a bright career awaited him.

At the end of 1828, Gogol is supposed to have sought out Alexander Pushkin, the reigning literary star in St. Petersburg, for sponsorship and advice. He was rebuffed, the story goes, by Pushkin's butler, who refused to awaken the great poet after a night of gambling. Gogol then began a series of minor civil posts, received through the importuned influence of Troschinsky. His attempt to self-publish his schoolboy poem, "Hans Küchelgarten," under the pseudonym V. Alov was an embarrassing disaster for him, and he fled for six weeks to Germany, offering such fanciful excuses by letter to his mother that she erroneously concluded that he had contracted a venereal disease. He returned to St. Petersburg and persisted in his writing, changing his emphasis to prose works of Ukrainian life and superstitions. With the circulation of these works under the name Nikolai Gogol, he soon won the sponsorship of Pushkin and of Vasily Zhukovsky, the poet and translator.

In the 1830's, Gogol was given the care of two of his sisters, who had come to St. Petersburg to find suitable husbands. This responsibility necessitated his working as a tutor and teacher. At first, upon Zhukovsky's recommendation, he taught history at a young women's finishing school, the Patriotic Institute, but he complained to acquaintances that it vexed him to bestow his insights on such "puny intellects" as his students there possessed. Women, apart from his mother and sisters, were always beneath his concern. He never had, or sought, romantic involvement with any woman. Indeed, current scholars debate the evidence for his struggle with a latent homosexuality. His effusive and often saccharine letters to male acquaintances seem to support the contention that the objects of his romantic feelings were male.

As Gogol's first collection of stories, *Vechera na Khutore bliz Dikanki* (1831-1832; *Evenings on a Farm near Dikanka*, 1926), gained popularity, he was struggling through a professorship in world history at St. Petersburg University, a position for which he had no appropriate credentials or erudition. Yet the publication of his *Arabeski* (1835; *Arabesques*, 1982), a miscellany of lectures, essays, and stories; of his *Mirgorod* (1835; English translation, 1928), a collection of four stories; and of his fantastic short story "Nos" (1836; "The Nose") gave him financial independence at last, and he was able to cease his labors in academia. Pushkin had given him the idea for a play about a man who is mistaken by provincial officials for a visiting government inspector general; but the staging and reception of *Revizor* (1836; *The Inspector General*, 1890) so upset Gogol that he left St. Petersburg for Europe, returning only twice for visits in the next twelve years.

It was also Pushkin who gave Gogol the core ideas of both *The Inspector General* and his great novel, *Myortvye dushi* (part 1, 1842; part 2, 1855; *Dead Souls*, 1887). The basic idea of this work was that a swindler might make money by buying the legal titles to deceased serfs, or "souls," whose names were still listed on the decennial census rolls. Gogol's subsequent characterization of the real "dead souls," who were the dead serfs' greedy or oblivious owners, was acclaimed by the seminal socialist literary critic Vissarion Belinsky as Russia's most accomplished literary indictment of the institution of serfdom. Belinsky hailed Gogol as an abolitionist and a social critic of the first magnitude and urged him to continue his literary endeavors in this vein. Yet Belinsky was misinterpreting Gogol's motivation in writing *Dead Souls*. Gogol was not primarily a socially conscious writer, though he came to think that he should be, trying to meet the expectations of Belinsky and others of his time.

In 1842, Gogol's short story "The Overcoat" was published. The pitiful protagonist of this work, Akaky Akakievich, whose demise was occasioned by his attempt to procure a new overcoat, became the epitome of the "little man" theme in the "laughter through tears" point of view. Gogol's portrayal sprang from his own deep feelings of human inadequacy and from his religious conception of divine retribution for wrongs done. Once again, however, the social critics misinterpreted him and proclaimed his work as an example of literature with a sociopolitical message. They clamored for him to complete the second part of *Dead Souls*, expecting to obtain therein his guidance in the social and political concerns of the day.

After 1842, Gogol struggled more and more with the loss of his inspiration. The social and political expectations that his previous works had elicited from others were not in accord with his own growing religious mysticism. The act of literary creation became ever more difficult for him. He traveled from place to place, at last sending in his *Vybrannye mesta iz perepiski s druzyami* (1847; *Selected Passages from Correspondence with Friends*, 1969) for publication in Moscow. The critics were mystified by this intensely personal call for the spiritual regeneration of Russia along religious lines. Belinsky was incensed and wrote a famous open letter to Gogol in which he expressed his sense of disappointment and betrayal. As a result, Gogol felt even more estranged from his beloved country and its problems. His efforts to complete the second part of *Dead Souls*, the work that he felt might ransom him with his readership, became even more belabored.

In the spring of 1848, Gogol traveled to Jerusalem, hoping to find spiritual peace. He returned to Moscow still without hope, but he was impressed with the spiritual guidance that he was offered by Father Matthew Konstantinovsky, former archbishop of Rzhev, who had taken to giving his guidance in Moscow to the nobles gathered for that purpose by Count Alexander Tolstoy, an ex-diplomat and very conservative religious scholar. Konstantinovsky advised Gogol to renounce literary pursuits altogether in the interest of saving his soul. This advice only tormented Gogol's soul further, since literary pursuits were tantamount to living and breathing for him. He therefore decided to travel again, to Odessa, to see his mother in Sorochintsy, and to various monasteries, but finally he returned to Moscow in early 1852.

On the last day of January, 1852, Gogol was staying at the Moscow home of Count Tolstoy. Gogol was deeply under the influence of Konstantinovsky, who was berating him for his continued attempts to find salvation in "pagan" literature. Gogol woke a servant boy in the middle of the night to aid him in burning his manuscripts for the second part of *Dead Souls* in the household furnace. The boy pleaded with Gogol to stop, but Gogol continued until the work of his past decade of life was destroyed. He lived only a few days after this, summoning the doctors to bleed him with leeches to correct stomach pangs that were the result of his fasting. The loss of blood in his weakened condition caused his death in Moscow on March 4, 1852. All the leading intellectuals of Moscow society attended his funeral. His gravestone in the cemetery of St. Daniel's Monastery is inscribed with the words that he chose from the Book of *Jeremiah*: "For they will laugh at my bitter words."

Analysis

Early in his literary career, Gogol strove to entertain his more cosmopolitan Russian readers with tales of Ukrainian folk customs and superstitions. Supernatural tales were very popular at that time, and the main literary method was to structure a story in such a way that the events related could be attributed either to natural or to supernatural causes. The tension between the two possibilities of interpretation was a key aspect of the narration. Occurrences of spontaneous human combustion, as Gogol relates in "St. John's Eve" (from *Evenings on a Farm near Dikanka*) and in "Viy" (from *Mirgorod*) and again later in *Dead Souls*, can be seen either as evidence of unknown natural processes or as divine intercession in human events.

As Gogol's career matured, he began to deviate from the prevailing modes of prose narration, both in theme and in method. Indeed, his innovations in these areas defined his greatness as a writer. *Taras Bulba* (1835, 1842; English translation, 1886) was a harbinger of thematic innovation, with its treatment of a father's killing of his own son for reasons of obsessive pride. This story also shows the transcendence of the narration itself over its relation to reality, a later Gogol hallmark. That is, the time frame of *Taras Bulba* is hard to define, the specific ethnic conflicts between Cossacks and Turks and Poles are only vaguely explored, if at all. The time line of the narrative misses subtleties of season or of reasonable travel time between the cities depicted. Yet the reader is swept into the relationships of the characters and into their actions by the power of Gogol's narration. By the time of his *Arabesques* collection, Gogol had essentially abandoned the tales of Ukrainian life and was writing stories that were intended not only to entertain and amuse but also to edify and mystify. The struggle between good and evil and its consequences to ordinary people gained primacy in Gogol's characterizations.

Long a part of Slavic narrative technique is the "telling of what is not." Gogol elevated this technique to literary use and availed himself of it on a multitude of levels. He deliberately sought to bring into the reader's attention details that other writers would not consider worth mentioning——descriptions of meals eaten, street signs passed, dogs encountered. In *Dead Souls*, Gogol justifies his fixation on detail by writing that "microscopes, revealing the movements of unseen creatures, are just as wonderful as telescopes, which give us a new view of the sun." The reader is deluged with what is not of significance to the main plot, as well as with what is. Digression follows digression until the point is almost, but not quite, lost. Characters are created and explored and then suddenly dropped.

In Gogol's earlier work, his satire is largely devoid of sympathy for its human objects. The epigraph to his play *The Inspector General* quotes a Russian popular saying, "If your face is skew don't blame the mirror." In his later "Confession by an Author," Gogol writes that he "resolved in *The Inspector General* to pile all the rubbish of Russia together . . . and laugh at the whole lot." Provincial officials are parodied as petty, corrupt, venal, and downright foolish in their attempts to find favor in the eyes of Khlestakov, a St. Petersburg clerk whom they mistakenly believe is a government *inspector general.* Khlestakov soon assumes the pose with relish but is revealed as a fraud when the local postmaster reads his letter to a friend in which, to their horror, the parodied provincial officials are ridiculed.

As Gogol matured as a writer, he developed more sympathy for his objects of ridicule, obviously identifying with them personally as a human being caught in the clash of forces, both social and spiritual, beyond human control. In "The Overcoat," the reader can feel Gogol's sympathy for the tormented Akaky Akakievich, the office copy clerk who is the butt of his coworkers' pranks. Gogol gives Akaky a supernatural revenge for the cruelty and the slights. In *Dead Souls*, Gogol summarized his relationship with his characters in this way: "Supernatural powers have ordained that I should walk hand in hand with my odd heroes, observing the life that flows majestically past me, conveying it through laughter, which the world can hear, while seeing it myself through tears it never suspects." This "laughter through tears" is the most lasting literary legacy of Nikolai Gogol.

THE DIARY OF A MADMAN

First published: "Zapiski sumasshedshego," 1835 (English translation, 1922)
Type of work: Short story (in diary form)

The reader witnesses the progression of a man's insanity in twenty entries from his diary.

In "The Diary of a Madman," the eccentric clerk Poprishchin is infatuated with the daughter of his office director. He records in his diary that he has intercepted a letter from her dog to another dog. The contents eventually lead him to conclude that "women are in love with the Devil," a fact that only he has discovered. Soon, he ceases going to work, where his main task is to sharpen the director's quills, because he has become the king of Spain, although "Spain and China are one and the same country." The flimsy moon, he relates, is inhabited by people's noses, and that is why they cannot see them on their own faces.

Poprishchin (whose name evokes the Russian word for "pimple") records "October 3" as his first diary entry. Entries for "October 4," "November 6," and "November 8" follow. Yet as his insanity becomes more and more pervasive and debilitating, the entries are given dates such as "the 43rd Day of April in the year 2000," or "The 34th of yrae yraurbeF 349." The reader begins to see shadows of reality in Poprishchin's ramblings, as when he mentions the "Spanish court custom" requiring that his head be shaved and that water be dripped on it. In his last entry, Poprishchin longs for escape. He wants to return to his peasant home and to his mother, saying,

> O mother, mother, save your unhappy son! Let a tear fall on his aching head! See how they torture him! Press the poor orphan to your bosom! He has no rest in this world; they hunt him from place to place.
>
> Mother, mother, have pity on your sick child! And do you know that the Bey of Algiers has a wart under his nose?

THE NOSE

First published: "Nos," 1836 (English translation, 1915)
Type of work: Short Story

A St. Petersburg city official awakens without a nose and takes several courses of remedial action to no effect before the nose's mysterious return.

Much has been made of the "nose" theme in Gogol's work "The Nose." The American writer Vladimir Nabokov, in his interpretation, rejects the Freudian view that, in Gogol's topsy-turvy world, the nose represents a misplaced phallus, and that his literary fixation on noses, sneezes, snuff, stinks, scents, and the like evidences his own uncertain sense of sexual identity. Instead, Nabokov attributes Gogol's "olfactivism" to a general nasal consciousness in the Russian culture that was made more acute in Gogol's work because of the peaked prominence of his own nose. Whatever the origin, Gogol's tale is "verily a hymn to that organ."

St. Petersburg barber Ivan Yakovlevich awakes to find a nose baked into his breakfast bread. He recognizes the nose as that of his recent customer, Major Platon Kovalyov, a collegiate assessor in the municipal government. Harangued by his wife, he seeks to dispose of the nose by wrapping it in a cloth and throwing it into the water below the Isaac Bridge. He is observed in this act, however, by a policeman. Major Kovalyov awakens, looks in the mirror, and notices that his nose is missing. He is most upset about this, and so he covers his face with a handkerchief and walks out onto Nevsky Prospect to seek aid. His sense of embarrassment prevents him from approaching anyone, however, and his discomfiture is greatly increased when, in front of a confectionary shop, he encounters his nose exiting a carriage. Since his nose is wearing the uniform of an official of higher rank than his, Kovalyov importunes the nose very politely to return to his face. The nose, however, is indignant and denies that there can be any close ties between them, before haughtily walking away.

Kovalyov goes to seek the aid of the chief of police, but the chief of police is not at home. Kovalyov realizes that he must act on his own to effect the return of his nose. He contemplates advertising in the newspaper for its return but rejects the idea. At this point, the policeman who has observed Ivan Yakovlevich throwing the nose off the Isaac Bridge comes to Kovalyov's house to inform him that the nose "had been arrested just as it was getting into a carriage for Riga." The nose is now returned to Kovalyov in its cloth wrapping. Kovalyov is very grateful, but he does not know how to stick the nose back onto his face. A physician whom he consults on the matter is no help at all.

Thinking things over, Kovalyov concludes that the loss of his nose is the result of a spell put on him by his superior's wife, Madame Podtochina, whose ire was raised at him when he refused to marry her daughter. He writes Madame Podtochina a letter, demanding that she restore his nose to its rightful place or face "legal procedures." Kovalyov's quandary continues until "April 7th," when he awakens to find his nose returned to its proper place in the middle of his face.

The notion of a nose disappearing from a man's face, assuming human size, rank, and uniform, is Gogol's way of expressing life's absurdity. The reader's sense of expected reality is violated. Is this the relation of dreams? Is it the rambling of a madman? Are there unexplained facts behind it all? What does it mean? Many authors since have included similar violations of expected reality in their literary art. Franz Kafka's *Die Verwandlung* (1915; *The Metamorphosis*, 1936) comes to mind. Yet Gogol characterizes the entire story within the narrative as one of those "strange things" that "happen all the time." "Whatever you might say," he writes in the famous concluding sentences, "such things do happen, rarely perhaps, but they do."

THE OVERCOAT

First published: "Shinel," 1842 (English translation, 1915)
Type of work: Short story

A downtrodden copy clerk saves for months to buy an overcoat, but, before he can enjoy it, it is stolen, and, as a result, he dies.

In many a workplace, there is one person who serves as the object of the others' cruel amusement. In "The Overcoat," that person is Akaky Akakievich Bashmachkin, a poor office worker whose very name reminds a Russian of excrement-befouled boots (from "kaka," the child's word for "excrement," and "bashmak" for "boot" or "shoe"). His coworkers poke endless fun at him. They tear paper into confetti and sprinkle it over his head. Akaky protests only when the torment becomes extreme. Otherwise, he is content to work as a copy clerk, keeping his pencils sharp and copying document after document all day.

The fiercely cold St. Petersburg winter forces Akaky to consider the purchase of a new overcoat, since his old coat had worn to complete transparency and was useless. The tailor, Petrovich, suggests the possibility of owning a splendid new coat with a "catskin collar that could pass for marten." After months of the most sacrificing parsimony (so many months, in fact, that it would have been summer and the coat not needed, but Gogol's narrative logic is not fazed by this fact), Akaky saves the needed eighty rubles to buy the coat. He immediately wears it to work and basks for the first time in the admiration of his coworkers. One of them even invites Akaky to a birthday party. Yet on the way home after the party, a group of "people with moustaches," one of whom had a "fist the size of a civil servant's head," accosted him and stripped him of his new coat.

Akaky knows that seeking redress for such a crime from the police is futile. Instead, he makes an appointment to see a "very important person." This "very important person," however, only sees Akaky as someone else to intimidate. He booms out three sets of three questions at Akaky (there is much triplicity in Gogol's work): "Are you aware who you are talking to?" "Do you realize who is standing before you?" and "Do you hear me?" Akaky flees this person's office in terror, goes home coatless through the winter wind, and takes to bed with a swollen throat and a fever. In three days, he is dead. It takes another three days for his office to miss him and replace him with another copy clerk, whose letters were written "in a hand quite unlike Akaky Akakievich's upright ciphers, sloping heavily to one side."

Yet the sad story is not ended. A mysterious ghost begins to haunt St. Petersburg near the area of the department. The ghost accosts people and strips them of their coats. Indeed the "very important person," whose conscience had begun to trouble him over his treatment of Akaky, is accosted by the ghost and has his coat stolen as well. The reader feels that, in death, Akaky is wreaking his revenge on those who slighted him in life. The coat-stealing ghost is not seen again after the robbery of the "very important person's" coat. Another ghost, though, is seen by a cowardly constable, who is taken aback by the "much taller" apparition's "enormous moustache" and a "fist such as you would see on no living man." With this baffling inclusion, Gogol ends his classic story of the "little man" and his mistreatment by society.

"The Overcoat" has been a very influential story in world literature. Many literary works that treat the problems of an individual in a callous society with some psychological depth and empathy owe a debt to Gogol. The Russian novelist Fyodor Dostoevski's famous remark that "We all came out from Gogol's Overcoat" still held true through much of the twentieth century. The "little tramp" films of the English actor Charles Chaplin also embody Gogolesque aspects of the "little man" and the "laughter through tears" character type.

DEAD SOULS

First published: *Myortvye dushi*, part 1, 1842; part 2, 1855 (English translation, 1887)
Type of work: Novel

A con artist plans to purchase "dead souls," or serfs, from a number of provincial landowners who turn out to be the real "dead souls."

In Gogol's time, a Russian landowner could buy and sell serfs, or "souls," like any other property. The serfs were counted for the purpose of tax assessment every ten years. Thus, a landowner still had to pay taxes on the value of serfs that had died until the next ten-year census could legally record the deaths. In *Dead Souls*, a prose novel subtitled "A Poem," Gogol's hero, Pavel Ivanovich Chichikov, plans to buy the titles to these "dead souls" so as to use them as collateral to obtain a large loan. He comes to a small provincial town and begins to proposition the local landowners: the slothful Manilovs (the "kind-manners"), the slovenly Plewshkin ("Mr. Spitoon"), the coarse Sobakievich ("Mr. Dog"), the cautious Madame Korobachka ("Mrs. Box"), and the bully and cheat Nozdryov ("Mr. Nostrils"). These landowners are revealed to be so petty and avaricious that not even Chichikov's amazing offer can be worked to his advantage on them. Some stall, some refuse for no obvious reasons, some promise and then renege, while others want "in on the deal." In the end, Chichikov, having concluded that the landowners are a hopeless lot, leaves for other regions.

Throughout *Dead Souls*, Gogol presents Russian life as a mosaic of strangely intersecting inanities. He makes his authorial presence felt as a first-person commentator. His commentator's stance is curiously unresolved. Though he likens Russia to the "fastest troika imaginable . . . racing headlong . . . inspired by God," he seems most insistent, with his wordy, tongue-in-cheek prose, in portraying the life within its borders as inalterably superficial.

Summary

Nikolai Gogol was a man with more than his share of neuroses. He was confident of his narrative gift yet lived in fear that his inspiration would wane. He was misinterpreted in his lifetime, and he died in mental and spiritual frustration. Yet he has given world literature some of its most laughable, and yet pathetic, prose. In most of his mature works, he laid bare the banality and the pettiness (signifying the manifestation of false values) underlying all human pretense. For Gogol, humor was the most effective way to call for human sincerity. Digressions were the way that he chose to address the central aspects of human life. Trivia was his path to finding what was most important.

Bibliography

Gippius, V. V. *Gogol*. Edited and translated by Robert A. Maguire. Reprint. Durham, N.C.: Duke University Press, 1989.

Karlinsky, Simon. *The Sexual Labyrinth of Nikolai Gogol*. Cambridge, Mass.: Harvard University Press, 1976.

Lindstrom, Thais S. *Nikolay Gogol*. New York: Twayne, 1974.

Magarshack, David. *Gogol: A Life*. London: Faber & Faber, 1957.

Nabokov, Vladimir. *Nikolai Gogol*. New York: New Directions, 1961.

Rancour-Laferriere, Daniel. *Out from Under Gogol's Overcoat: A Psychoanalytic Study*. Ann Arbor, Mich.: Ardis Publishers, 1982.

Rowe, William Woodin. *Through Gogol's Looking Glass: Reverse Vision, False Focus, and Precarious Logic*. New York: New York University Press, 1976.

Setchkarev, Vsevolod. *Gogol: His Life and Works*. Translated by Robert Kramer. New York: New York University Press, 1965.

Troyat, Henri. *Divided Soul: The Life of Gogol*. Translated by Nancy Amphoux. New York: Minerva Press, 1975.

Lee B. Croft

MAGILL'S
SURVEY
OF
WORLD
LITERATURE

GLOSSARY

Aesthetics: The branch of philosophy that studies the beautiful in nature and art, including how beauty is recognized in a work of art and how people respond to it. In literature, the aesthetic approach can be distinguished from the moral or utilitarian approach; it was most fully embodied in the movement known as aestheticism in the late nineteenth century.

Alienation: The German dramatist Bertolt Brecht developed the theory of alienation in his epic theater. Brecht sought to create an audience that was intellectually alert rather than emotionally involved in a play by using alienating techniques such as minimizing the illusion of reality onstage and interrupting the action with songs and visual aids.

Allegory: A literary mode in which characters in a narrative personify abstract ideas or qualities and so give a second level of meaning to the work, in addition to the surface narrative. Two famous examples of allegory are Edmund Spenser's *The Faerie Queene* (1590, 1596) and John Bunyan's *The Pilgrim's Progress* (1678). For modern examples, see the stories and novels of Franz Kafka.

Alliteration: A poetic technique in which consonant repetition is focused at the beginning of syllables, as in "Large mannered motions of his mythy mind." Alliteration is used when the poet wishes to focus on the details of a sequence of words and to show the relationships between words in a line.

Angry young men: The term used to describe a group of English novelists and playwrights in the 1950's and 1960's, whose work stridently attacked what it saw as the outmoded political and social structures (particularly the class structure) of post-World War II Britain. John Osborne's play *Look Back in Anger* (1956) and Kingsley Amis' *Lucky Jim* (1954) are typical examples.

Angst: A pervasive feeling of anxiety and depression often associated with the moral and spiritual uncertainties of the twentieth century, as expressed in the existentialism of writers such as Jean-Paul Sartre and Albert Camus.

Antagonist: A character in fiction who stands in opposition or rivalry to the protagonist. In William Shakespeare's *Hamlet* (c. 1600-1601), for example, King Claudius is the antagonist of Hamlet.

Anthropomorphism: The ascription of human characteristics and feelings to animals, inanimate objects, or gods. The gods of Homer's epics are anthropomorphic, for example. Anthropomorphism occurs in beast fables, such as George Orwell's *Animal Farm* (1945). The term "pathetic fallacy" carries the same meaning: Natural objects are invested with human feelings. *See also* Pathetic fallacy.

Antihero: A modern fictional figure who tries to define himself and establish his own codes, or a protagonist who simply lacks traditional heroic qualities, such as Jim Dixon in Kingsley Amis' *Lucky Jim* (1954).

Aphorism: A short, concise statement that states an opinion, precept, or general truth, such as Alexander Pope's "Hope springs eternal in the human breast."

Apostrophe: A direct address to a person (usually absent), inanimate entity, or abstract quality.

Archetype: The term was used by psychologist Carl Jung to describe what he called "primordial images" that exist in the "collective unconscious" of humankind and are manifested in myths, religion, literature, and dreams. Now used broadly in literary criticism to refer to character types, motifs, images, symbols, and plot patterns recurring in many different literary forms and works. The embodiment of archetypes in a work of literature can make a powerful impression on the reader.

Aristotelian unities: A set of rules for proper dramatic construction formulated by Italian and French critics during the Renaissance, purported to be derived from the *De poetica* (c. 334-323 B.C.; *Poetics*) of Aristotle. According to the "three unities," a play should have no scenes irrelevant to the main action, should not cover a period of more than twenty-four hours, and should not occur in more than one place or locale. In fact, Aristotle insists only on unity of action in a tragedy.

Assonance: A term for the association of words with identical vowel sounds but different consonants: "stars," "arms," and "park," for example, all contain identical *a* (and *ar*) sounds.

***Auto sacramental*:** A Renaissance development of the medieval open-air Corpus Christi pageant in Spain. A dramatic, allegorical depiction of a sinful soul wavering and transgressing until the intervention of Divine Grace restores order. During a period of prohibition of all secular drama in Spain, from 1598 to 1600, even Lope de Vega Carpio adopted this form.

Autobiography: A form of nonfiction writing in which the author narrates events of his or her own life. Autobiography differs from memoir in that the latter focuses on prominent people the author has known and great events that he has witnessed, rather than on his own life.

Ballad: Popular ballads are songs or verse that tell dramatic, usually impersonal, tales. Supernatural events, courage, and love are frequent themes, but any experience that appeals to ordinary people is acceptable material. Literary ballads—narrative poems based on the popular ballads—have frequently been in vogue in English literature, particularly during the Romantic period. One of the most famous is Samuel Taylor Coleridge's *The Rime of the Ancient Mariner* (1798).

Baroque: The term was first used in the eighteenth century to describe an elaborate and grandiose type of architecture. It is now also used to refer to certain stylistic features of Metaphysical poetry, particularly the poetry of Richard Crashaw. The term can also refer to post-Renaissance literature, 1580-1680.

***Bildungsroman*:** Sometimes called the "novel of education," or "apprenticeship novel," the *Bildungsroman* focuses on the growth of a young protagonist who is learning about the world and finding his place in life; a typical example is James Joyce's *A Portrait of the Artist as a Young Man* (1916).

GLOSSARY

Blank verse: A term for unrhymed iambic pentameter, blank verse first appeared in drama in Thomas Norton and Thomas Sackville's *Gorboduc*, performed in 1561, and later became the standard form of Elizabethan drama. It has also commonly been used in long narrative or philosophical poems, such as John Milton's *Paradise Lost* (1667, 1674).

Bourgeois novel: A novel in which the values, the preoccupations, and the accoutrements of middle-class or bourgeois life are given particular prominence. The heyday of the genre was the nineteenth century, when novelists as varied as Jane Austen, Honoré de Balzac, and Anthony Trollope both criticized and unreflectingly transmitted the assumptions of the rising middle class.

Burlesque: A work that by imitating attitudes, styles, institutions, and people aims to amuse. Burlesque differs from satire in that it aims to ridicule simply for the sake of amusement rather than for political or social change.

Capa y espada: Spanish for "cloak and sword." A term referring to the Spanish theater of the sixteenth and seventeenth centuries dealing with love and intrigue among the aristocracy. The greatest practitioners were Lope de Vega Carpio and Pedro Calderón de la Barca. The term *comedia de ingenio* is also used.

Catharsis: A term from Aristotle's *De poetica* (c. 334-323 B.C.; *Poetics*) referring to the purgation of the emotions of pity and fear in the spectator aroused by the actions of the tragic hero. The meaning and the operation of the concept have been a source of great, and unresolved, critical debate.

Celtic romance: Gaelic Celts invaded Ireland in about 350 B.C.; their epic stories and romances date from this period until about A.D. 450. The romances are marked by a strong sense of the Otherworld and of supernatural happenings. The Celtic romance tradition influenced the poetry of William Butler Yeats.

Celtic Twilight: Sometimes used synonymously with the term Irish Renaissance, which was a movement beginning in the late nineteenth century which attempted to build a national literature by drawing on Ireland's literary and cultural history. The term, however, which is taken from a book by William Butler Yeats titled *The Celtic Twilight* (1893), sometimes has a negative connotation. It is used to refer to some early volumes by Yeats, which have been called self-indulgent. The poet Algernon Charles Swinburne said that the Celtic Twilight manner "puts fever and fancy in the place of reason and imagination."

Chamber plays: Refers to four plays written in 1907 by the Swedish dramatist August Strindberg. The plays are modeled on the form of chamber music, consisting of motif and variations, to evoke a mood or atmosphere (in these cases, a very sombre one). There is no protagonist but a small group of equally important characters.

Character: A personage appearing in any literary or dramatic work. Characters can be presented with the depth and complexity of real people (sometimes called "round" characters) or as stylized functions of the plot ("flat" characters).

Chorus: Originally a group of singers and dancers in religious festivals, the chorus evolved into the dramatic element that reflected the opinions of the masses or commented on the action in Greek drama. In its most developed form, the chorus consisted of fifteen members: seven reciting the strophe, seven reciting the antistrophe, and the leader interacting with the actors. The chorus has been used in all periods of drama, including the modern period.

Classicism: A literary stance or value system consciously based on the example of classical Greek and Roman literature. While the term is applied to an enormous diversity of artists in many different periods and in many different national literatures, it generally denotes a cluster of values including formal discipline, restrained expression, reverence of tradition, and an objective, rather than subjective, orientation. Often contrasted with Romanticism. *See also* Romanticism.

***Comédie-Française*:** The first state theater of France, composed of the company of actors established by Molière in 1658. The company took the name *Comédie-Française* in 1680. Today, it is officially known as the *Theatre Français (Salle Richelieu)*.

Comedy: Generally, a lighter form of drama (as contrasted with tragedy) that aims chiefly to amuse and ends happily. The comic effect typically arises from the recognition of some incongruity of speech, action, or character development. The comic range extends from coarse, physical humor (called low comedy) to a more subtle, intellectual humor (called high comedy).

Comedy of manners: A form of comedy that arose during the seventeenth century, dealing with the intrigues (particularly the amorous intrigues) of sophisticated, witty members of the upper classes. The appeal of these plays is primarily intellectual, depending as they do on quick-witted dialogue and clever language. For examples, see the plays of Restoration dramatists William Congreve, Sir George Etherege, and William Wycherley. *See also* Restoration comedy/drama.

***Commedia dell'arte*:** Dramatic comedy performed by troupes of professional actors, which became popular in the mid-sixteenth century in Italy. The troupes were rather small, consisting of perhaps a dozen actors who performed stock roles in mask and improvised on skeletal scenarios. The tradition of the *commedia*, or masked comedy, was influential into the seventeenth century and still exerts some influence.

Conceit: A type of metaphor, the conceit is used for comparisons that are highly intellectualized. When T. S. Eliot, for example, says that winding streets are like a tedious argument of insidious intent, there is no clear connection between the two, so the reader must apply abstract logic to fill in the missing links.

Conversation poem: Conversation poems are chiefly associated with the poetry of Samuel Taylor Coleridge. These poems all display a relaxed, informal style, quiet settings, and a circular structure—the poem returns to where it began, after an intervening meditation has yielded some insight into the speaker's situation.

GLOSSARY

Cubism: A term borrowed from Cubist painters. In literature, cubism is a style of poetry, such as that of E. E. Cummings, Kenneth Rexroth, and Archibald MacLeish, which first fragments an experience, then rearranges its elements into some new artistic entity.

Dactyl: The dactylic foot, or dactyl, is formed of a stress followed by two unstressed syllables, as in the words "Washington" and "manikin." "After the pangs of a desperate lover" is an example of a dactylic line.

Dadaism: Dadaism arose in France during World War I as a radical protest in art and literature against traditional institutions and values. Part of its strategy was the use of infantile, nonsensical language. After World War I, when Dadaism was combined with the ideas of Sigmund Freud, it gave rise to the Surrealist movement.

Decadence: The period of decline that heralds the ending of a great age. The period in English dramatic history immediately following William Shakespeare is said to be decadent, and the term "Decadents" is applied to a group of late-nineteenth and early twentieth century writers who searched for new literary and artistic forms as the Victorian Age came to a close.

Detective story: The "classic" detective story (or "mystery") is a highly formalized and logically structured mode of fiction in which the focus is on a crime solved by a detective through interpretation of evidence and clever reasoning. Many modern practitioners of the genre, however, such as Raymond Chandler, Patricia Highsmith, and Ross Macdonald, have placed less emphasis on the puzzlelike qualities of the detective story and have focused instead on characterization, theme, and other elements of mainstream fiction. The form was first developed in short fiction by Edgar Allan Poe; Jorge Luis Borges has also used the convention in short stories.

Dialectic: A philosophical term meaning the art of examining opinions or ideas logically. The dialectic method of Georg Wilhelm Friedrich Hegel and Karl Marx was based on a contradiction of opposites (thesis and antithesis) and their resolution (synthesis). In literary criticism, the term has sometimes been used by Marxist critics to refer to the structure and dynamics of a literary work in its sociological context.

Dialogue: Speech exchanged between characters, or even, in a looser sense, the thoughts of a single character. Dialogue serves to characterize, to further the plot, to establish conflict, and to express thematic ideas.

Doppelgänger: A double or counterpart of a person, sometimes endowed with ghostly qualities. A fictional *Doppelgänger* often reflects a suppressed side of his personality, as in Fyodor Dostoevski's novella *Dvoynik* (1846; *The Double*, 1917) and the short stories of E. T. A. Hoffmann. Isaac Bashevis Singer and Jorge Luis Borges, among other modern writers, have also employed the *Doppelgänger* with striking effect.

Drama: Generally speaking, any work designed to be represented on a stage by actors (Aristotle defined drama as "the imitation of an action"). More specifically, the term has come to signify a play of a serious nature and intent that may end either happily (comedy) or unhappily (tragedy).

Dramatic irony: A situation in a play or a narrative in which the audience knows something that the character does not. The irony lies in the different meaning that the character's words or actions have for himself and for the audience. A common device in classical Greek drama. Sophocles' *Oidipous Tyrannos* (429 B.C.; *Oedipus Tyrannus*) is an example of extended dramatic irony.

Dramatic monologue: In dramatic monologue, the narrator addresses a persona who never speaks but whose presence greatly influences what the narrator tells the reader. The principal reason for writing in dramatic monologue is to control the speech of the major persona by the implied reaction of the silent one. The effect is one of continuing change and often surprise. The technique is especially useful for revealing characters slowly and for involving the reader as another silent participant.

Dramatic verse: Poetry that employs dramatic form or technique, such as dialogue or conflict, to achieve its effects. The term is used to refer to dramatic monologue, drama written in verse, and closet dramas.

***Dramatis personae*:** The characters in a play. Often, a printed listing defining the characters and specifying their relationships.

Dream vision: An allegorical form common in the Middle Ages, in which the narrator or a character falls asleep and dreams a dream that becomes the actual framed story.

Dystopian/Utopian novel: A dystopian novel takes some existing trend or theory in present-day society and extends it into a fictional world of the future, where the trend has become more fully manifested, with unpleasant results. Aldous Huxley's *Brave New World* (1932) is an example. The utopian novel is the opposite: It presents an ideal society. The first utopian novel was Sir Thomas More's *Utopia* (1516).

Elegy: A long, rhymed, formal poem whose subject is meditation upon death or a lamentable theme. The pastoral elegy uses a pastoral scene to express grief at the loss of a friend or important person. *See also* Pastoral.

Elizabethan Age: Of or referring to the reign of Queen Elizabeth I of England, lasting from 1558 to 1603, a period of important developments and achievements in the arts in England, particularly in poetry and drama. The era included such literary figures as Edmund Spenser, Christopher Marlowe, William Shakespeare, and Ben Jonson. Sometimes referred to as the English Renaissance.

English novel: The first fully realized English novel was Samuel Richardson's *Pamela* (1740-1741). The genre took firm hold in the second half of the eighteenth century, with the work of Daniel Defoe, Henry Fielding, and Tobias Smollett, and reached its full flowering in the nineteenth century, in which great novelists such as Jane Austen, Charles Dickens, William Makepeace Thackeray, Anthony

Trollope, Thomas Hardy, and George Eliot produced sweeping portraits of the whole range of English life in the period.

Enlightenment: A period in Western European cultural history that began in the seventeenth century and culminated in the eighteenth. The chief characteristic of Enlightenment thinkers was their belief in the virtue of human reason, which they believed was banishing former superstitious and ignorant ways and leading to an ideal condition of human life. The Enlightenment coincides with the rise of the scientific method.

Epic: Although this term usually refers to a long narrative poem that presents the exploits of a central figure of high position, the term is also used to designate a long novel that has the style or structure usually associated with an epic. In this sense, for example, Herman Melville's *Moby Dick* (1851) and James Joyce's *Ulysses* (1922) may be called epics.

Epigram: Originally meaning an inscription, an epigram is a short, pointed poem, often expressing humor and satire. In English literature, the form flourished from the Renaissance through the eighteenth century, in the work of poets such as John Donne, Ben Jonson, and Alexander Pope. The term also refers to a concise and witty expression in prose, as in the plays of Oscar Wilde.

Epiphany: Literally, an epiphany is an appearance of a god or supernatural being. The term is used in literary criticism to signify any moment of heightened awareness, or flash of transcendental insight, when an ordinary object or scene is suddenly transformed into something that possesses eternal significance. Especially noteworthy examples are found in the works of James Joyce.

Epistle: The word means "letter," but epistle is used to refer to a literary form rather than a private composition, usually written in dignified style and addressed to a group. The most famous examples are the epistles in the New Testament.

Epistolary novel: A work of fiction in which the narrative is carried forward by means of letters written by the characters. Epistolary novels were especially popular in the eighteenth century. Examples include Samuel Richardson's *Pamela* (1740-1741) and *Clarissa* (1747-1748).

Epithet: An adjective or adjectival phrase that expresses a special characteristic of a person or thing. "Hideous night," "devouring time," and "sweet silent thought" are epithets that appear in William Shakespeare's sonnets.

Essay: A brief prose work, usually on a single topic, that expresses the personal point of view of the author. The essay is usually addressed to a general audience and attempts to persuade the reader to accept the author's ideas.

Everyman: The central character in the work by the same name, the most famous of the English medieval morality plays. It tells of how Everyman is summoned by Death and of the parts played in his journey by characters named Fellowship, Cousin, Kindred, Goods, Knowledge, Confession, Beauty, Strength, Discretion, Five Wits, and Good Deeds. Everyman has proved lastingly popular; there have been many productions even in the twentieth century. More generally, the term means the typical, ordinary person.

Existentialism: A philosophy or attitude of mind that has gained wide currency in religious and artistic thought since the end of World War II. Typical concerns of existential writers are humankind's estrangement from society, its awareness that the world is meaningless, and its recognition that one must turn from external props to the self. The works of Jean-Paul Sartre and Franz Kafka provide examples of existentialist beliefs.

Experimental novel: The term is associated with novelists such as Dorothy Richardson, Virginia Woolf, and James Joyce in England, who experimented with the form of the novel, using in particular the stream-of-consciousness technique.

Expressionism: Beginning in German theater at the start of the twentieth century, expressionism became the dominant movement in the decade following World War I. It abandoned realism and relied on a conscious distortion of external reality in order to portray the world as it is "viewed emotionally." The movement spread to fiction and poetry. Expressionism influenced the novels of Franz Kafka and James Joyce.

Fable: One of the oldest narrative forms, usually taking the form of an analogy in which animals or inanimate objects speak to illustrate a moral lesson. The most famous examples are the fables of Aesop, who used the form orally in 600 B.C.

Fabliau: A short narrative poem, popular in medieval French literature and during the English Middle Ages. Fabliaux were usually realistic in subject matter and bawdy; they made a point of satirizing the weaknesses and foibles of human beings. Perhaps the most famous are Geoffrey Chaucer's "The Miller's Tale" and "The Reeve's Tale."

Fairy tale: A form of folktale in which supernatural events or characters are prominent. Fairy tales usually depict a realm of reality beyond that of the natural world in which the laws of the natural world are suspended.

Fantasy: A literary form that makes a deliberate break with reality. Fantasy literature may use supernatural or fairy-tale events in which the ordinary commonsense laws of the everyday world do not operate. The setting may be unreal. J. R. R. Tolkien's fantasy trilogy, *The Lord of the Rings* (1955), is one of the best-known examples of the genre.

Farce: From the Latin *farcire*, meaning "to stuff." Originally an insertion into established Church liturgy in the Middle Ages, farce later became the term for specifically comic scenes inserted into early liturgical drama. The term has come to refer to any play that evokes laughter by such low-comedy devices as physical humor, rough wit, and ridiculous and improbable situations and characters.

Femme fatale: The "fatal woman" is an archetype that appears in myth, folklore, religion, and literature. Often she is presented as a temptress or a witch who ensnares, and attempts to destroy, her male victim. A very common figure in Romanticism, the fatal woman often appears in twentieth century American literature.

Figurative language: Any use of language that departs from the usual or ordinary meaning to gain a poetic or otherwise special effect. Figurative language embodies various figures of speech, such as irony, metaphor, simile.

First person: A point of view in which the narrator of a story or poem addresses the reader directly, often using the pronoun "I," thereby allowing the reader direct access to the narrator's thoughts.

Folklore: The traditions, customs, and beliefs of a people expressed in nonliterary form. Folklore includes myths, legends, fairy tales, riddles, proverbs, charms, spells, and ballads and is usually transmitted through word of mouth. Many literary works contain motifs that can be traced to folklore.

Foreshadowing: A device used to create suspense or dramatic irony by indicating through suggestion what will take place in the future. The aim is to prepare the reader for the action that follows.

Frame story: A story that provides a framework for another story (or stories) told within it. The form is ancient and is used by Geoffrey Chaucer in *The Canterbury Tales* (1387-1400). In modern literature, the technique has been used by Henry James in *The Turn of the Screw* (1898), Joseph Conrad in *Heart of Darkness* (serial, 1899; book, 1902), and John Barth in *Lost in the Funhouse* (1968).

Free verse: Verse that does not conform to any traditional convention, such as meter, rhyme, or form. All poetry must have some pattern of some kind, however, and there is rhythm in free verse, but it does not follow the strict rules of meter. Often the pattern relies on repetition and parallel construction.

Genre: A type or category of literature, such as tragedy, novel, memoir, poem, or essay; a genre has a particular set of conventions and expectations.

German Romanticism: Germany was the first European country in which the Romantic movement took firm grip. Poets Novalis and Ludwig Tieck, philosopher Friedrich Wilhelm Joseph Schelling, and literary theorists Friedrich and August Wilhelm Schlegel were well established in Jena from about 1797, and they were followed, in the second decade of the nineteenth century, by the Heidelberg group, including novelist and short-story writer E. T. A. Hoffmann and poet Heinrich Heine.

Gnomic: Aphoristic poetry, such as the wisdom literature of the Bible, which deals with ethical questions. The term "gnomic poets" is applied to a group of Greek poets of the sixth and seventh century B.C.

Gothic novel: A form of fiction developed in the late eighteenth century that focuses on horror and the supernatural. An example is Mary Shelley's *Frankenstein* (1818). In modern literature, the gothic genre can be found in the fiction of Truman Capote.

Grand Tour: Fashionable during the eighteenth century in England, the Grand Tour was a two- to three-year journey through Europe during which the young aristocracy and prosperous, educated middle classes of England deepened their knowledge of the origins and centers of Western civilization. The tour took a standard route; Rome and Naples were usually considered the highlights.

Grotesque: Characterized by a breakup of the everyday world by mysterious forces, the form differs from fantasy in that the reader is not sure whether to react with humor or with horror. Examples include the stories of E. T. A. Hoffmann and Franz Kafka.

Hagiography: Strictly defined, hagiography refers to the lives of the saints (the Greek word *hagios* means "sacred"), but the term is also used in a more popular sense, to describe any biography that grossly overpraises its subject and ignores his or her faults.

Heroic couplet: A pair of rhyming iambic pentameter lines traditionally used in epic poetry; a heroic couplet often serves as a self-contained witticism or pithy observation.

Historical fiction: A novel that depicts past historical events, usually public in nature, and that features real, as well as fictional, people. Sir Walter Scott's Waverley novels established the basic type, but the relationship between fiction and history in the form varies greatly depending on the practitioner.

Hubris: Greek term for "insolence" or "pride," the characteristic or emotion in the tragic hero of ancient Greek drama that causes the reversal of his fortune, leading him to transgress moral codes or ignore warnings.

Humanism: A human-centered, rather than God-centered, view of the universe. In the Renaissance, Humanism devoted itself to the revival of classical culture. A reaction against medieval Scholasticism, Humanism oriented itself toward secular concerns and applied classical ideas to theology, government, literature, and education. In literature, the main virtues were seen to be restraint, form, and imitation of the classics. *See also* Renaissance.

Iambic pentameter: A metrical line consisting of five feet, each foot consisting of one unstressed syllable followed by one stressed syllable: "So long as men can breathe or eyes can see." Iambic pentameter is one of the commonest forms of English poetry.

Imagery: Often defined as the verbal stimulation of sensory perception. Although the word betrays a visual bias, imagery, in fact, calls on all five senses. In its simplest form, imagery re-creates a physical sensation in a clear, literal manner; it becomes more complex when a poet employs metaphor and other figures of speech to re-create experience.

Impressionism: A late nineteenth century movement composed of a group of painters including Paul Cézanne, Édouard Manet, Claude Monet, and Pierre-Auguste Renoir, who aimed in their work to suggest the impression made on the artist by a scene rather than to reproduce it objectively. The term has also been applied to French Symbolist poets such as Paul Verlaine and Stéphane Mallarmé, and to writers who use the stream-of-consciousness technique, such as James Joyce and Virginia Woolf.

Irony: Recognition of the difference between real and apparent meaning. Verbal irony is a rhetorical trope wherein x is uttered and "not x" is meant. In the New Criticism, irony, the poet's recognition of incongruities, was thought to be the master trope in that it was essential to the production of paradox, complexity, and ambiguity.

Jacobean: Of or pertaining to the reign of James I of England, who ruled from 1603 to 1623, the period immediately following the death of Elizabeth I, which saw tremendous literary activity in poetry and drama. Many writers who achieved fame during the Elizabethan Age, such as William Shakespeare, Ben Jonson, and John Donne, were still active. Other dramatists, such as John Webster and Cyril Tourneur, achieved success almost entirely during the Jacobean era.

Jungian psychoanalysis: Refers to the analytical psychology of the Swiss psychiatrist Carl Jung. Jung's significance for literature is that, through his concept of the collective unconscious, he identified many archetypes and archetypal patterns that recur in myth, fairy tale, and literature and are also experienced in dreams.

Kafkaesque: Refers to any grotesque or nightmare world in which an isolated individual, surrounded by an unfeeling and alien world, feels himself to be caught up in an endless maze that is dragging him down to destruction. The term is a reference to the works of Austrian novelist and short-story writer Franz Kafka.

Leitmotif: From the German, meaning "leading motif." Any repetition—of a word, phrase, situation, or idea—that occurs within a single work or group of related works.

Limerick: A comic five-line poem employing an anapestic base and rhyming *aabba*, in which the third and fourth lines are shorter (usually five syllables each) than the first, second, and last lines, which are usually eight syllables each.

Linear plot: A plot that has unity of action and proceeds from beginning to middle to end without flashbacks or subplots, thus satisfying Aristotle's criterion that a plot should be a continuous sequence.

Literary criticism: The study and evaluation of works of literature. Theoretical criticism sets forth general principles for interpretation. Practical criticism offers interpretations of particular works or authors.

Lyric poetry: Lyric poetry developed when music was accompanied by words, and although the "lyrics" were later separated from the music, the characteristics of lyric poetry have been shaped by the constraints of music. Lyric poems are short, more adaptable to metrical variation, and usually personal compared with the cultural functions of narrative poetry. Lyric poetry sings of the self; it explores deeply personal feelings about life.

Magical Realism: Imaginary or fantastic scenes and occurrences presented in a meticulously realistic style. The term has been applied to the fiction of Gabriel

García Márquez, Jorge Luis Borges, Günter Grass, John Fowles, and Salman Rushdie.

Masque: A courtly entertainment popular during the first half of the seventeenth century in England. It was a sumptuous spectacle including music, dance, and lavish costumes and scenery. Masques often dealt with mythological or pastoral subjects, and the dramatic action often took second place to pure spectacle.

Melodrama: Originally a drama with music (*melos* is Greek for "song"). By the early nineteenth century, it had come to mean a play in which characters are clearly either virtuous or evil and are pitted against one another in suspenseful, often sensational situations. The term took on a pejorative meaning, which it retains: any dramatic work characterized by stereotyped characters and sensational, improbable situations.

Metafiction: Refers to fiction that manifests a reflexive tendency, such as Vladimir Nabokov's *Pale Fire* (1962), and John Fowles's *The French Lieutenant's Woman* (1969). The emphasis is on the loosening of the work's illusion of reality to expose the reality of its illusion. Such terms as "irrealism," "postmodernist fiction," and "antifiction" are also used to refer to this type of fiction. *See also* Postmodernism.

Metaphor: A figure of speech in which two dissimilar objects are imaginatively identified (rather than merely compared) on the assumption that they share one or more qualities. The term is often used in modern criticism in a wider sense, to identify analogies of all kinds in literature, painting, and film.

Metaphysical poetry: A type of poetry that stresses the intellectual over the emotional; it is marked by irony, paradox, and striking comparisons of dissimilar things, the latter frequently being farfetched to the point of eccentricity. Usually used to designate a group of seventeenth century English poets, including John Donne, George Herbert, Andrew Marvell, and Thomas Traherne.

Meter: Meter is the pattern of language when it is forced into a line of poetry. All language has rhythm, but when that rhythm is organized and regulated in the line so as to affect the meaning and emotional response to the words, then the rhythm has been refined into meter. The meter is determined by the number of syllables in a line and by the relationship between them.

Mock epic: A literary form that burlesques the epic by taking a trivial subject and treating it in a grand style, using all the conventions of epic, such as invocation to the deity, long and boastful speeches of the heroes, and supernatural machinery. Alexander Pope's *The Rape of the Lock* (1712, 1714) is probably the finest example in English literature. The term is synonymous with mock heroic. *See also* Mock hero.

Mock hero: The hero of a mock epic. *See also* Mock epic.

Modernism: A term used to describe the characteristic aspects of literature and art between World War I and World War II. Influenced by Friedrich Nietzsche, Karl Marx, and Sigmund Freud, modernism embodied a lack of faith in Western civilization and culture. In poetry, fragmentation, discontinuity, and irony were common; in fiction, chronological disruption, linguistic innovation, and the stream-of-consciousness technique; in theater, expressionism and Surrealism.

Morality play: A dramatic form in the late Middle Ages and the Renaissance containing allegorical figures (most often virtues and vices) that are typically involved in the struggle over a person's soul. The anonymously written *Everyman* (1508) is one of the most famous medieval examples of this form.

Motif: An incident, situation, or device that occurs frequently in literature. Motif can also refer to particular words, images, and phrases that are repeated frequently in a single work. In this sense, motif is the same as leitmotif. Motif is similar to theme, although the latter is usually more abstract.

Myth: An anonymous traditional story, often involving supernatural beings, or the interaction between gods and humans, and dealing with the basic questions of how the world and human society came to be. Myth is an important term in contemporary literary criticism. The critic Northrop Frye, for example, has said that "the typical forms of myth become the conventions and genres of literature." He means that the genres of comedy, romance, tragedy, and irony (satire) correspond to seasonal myths of spring, summer, autumn, and winter.

Narrative: An account in prose or verse of an event or series of events, whether real or imagined.

Narrator: The character who recounts the narrative. There are many different types of narrator. The first-person narrator is a character in the story and can be recognized by his use of "I"; third-person narrators may be limited or omniscient. In the former, the narrator confines himself to knowledge of the minds and emotions of one or at most a few characters. In the latter, the narrator knows everything, seeing into the minds of all the characters. Rarely, second-person narration may be used (an example can be found in Edna O'Brien's *A Pagan Place*, published in 1970).

Naturalism: The application of the principles of scientific determinism to fiction. Although it usually refers more to the choice of subject matter than to technical conventions, conventions associated with the movement center on the author's attempt to be precise and objective in description and detail, regardless of whether the events described are sordid or shocking. Naturalism flourished in England, France, and America in the late nineteenth and early twentieth centuries.

Neoclassicism: A term used to describe the classicism that dominated English literature from the Restoration to the late eighteenth century. Modeling itself on the literature of ancient Greece and Rome, neoclassicism exalted the virtues of proportion, unity, harmony, grace, decorum, taste, manners, and restraint. It valued realism and reason over imagination and emotion. *See also* Rationalism, Realism.

Neorealism: A movement in modern Italian literature, extending from about 1930 to 1955. Neorealism was shaped by opposition to Fascism, and by World War II and the Resistance. Neorealist literature therefore exhibited a strong concern with social issues and was marked by pessimism regarding the human condition. Its practitioners sought to overcome the gap between literature and the masses, and its subject matter was frequently drawn from lower-class life. Neorealism is associated preeminently with the work of Italo Calvino.

Nonsense literature/verse: Nonsense verse, such as that written by Edward Lear and Lewis Carroll, makes use of invented words that have no meaning, portmanteau words, and so-called macaroni verse, in which words from different languages are mingled. The verse holds the attention because of its strong rhythms, appealing sounds, and, occasionally, the mysterious atmosphere that it creates.

Novel of education: See *Bildungsroman*.

Novel of ideas: A novel in which the characters, plot, and dialogue serve to develop some controlling idea or to present the clash of ideas. Aldous Huxley's *Eyeless in Gaza* (1936) is a good example.

Novel of manners: The classic example of the form might be the novels of Jane Austen, wherein the customs and conventions of a social group of a particular time and place are realistically, and often satirically, portrayed.

Novella: An Italian term meaning "a little new thing" that now refers to that form of fiction longer than a short story and shorter than a novel.

Objective correlative: A key concept in modern formalist criticism, coined by T. S. Eliot in *The Sacred Wood* (1920). An objective correlative is a situation, an event, or an object that, when presented or described in a literary work, expresses a particular emotion and serves as a precise formula by which the same emotion can be evoked in the reader.

Ode: The ode is a lyric poem that treats a unified subject with elevated emotion, usually ending with a satisfactory resolution. There is no set form for the ode, but it must be long enough to build intense emotional response. Often the ode will address itself to some omnipotent source and will assume a spiritual hue.

Oxford Movement: A reform movement in the Church of England that began in 1833, led by John Henry (later Cardinal) Newman. The Oxford Movement aimed to combat liberalism and the decline of the role of faith in the Church and to restore it to its former ideals. It was attacked for advocating what some saw as Catholic doctrines; as a result, Newman left the Church of England and became a Roman Catholic in 1845.

Panegyric: A formal speech or writing in praise of a particular person or achievement; a eulogy. The form dates back to classical times; the term is now often used in a derogatory sense.

Parable: A short, simple, and usually allegorical story that teaches a moral lesson. In the West, the most famous parables are those told in the Gospels by Christ.

Parody: A literary work that imitates or burlesques another work or author, for the purpose of ridicule. Twentieth century parodists include E. B. White and James Thurber.

Pastoral: The term derives from the Latin "pastor," meaning "shepherd." Pastoral is a literary mode that depicts the country life in an idealized way; it originated in classical literature and was a popular form in English literature from 1550 to 1750. Notable pastoral poems include John Milton's "Lycidas" and Percy Bysshe Shelley's *Adonais.*

Pathetic fallacy: The ascribing of human characteristics or feelings to inanimate objects. The term was coined by John Ruskin in 1856, who disapproved of it, but it is now used without any pejorative sense.

Persona: *Persona* means literally "mask": It is the self created by the author and through whom the narrative is told. The persona is not to be identified with the author, even when the two may seem to resemble each other. The narrative persona in Lord Byron's *Don Juan* (1819-1824, 1826), for example, may express many sentiments of which Byron would have approved, but he is nonetheless a fictional creation who is distinct from the author.

Personification: A figure of speech that ascribes human qualities to abstractions or inanimate objects.

Petrarchan sonnet: Named after Petrarch, a fourteenth century Italian poet, who perfected the form, which is also known as the Italian sonnet. It is divided into an octave, in which the subject matter, which may be a problem, a doubt, a reflection, or some other issue, is raised and elaborated, and a sestet, in which the problem is resolved. The rhyme scheme is usually *abba abba ced cde, cdc cdc,* or *cde dce.*

Philosophical dualism: A theory that the universe is explicable in terms of two basic, conflicting entities, such as good and evil, mind and matter, or the physical and the spiritual.

Picaresque: A form of fiction that revolves around a central rogue figure, or picaro, who usually tells his own story. The plot structure of a picaresque novel is usually episodic, and the episodes usually focus on how the picaro lives by his wits. The classic example is Henry Fielding's *The History of Tom Jones, a Foundling* (1749).

Pindaric ode: Odes that imitate the form of those composed by the ancient Greek poet Pindar. A Pindaric ode consists of a strophe, followed by an antistrophe of the same structure, followed by an epode. This pattern may be repeated several times in the ode. In English poetry, Thomas Gray's "The Bard" is an example of a Pindaric ode.

Play: A literary work that is written to be performed by actors who speak the dialogue, impersonate the characters, and perform the appropriate actions. Usually, a play is performed on a stage, and an audience witnesses it.

Play-within-the-play: A play or dramatic fragment performed as a scene or scenes within a larger drama, typically performed or viewed by the characters of the larger drama.

Plot: Plot refers to how the author arranges the material not only to create the sequence of events in a play or story but also to suggest how those events are connected in a cause-and-effect relationship. There are a great variety of plot patterns, each of which is designed to create a particular effect.

Poem: A unified composition that uses the rhythms and sounds of language, as well as devices such as metaphor, to communicate emotions and experiences to the reader.

Poet laureate: The official poet of England, appointed for life by the English sovereign and expected to compose poems for various public occasions. The first official laureate was John Dryden in the seventeenth century. In the eighteenth century, the laureateship was given to a succession of mediocrities, but since the appointment of William Wordsworth in 1843, the office has generally been regarded as a substantial honor.

Polemic: A work that forcefully argues an opinion, usually on a controversial religious, political, or economic issue, in opposition to other opinions. John Milton's *Areopagitica* (1644) is one of the best known examples in English literature.

Postmodernism: The term is loosely applied to various artistic movements that have succeeded modernism, particularly since 1965. Postmodernist literature is experimental in form and reflects a fragmented world in which order and meaning are absent.

Pre-Raphaelitism: Refers to a group of nineteenth century English painters and writers, including Dante Gabriel Rossetti, Christina Rossetti, and William Morris. The Pre-Raphaelites were so called because they rebelled against conventional methods of painting and wanted to revert to what they regarded as the simple spirit of painting that existed before Raphael, particularly in its adherence to nature; they rejected all artificial embellishments. Pre-Raphaelite poetry made much use of symbolism and sensuousness, and showed an interest in the medieval and the supernatural.

Prose poem: A type of poem ranging in length from a few lines to three or four pages; most occupy a page or less. The distinguishing feature of the prose poem is its typography: it appears on the page like prose, with no line breaks. Many prose poems employ rhythmic repetition and other poetic devices not found in prose, but others do not; there is enormous variety in the genre.

Protagonist: Originally, in the Greek drama, the "first actor," who played the leading role. The term has come to signify the most important character in a drama or story. It is not unusual for there to be more than one protagonist in a work.

Proverb: A wise and pithy saying, authorship unknown, that reflects some observation about life. Proverbs are usually passed on through word of mouth, although they may also be written, as for example, the Book of Proverbs in the Bible.

Psychological novel: Once described as an interpretation of "the invisible life," the psychological novel is a form of fiction in which character, especially the inner life of characters, is the primary focus, rather than action. The form has characterized much of the work of Henry James, James Joyce, Virginia Woolf, and William Faulkner. *See also* Psychological realism.

Psychological realism: A type of realism that tries to reproduce the complex psychological motivations behind human behavior; writers in the late nineteenth century and early twentieth century were particularly influenced by Sigmund Freud's theories. *See also* Psychological novel.

Pun: A pun occurs when words with similar pronunciations have entirely different meanings. The result may be a surprise recognition of an unusual or striking connection, or, more often, a humorously accidental connection.

Quest: An archetypal theme identified by mythologist Joseph Campbell and found in many literary works. Campbell describes the heroic quest in three fundamental stages: departure (leaving the familiar world), initiation (encountering adventures and obstacles), and return (bringing home a boon to transform society).

Rabelaisian: The term is a reference to the sixteenth century French satirist and humorist François Rabelais. "Rabelaisian" is now used to refer to any humorous or satirical writing that is bawdy, coarse, or very down to earth.

Rationalism: A system of thought that seeks truth through the exercise of reason rather than by means of emotional response or revelation, or traditional authority. In literature, rationalism is associated with eighteenth century neoclassicism. *See also* Neoclassicism.

Realism: A literary technique in which the primary convention is to render an illusion of fidelity to external reality. Realism is often identified as the primary method of the novel form; the realist movement in the late nineteenth century coincided with the full development of the novel form.

Renaissance: The term means "rebirth" and refers to a period in European cultural history from the fourteenth to the early seventeenth century, although dates differ widely from country to country. The Renaissance produced an unprecedented flowering of the arts of painting, sculpture, architecture, and literature. The period is often said to mark the transition from the Middle Ages to the modern world. The questing, individualistic spirit that characterized the age was stimulated by an increase in classical learning by scholars known as Humanists, by the Protestant Reformation, by the development of printing, which created a wide market for books, by new theories of astronomy, and by the development of other sciences that saw natural laws at work where the Middle Ages had seen occult forces. *See also* Humanism.

Restoration comedy/drama: The restoration of the Stuart dynasty brought Charles II to the English throne in 1660. In literature, the Restoration period extends from 1660 to 1700. Restoration comedy is a comedy of manners, which centers around complicated plots full of the amorous intrigues of the fashionable upper classes. The humor is witty, but the view of human nature is cynical. Restoration dramatists include William Congreve, Sir George Etherege, and William Wycherley. In serious, or heroic, drama, the leading playwright was John Dryden. *See also* Comedy of manners.

Roman à clef: A fiction wherein actual persons, often celebrities of some sort, are thinly disguised. Lady Caroline Lamb's *Glenarvon* (1816), for example, contains a thinly veiled portrait of Lord Byron, and the character Mark Rampion in Aldous Huxley's *Point Counter Point* (1928) strongly resembles D. H. Lawrence.

Romance: Originally, any work written in Old French. In the Middle Ages, romances were about knights and their adventures. In modern times, the term has also been used to describe a type of prose fiction in which, unlike the novel, realism plays little part. Prose romances often give expression to the quest for transcendent truths.

Romanticism: A movement of the late eighteenth century and the nineteenth century that exalted individualism over collectivism, revolution over conservatism, innovation over tradition, imagination over reason, and spontaneity over restraint. Romanticism regarded art as self-expression; it strove to heal the cleavage between object and subject and expressed a longing for the infinite in all things. It stressed the innate goodness of human beings and the evils of the institutions that would stultify human creativity. The major English Romantic poets are William Blake, Lord Byron, Samuel Taylor Coleridge, John Keats, Percy Bysshe Shelley, and William Wordsworth.

Satire: A form of literature that employs the comedic devices of wit, irony, and exaggeration to expose, ridicule, and condemn human folly, vice, and stupidity. Justifying satire, Alexander Pope wrote that "nothing moves strongly but satire, and those who are ashamed of nothing else are so of being ridiculous."

Scene: A division of action within an act (some plays are divided only into scenes instead of acts). Sometimes, scene division indicates a change of setting or locale; sometimes, it simply indicates the entrances and exits of characters.

Science fiction: Fiction in which real or imagined scientific developments or certain givens (such as physical laws, psychological principles, or social conditions) form the basis of an imaginative projection, frequently into the future. Classic examples are the works of H. G. Wells and Jules Verne.

Sentimental novel: A form of fiction popular in the eighteenth century in which emotionalism and optimism are the primary characteristics. The best-known examples are Samuel Richardson's *Pamela* (1740-1741) and Oliver Goldsmith's *The Vicar of Wakefield* (1766).

Shakespearean sonnet: So named because William Shakespeare was the greatest English sonneteer, whose ranks also included the earl of Surrey and Thomas Wyatt. The Shakespearean sonnet consists of three quatrains and a concluding couplet, rhyming *abab cdcd efef gg*. The beginning of the third quatrain marks a turn in the argument.

GLOSSARY

Short story: A concise work of fiction, shorter than a novella, that is usually more concerned with mood, effect, or a single event than with plot or extensive characterization.

Simile: A type of metaphor in which two things are compared. It can usually be recognized by the use of the words "like," "as," "appears," or "seems."

Skaz: A term used in Russian criticism to describe a narrative technique that presents an oral narrative of a lowbrow speaker.

Soliloquy: An extended speech delivered by a character alone on stage, unheard by other characters. Soliloquy is a form of monologue, and it typically reveals the intimate thoughts and emotions of the speaker.

Song: A lyric poem, usually short, simple, and with rhymed stanzas, set to music.

Sonnet: A traditional poetic form that is almost always composed of fourteen lines of rhymed iambic pentameter; a turning point usually divides the poem into two parts, with the first part (octave) presenting a situation and the second part (sestet) reflecting on it. The main sonnet forms are the Petrarchan sonnet and the English (sometimes called Shakespearean) sonnet.

Stanza: When lines of poetry are meant to be taken as a unit, and the unit recurs throughout the poem, that unit is called a stanza; a four-line unit, a quatrain, is one common stanza. Others include couplet, *ottava rima*, and the Spenserian stanza.

Story line: The story line of a work of fiction differs from the plot. Story is merely the events that happen; plot is how those events are arranged by the author to suggest a cause-and-effect relationship. *See also* Plot.

Stream of consciousness: A narrative technique used in modern fiction by which an author tries to embody the total range of consciousness of a character, without any authorial comment or explanation. Sensations, thoughts, memories, and associations pour forth in an uninterrupted, prerational, and prelogical flow. For examples, see James Joyce's *Ulysses* (1922), Virginia Woolf's *To the Lighthouse* (1927), and William Faulkner's *The Sound and the Fury* (1929).

Sturm und Drang: A dramatic and literary movement in Germany during the late eighteenth century. Translated as "Storm and Stress," the movement was a reaction against classicism and a forerunner of Romanticism, characterized by extravagantly emotional language and sensational subject matter.

Surrealism: A revolutionary approach to artistic and literary creation, Surrealism argued for complete artistic freedom: The artist should relinquish all conscious control, responding to the irrational urges of the unconscious mind. Hence the bizarre, dreamlike, and nightmarish quality of Surrealistic writing. In the 1920's and 1930's, Surrealism flourished in France, Spain, and Latin America. (After World War II, it influenced such American writers as Frank O'Hara, John Ashberry, and Nathanael West.)

Symbol: A literary symbol is an image that stands for something else; it may evoke a cluster of meanings rather than a single specific meaning.

Symbolism: A literary movement encompassing the work of a group of French writers in the latter half of the nineteenth century, a group that included Charles Baudelaire, Stéphane Mallarmé, and Paul Verlaine. According to Symbolism, there is a mystical correspondence between the natural and spiritual worlds.

Theater of Cruelty: A term, coined by French playwright Antonin Artaud, which signifies a vision in which theater becomes an arena for shock therapy. The characters undergo such intense physical and psychic extremities that the audience cannot ignore the cathartic effect in which its preconceptions, fears, and hostilities are brought to the surface and, ideally, purged.

Theater of the Absurd: Refers to a group of plays that share a basic belief that life is illogical, irrational, formless, and contradictory, and that humanity is without meaning or purpose. Practitioners, who include Eugène Ionesco, Samuel Beckett, Jean Genet, Harold Pinter, Edward Albee, and Arthur Kopit, abandoned traditional theatrical forms and coherent dialogue.

***Théâtre d'avant-garde*:** A movement in late nineteenth century drama in France, which challenged the conventions of realistic drama by using Symbolist poetry and nonobjective scenery.

Third person: Third-person narration occurs when the narrator has not been part of the event or affected it and is not probing his own relationship to it but is only describing what happened. He does not allow the intrusion of the word *I.* Third-person narration establishes a distance between reader and subject, gives credibility to a large expanse of narration that would be impossible for one person to experience, and allows the narrative to include a number of characters who can comment on one another as well as be the subjects of commentary by the participating narrator.

Tragedy: A form of drama that is serious in action and intent and that involves disastrous events and death; classical Greek drama observed specific guidelines for tragedy, but the term is now sometimes applied to a range of dramatic or fictional situations.

Travel literature: Writing that emphasizes the author's subjective response to places visited, especially faraway, exotic, and culturally different locales.

Trilogy: A novel or play written in three parts, each of which is a self-contained work, such as William Shakespeare's *Henry VI* (*Part I*, 1592; *Part II*, c. 1590-1591; *Part III*, c. 1590-1591). Modern examples include C. S. Lewis' Space Trilogy (1938-1945) and William Golding's Sea Trilogy (1980-1989).

Trope: Trope means literally "turn" or "conversion"; it is a figure of speech in which a word or phrase is used in a way that deviates from the normal or literal sense.

***Verismo*:** Refers to a type of Italian literature that deals with the lower classes and presents them realistically using language that they would use. Called *verismo* because it is true to life, and, from the writer's point of view, impersonal.

Verse: Verse is a generic name for poetry. Verse also refers in a narrower sense to poetry that is humorous or merely superficial, as in "greeting-card verse." Finally, English critics sometimes use "verse" to mean "stanza," or, more often, to mean "line."

Verse drama: Verse drama was the prevailing form for Western drama throughout most of its history, comprising all the drama of classical Greece and continuing to dominate the stage through the Renaissance, when it was best exemplified by the blank verse of Elizabethan drama. In the seventeenth century, however, prose comedies became popular, and in the nineteenth and twentieth centuries verse drama became the exception rather than the rule.

Victorian novel: Although the Victorian period extended from 1837 to 1901, the term "Victorian novel" does not include works from the later decades of Queen Victoria's reign. The term loosely refers to the sprawling works of novelists such as Charles Dickens and William Makepeace Thackeray, which are characterized by a broad social canvas.

Villanelle: A French verse form assimilated by English prosody. It is usually composed of nineteen lines divided into five tercets and a quatrain, rhyming *aba*, *bba*, *aba*, *aba*, *abaa*. The third line is repeated in the ninth and fifteenth lines. Dylan Thomas' "Do Not Go Gentle into That Good Night" is a modern example of a successful villanelle.

Well-made play: From the French term *pièce bien faite*, a type of play constructed according to a "formula" that originated in nineteenth century France. The plot often revolves around a secret known only to some of the characters, which is revealed at the climax and leads to catastrophe for the villain and vindication or triumph for the hero. The well-made play influenced later dramatists such as Henrik Ibsen and George Bernard Shaw.

Weltanschauung: A German term translated as "worldview," by which is meant a comprehensive set of beliefs or assumptions by means of which one interprets what goes on in the world.

Zeitgeist: A German term meaning the spirit of the times, the moral or intellectual atmosphere of any age or period. The *Zeitgeist* of the Romantic Age, for example, might be described as revolutionary, restless, individualistic, and innovative.

LIST OF AUTHORS

PLOUTARCHOS, MESTRIOS.
   See PLUTARCH.
PLUTARCH, **5**-1514
POPE, ALEXANDER, **5**-1521
POQUELIN, JEAN-BAPTISTE.
   See MOLIÈRE.
POWELL, ANTHONY, **5**-1533
PRITCHETT, V. S., **5**-1545
PROUST, MARCEL, **5**-1557
PUSHKIN, ALEXANDER, **5**-1565
PYM, BARBARA, **5**-1575

RABELAIS, FRANÇOIS, **5**-1586
RACINE, JEAN, **5**-1594
RICHARDSON, SAMUEL, **5**-1602
RICHLER, MORDECAI, **5**-1610
RILKE, RAINER MARIA, **5**-1620
RIMBAUD, ARTHUR, **5**-1632
ROUSSEAU, JEAN-JACQUES, **5**-1644
ROY, GABRIELLE, **5**-1656
RUSHDIE, SALMAN, **5**-1665
RUSKIN, JOHN, **5**-1673

SARTRE, JEAN-PAUL, **5**-1684
SAYERS, DOROTHY L., **5**-1693
SCHILLER, FRIEDRICH, **5**-1701
SCOTT, SIR WALTER, **5**-1709
SENECA, **5**-1717
SHAKESPEARE, WILLIAM, **5**-1725
SHAW, GEORGE BERNARD, **5**-1737
SHELLEY, MARY, **5**-1749
SHELLEY, PERCY BYSSHE, **5**-1757
SHIKIBU, MURASAKI. *See*
   MURASAKI SHIKIBU
SIDNEY, SIR PHILIP, **5**-1768
SINGER, ISAAC BASHEVIS, **5**-1780
SIRIN, V. *See* NABOKOV, VLADIMIR.
SOLZHENITSYN, ALEKSANDR,
   5-1792
SOPHOCLES, **5**-1803
SPARK, MURIEL, **6**-1813
SPENSER, EDMUND, **6**-1824

STENDHAL, **6**-1836
STERNE, LAURENCE, **6**-1844
STEVENSON, ROBERT LOUIS, **6**-1852
STOPPARD, TOM, **6**-1862
STRAUSSLER, TOMAS.
   See STOPPARD, TOM.
STRINDBERG, AUGUST, **6**-1873
SWIFT, JONATHAN, **6**-1885
SWINBURNE, ALGERNON
   CHARLES, **6**-1896
SYNGE, JOHN MILLINGTON, **6**-1904

TENNYSON, ALFRED, LORD, **6**-1912
THACKERAY, WILLIAM
   MAKEPEACE, **6**-1923
THOMAS, DYLAN, **6**-1931
TOLKIEN, J. R. R., **6**-1944
TOLSTOY, LEO, **6**-1955
TROLLOPE, ANTHONY, **6**-1967
TU FU, **6**-1974
TURGENEV, IVAN, **6**-1982

VARGAS LLOSA, MARIO, **6**-1990
VEGA CARPIO, LOPE DE, **6**-1998
VERGIL, **6**-2006
VERLAINE, PAUL, **6**-2018
VERNE, JULES, **6**-2026
VOLTAIRE, **6**-2034

WALCOTT, DEREK, **6**-2046
WAUGH, EVELYN, **6**-2058
WELLS, H. G., **6**-2071
WIESEL, ELIE, **6**-2082
WILDE, OSCAR, **6**-2091
WODEHOUSE, P. G., **6**-2103
WOOLF, VIRGINIA, **6**-2112
WORDSWORTH, WILLIAM, **6**-2124

YEATS, WILLIAM BUTLER, **6**-2136
YEVTUSHENKO, YEVGENY, **6**-2148

ZOLA, ÉMILE, **6**-2156